# Philosophers in Depth

**Series Editor**
Constantine Sandis
Department of Philosophy
University of Hertfordshire
Hatfield, UK

*Philosophers in Depth* is a series of themed edited collections focusing on particular aspects of the thought of major figures from the history of philosophy. The volumes showcase a combination of newly commissioned and previously published work with the aim of deepening our understanding of the topics covered. Each book stands alone, but taken together the series will amount to a vast collection of critical essays covering the history of philosophy, exploring issues that are central to the ideas of individual philosophers. This project was launched with the financial support of the Institute for Historical and Cultural Research at Oxford Brookes University, for which we are very grateful.

Constantine Sandis

More information about this series at
http://www.palgrave.com/gp/series/14552

Christos Hadjioannou
Editor

# Heidegger on Affect

palgrave
macmillan

*Editor*
Christos Hadjioannou
Faculty of Philosophy
Sofia University St Kliment Ohridski
Sofia, Bulgaria

Philosophers in Depth
ISBN 978-3-030-24638-9          ISBN 978-3-030-24639-6    (eBook)
https://doi.org/10.1007/978-3-030-24639-6

Cover illustration: © Constantinos Taliotis

This Palgrave Macmillan imprint is published by the registered company Springer Nature Switzerland AG
The registered company address is: Gewerbestrasse 11, 6330 Cham, Switzerland

*For my daughter Polyxeni*

# Acknowledgements

I would like to thank Professor Dermot Moran who was my mentor during my Government of Ireland Postdoctoral Fellowship, during which most work for this volume took place. I would like to thank all the contributors for their excellent essays. I would also like to thank the following sponsors of the conference, which gave the opportunity to contributors to present drafts of their chapters and receive feedback: the Irish Research Council, the College of Sciences and Law Scheme Funding (University College Dublin), SEED Funding (University College Dublin), The Mind Association, the Embassy of the Federal Republic of Germany (Dublin), and the School of Philosophy (University College Dublin). Special thanks to the Ph.D. students, Luca Banfi and Georgios Petropoulos, for assisting me with organizing the conference. I would like to thank Helen Kenny for the invaluable administrative help as well as my colleagues, Anya Daly, Anna Bortolan and Elisa Magri, for their support and their friendship during my IRC Fellowship.

I would like to thank Constantine Sandis, the editor of this series, who believed in this volume and supported it. I would like to thank my Ph.D. supervisor, Professor Tanja Staehler, for her support. I would like to thank Professor Daniel Dahlstrom for the support and useful advice. I would like to thank Leoni and Fred for their hospitality. I would like to thank Brendan George, Lauriane Piette and April James, of Palgrave Macmillan, for their support and patience.

I would like to thank my friend and mentor, Mahon O'Brien, for all the support. It's so invaluable I can't repay it back.

I would like to thank Larry Hatab—my first mentor who started me thinking about such things. Larry, get well soon!

I would like to thank my family Kyriaki, Miltiades and Louis, for their love and support.

Special thanks go to Constantinos Taliotis for granting permission to use the wonderful photograph he took of Lake Biwa in Shiga Valley (Japan).

Most of all, I would like to thank my wife, Irene, for her love, friendship, support, inspiration, and for all the fun.

# Introduction

Affective phenomena play a significant role in Heidegger's philosophy. His analyses of angst in *Being and Time* (*BT*), and of boredom in the *Fundamental Concepts of Metaphysics: World, Finitude, Solitude* (*FCM*), have been the obvious reference points for scholars who wished to show the importance Heidegger ascribes to affective phenomena. Much has been written on angst partly because it is the fundamental mood (*Grundstimmung*) analyzed in *BT* which is widely accepted as Heidegger's magnum opus. However, it is far from certain that we achieved clarity even on such a basic theme as angst.

Despite the fact that affective phenomena are central to all of Heidegger's work, and his analyses of mood have been so influential in existentialism, hermeneutics, phenomenology, but also theology and cultural studies, no single collection of essays has been exclusively dedicated to this theme. This volume brings together the work of leading interpreters of Heidegger's thought on this theme. The volume does not simply genuflect before Heidegger but includes essays which are critical of Heidegger's work.

Generally speaking, activity has been linked to the process of "creating" and passivity to the process of "receiving" (see Zaborowski 2010).

Both had already been posited by Plato, as two basic characteristics of being. In Aristotle, we meet these two characteristics as the last two of his categories, the ninth and the tenth: "[...] how active, what doing (or Action), how passive, what suffering (Affection)" (Zaborowski 2010, 2). Affect (*affectus*) along with *passio* were used commonly as philosophical translations of the Greek term *pathos* (Zaborowski 2010, 7). There exists a long history of affective phenomena that began with the ancient Greeks and has gone on to Sartre and to Hartmann, while undergoing a dynamic transformation: "from *thumos* to *pathos* and *affectus*, then from passion to emotion and feeling" (Ibid.). Heidegger's philosophy has extensively covered affective phenomena, despite the fact that he did not develop full clarity on the distinction between emotion, feeling, passion, affect, and mood.

Heidegger's treatment of affective phenomena is terminologically disparate and inconsistent. Whilst he does at various times (for example, in his Nietzsche lectures) acknowledge distinctions between affect, mood, emotion, feeling, and passion, he does not conscientiously define them, or keep them distinct. However, in *BT*, and indeed in most of his work, his accounts of affective phenomena are indicated by the words *Stimmung* (mood) and *Befindlichkeit* (disposition).[1] But throughout his long career, Heidegger uses various words and concepts in order to indicate affective phenomena: *Empfindung, Gemüt, Affekt, Gefühl, Befindlichkeit* (and *Grundbefindlichkeit*), *Sichbefinden, Stimmung* (and *Grundstimmung*), *Gestimmtsein, Gestimmtheit, Leidenschaft, Motivation, Disposition,* πάθος, διάθεσις, *affectio*. Some of these notions are consistently used in a pejorative sense (despite the lack of a clear definition), or in the context of his encounter (*Auseinandersetzung*) with the notions used by other philosophers (and thus, neither simply dismissively nor approvingly). In any case, most of the notions that Heidegger uses in his own phenomenological descriptions of affective phenomena, appear, disappear, and sometimes reappear throughout his career, in inconsistent ways.

These inconsistencies though are not only characteristic of Heidegger's terminology for affective phenomena, but are also characteristic of most of the central notions in his work, and an inevitable "product" of his own method and hermeneutic style of philosophizing. Let us recall that he himself chose to include all of his manuscripts (published material, lecture material, even his private notebooks) in the complete edition (*Gesamtausgabe*) of his work, and prefaced it with the motto "*Wege—nicht Werke*" meaning "Ways—not works", because he considered his philosophical path to be one ridden with failed (but not futile) attempts to give expression to the problem of the meaning of Being. So whilst the deeper problem maintains a certain unity, Heidegger's style, angle, and (unavoidably) *words* used vary, as does the "success" and cogency of each "attempt".[2] Affective phenomena are always a fundamental part, and always form a constitutive ground of the world, and of the various epochs of the history of Being. At the same time, they are constitutive of any *understanding* of Being, and hence each way of understanding Being is grounded in affect (mood), and affect is also what supplies the impetus behind the transition from one way of understanding Being (and world) to another. Affects have operated as what might be described as a transcendental "normalizing", providing the *ground* for disclosure, the origin of authentic ontological understanding, the defining character of each historical epoch, as well as the enactmental urgency (*Notwendigkeit*) that will bring about Heidegger's, famously elusive, "other" beginning.

The volume comprises twelve chapters. In Chapter 1, entitled "Being, Nothingness and Anxiety", Mahon O'Brien re-examines Heidegger's analysis of moods in *BT* against the backdrop of his famous 1929 inaugural lecture ('What is Metaphysics?') and his 1940s retrospectives on the same lecture along with some related discussions in his 1935 lecture course—*Introduction to Metaphysics*. The chapter argues that Heidegger's major concern in his early account of moods is best understood as an attempt to identify the role that absence plays in Dasein's barest affective states which testify once more to the constant interplay of presence and absence in terms of what it means for anything to be. Though Heidegger looks to clarify his position in later writings, his account of moods is frequently misunderstood by commentators who see Heidegger's early work as existentialist, humanist and/or anthropological in ways that fail to appreciate how his discussions in the existential analytic and the subsequent account of authenticity are, in fact, fledgling attempts to begin to sketch out the possibility of moving beyond the metaphysics of presence.

In Chapter 2, entitled "Heidegger: πάθος as the Thing Itself", Thomas Sheehan argues that Heidegger's phenomenological readings of Aristotle on πάσχειν and πάθος revolutionized the phenomenology of affect, and he carried that revolution into his later work on πάθος, *Lichtung*, and *Ereignis*. The chapter argues that πάθος, read as *Dasein's* thrownness or appropriation, is *die Sache selbst* of Heidegger's thought.

In Chapter 3, entitled "The Affects of Rhetoric and Reconceiving the Nature of Possibility", Niall Keane looks at the genesis of Heidegger's reflections on affect, embodied speaking together, the nature of possibility and the critique of actuality, which form the soil in which the later existential analysis of *BT* sinks its roots. These original reflections are to be found in the 1924 summer semester lecture course entitled *Basic Concepts of Aristotelian Philosophy*. On the basis of this, the chapter shows how the early lectures help us understand what happens to Heidegger's reflections on affect, *dynamis*, and being together with others, shapes the development of his later critique of the metaphysics of actuality in both *BT* and in the *Contributions to Philosophy*.

In Chapter 4, entitled "Angst as Evidence: Shifting Phenomenology's Measure", Christos Hadjioannou argues that an important aspect of *BT* is to radicalize the basic concept of evidence that is operative in Husserlian phenomenology, conceived in terms of apodictic certainty, which commits Husserl to mentalist evidentialism. Heidegger overcomes mentalist evidentialism and relaunches phenomenology on the basis of a different "epistemic" measure, which turns phenomenology into a hermeneutics of facticity. The chapter specifically analyzes the fundamental mood of angst in terms of evidence, so as to better illustrate the methodological role it plays in *BT*. Angst serves as the hermeneutic equivalent to what analytic epistemologists call "justifier of knowledge", that is, it takes on the function of *evidence* that phenomenologically grounds the interpretation of the basic structures of Dasein, as these are disclosed in authentic existence.

In Chapter 5, entitled "Missing in Action: Affectivity in *Being and Time*", Daniel O. Dahlstrom argues that despite the importance that Heidegger assigns to affectivity structurally in *BT*, accounts of the relevant sorts of affectivity are frequently and, in some cases, perhaps even egregiously missing from existential analyses that form the centerpiece of the work. The aim of the chapter is to demonstrate as much. After recounting the considerable insights of Heidegger's general account of disposedness and affectivity and the fundamental status he assigns to them, the focus of the paper turns to the secondary status often accorded them in the first half of *BT* and the seemingly crucial absence of an adequate account of the affective dimension of authentic existence, in the second half of the work. After making the argument that, according to Heidegger's own criterion, the adequate rootedness of the existential analysis demands a more robust account of the affective character of existing authentically, the chapter concludes with an open question about the mood of undertaking the existential analysis itself.

In Chapter 6, entitled "Affect and Authenticity: Three Heideggerian Models of Owned Emotion", Denis McManus explores the notion of an authentic affective life by examining three models of Heideggerian authenticity in light of his remarks on emotion. In addition to the familiar "decisionist model," the chapter examines what he calls the "standpoint model" and the "all things considered judgment model" (AJM). Each of these models suggests a distinctive picture of what authenticity in one's affective life might be, and considering the plausibility of these pictures provides an interesting way to re-consider the plausibility of those models. The chapter argues that authentic affect as the decisionist model understands it requires a level of control over our emotions that is inherently implausible and incompatible with Heidegger's understanding of them, and that the standpoint model's understanding of authentic affect requires a uniformity in our emotions which should be rejected on the same grounds. Ultimately, the chapter argues in favor of the AJM on the grounds that its picture of affective authenticity—an openness to the many ways in which my situation matters to me, touches me and moves me whether I like it or not—is both truer to our actual emotional lives and more harmonious with Heidegger's own understanding of these matters.

In Chapter 7, entitled "Finding Oneself, Called", Katherine Withy situates Heidegger's account of moods and affects in its original philosophical and methodological home: his account of disclosing as our original human openness. The dimension of disclosing to which affects belong is finding, or findingness (*Befindlichkeit*). The chapter argues that to be finding is to be called by vocational projects (e.g., in ground-moods like angst and boredom) and to be called by the solic-itings of entities, not only in being mooded but also in sensing and in being normatively responsive (among others). This wider perspective on Heidegger's thinking of affectivity yields the proper context in which to understand and assess what he says about moods, as well as a powerful framework within which to understand affective disclosing generally, as the phenomenon of finding oneself called.

In Chapter 8, entitled "Is Profound Boredom Boredom?", Andreas Elpidorou and Lauren Freeman turn to Heidegger's thorough phe-nomenological investigations of the nature of boredom. In his 1929–1930 lecture course, *The Fundamental Concepts of Metaphysics: World, Finitude, Solitude*, Heidegger goes to great lengths to distinguish between three different types of boredom and to explicate their respec-tive characters. Elpidorou and Freeman undertake a study of the nature of profound boredom with the aim of investigating its place within contemporary psychological and philosophical research on boredom. Although boredom used to be a neglected emotional experience, it is no more. Boredom's causal antecedents, effects, experiential profile, and neurophysiological correlates have become topics of active study; as a consequence, a proliferation of claims and findings about bore-dom has ensued. Such a situation provides an opportunity to scrutinize Heidegger's claims and to try to understand them both on their own terms and in light of contemporary understanding of boredom.

In Chapter 9, entitled "Truth, Errancy, and Bodily Dispositions in Heidegger's Thought", Daniela Vallega-Neu argues that while Heidegger has written much about the relation between attunements and truth in terms of the unconcealment of being, he has written little if not nothing about the relation between attunements and errancy (*Irre*). In her chap-ter, she questions the link between attunement and errancy (the turn toward beings) in the context of Heidegger's questioning of being as such, but also relates this to Heidegger's mostly missing considerations of the lived body (*Leib*). Vallega-Neu shows the limits of Heidegger's account of attunements when it comes to "being with" beings and the question of the body, but also supplements Heidegger's accounts of attunement by suggesting how we could begin to think them in relation to the body. In order to mark a difference between, on the one hand, fundamental attunements and, on the other hand, attunements in so far as they relate to specific things or events and involve our body, Vallega-Neu speaks of the latter as bodily dispositions. In the last part of the chapter, she puts into question that very distinction and suggests that even when it comes to fundamental attunements, these occur through or with bodily dispositions. That Heidegger failed to take these into account may have to do with "his" errancies.

In Chapter 10, entitled "Love as Passion: Epistemic and Existential Aspects of Heidegger's Unknown Concept", Tatjana Noemi Tömmel argues against the assumption that Heidegger never wrote a single word on love. Heidegger's philosophy is not without love: a careful reading of his writings including lecture courses, notes, and correspondence reveals that love is not only featured as a notion among others in his works, but in fact plays a major role in the development of his thoughts. The chapter focuses on the most important epistemic, existential and social aspects of love in Heidegger: The first part analyzes the relation between love and cognition. Influenced by Plato, Augustine, medieval mystics and Max Scheler, Heidegger discusses the epistemic function of love in his earliest writings and later conceives a concept of philosophy in which love actualizes *Dasein's* primordial transcendence and is therefore the "foundation of phenomenological understanding" (*GA* 16, 185). The second part focuses on Heidegger's early Freiburg and Marburg years and shows how love becomes the key to leading an authentic life, usually associated with anxiety and death. Decades before 'event' or 'enowning' (*Ereignis*) becomes the focal point of his thinking, Heidegger describes the beginning of love as a true break-out, which transforms existence for good. The third part discusses the interpersonal or social dimension of Heidegger's concept of love. Like the kind of solicitude that 'leaps ahead,' love is focused on the other's authentic existence. By discussing love's role for cognition and truth, sociality and authenticity, the chapter gives an overview of Heidegger's little known concept of love, thus trying to gain a more differentiated image of the "socio-ontological deficits" (Schmidt 2005) of his analysis of *Dasein*.

In Chapter 11, entitled "The Ethics of Moods", François Raffoul explores the *ethical* scope of moods. Raffoul argues that to be in a mood, to be thrown in a mood, engages a certain response, already a responsibility, an ethical relation. It may be objected that moods display a kind of radical opaqueness, withdrawal, and even unintelligibility (one does not know why one is in such or such a mood) that seem to prevent any possible appropriation in an ethical response. Raffoul argues that this expropriation precisely calls us to an *ethical* response, an original responsibility that allows us to speak of an "ethics of moods." Ultimately, the ethics of moods is a responsibility for finitude itself, for the *secret* of moods, a being-responsible in which it is a matter, not of overcoming moods, but of assuming their mystery, of respecting their secret, and as it were being their enigma.

In Chapter 12, Jan Slaby and Gerhard Thonhauser argue that Heidegger's ontological account of affectivity provides an interesting angle to consider questions of politics. On the one hand, one might take some of what Heidegger wrote on affectivity in the late 1920s and early 1930s—usually couched in the idiom of *Stimmungen* (moods) and *Befindlichkeit*—as a foreshadowing of his involvement with Nazi politics, culminating in his time as *Führer-Rektor* of Freiburg University (1933/1934). On the other hand, Heidegger's views on affectivity might be taken as a starting point for an ontological perspective on the political as such. His perspective on *Befindlichkeit* as *disclosive postures* can prepare such a reading, while especially his views on the ontological character of *anxiety* and *boredom* lead into the founding dimension of the political as such.

This is because these affective orientations reveal the ungroundedness and thus radical contingency of existence. The flip side of this ungroundedness is the inevitability for self-determination—in other words: the need for *deciding the undecidable*. Although Heidegger's own politics—at least in the early 1930s—did not explicitly relate to the affectively disclosed ungroundedness of existence, but rather curtailed this openness and indeterminacy in an individualistic and decisionistic closure, Slaby and Thonhauser argue that Heidegger's view yields to a radically political reading. Not least, this is evidenced in much of French political thought since the 1960s which heavily draws on

Heidegger's *ontological difference*. The political as such does not refer to politics as a sub-system of society, but to the questioning of the foundations of politics, which turn out to be necessarily "contingent foundations" (Butler 1992). The chapter aims to trace this line of thought back to its origins in Heidegger's works, in order to assess the potentials and pitfalls of 'Heidegger on politics'.

For the sake of simplicity, references to *Being and Time* use the pagination of the German original (*SZ*), given in both available English translations. References to other works by Heidegger use acronyms given in the Abbreviations section, followed by page numbers.

## Notes

1. Each contributor has translated these notions in the way they preferred. There is no consensus among scholars on this issue. I translate *Stimmung* as "mood" and *Befindlichkeit* as "disposition". For a justification of my translation, please see Chapter 4 in this volume.
2. The publication of Heidegger's *Black Notebooks* rekindled the uncertainty and aporia about Heidegger's philosophical ways vis-á-vis their relation to National Socialism and antisemitism. His philosophy needs to be approached with intellectual honesty, critical judgment and sobriety, rather than with knee-jerk reactions and confirmation biases. In my opinion, while there is evidence to suggest that *some* of Heidegger's concepts (words) are sometimes employed in an antisemitic context, it is not evident that Heidegger's entire philosophy is inherently antisemitic: some of it can be said to be *compliant* with antisemitism and fascism, but some of it is clearly incompatible with any sort of totalitarian ideas, including antisemitism and fascism. (See Hadjioannou 2017).

## References

Butler, Judith. 1992. "Contingent Foundations: Feminism and the Question of 'Postmodernism'". In *Feminists Theorize the Political*, edited by J. Butler and J. W. Scott, 345–456. New York: Routledge.

Hadjioannou, Christos. 2017. "What Can We Do with Heidegger in the Twenty-First Century?" *The Journal of the British Society for Phenomenology* 48 (4): 350–359. https://doi.org/10.1080/00071773.2017.1286154.

Schmidt, Michael. 2005. *Ekstatische Transzendenz. Ludwig Binswangers Phänomenologie der Liebe und die Aufdeckung der sozialontologischen Defizite in Heideggers* Sein und Zeit. Würzburg: Königshausen & Neumann.

Zaborowski, Robert. 2010. "From *Thumos* to emotion and feeling. Some observations on the passivity and activity of affectivity", *History and Philosophy of Psychology* 12 (1): 1–25.

# Contents

# Notes on Contributors

**Daniel O. Dahlstrom** is John R. Silber Professor of Philosophy and Chair of the Department of Philosophy at Boston University. He has authored numerous studies of Heidegger's thought including *Heidegger's Concept of Truth* (Cambridge University Press, 2001) and *The Heidegger Dictionary* (Bloomsbury, 2013). In addition to translating Heidegger's first Marburg lectures, *Introduction to Phenomenological Research* (Indiana, 2005), he has edited *Interpreting Heidegger: Critical Essays* (Cambridge, 2011), *Gatherings*, the Heidegger Circle's annual from 2010–2014, and *Kant and His German Contemporaries II* (Cambridge, 2018). He is also the author of *Philosophical Legacies: Essays on the Thought of Kant, Hegel, and Their Contemporaries* (Catholic University, 2008) and *Identity, Authenticity, and Humility* (Marquette, 2017).

**Andreas Elpidorou** is Associate Professor in the Department of Philosophy at the University of Louisville. He specializes in the philosophical study of the mind with an emphasis on emotions and consciousness. In addition to having published numerous journal articles and book chapters, he is the author of *Propelled! How Boredom, Frustration, and Anticipation Can Lead Us to the Good Life* (Oxford University Press, 2020), the co-author of *Consciousness and Physicalism:*

*A Defense of a Research Program* (Routledge, 2018), and the co-editor of *Philosophy of Mind and Phenomenology: Conceptual and Empirical Approaches* (Routledge, 2016).

**Lauren Freeman** is Associate Professor of Philosophy at the University of Louisville. She is also an affiliated faculty member in the Department of Women's, Gender, and Sexuality Studies and a core faculty member in the M.A. program in Bioethics and Medical Humanities. She works in the areas of feminist bioethics, analytic feminism, phenomenology, and philosophy of emotion. She also has written on implicit bias and stereotype threat. Lauren has co-edited a special issue of *Phenomenology and the Cognitive Sciences* on the topic of the phenomenology and science of emotions and has edited a special issue of the *International Journal of Feminist Approaches to Bioethics* on the topic of feminist phenomenological approaches to bioethics, medicine, and health. She is currently the editor of *The American Philosophical Association's Newsletter on Feminism and Philosophy*. Lauren is co-editing *Microaggressions and Philosophy* (Routledge, 2019) and co-writing *Microaggressions in Medicine.*

**Christos Hadjioannou** is Postdoctoral Fellow at Faculty of Philosophy, Sofia University "St Kliment Ohridski". He was Government of Ireland Postdoctoral Fellow at University College Dublin, and DAAD scholar at Freie Universität Berlin. His Ph.D. thesis was entitled *The Emergence of Mood in Heidegger's Phenomenology* (University of Sussex, 2015). He has published on Heidegger and Husserl, and is working towards a monograph on Heidegger's phenomenology of mood, as well as a book on Heidegger's relation to Stoic philosophy. He co-edited *Heidegger on Technology* (Routledge, 2018) with Aaron J. Wendland and Christopher Merwin, and *Towards a New Human Being* (Palgrave Macmillan, 2019) with Luce Irigaray and Mahon O'Brien.

**Niall Keane** is Senior Lecturer of Philosophy at Mary Immaculate College, University of Limerick, Ireland. He co-authored with Chris Lawn *The Gadamer Dictionary* (2011) and translated Mauro Carbone's *An Unprecedented Deformation: Marcel Proust and the Sensible Ideas* (2010). He also co-edited with Chris Lawn *The Blackwell Companion to Hermeneutics* (2016). He has written several articles on Martin Heidegger and other philosophers.

**Denis McManus** is Professor of Philosophy at the University of Southampton. He is the author of *The Enchantment of Words: Wittgenstein's* Tractatus Logico-Philosophicus (Oxford University Press, 2006) and *Heidegger and the Measure of Truth* (Oxford University Press, 2012). He is the editor of *Wittgenstein and Scepticism* (Routledge, 2004) and *Heidegger, Authenticity and the Self: Themes From Division Two of* Being and Time (Routledge, 2015). Denis is currently working on a range of issues, including the nature of responsibility, selfhood and self-knowledge, and the possibility of objectivity and ontological knowledge-much of this work shaped by his study of Wittgenstein and Heidegger.

**Mahon O'Brien** is Senior Lecturer in Philosophy at the University of Sussex. He has held posts at Universities and Research Institutes in Boston, Vienna and Dublin before taking up his position at the University of Sussex. His work to date has largely been concerned with issues in phenomenology, in particular, the work of Martin Heidegger. His first book was on Heidegger and the question of authenticity (*Heidegger and Authenticity: From Resoluteness to Releasement*. Continuum, 2011). His second book offers a new approach to the Heidegger Controversy and, in particular, examines the notion of an authentic historical community in Heidegger's thought (*Heidegger, History and the Holocaust*. Bloomsbury, 2015). He recently co-edited a volume of essays with Luce Irigaray and Christos Hadjioannou (*Towards a New Human Being*. Palgrave Macmillan, 2019) while a short intellectual biography on Heidegger will come out later this year (*Heidegger's Life and Thought: A Tarnished Legacy*. Rowman & Littlefield, 2019).

**François Raffoul** is Professor of Philosophy and French Studies at Louisiana State University. He is the author of *Heidegger and the Subject* (Prometheus Books, 1999), *A Chaque fois Mien* (Galilée, Paris, 2004), *The Origins of Responsibility* (Indiana University Press, 2010) and *Thinking the Event* (forthcoming with Indiana University Press). He is the co-editor of several volumes, *Disseminating Lacan* (1996), *Heidegger and Practical Philosophy* (2002), *Rethinking Facticity* (2008), *French Interpretations of Heidegger* (2008), and *The Bloomsbury Companion to Heidegger* (2013, 2016). He is the translator and co-translator of several French philosophers, in particular Jacques Derrida

(*"Ulysses Gramophone: Hear Say Yes in Joyce"*, in *Derrida and Joyce: Texts and Contexts*, SUNY Press, 2013), Dominique Janicaud's *Heidegger in France* (Indiana University Press, 2015), Jean-Luc Nancy's *The Title of the Letter: A Reading of Lacan* (1992), *The Gravity of Thought* (1998), *The Creation of the World or Globalization* (2007) and *Identity* (Fordham University Press, 2014). He is also the co-translator of Martin Heidegger's last seminars, *Four Seminars* (Indiana University Press, 2003). He is the co-editor of a book series at SUNY Press on *Contemporary French Thought*.

**Thomas Sheehan** teaches religious studies and philosophy at Stanford University. He specializes in contemporary European philosophy and its relation to religious questions, with particular interests in Heidegger and Roman Catholicism. His books include: *Making Sense of Heidegger: A Paradigm Shift* (2015); Martin Heidegger, *Logic: The Question of Truth* (trans., 2010); *Becoming Heidegger* (2007); *Edmund Husserl: Psychological and Transcendental Phenomenology and the Encounter With Heidegger* (1997); *Karl Rahner: The Philosophical Foundations* (1987); *The First Coming: How the Kingdom of God Became Christianity* (1986); and *Heidegger, the Man and the Thinker* (1981).

**Jan Slaby** is Professor of Philosophy at Free University Berlin, Germany. His research areas are philosophy of mind, especially emotion and affect, agency, self-consciousness and personhood in general. Areas of expertise include philosophical anthropology, phenomenology, social and political philosophy, philosophy of science and science studies (especially concerning psychology, psychiatry and neuroscience). He is the author of numerous articles on theories of emotion and affect.

**Gerhard Thonhauser** works at the Institute of Philosophy at TU Darmstadt. He was an Erwin Schrödinger Fellow of the Austrian Science Fund associated with the Collaborative Research Centre »Affective Societies« at Freie Universität Berlin. He holds a Ph.D. in philosophy and MAs in philosophy and political science from the University of Vienna, where he worked as a DOC-fellow of the Austrian Academy of Sciences and a predoctoral fellow. His research focuses on social and political philosophy, and theories of emotion and affectivity from a phenomenological perspective. He is the author of *Ein rätselhaftes Zeichen. Zum Verhältnis von Martin Heidegger und Søren Kierkegaard* (2016), and co-editor of *From Conventionalism to Social Authenticity. Heidegger's Anyone and Contemporary Social Theory* (2017).

**Tatjana Noemi Tömmel** studied Comparative Literature and Philosophy in Munich, Berlin and Paris, and holds a doctorate in Philosophy from the Goethe University Frankfurt am Main. In 2012–2013, she worked as Marie Curie Early Stage Researcher at the Center for Subjectivity Research at the University of Copenhagen/Denmark. Since 2013, she has been a Postdoctoral Researcher at the Department of Philosophy at Berlin Technical University, currently working on the social and political implications of the Jewish Enlightenment's aesthetic. Her work brought her twice to the United States: During her Ph.D. she was a visiting scholar at Yale University (2009/2010), and in autumn 2016 she was at Columbia University. Her work centres on social philosophy, ethics and aesthetics; in 2013 she published her first book *Wille und Passion. Der Liebesbegriff bei; Heidegger und Arendt (Will and Passion: The Concept of Love in Heidegger and Arendt).*

**Daniela Vallega-Neu** is Professor of Philosophy at University of Oregon. Her most recent research focused on Heidegger's non-public writings as well as on rethinking time as the temporalizing of things and events. Her latest book, entitled *Heidegger's Poetic Writings: From* Contributions to Philosophy *to* The Event (Indiana University Press, 2018), traces and questions shifts of themes and concepts in Heidegger's non-public writings from *Contributions to Philosophy* to *Das* Ereignis. She co-translated Heidegger's *Contributions to Philosophy (Of the Event)* (Indiana University Press, 2011) and wrote a widely used introduction to this book: *Heidegger's* Contributions to Philosophy: *An Introduction* (Indiana University Press, 2003). In her work on time, she approaches time in terms of the rhythmic articulation of things and events such that time is first and foremost *of* things and events in their encroaching occurrences.

**Katherine Withy** is Associate Professor of Philosophy at Georgetown University. She works on the nature of finitude in Heidegger's philosophy—not only the finitude of human beings (e.g. in moods), but also the finitude of being (e.g. its self-concealing character) and the finitude of meaning (especially in world collapse). Her book, *Heidegger on Being Uncanny*, was published by Harvard University Press in 2015.

# Martin Heidegger Abbreviations

BCAP      *Basic Concepts of Aristotelian Philosophy.* Trans. Robert D. Metcalf and Mark B. Tanzer. Bloomington, IN: Indiana University Press, 2009.

BP      *The Basic Problems of Phenomenology*, Revised ed. Ed. Albert Hofstadter. Bloomington, IN: Indiana University Press, 1988.

BQ      *Basic Questions of Philosophy: Selected "Problems" of "Logic."* Trans. Richard Rojcewicz and André Schuwer. Bloomington, IN: Indiana University Press, 1994.

BT      *Being and Time.* Trans. John Macquarrie and Edward Robinson. New York, NY: Harper & Row, 1962.

BW      *Basic Writings.* Ed. David Farrell Krell. New York, NY: HarperCollins, 1993.

CP      *Contributions to Philosophy (Of the Event).* Trans. Richard Rojcewicz and Daniela Vallega-Neu. Bloomington, IN: Indiana University Press, 2012.

CT      *The Concept of Time.* Trans. William McNeill. Oxford: Blackwell, 1992.

EHP      *Elucidations of Hölderlin's Poetry.* Trans. Keith Hoeller. Amherst, NY: Humanity Books, 2000.

ET      *The Essence of Truth: On Plato's Parable of the Cave Allegory and Theaetetus.* Trans. Ted Sadler. London: Continuum, 2002.

FCM         *The Fundamental Concepts of Metaphysics: World, Finitude,*
            *Solitude.* Trans. William McNeill and Nicholas Walker.
            Bloomington, IN: Indiana University Press, 1995.

HCT         *History of the Concept of Time: Prolegomena.* Trans. Theodore
            Kisiel. Bloomington, IN: Indiana University Press, 1985.

HGR         *Hölderlin's Hymns "Germania" and "The Rhine."* Trans. William
            McNeill and Julia Ireland. Bloomington, IN: Indiana University
            Press, 2014.

IM          *An Introduction to Metaphysics.* Trans. Gregory Fried and Richard
            Polt. New Haven, CT: Yale University Press, 2000.

IPR         *An Introduction to Phenomenological Research.* Trans. Daniel O.
            Dahlstrom. Bloomington, IN: Indiana University Press, 2005.

MFL         *The Metaphysical Foundations of Logic.* Trans. Michael Heim.
            Bloomington, IN: Indiana University Press, 1992.

N           *Nietzsche* (4 vols., volume number indicated by Roman numeral).
            Trans. David Farrell Krell. New York, NY: Harper & Row,
            1979–1987.

PIA         *Phenomenological Interpretations of Aristotle: Initiation*
            *into Phenomenological Research.* Trans. Richard Rojcewicz.
            Bloomington, IN: Indiana University Press, 2001.

PICA        *Phenomenological Interpretations in Connection with Aristotle: An*
            *Indication of the Hermeneutical Situation.* Trans. John van Buren,
            in Heidegger, ed. John van Buren, *Supplements: From the Earliest*
            *Essays to* Being and Time *and Beyond.* New York: SUNY Press,
            2002.

PM          *Pathmarks.* Trans. William McNeill. Cambridge: Cambridge
            University Press, 1998.

PRL         *The Phenomenology of Religious Life.* Trans. Matthias Frisch and
            Jennifer Anna Gosetti-Ferencei. Bloomington, IN: Indiana
            University Press, 2004.

PS          *Plato's Sophist.* Trans. Richard Rojcewicz and André Schuwer.
            Bloomington, IN: Indiana University Press, 1997.

Supp        *Supplements: From the Earliest Essays to* Being and Time *and*
            *Beyond.* Ed. John van Buren. Albany, NY: SUNY Press, 2002.

SZ          *Sein und Zeit (1927).* Tübingen: Max Niemeyer Verlag GmbH &
            Co., 1993.

WCT         *What Is Called Thinking?* Trans. Fred D. Wieck and J. Glenn Gray.
            New York, NY: Harper & Row, 1968.

| | |
|---|---|
| *WIP* | *What Is Philosophy?* Trans. Jean T. Wilde and William Kluback. New Haven, CT: College & University Press, 1958. |
| *WM* | *What Is Metaphysics?*, in *Pathmarks*. Trans. William McNeill. Cambridge: Cambridge University Press, 1998: 82–96. |
| *Zo* | *Zollikon Seminars: Protocols—Conversations—Letters.* Ed. Medard Boss, Trans. Mayr and Richard Askay. Evanston, IL: Northwestern University Press, 2001. |
| *GA 1* | *Frühe Schriften.* Gesamtausgabe vol. 1, ed. Friedrich-Wilhelm von Hermann. Frankfurt am Main: Vittorio Klostermann, 2018. |
| *GA 5* | *Holzwege (1935–1946).* Gesamtausgabe vol. 5, ed. Friedrich Wilhelm von Hermann. Frankfurt am Main: Vittorio Klostermann, 2003. |
| *GA 6.1* | *Nietzsche I (1936–1939).* Gesamtausgabe vol. 6.1, ed. Brigitte Schillbach. Frankfurt am Main: Vittorio Klostermann, 1996. |
| *GA 6.2* | *Nietzsche II (1939–1946).* Gesamtausgabe 6.2, ed. Brigitte Schillbach. Frankfurt am Main: Vittorio Klostermann, 1997. |
| *GA 8* | *Was heißt Denken? (1951–1952).* Gesamtausgabe vol. 8, ed. Paola Ludivika Coriando. Frankfurt am Main: Vittorio Klostermann, 2002. |
| *GA 9* | *Wegmarken (1919–1961).* Gesamtausgabe vol. 9, ed. Friedrich Wilhelm von Herrmann. Frankfurt am Main: Vittorio Klostermann, 2004. |
| *GA 11* | *Identität und Differenz (1955–1957).* Gesamtausgabe vol. 11, ed. Friedrich-Wilhelm von Herrmann. Frankfurt am Main: Vittorio Klostermann, 2006. |
| *GA 12* | *Unterwegs zur Sprache (1950–1959).* Gesamtausgabe vol. 12, ed. Friedrich-Wilhelm von Herrmann. Frankfurt am Main: Vittorio Klostermann, 2018. |
| *GA 16* | *Reden und andere Zeugnisse eines Lebensweges (1910–1976).* Gesamtausgabe vol. 16, ed. Hermann Heidegger. Frankfurt am Main: Vittorio Klostermann, 2000. |
| *GA 18* | *Grundbegriffe der aristotelischen Philosophie.* Gesamtausgabe vol. 18, ed. Mark Michalski. Frankfurt am Main: Vittorio Klostermann, 2002. |
| *GA 19* | *Platon: Sophistes.* Gesamtausgabe vol. 19, ed. Ingeborg Schüßler. Frankfurt am Main: Vittorio Klostermann, 2018. |
| *GA 20* | *Prolegomena zur Geschichte des Zeitbegriffs.* Gesamtausgabe vol. 20, ed. Petra Jaeger. Frankfurt am Main: Klostermann, 1994. |

GA 21      *Logik. Die Frage nach der Wahrheit.* Gesamtausgabe vol. 21, ed.
           Walter Biemel. Frankfurt am Main: Vittorio Klostermann, 1995.

GA 24      *Die Grundprobleme der Phänomenologie.* Gesamtausgabe
           vol. 24, ed. Friedrich-Wilhelm von Herrmann. Frankfurt am
           Main: Vittorio Klostermann, 1997.

GA 26      *Metaphysische Anfangsgründe der Logik im Ausgang von Leibniz.*
           Gesamtausgabe vol. 26, ed. Klaus Held. Frankfurt am Main:
           Vittorio Klostermann, 2007.

GA 27      *Einleitung in die Philosophie.* Gesamtausgabe vol. 27, ed. Otto
           Saame and Ina Saame-Speidel. Frankfurt am Main: Vittorio
           Klostermann, 2001.

GA 29/30   *Die Grundbegriffe der Metaphysik: Welt—Endlichkeit—Einsamkeit.*
           Gesamtausgabe vol. 29/30, ed. Friedrich-Wilhelm von Herrmann.
           Frankfurt am Main: Vittorio Klostermann, 2004.

GA 38      *Logik als die Frage nach dem Wesen der Sprache.* Gesamtausgabe
           vol. 38, ed. Günter Seubold. Frankfurt am Main: Vittorio
           Klostermann,1998.

GA 39      *Hölderlins Hymnen „Germanien" und „Der Rhein".* Gesamtausgabe
           vol. 39, ed. Susanne Ziegler. Frankfurt am Main: Vittorio
           Klostermann, 1999.

GA 43      *Nietzsche: Der Wille zur Macht als Kunst.* Gesamtausgabe vol.
           43, ed. Bernd Heimbüchel. Frankfurt am Main: Vittorio
           Klostermann, 1985.

GA 52      *Hölderlins Hymne „Andenken."* Gesamtausgabe vol. 52, ed. Curd
           Ochwadt. Frankfurt am Main: Vittorio Klostermann, 1992.

GA 58      *Grundprobleme der Phänomenologie.* Gesamtausgabe vol. 58,
           ed. Hans-Helmuth Gander. Frankfurt am Main: Vittorio
           Klostermann, 2010.

GA 60      *Phänomenologie des religiösen Lebens.* Gesamtausgabe vol. 60, ed.
           Claudius Strube. Frankfurt am Main: Vittorio Klostermann,
           2011.

GA 61      *Phänomenologische Untersuchungen zu Aristoteles.* Gesamtausgabe
           vol. 61, ed. Walter Bröcker and Käte Bröcker-Oltmanns.
           Frankfurt am Main: Vittorio Klostermann, 1994.

GA 63      *Ontologie (Hermeneutik der Faktizität).* Gesamtausgabe vol. 63,
           ed. Käte Bröcker-Oltmanns. Frankfurt am Main: Klostermann,
           2018.

GA 64     *Der Begriff der Zeit (1924).* Gesamtausgabe vol. 64, ed.
          Friedrich-Wilhelm von Herrmann. Frankfurt am Main: Vittorio
          Klostermann, 2004.
GA 65     *Beiträge zur Philosophie (Vom Ereignis)*, Gesamtausgabe vol. 65,
          ed. Friedrich-Wilhelm von Herrmann. Frankfurt am Main:
          Vittorio Klostermann, 2003.
GA 66     *Besinnung (1938/1939).* Gesamtausgabe vol. 66, ed. Friedrich-
          Wilhelm von Herrmann. Frankfurt am Main: Vittorio
          Klostermann, 1997.
GA 70     *Über den Anfang (1941).* Gesamtausgabe vol. 70, ed. Paola-
          Ludovika Coriando. Frankfurt am Main: Vittorio Klostermann,
          2005.
GA 73     *Zum Ereignis-Denken.* Gesamtausgabe vol. 73, ed. Peter Trawny.
          Frankfurt am Main: Vittorio Klostermann, 2013.
GA 75     *Zu Hölderlin—Griechenlandreisen.* Gesamtausgabe vol. 75, ed.
          Curd Ochwadt. Frankfurt am Main: Vittorio Klostermann, 2000.
GA 78     *Der Spruch des Anaximander.* Gesamtausgabe vol. 78, ed. Ingeborg
          Schüssler. Frankfurt am Main: Vittorio Klostermann, 2010.
GA 83     *Seminare: Platon—Aristoteles—Augustinus.* Gesamtausgabe
          vol. 83, ed. Mark Michalski. Frankfurt am Main: Vittorio
          Klostermann, 2012.
GA 90     *Zu Ernst Jünger.* Gesamtausgabe vol. 90, ed. Peter Trawny.
          Frankfurt am Main: Vittorio Klostermann, 2004.
GA 95     *Überlegungen VII–XI (Schwarze Hefte 1938/1939).*
          Gesamtausgabe vol. 95, ed. Peter Trawny. Frankfurt am Main:
          Vittorio Klostermann, 2014.

# List of Tables

# 1

# Being, Nothingness and Anxiety

## Mahon O'Brien

## 1  Being and Nothing

One of Heidegger's great disappointments in the immediate aftermath of the publication of *Being and Time* (*BT*), and something he bemoans frequently to the end of his life, are the myriad ways in which his early masterpiece was misread. Heidegger's 1927 text was misinterpreted variously as a kind of existentialism, as being nihilistic, preoccupied with the bleak nature of an absurd human condition in the face of an inevitable death, a contribution to philosophical anthropology, psychology, humanism, subjectivism—the list goes on and on. In some ways then, this paper is a modest attempt at a bit of housekeeping on Heidegger's behalf by returning to the question of the role of moods in *BT* as part of what has been a general strategy of mine in previous work, namely, to forestall or undermine readings of Heidegger in the literature which begin from the hermeneutic presupposition that the later Heidegger

M. O'Brien (✉)
University of Sussex, Brighton, UK
e-mail: mahon.o-brien@sussex.ac.uk

© The Author(s) 2019

C. Hadjioannou (ed.), *Heidegger on Affect*, Philosophers in Depth,
https://doi.org/10.1007/978-3-030-24639-6_1

exists only at the expense of the Heidegger that writes *BT*.[1] As Heidegger writes in his 1949 "Introduction to 'What Is Metaphysics?'":

> If, as we unfold the question concerning the truth of Being, we speak of overcoming metaphysics, this means: recalling Being itself. Such recalling goes beyond the traditional failure to think the ground of the root of philosophy. The thinking attempted in *Being and Time* sets out on the way to prepare an overcoming of metaphysics, so understood. (*PM* 279)

In a 1943 "Postscript to 'What Is Metaphysics?'" Heidegger suggests that his basic question "springs from a thinking that has already entered into the overcoming of metaphysics" (*PM* 231). Heidegger further argues (as he will again, famously, in "Letter on Humanism"[2]—though in a way that has been routinely misinterpreted) that any such attempts to overcome "must continue to speak the language of that which they help overcome" (*PM* 231). Furthermore, Heidegger, in returning to some of the key ideas animating *BT*, while re-assessing a lecture first delivered two years after he published that text, reminds his readers that his key question is related to the Leibnizian question.[3] He famously revisits the Leibnizian question in his 1935 lecture course, *Introduction to Metaphysics* (*IM*), (where he has routinely been thought to have effected a turn away from *BT*) identifying it as the fundamental question for Western metaphysics (which he has by now diagnosed as a metaphysics of presence)—a metaphysics that he wants to overcome. As he writes in another 1940s retrospective on the 1929 lecture:

> Metaphysics does not ask this question [the Being question/*Seinsfrage*] because it thinks Being only by representing being as beings. It means beings as a whole, although it speaks of Being. It names Being and means beings as beings. From its beginning to its completion, the propositions of metaphysics have been strangely involved in a persistent confusion of beings and Being. (Introduction to "What Is Metaphysics?" in *PM* 281)

In the 1929 lecture, Heidegger anticipates much of what he will discuss in his famous 1935 lecture course concerning the question of the nothing and the related ways that he attempts to put pressure on the tradition. He dismisses again what he takes to be stock objections which rely on the principle of non-contradiction since that approach, for Heidegger, has already conflated being with presence and has made a decision about the meaning of being, unwitting or otherwise, which he wishes to call into question. In the 1935 lecture course where Heidegger began to try and unfold many of the motivating ideas and themes behind *BT*,[4] be begins with Leibniz's famous question:

> Why are there beings at all instead of nothing? That is the question…this is obviously the first of all questions. Of course, it is not the first ques-tion in the chronological sense. Individuals as well as peoples ask many questions in the course of their historical passage through time. They explore, investigate, and test many sorts of things before they run into the question 'Why are there beings at all instead of nothing?' Many never run into this question at all, if running into the question means not only hearing and reading the interrogative sentence as uttered, but asking the question, that is, taking a stand on it, posing it, compelling oneself into the state of this questioning.

Heidegger is asking, when we pose this question of being and non-being or nothing, whether we have an adequate sense of 'being'? What do we mean by this word 'being'—what does this verb so commonly invoked bring to the party? Of course, the obvious answer is 'presence' and, for this reason, Leibniz's own question focuses on the simple issue of presence versus absence. As Heidegger says in one of the later reflec-tions on his famous inaugural lecture ("What Is Metaphysics?"):

> Is it perhaps from this that the as yet unshaken presumption has entered all metaphysics that an understanding of 'Being' may simply be taken for granted and that the Nothing can therefore be dealt with more easily than beings? That is indeed the situation regarding Being and Nothing. If it were different, then Leibniz could not have said in the same place by way of an explanation: 'Car le rien est plus simple et plus facile que quelque chose [For the nothing is simpler and easier than any thing].' ("Introduction to 'What Is Metaphysics?'" *PM* 190)

Heidegger notes something that he considers both non-trivial and which he thinks the tradition has not adequately dealt with. We say of many things that they 'are' in various ways when it is not clear that that means that they exist as fully *present* or actualized before us. For example, if I say that I see a clearing in the forest, or a gap in the hedge—I say that there 'is' a gap. But what does it mean to say that there is a 'gap', literally an absence of trees in one instance or foliage on the side of the road on the other? Someone might try to counter that that is just a trick of language; that all we mean is that there is a space where no trees are growing or no hedge is growing. But, think of how else we might express this—'there *are no trees* in that part of the forest' or 'there *is nothing* between those two pieces of hedge'.[5] What do we mean with this verb 'being'—what does the term itself actually *mean*? One might be tempted to go the route of First Order logic here and suggest that if we rewrite the sentences using existential quantifiers that this kind of problem dissolves but Heidegger believes that that is because the logician has already assumed that being means presence (understood here as continuous presence) and that any talk of 'the nothing' as somehow 'being' is literally nonsense. For the logician then, they might try to rewrite similar kinds of sentences by translating them into other sentences that appear to have the same meaning, which can, in turn, be translated using existential quantifiers. And, using something like this approach, one can say that there is no problem and that one does not have to posit the presence of absence in an ideal language in order to understand the statement that there is a gap or clearing in the forest. However, Heidegger is unsatisfied with this kind of approach and anticipates it and rejects it in *IM* as well as in his 1940s retrospectives on his 1929 essay ("What Is Metaphysics") which was famously attacked by Carnap in a 1932 paper (see Carnap 1932).[6] It is worth bearing in mind here that Heidegger had spent some time studying mathematics and logic and described himself as an 'ahistorical mathematician' before his breakthroughs in the 1920s. Of course, that is not to suggest that Heidegger was fully au fait with the latest developments in the philosophical logic of his day.[7] But neither is this the perversely vainglorious innumeracy or ill-informed prejudice of some literary crank with no real facility for mathematics or logic.

In his 1935 lecture course, in order to illustrate his point with respect to the role of the nothing in terms of what it means for anything 'to be', Heidegger takes an immediate example from the lecture hall—a piece of chalk:

> The piece of chalk here is an extended, relatively stable, definitely formed, grayish-white thing, and furthermore, a thing for writing. As certainly as it belongs precisely to this thing to lie here, the capacity not to be here and not to be so big also belongs to it. The possibility of being drawn along the blackboard and used up is not something that we merely add onto the thing with our thought. The chalk itself, as this being, *is* in this possibility; otherwise it would not be chalk as a writing implement. Every being, in turn, has this Possible in it, in a different way in each case. This possible belongs to the chalk. (*IM* 32)

In other words, so Heidegger wants to say, what the chalk means, what we take it to mean when we say that the chalk 'is' in various ways, amounts to more than simply stating that the chalk is 'present' or 'actual'. Of course it *is* present in various ways, but it can also be understood in all manner of *possible* ways that involve more than what is actually present at any given moment. Moreover, this is a fundamental part of what it *means* for things to *be*. For Heidegger, the logician will be tempted to respond that when anyone says of the chalk that 'the chalk is' that this is adequately represented by the propositional form ∃xCx—there exists some entity/x such that that entity/x is a piece of chalk. Heidegger very clearly has Carnap and the logical positivists in mind here and explicitly targets the principle of non-contradiction:

> Whoever talks about Nothing does not know what he is doing. In speaking about Nothing, he makes it into a something. By speaking this way, he speaks against what he means. He contra-dicts himself. But self-contradictory speech is an offense against the fundamental rule of speech (*logos*), against 'logic.' Talking about Nothing is illogical. Whoever talks and thinks illogically is an unscientific person. Now whoever goes so far as to talk about Nothing within philosophy, which after all is the home of logic, deserves all the more to be accused of offending against the fundamental rule of all thinking. Such talk about Nothing consists in utterly

senseless propositions. Moreover, whoever takes Nothing seriously takes the side of nullity. He obviously promotes the spirit of negation and serves disintegration. Talking about Nothing is not only completely contrary to thought, but it undermines all culture and faith. Whatever both disregards the fundamental law of thinking and also destroys faith and the will to construct is pure nihilism. (*IM* 25–26)

The obvious suggestion here is that one should perhaps simply ignore the question or issue of the Nothing. However, Heidegger notes that we already began with this question as a question that we received from the tradition and he further notes that the question of being was always posed in conjunction with the question of Nothingness from that same tradition:

Our introduction of talk about Nothing here is not a careless and overly enthusiastic manner of speaking, nor our own invention, but merely strict respect for the originary tradition regarding the sense of the fundamental question. (*IM* 26)

And yet, as Heidegger suggests, it may well be the case that the belief that this notion of 'Nothing' and/or any discussion of it as being tantamount to nihilism or a confounding of the fundamental and immutable laws of thinking rests on a misunderstanding. He reiterates then his opposition to the idea that rules of logic such as the principle of non-contradiction necessarily operate as the rules upon which any understanding of anything whatsoever must be based since this thinking itself rests upon a misunderstanding when it comes to the being question:

For it cannot be decided so readily whether logic and its fundamental rules can provide any measure for the question about beings as such. It could be the other way around, that the whole logic that we know and that we treat like a gift from heaven is grounded in a very definite answer to the question about beings, and that consequently any thinking that simply follows the laws of thought of established logic is intrinsically incapable of even beginning to understand the question about beings, much less of actually unfolding it and leading toward an answer. In truth, it is only an illusion of rigor and scientificity when one appeals to the principle of contradiction, and to logic in general, in order to prove that all thinking and all talk about Nothing is contradictory and therefore senseless. 'Logic' is then taken as a tribunal, secure for all eternity, and it goes without saying that no rational human being will call into doubt its authority as the first and last court of appeal. Whoever speaks against logic is suspected, implicitly or explicitly, of arbitrariness. The mere suspicion already counts as an argument and an objection, and one takes oneself to be exempted from further, authentic reflection. (*IM* 27)

The question of nothingness has always, in our philosophical tradition, gone hand in hand with the question of being. We normally begin with 'beings' and, beings of course 'are':

They are given to us, they are in front of us and can thus be found before us at any time, and are also known to us within certain domains. Now the beings given to us in this way are immediately interrogated as to their ground. The question advances directly toward a ground. Such a method just broadens and enlarges, as it were, a procedure that is practised every day. Somewhere in the vineyard, for example, an infestation turns up, something indisputably present at hand. One asks: where does this come from, where and what is its ground? Similarly, as a whole, beings are present at hand. One asks: where and what is the ground? This kind of questioning is represented in the simple formula: Why are there beings? Where and what is their ground? Tacitly one is asking after another, higher being. But there the question does not pertain at all to beings as a whole and as such. (*IM* 30)

One can see then that Heidegger is trying to identify a misstep that we have commonly taken when it comes to thinking about being and beings. We begin with things that are there for us and immediately begin to wonder as to why they are there, what is the cause of these beings. And traditionally— one closed off that line of questioning with the idea of a higher being that caused all the other beings. But this misses something for Heidegger since it glosses over the question as to what we mean by 'being' and simply asks for the cause (the why) of things that are present. This is to assume that what 'being' means when we say that beings 'are' reduces to 'presence'— that is, 'existent', and thus we have taken for granted precisely the issues that Heidegger thinks are open to further questioning. If one considers the original question again "Why are there beings at all instead of nothing?"—we notice now that one cannot accept the prejudice concerning logic and non-contradiction since we cannot in this case simply take beings as given in the first place according to the scope of this originary question. Rather we have to consider the possibility of there not being beings. The addition of the nothing to our question in this instance:

> Prevents us, in our questioning, from beginning directly with beings as unquestionably given, and having already begun, already moving on to the ground we are seeking which is also in being. Instead, these beings are held out in a questioning manner into the possibility of not-Being. (*IM* 30)

Heidegger is convinced that traditional approaches miss out on all of the possibilities inherent in what we 'mean', for example, when we say that the chalk *is* here, or there, or *is* something or other. Part of what it means for the chalk to be a particular piece of chalk is its possibility of being used up when drawn along the blackboard and thus to no longer be—this is part of what it means for the chalk to be—it 'is' in this possibility. But, Heidegger goes on to argue:

> Of course, when we look for this Possible in the chalk, we are accustomed and inclined to say that we do not see it and do not grasp it. But that is a prejudice. The elimination of this prejudice is part of the unfolding of our question. For now, this question should just open up beings, in their wavering between not-Being and Being. Insofar as beings stand up against the extreme possibility of not-Being, they themselves stand in Being, and yet they have never thereby overtaken and overcome the possibility of not-Being. (*IM* 32–33)

Heidegger goes on to ask:

> How are we even supposed to inquire into the ground for the Being of beings, let alone be able to find it out, if we have not adequately conceived, understood and grasped Being itself? This enterprise would be just as hopeless as if someone wanted to explain the cause and ground of a fire and declared that he need not bother with the course of the fire or the investigation of its scene.
>
> So it turns out that the question 'Why are there beings at all instead of nothing?' forces us to the prior question: '*How does it stand with Being?*' (*IM* 34)

Heidegger is convinced then that there is a fundamental problem which has led philosophy astray from the time of the Presocratic philosophers. In short, the Western tradition has taken the meaning of being itself to be self-evident and thus overlooked an important philosophical dimension to the way things become meaningful for us and how we in turn project meanings onto the world around us and this has generated a whole series of pseudo problems. Without getting too far ahead of ourselves, Heidegger believes that we have inherited a philosophical tradition, which, for all its variety, vagaries and conflicting views, is based on an underlying prejudice, namely, that things or objects given to us in experience, appear to us as continuously present. What is suppressed, however, is the role that *absence* or *nothingness* plays in our experience and how most of our experience involves a constant interplay of presence and absence. Nothing/no object is ever fully there and available to us as completely present in every particularity/possibility; indeed, Heidegger believes that this is obvious even in our experience of ordinary, everyday objects such as the chalk. When I say—'I see a piece of chalk over there'—I mean or intend *that* piece of chalk and *part* of what I mean or intend are aspects and possibilities of the chalk that are not actually present, or there, or continuously there before me. Heidegger is invoking a famous idea of Husserl's here, namely, the notion of 'intentionality'. Indeed, Heidegger believed this to be one of Husserl's most important philosophical insights. Husserl realized that the way things appear to us involves a significant amount of 'intentional' work done by us in terms of meaning or intending the things that we perceive. If one considers something in the room or place they are sitting for a moment—perhaps a lamp in the corner, a picture on the wall, a car passing by the window outside or in the distance; now consider what one *actually* perceives. One sees one particular side, perhaps, of a lampshade; a good deal of the object may actually be obscured from one's view and yet we don't say that we see a part of a conical surface attached to what appears to be a supporting stem—we say that we see a lamp. In other words, we imagine the rest of the lamp to exist, we fill out the profile of the lamp imaginatively and synthesize this with what we currently perceive such that our intentional experience is not of something partially obscured but a fully conceived thing. Similarly with the picture on the wall, we imagine that it is three-dimensional, has depth and that there is a wall and hanging nail supporting the picture and the frame. In terms of the passing car, one might well say that they have heard a passing car, but what was actually given to them in terms of bare perception? It may only have been a sound or a series of sounds that reached one's ears and yet what they 'heard' was not a series of bare auditory sensations, what they 'heard' was a car that was not slowing down to turn into their driveway, rather they heard the sound of a car travelling with sufficient speed so as to suggest that it was driving on by the house. They *hear*, in that case, something very different to what they hear when they hear their spouse's car turning into the driveway, the unmistakeable sound of the way they let the car idle before turning in and the full, vibrating baritone of the heavy diesel engine of that particular vehicle. As Heidegger explains in "The Origin of the Work of Art":

> We never really first perceive a throng of sensations, e.g., tones and noises, in the appearance of things – as this thing-concept alleges; rather we hear the storm whistling in the chimney, we hear the three-motored plane, we hear the Mercedes in immediate distinction from the Volkswagen. Much closer to us than all sensations are the things themselves. We hear the door shut in the house and never hear acoustical sensations or even mere sounds. In order to hear a bare sound we have to listen away from things, divert our ear from them, i.e., listen abstractly. (*BW* 151–152)

Similarly with other objects which are 'experienced'—what the perceiver may actually be presented with is often a rather partial, obscured view and yet their imagination spontaneously fills out the rest of the profile of the thing which they don't actually see—the back of the lampshade which is absent is somehow made present by the imagination without actually being directly perceived during that experience. This insight fits nicely with Heidegger's belief that we artificially render everything as fully present to ourselves without realizing that some of the aspects and features which we make 'present' are not actually present in our experience, rather we project them onto our experience and, when we forget or suppress this activity, we are left with a skewed metaphysical picture whereby the temporal, historical character of existence is concealed from us.

# 2     Why Moods?

When introducing the traditional and, Heidegger suggests, 'first' question of metaphysics in the 1935 lecture course, that is, Leibniz's question, Heidegger claims that:

> we are each touched once, maybe even now and then, by the concealed power of this question, without properly grasping what is happening to us. In great despair, for example, when all weight tends to dwindle away from things and the sense of things grows dark, the question looms. Perhaps it strikes only once, like the muffled tolling of a bell that resounds into Dasein and gradually fades away. The question is there in heartfelt joy, for then all things are transformed and surround us as if for the first time, as if it were easier to grasp that they were not than that they are, and are as they are. The question is there in a spell of boredom, when we are equally distant from despair and joy, but when the stubborn ordinariness of beings lays open a wasteland in which it makes no difference to us whether beings are or are not – and then, in a distinctive form, the question resonates again: Why are there beings at all instead of nothing? (*IM* 1–2)

Closely read, one can see that this passage contains a series of buried allusions to the role that 'bare moods' or states-of-mind/dispositions could play in terms of how they phenomenally attest to the manner in which Dasein is the open site for the interplay of presence and absence. That is, that again in this passage, what Heidegger is underlining is the phenomenal importance of moods in terms of how they disclose more than what is simply present. Instead, they are a constant source of evidence of movement and interplay between presence and absence.[8] He is trying that is, to show how there is a liminal awareness of 'more than this', 'more than what is just present' constantly attested to in our affectivity. Heidegger introduced this idea in *Being and Time*, and attempts to explain it more succinctly in 1935 and in the 1929 lecture through some simple examples involving the role that possibilities play in the manner in which anything can be taken by us to be.

In terms of Leibniz's question, Heidegger, as we saw, believes that he must pose another, deeper question—the question concerning the *meaning* of Being which already demands a re-examination as evidenced by the way the 'nothing' in Leibniz's question is simply passed over. We need to return to this question, so Heidegger argues, unencumbered with the presuppositions of the metaphysics of presence. For Heidegger, then, the 'nothing' is dismissed as a result of a fateful prejudice concerning the meaning of Being which has dominated Western thought since the time of the Presocratics. Being has, since that time, been discussed always and everywhere in terms of beings and, thus, as reducing always and everywhere to 'presence'. The principle of non-contradiction is routinely invoked to dismiss all talk of the Nothing as simply wrongheaded, illogical, unscientific, in short, as contradictory. After all, to talk of Nothing as 'being' in any way is to treat it as a being and one simply cannot make nothingness into something—but again this is already to have conflated being with beings.[9] And again, for Heidegger, this is already to have decided in advance that being reduces to presence, that it is present, or that it is itself *a* being and not nothing.

In the 1929 lecture, when his sights are set squarely on the role of nothingness, Heidegger returns to his *BT* account of states-of-mind or the bare moods which all of our experience presupposes and which themselves attest to the way we find ourselves already thrown open as a site for the interplay of presence and absence as finite transcendences. Part of what we are held out into, even in this early account in *BT*, is the nothing and Heidegger returns to and defends this idea in 1929, in 1935 and again in his 1940s introduction and postscript to the 1929 lecture. And again, this seems to invite us to begin to think of *BT* itself as very much anticipating the continuing attempts to resist the metaphysics of presence for the rest of his career. In 1929, for example, Heidegger will state:

> The founding mode of attunement [*die Befindlichkeit der Stimmung*] not only reveals beings as a whole in various ways, but this revealing – far from being merely incidental – is also the basic occurrence of our Da-sein. (*BW* 100)

Heidegger is quick to distinguish this notion, which is called a 'bare mood' or basic attunement in *BT*, from feelings which are in fact a way of diverting us away from the 'nothing' which is what he is looking to investigate. Such feelings, psychic phenomena, directed or thematic moods, if you like, are taken up with things or matters in the world of everyday concern. Heidegger is looking for something else, however; he asks:

> Does such an attunement, in which man is brought before the nothing itself, occur in human existence? This can and does occur, although rarely enough and only for a moment, in the fundamental mood of anxiety. By this anxiety we do not mean the quite common anxiousness, ultimately reducible to fearfulness, which all too readily comes over us. Anxiety is basically different from fear. We become afraid in the face of this or that particular being that threatens us in this or that particular respect. (*BW* 100)

Heidegger is thinking of a kind of anxiety that is not specifically directed then. He is thinking of a 'fundamental mood', something which is there, simmering away behind all our directed experience and which reaches up fully into our conscious awareness only rarely. But there is some sense of it whispering away in the background, just out of earshot, in a manner that we perhaps register as background noise that never leaves us entirely alone in any particular moment of existence. When anxiety comes into full view for us, we are not anxious in a specific way, we are anxious before nothing in particular; all things that normally have significance are suddenly robbed of that same significance, they recede from our concern and we are left anxious about, nothing in particular, anxious over, if you like, nothing. Heidegger believes in fact that in the most basic occurrence of Dasein, the nothing is revealed; this is what anxiety discloses, but anxiety understood now as a fundamental mood, a bare mood, a basic attunement of our awareness, a fundamental dispositional state. And, the nature of our everyday evasion, our absorption with things, is itself phenomenological testament to the nothingness which is disclosed in our most basic disposition/disposedness. We are normally turned toward things, we are preoccupied in one way or another and turned away from the prior experience of the Nothing. Our 'turned-awayness' testifies in fact to the

Nothing which we are held out into—the manner in which we are a transcendence in that we are already beyond beings as a whole. To be Dasein, is in a way, to be non-static, moving, thus there is this constant bare sense of 'more than now', 'more than this' constantly at work in our awareness.

This *seems* to be an uncontroversial gloss of some of the fundamental impulses behind Heidegger's thinking in the 1920s that he returns to and reinforces in the 1930s and 1940s. And yet, if these *are* uncontroversial pieces of analysis and summary, that is somewhat surprising, since the ramifications of this quick overview put pressure on some entrenched views concerning the discontinuity of the later Heidegger's project with the so-called early one and force us to take stock of and indeed rethink what, in fact, Heidegger's interest in moods might be! One of the claims that I wish to make then is that Heidegger had already carefully laid the groundwork for everything I've alluded to so far in this essay in *BT*. His 1927 text is thereby understood as, at least in part, a nascent attempt to overcome the metaphysics of presence. And, as it turns out, Heidegger goes to considerable lengths in the earlier text to unpack what he takes to be phenomenally evident in the barest experiences available to Dasein prior to all abstraction and which any engaged absorption in the world of our concern already presupposes and operates in the mode of a turning away from. Heidegger very much anticipates and introduces all of the key ideas and arguments that the later concerns with the nothing will be based on in his 1927 text.

*   *   *

In *BT*, Heidegger introduces the concept of mood (*Stimmung*), in the context of what Macquarrie and Robinson translate as state-of-mind/disposition (*Befindlichkeit*). Heidegger's claim is that our basic state-of-mind, quite literally, the way we find ourselves, is such that we are always in some kind of bare mood. There is some kind of minimal affectivity to our awareness ever before we thematize that affect and what Heidegger will try to show is that it is already itself indicative of nothingness, even if the provisional notion that he focuses on in the earlier text is time.

Heidegger clarifies again at the beginning of his discussion

> In the preparatory stage of the existential analytic of Dasein, we have for
> our leading theme this entity's basic state, Being-in-the-world. Our first
> aim is to bring into relief phenomenally the unitary primordial structure
> of Dasein's Being, in terms of which its possibilities and the ways for it 'to
> be' are ontologically determined. (*SZ* 131)

The key thing to note here is the use of the term "possibilities" and the
phrase "ways for it [Dasein] 'to be'". The importance of the role that
possibility plays in *BT* cannot be overstated. Also important to note is
the stated aim of getting the unitary primordial structure of Dasein's
being into view since it is a state-of-mind which will attest to the fact
(and when investigated will show how) that this happens by confronting Dasein with its 'there' before it actually turns toward anything
specific within the world of its quotidian concern, which is typically a
turning away from what is attested to in such bare moods. What allows
us to get a view of the unitary primordial structure of Dasein's being is
something like *angst*—which Heidegger, I believe, wants to characterize as a bare sense of 'more than this', 'more than what is present now',
which is the most basic level of our affective awareness at any given
moment into which we find ourselves thrown. And, the more than this,
the more than now, the not now, and not here, points to the nothingness, the abyss which haunts the edges of presence, the nothing which is
the necessary correlate of anything that is.

Heidegger makes another claim shortly afterwards, which is related to
this and consistent with the idea that he is not looking here to make any
kind of contribution to psychology or anthropology:

> If need be, there still remains the possibility of broadening out the anal-
> ysis by characterizing comparatively the variations of concern and its
> circumspection, of solicitude and the considerateness which goes with
> it; there is also the possibility of contrasting Dasein with entities whose
> character is not that of Dasein by a more precise explication of the Being
> of all possible entities within-the-world. Without question, there are still
> unfinished tasks lying in this field. What we have hitherto set forth needs
> to be rounded out in many ways by working out fully the existential *a*

*priori* of philosophical anthropology and taking a look at it. But this is not the aim of our investigation. *Its aim is one of fundamental ontology.* (*SZ* 131; Heidegger's emphasis)

Heidegger is *not* looking to contribute to an existentialism, humanism or psychology or to say anything specifically about the human condition. Of course, human beings will ultimately be affected by adequately posing the question concerning the meaning of being in general since humans are affected by the question and the answer; as Heidegger says a number of times, we are 'implicated' in the answer—one can find Heidegger reiterating this very point in his famous "Letter on Humanism". Notwithstanding, Heidegger is, even here, already interested in what is going to become his lifelong attempt to overcome the metaphysics of presence.[10] The goal is always then something like the meaning of being in general; it is not his intention or desire to simply contribute to psychology. Heidegger wants to overcome the metaphysics of presence. And, with this in mind, Heidegger is looking for phenomenal evidence that the being which is the subject of investigation in *BT*, Dasein, offers us some phenomenal clues or evidence as to how already, in the most basic state of Dasein's awareness, there is some sense of more than what is just present. This, in turn, leads Heidegger to look at the most basic affective state of our 'thereness'.[11]

The aspect of the existential constitution of the there that we are interested in, in particular, is being-there as a 'state-of-mind' (*Befindlichkeit*).[12] The way one 'finds' oneself (which is what the German term picks out quite literally) is clearly what most of us would mean when we ask after someone's state-of-mind, what is typically referred to in the literature today as 'disposition'. And, the answer, Heidegger suggests, is always going to involve a 'mood' or 'attunement' (*Stimmung*). Heidegger immediately qualifies the sense in which he is going to discuss moods and, again, stresses his interest in looking at moods as an existentiale, that is, as a basic structural component of Dasein, a way that it can be:

Prior to all psychology of moods, a field which in any case still lies fallow, it is necessary to see this phenomenon as a fundamental *existentiale*, and to outline its structure. (*SZ* 134)

A lot of the misconceptions concerning Heidegger's treatment of angst in *BT* and again in his 1929 inaugural lecture, then, are owing to a failure to see the context within which these analyses occur. As we can see from some of the passages already quoted, Heidegger continually emphasizes the fact that his goal in *BT* is not to contribute to anything like a discussion of our psychological states or feelings about x or y[13]; he is not trying to write about the human condition per se, this is *not* existentialism or humanism.[14] And again, it is worth noting that one of the most common interpretive viruses that infects new readers of *BT*, influenced by generations of carriers of this same interpretive contagion, is the assumption that the later Heidegger rejects *BT* owing to its excessive reliance on traditional subjectivity or that *BT* is a Dasein-oriented story, his humanist, existentialist phase and so on. Heidegger is interested in the question concerning the way being becomes meaningful and he first looks to tackle this question by looking at the being whose own being is an issue and is meaningful for it—Dasein. But even this task should not be taken as a Dasein-oriented story; the aim is the meaning of being in general. So, what we should be on the look out for, ultimately, are the ways in which Heidegger investigates the role that possibility (and thus 'absence') plays in Dasein's being-in-the-world such that he can find some phenomenal evidence to justify the attempt at a fundamental ontology, which, in turn, would be a departure from the metaphysics of presence. After all, this is what the question concerning the meaning of Being is concerned with. This interpretive failure on the part of readers of *BT* is not localized to this particular topic—it is one of the main reasons that the account of authenticity, for example, is routinely misinterpreted and it stands as the most consistent pattern of interpretive failure in terms of the general understanding of Heidegger's various accounts of being-in-the-world, the call of conscience, being-towards-death, anxiety and so on. To paraphrase his conclusion from above—the aim is a fundamental ontology, which, I am suggesting here, is a nascent attempt to get beyond the metaphysics of presence. To do so, Heidegger needs to find a way to identify the interplay of presence and absence in the way anything 'is' for Dasein, including Dasein's own self. This is going to involve identifying the role that 'possibility' plays in Dasein's self-understanding at any given moment, very much in the way that in 1935, Heidegger will famously characterize the features which lie as possibilities for the chalk, but which are not currently 'present', as part of what it means for the chalk to be this or that piece of chalk. In terms of Dasein, anxiety is the mood which attests to the role that the not-yet, the possible, and thus the non-present or the Nothing play in Dasein's existence and it is from *this* standpoint that Heidegger is interested in anxiety:

> In having a mood, Dasein is always disclosed moodwise as that entity to which it has been delivered over in its Being; and in this way it has been delivered over to the Being which, in existing, it has to be. 'To be disclosed' does not mean 'to be known as this sort of thing'. And even in the most indifferent and inoffensive everydayness the Being of Dasein can burst forth as a naked 'that it is and has to be'. The pure 'that it is' shows itself, but the 'whence' and the 'whither' remain in darkness. The fact that it is just as everyday a matter for Dasein not to 'give in' ['nach-gibt'] to such moods – in other words, not to follow up [nachgeht] their disclosure and allow itself to be brought before that which is disclosed – is no evidence *against* the phenomenal facts of the case, in which the Being of the 'there' is disclosed moodwise in its 'that-it-is', it is rather evidence for it. In an *ontico*-existentiell sense, Dasein for the most part evades the Being which is disclosed in the mood. In an *ontologico*-existential sense, this means that even in that to which a mood pays no attention, Dasein is unveiled in its Being-delivered-over to the 'there'. In the evasion itself the 'there' *is* something disclosed. (*SZ* 135)

Heidegger is introducing a feature of Dasein's being-in-the-world which is crucial to his account—namely 'throwness' (*Geworfenheit*). We operate in such a way that it can often seem as though we are absorbed in one project before moving on to another, there is a surface story to our activities which we do not interrogate as to their ultimate signifi-cance since we normally look to avoid or evade what is disclosed to us in the basic, thrown character of the 'da' of everyday Dasein. Part of what is disclosed, is the nullity at the heart of Dasein. Heidegger will later say that Dasein is the null basis of a nullity and our underlying angst is a constant testament to that phenomenal fact. He will go fur-ther into this notion of anxiety in paragraph 40 of *BT*; this is what he will look to examine in his 1929 inaugural lecture, underline in the

1940s introduction and postscript to that lecture, and it emerges once again in the context of the fundamental question of metaphysics (Why are there beings at all instead of nothing) in his 1935 lecture course—*Introduction to Metaphysics*. Here, as he introduces the notion of throwness, Heidegger writes:

> This characteristic of Dasein's being – this 'that it is' – is veiled in its 'whence' and 'whither', yet disclosed in itself all the more unveiledly; we call it the '*throwness*' of this entity into its 'there'. The expression 'throwness' is meant to suggest the *facticity of its being delivered over*. (*SZ* 135)

Experiencing its 'there' is not the same as experiencing itself in terms of its thatness, where its thatness reduces to pure presence, i.e., where we are thinking the way we would of an object which is present-at-hand and can be posited as being there as a fully actualized object with properties. Again, this is always something that Heidegger is trying to move us away from. Instead then:

> The 'that it is' which is disclosed in Dasein's state-of-mind must rather be conceived as an existential attribute of the entity which has Being-in-the-world as its way of Being. (*SZ* 135)

And to be-in-the-world, understood now as 'a way to be', is always going to be directional, a being-towards, absorbed for the most part in all kinds of projects. What we are, most basically then, before any abstraction, is always already thrown such that we are as a 'way to be' which means towards possibilities. Heidegger in turn is going to look for that bare mood which colours our basic thrown situation and which attests to the fundamental possibility which is constitutive of the way any other possibilities can be meaningful for us. In other words, as long as Dasein is, it has at least one constant possibility which constitutively shapes all of our other possibilities, namely, the possibility *not*-to-be. For the most part we are immersed in possibilities which, in a way, allow us to escape or evade the starkness of the nullity which is at the heart of the 'da' of Dasein. However, these possibilities in turn, phenomenally attest to the manner in which we are ultimately temporal, historical, finite transcendences. His excavation of the basic underlying fact that we are always and ever delivered over to our 'there' such that we find ourselves in some kind of mood testifies to this.[15] To continue, one might well claim to be assured about where they are coming from and what they are up to, or be able to issue an exact theoretical account of what they are taken up with at any given moment. This does not entail, however, that what is disclosed by moods can be compared with "what Dasein is acquainted with, knows, and believes 'at the same time' when it has such a mood" (*SZ* 135–136). It is this notion of possibility, itself run through with nullity and nothingness, which Heidegger is alluding to when he mentions the "burdensome character of Dasein" even if, for the most part, in our inauthentic everydayness we turn away from the reality of this situation. Moreover, fundamental moods are prior to (if you like, they outstrip) any evasion or specific moods about things in the world and bring:

> Dasein before the 'that-it-is' of its 'there', which, as such, stares it in the face with the inexorability of an enigma. From the existential-ontological point of view, there is not the slightest justification for minimizing what is 'evident' in states-of-mind, by measuring it against the apodictic certainty of a theoretical cognition of something which is purely present-at-hand. (*SZ* 136)

Heidegger has thus worked his way to a position where he can begin to examine states-of-mind in our everyday situation and thus determine phenomenologically, in keeping with the avowed goal of a hermeneutics of facticity, the role that nothingness and possibility play in the manner in which Dasein can understand anything to be or that anything can be meaningful for Dasein. Heidegger makes a further point that bears on how we think of the role of moods in his thinking at this structural, existential level:

> From what has been said we can see already that a state-of-mind is very remote from anything like coming across a psychical condition by the kind of apprehending which first turns around and then back. Indeed it is so far from this, that only because the 'there' has already been disclosed in

a state-of-mind can immanent reflection come across 'Experiences' at all. The 'bare mood' discloses the 'there' more primordially, but correspondingly it *closes* it *off* more stubbornly than any *not*-perceiving. (*SZ* 136)

In other words, when we are taken up with a mood which is directed precisely within our world of immediate concern, a bad mood, perhaps, we are diverted away from the nature of mood as a primordial state-of-mind which phenomenally attests or discloses Being-in-the-world as a whole, which indicates, in turn, the absence that corresponds to the presence of anything or anybody within the world and the role that possibility plays in the meaning of anything which currently is taken to be in a specific way. Thus it is a mistake to simply conflate mood, in the sense that Heidegger is talking about here, a bare mood, a state-of-mind with the psychical. Mood, as a bare mood:

has already disclosed, in every case, Being-in-the-world as a whole, *and makes it possible first of all to direct oneself towards something.* Having a mood is not related to the psychical in the first instance, and it is not an inner condition which then reaches forth in an enigmatical way and puts its mark on Things and persons. (*SZ* 137)

Before Heidegger turns specifically to anxiety, he offers a detailed examination of Dasein as it is in fallen everydayness where Dasein has fled from what he thinks it is faced with before we begin to reflect on things and as a result of which we immerse ourselves in a world of feigned continuous presence. In short, what is laid bare for us is ourselves as a thrown-openness for the emergence of being, a clearing in which presence and absence are interlinked. However, even if ordinarily we have turned away from that which we are faced with in our basic state-of-mind and its bare moods, that does not mean that we are not afforded phenomenal clues which cash out at the existential-ontological level:

Within the ontical 'away from' which such turning-away implies, that in the face of which Dasein flees can be understood and conceptualized by 'turning-thither' in a way which is phenomenologically Interpretative. (*SZ* 185)

Anxiety then, at the level that Heidegger is discussing things, is not concerned with something specific within the world, some entity or other; that is, rather, fear, which for Heidegger is derivative insofar as it is parasitic on a disposition of that being that has *angst* as its most basic state-of-mind when it first finds itself as thrown being-in-the-world:

> the turning-away of falling is not a fleeing that is founded upon a fear of entities within-the-world. Fleeing that is so grounded is still less a character of this turning-away, when what this turning-away does is precisely to *turn thither* towards entities within-the-world by absorbing itself in them. *This turning-away of falling is grounded rather in anxiety, which in turn is what first makes fear possible.*
>
> To understand this talk about Dasein's fleeing in the face of itself in falling, we must recall that Being-in-the-world is a basic state of Dasein. *That in the face of which one has anxiety [das Wovor der Angst] is Being-in-the-world as such.* What is the difference phenomenally between that in the face of which anxiety is anxious [sich ängstet] and that in the face of which fear is afraid? That in the face of which one has anxiety is not an entity within-the-world. (*SZ* 186)

So, again, this is the anxiety that is there when Dasein is in a basic state-of-mind as simply thrown and disclosed as delivered over to its being-in-the-world and the sheer 'thatness' of what that entails, which involves more than just being that, that being, but is a constant sense of more than 'thatness' or 'thisness'. It is anxious in the face of the implications of its own situation and possibilities which are already implied in the way it is thrown into a situation bounded by temporal limits. Heidegger describes that in the face of which we are anxious as 'nothing in the world':

> In that in the face of which one has anxiety, the 'It is nothing and nowhere' becomes manifest. The obstinacy of the 'nothing and nowhere within-the-world' means as a phenomenon that *the world as such is that in the face of which one has anxiety.* The utter insignificance which makes itself known in the 'nothing and nowhere', does not signify that the world

is absent, but tells us that entities within-the-world are of so little importance in themselves that on the basis of this *insignificance* of what is within-the-world, the world in its worldhood is all that still obtrudes itself.

What oppresses us is not this or that, nor is it the summation of everything present-at-hand; it is rather the *possibility* of the ready-to-hand in general; that is to say, it is the world itself. (*SZ* 186–187)

As ready-to-hand—things express their possible and timely character and thus point to the possibility of the nothing, of no longer being, which is all part of what it means for them to be. The ready-to-handness of anything points to its function for us as part of a project which we are immersed in as part of perhaps some grander network of projects in the service of various things in the future. The timely, directional character of this ready-to-hand network of involvements itself attests to the temporal, finite nature of our existence and the constant 'passing away' and 'moving towards' of our existence and the eventual cessation of our own existence. We are assailed by the nothing each and every moment when we consider our sheer throwness and the role that our possibilities as being-in-the-world play. Anxiety then is like a primordial sense that the nothing haunts each waking moment, even in diversion, since it is the constant feeling of the not-yet that pulls us out of any sense of one moment to the next. To be-in-the-world is to be thrown such that one is towards one's possibilities and, part of what it means to be at any given moment, means to have been (which is no longer here) and to be towards (which is not yet here) and to be ultimately towards the main possibility of our being as human beings, to no longer be. Part of what it means to 'be' then, far from being opposed to nothing involves a confrontation with nothingness which itself is not a being, no more than being is itself a being. We are never quite there in the sense of being purely present. We are ever on the way and are as thrown since we were not here forever. The abyss of nothingness yawns all about us and, our being-in-the-world, even in its fallen evasion, is still structured according to the necessity of our being-towards-death. This ultimate possibility is constitutive of even our efforts to submerge ourselves in a tranquil everyday of phoney perpetual presence by way of evading our own necessary experience of the interplay of presence and absence.

And this is all that Heidegger wanted from his analysis of Dasein—from these and related insights concerning the being of that being whose own being is an issue for it, Heidegger hoped to embark on a destruction of the tradition of the metaphysics of presence. The attempts to get beyond, deconstruct or overcome the metaphysics of presence become Heidegger's lifelong task and, thus, seem perfectly congruent with what he first began to develop in his 1927 book. To conclude with a line from *BT*:

> The analytic of Dasein is not aimed at laying an ontological basis for anthropology; its purpose is one of fundamental ontology. (*SZ* 200)

## Notes

1. I noticed recently, for example, that Richard Capobianco tries to explain away a lot of the textual evidence which I will marshal in this paper by simply insisting that though Heidegger might have *wanted* to do what he claims to have done in his retrospectives on *Being and Time*, the fact of the matter is that it makes more sense to assume that the earlier text is mired in difficulties which require us to read the later Heidegger as discontinuous with the earlier Heidegger. For my part, I think this is a less than hermeneutically honest approach to a text and, what we find again, on the question of the role of angst in *Being and Time*, is that, read on its own terms, Heidegger's work anticipates and remains consistent with later developments in ways that the 'discontinuists' refuse to acknowledge (see Copabianco 2010, chapter four).
2. See *PM* 249–250.
3. Why is there something rather than nothing?
4. It is worth bearing in mind that Heidegger recommended the lecture course as a sort of companion piece to *BT*.
5. For a masterful and compelling treatment of negation and the notion of negative facts see Dahlstrom (2010).
6. It is arguably somewhat unfair to target Carnap specifically since few, if any, contemporary analytic philosophers would hold him aloft as pointing the way forward for their views concerning the role of logic, language and the relevance or non-relevance of metaphysics. However, the idea here is not to suggest that this response to Carnap

is a devastating blow to critics of metaphysics and/or Heidegger's thought. Notwithstanding, since Carnap himself explicitly challenges Heidegger's thinking and, since this challenge was seen to be successful to the extent that numerous analytic thinkers think that they can dismiss Heidegger's philosophy as nonsense as a result of Carnap's critique—demonstrating the failure of that critique itself already delegitimizes the position of those who refuse to read Heidegger exclusively on Carnap's say so. Focusing on Carnap is also helpful in that he states his position, however unsuccessfully, in very clear terms, and it also seems clear that Heidegger is explicitly responding to Carnap's positivism in his 1935 lectures, and in his 1940s introduction and postscript to the 1929 lecture that Carnap attacked. Everything here seems to revolve around a series of assumptions and presuppositions which Carnap insists upon but which Heidegger himself would clearly call into question. In a sense then, Carnap's entire approach to Heidegger's philosophy is somewhat question begging and I genuinely think this is something that would have been easily made clear had the two philosophers ever come head to head. It is a question ultimately of ontology, which is what Heidegger insists that metaphysics is synonymous with from the outset, a fact that is sadly misunderstood by Carnap. But, for Heidegger, our current ontology, and this has been the case for some time, is deficient and wrongheaded insofar as part of what must be taken to 'be', part of what 'is', is not itself a thing, nor can it be said to 'exist'. So, not all of our ontology can be covered by the notion of being understood as thingness or presence. However, Carnap clearly thinks that all of these issues are non-issues, which, if he had taken the trouble to read the introduction to *Being and Time*, he might have realized was an overly reductive view of things.

7. Neither do I mean to suggest that Heidegger's understanding of logic would have corresponded exactly with what we would think of as the field of logic today. The notion of logic had a much broader scope in the early decades of the twentieth century than it does today. Notwithstanding, Heidegger's conception of logic, though different to ours, is still relevant to the concerns of the Vienna circle and the likes of Carnap. He explicitly refers to positivism in some of his writings in the 30s and 40s when returning to discuss his 1929 essay. Stephan Käufer makes a compelling case concerning the importance of the contextual backdrop to Heidegger's claims concerning logic as a graduate student and indeed in his early years as a lecturer—that is, prior to the

publication of *BT*. Käufer argues, plausibly, that the notion of logic that loomed largest for Heidegger was a neo-Kantian one which was still some ways from the symbolic logic which was about to take centre stage in the late 1920s and 1930s. However, a number of points are worth bearing in mind here. Heidegger fastens on the law of con-contradiction in his 1929 lecture in a manner that clearly pits itself against what were the stock views of the logical positivism which was beginning to emerge as a result of interpretations of Wittgenstein's *Tractatus* and the work of members of the Vienna Circle. Moreover, in subsequent lecture courses in the 1930s, where Heidegger returns to the question of the nothing, he responds to his positivist critics and directly refers to the 'positivism' of the day. Granted Käufer is quite right that Heidegger is not sponsoring irrationalism—but to suppose that *none* of what he was arguing in 1929 was in any way relevant to the positivism that was emerging from the Vienna circle and which was already (rightly or wrongly) associated with Wittgenstein's 1912 *Tractatus* is excessive and doesn't really stand up to scrutiny. See Stefan Kaeufer. "On Heidegger on Logic," *Continental Philosophy Review* 34 (2001): 455–476.

8. In *GA* 95 Heidegger again invokes the importance of movement (see Heidegger 2017, 99–100). Dahlstrom also makes some telling observations in a paper in *The Review of Metaphysics*: "It would appear that these naysayers of negative facts construe the experience of real things (including the complex of perceptions, apprehensions, and judgments that such experience entails) as a static affair. Yet we see – we do not infer – movements and changes in states of affairs. In doing so, we see precisely that things do not remain at a standstill, that they are never quite what they were a moment ago or quite what they are about to be. To the extent that we see that something is moving, we see properties and relations, part/whole complexes making up corresponding states of affairs, many of which are anything but constant. Even where one sensation is dominant in the experience, what we apprehend in perception can be a steady interplay of presences and absences. Thus, we see the changing color of paint as we add tint to it, we feel the sweat dripping from our forehead, we savor a wine's lingering aftertaste, and we hear the fading strings of a symphony's first movement. These facts of movement and change can only be adequately characterized by invoking negation, and in this sense negative facts underlie the judgments, the convictions and beliefs, that emerge from the perceptual apprehension

of these movements. The import of these considerations is patent: in seeing that something changes or moves, we see that negative facts obtain." (Dahlstrom 2010, 266–267)

9. That is an offence against the much-revered principle of all principles, which is vouchsafed by the permanence of substance which, in turn, does not allow for any break in pure presence—a result that Kant relies on again in the first analogy of experience.

10. In *Being and Time* Heidegger hopes to find clues as to how to do as much from the phenomenal facts available from a hermeneutics of facticity.

11. Heidegger proposes to examine the 'da' of Dasein in two parts: "the existential Constitution of the 'there';" and the "everyday Being of the 'there', and the falling of Dasein" (*SZ* 133). For our part, we are going to focus on the existential constitution of the there, of *our thereness*.

12. State-of-mind in Macquarrie and Robinson translates 'Befindlichkeit' and though it is a translation which comes in for a certain amount of 'flak'—I think it actually works just fine when one considers the colloquial use of the term which, as one can tell from the translator's own notes on the phrase, is what they are trying to pick out.

13. In *GA* 95, for example, Heidegger writes that "*Being and Time* indicates the preparation of the decision toward *this possibility* by using the term 'disposition' ['*Stimmung*'] to name the 'feelings'. (At issue in that book is not a modification of the psychological-anthropological explanation of the emotional side of the human being, but rather a fundamental and different essential grounding of the human being in Da-sein, a grounding determined *purely* out of the question of being. The execution of this decisively recognized task was as defective as could be – but what is decisive remains the quite different questioning out of a quite different horizon.) Disposition (cf. winter semester 37 – 38) disposes the human being to his originary vocation of assignment in the stewardship of the truth of being. To be disposed does not mean to wallow in dispositions qua feeling and to feel these feelings; instead, it means: in appertaining to being, to *be* the 'there' qua the clearing of concealment as such. To feel feelings is to adhere obstinately to subjectivity; but to be disposed is to be transported into the open realm of the truth of being, such that being is thought not superveniently as the last pallor of what is represented as present-at-hand, but rather is first, constantly, and steadfastly experienced as the event (cf. *Beiträge*) and not objectively represented. The disposed human being receives

the vocation of his essence out of the basic disposition attuned to the event of appropriation. And the vocation is one toward Da-*sein*, toward being a ground for the truth of being. The essence of the human being now arises as essentially occurring out of being, and such essential occurrence is originary history – because arising out of the event itself" (Heidegger 2017, 119–120).

14. Heidegger makes one of many such disavowals pointedly in Volume 95 of the *Black Notebooks*: "Once and for all: I have nothing to do with the 'philosophy of existence'" (Heidegger 2017, 131).

15. This will of course give rise to the discussion of fallenness in the sections that follow and this account of inauthenticity itself has enjoyed a great deal of discussion in the secondary literature; however, for the purposes of getting through this structural recapitulation of the argument, we must forgo a consideration of these colorful and fascinating sections.

# References

Capobianco, Richard. 2010. *Engaging Heidegger*. Toronto, Buffalo and London: University of Toronto Press.

Carnap, Rudolf. 1932. "The Elimination of Metaphysics Through Logical Analysis of Language." *Erkenntnis* II: 10. Translated by Arthur Pap.

Dahlstrom, Daniel. 2010. "Negation and Being." *The Review of Metaphysics* 64 (December 2010): 247–271.

Heidegger, Martin. 2017. *Ponderings VII–XI: Black Notebooks 1938–1939*. Translated by Richard Rojcewicz. Bloomington: Indiana University Press.

Kaeufer, Stefan. 2001. "On Heidegger on Logic." *Continental Philosophy Review* 34: 455–476.

# 2

# Heidegger: πάθος as the Thing Itself

## Thomas Sheehan

What we do through all our waking hours (perhaps even during REM sleep) is make sense of stuff, whether of people, things, ideas, or experiences—whatever we happen to encounter.

We make sense of things even when we get it wrong, or go insane, or babble incoherently on our death beds. Antoine Roquentin in *Nausea* was making sense of things when he watched the seat on the Bouville tram turn into an animal's bloated and bleeding belly. Jean-Paul Sartre, his creator, was making sense of things when he saw pairs of crabs following him around Paris in the 1930s (Sartre sought out therapy from a young Jacques Lacan, and the crabs went away when he finally got bored of them.) (Gerassi 2009, 62–63).[1]

Heidegger argues we cannot *not* make sense of things because sense-making—the "disclosing" of things, whether correctly or not—is a fundamental element of our nature. We are the living beings who have λόγος, and therefore "the very being of ex-sistence is to make sense of things," not just occasionally or as an add-on, but necessarily (*GA* 21: 151).[2]

T. Sheehan (✉)
Stanford University, Stanford, CA, USA
e-mail: tsheehan@stanford.edu

© The Author(s) 2019
C. Hadjioannou (ed.), *Heidegger on Affect*, Philosophers in Depth,
https://doi.org/10.1007/978-3-030-24639-6_2

The core of Heidegger's work is about how and why we cannot *not* make sense of things. Put otherwise, his fundamental question about *der Sinn von Sein* is about how and why we must have access not just to things but above all to the *meanings* of things, indeed, to meaningfulness or intelligibility *at all*.

But wait. Wasn't Heidegger's basic question about "being" (*Sein*) rather than meaning or intelligibility (*Bedeutsamkeit* or *Sinn*)? No, once we take the phenomenological turn with Heidegger—the turn he took between 1915 and 1919—we see that all forms of *Sein* are in fact *Sinngebilde*, formations of sense. During a course from 1919–1920 he called on his students to see that their

> experience has whatever it experiences *in the character of meaningfulness*. Even the most trivial thing is meaningful (even though it remains trivial nonetheless). Even what is most lacking in value is meaningful. (*GA* 58: 104; my emphasis)[3]

And in 1924:

> For a long time now, I have been designating the ontological character of ex-sistence as *meaningfulness*. This ontological character is the primary one in which we encounter the world. (*GA* 18: 300)[4]

> We identify meaningfulness as the world's primary ontological characteristic. (*GA* 64: 24)[5]

Thus, in *Sein und Zeit* (*SZ*) Heidegger could declare that ontology is "the explicit inquiry into the *Sinn* of things" (*SZ* 12).[6]

What does this inevitable sense-making have to do with πάθος? I will argue that πάθος, as Heidegger interprets it, is "the thing itself," *die Sache selbst*, of Heidegger's work. There are four steps to the argument. The first step is to nail down the *goal* of Heidegger's work. The second is to work out what "transcendence" and "intentionality" mean. The third, an interlude, briefly sketches out Heidegger's phenomenological transformation of Aristotle. The fourth shows that facticity, read as πάθος, is *die Sache selbst*, what I'll call the "factum," that which is always already operative as the ultimate presupposition of everything human.

# 1    The Goal

The proper entrance into Heidegger's *Seinsfrage* is to realize he used the word *Sein* as only a provisional stand-in for *Anwesen*, the intelligibility or meaningful presence of whatever we encounter (*GA* 7: 234).[7] And the next step is to remember that *Anwesen* was not the goal of his work but only the starting point. Heidegger was after what *accounts* for intelligibility, its ἀρχή and αἰτία. Like Plato, his goal lay ἐπέκεινα τῆς οὐσίας (*Republic* 509b9), "beyond" all forms of *Anwesen*. He was after the <u>*Herkunft von Anwesen*</u>, the "whence" of intelligibility at all (*GA* 6.2: 304).[8]

Intelligibility occurs only in correlation with human beings. With that we have the arena within which to work out our question: the a priori, ever-operative, and ineluctable togetherness of human being as such and intelligibility as such (where "as such" means "in its essence," and "in its essence" means "in how-it-is-and-cannot-not-be"). Did Heidegger ever get any further than that?

The early Heidegger said we are "prisoners of meaningfulness," and he could equally have said that meaningfulness is the prisoner of human being (*GA* 58: 104).[9] The indissoluble bond of intelligibility and human being goes by several names in Heidegger's career. In *SZ* it was called *In-der-Welt-sein*, our structural engagement-with-meaning. He declares this to be our *daseinsmäßige Struktur*, which I render as "the existential structure of ex-sistence," intentionally misspelling and hyphenating the key terms in order to capture Heidegger's understanding of *Da-sein* as *Existenz* (Greek, ἐξ + ἵστημι, Latin, *ex + sistere*) (*GA* 83: 69).[10] Ex-sistence refers to the fact that we are necessarily (1) made-to-stand (2) out, ahead, and open as the field of intelligibility. More dynamically, human being is "thrown open" as the world of possible meaning.

To name the bond of ex-sistence and intelligibility, Heidegger in the 1930s used the term *Gegenschwung*, the reciprocal sameness (the *reci-proci-tas* or back-and-forth-ness) of *Da-<u>sein</u>* and *<u>Da</u>-sein*. That is:

- we hold open and *are* the field of intelligibility (*Da-<u>sein</u>*, as per *SZ* I.1–2),
- which field determines the meaning of all we encounter (*<u>Da</u>-sein* as per the projected *SZ* I.3 and the later work).

Drawing on his translation of δύναμις as *Eignung* (coming-into-its-own) Heidegger in *Beiträge zur Philosophie* began calling this bond "*Ereignis*," i.e., ex-sistence insofar as it has always already been ap-*propri*-ated to its proper status as the field of intelligibility. He also called the bond *Seyn* (an older spelling of the word *Sein*) and often discussed it in terms of "cor-respondence" (*Entsprechung*), a topic to which we shall return.

I call this bond the "factum," that which is always already operative in and as the being of ex-sistence. In *SZ* Heidegger declared it to be a "*unitary* phenomenon" (*SZ* 53)[11] that must never be split apart into "two"—ex-sistence on the one side and intelligibility on the other—which then might subsequently enter into a "relation". Heidegger was clear: there is no such relation because there are not "two" independent entities that need to be brought into relation. There is only the inseparable unity of *Seyn*, which itself is the indissoluble sameness of ex-sistence and intelligibility.

> Der Bezug ist jedoch nicht zwischen das Seyn und den Menschen eingespannt, als seien beide vordem bezuglos Seyn und Mensch. Der Bezug ist das Seyn selbst, und das Menschenwesen ist der selbe Bezug. (*GA* 73.1: 790)[12]

That is to say: There is no gap between ex-sistence and *Seyn* that needs to be bridged by a "relation". Intelligibility-as-such—the possibility of there being any meaning at all—is simply ex-sistence's way of being.

That notwithstanding, some Americans advance the worst parody of Heidegger's thinking by sundering that unity and turning "Being Itself" into a Metaphysical Something that subsists on its own, independent of Dasein. This Super-*Sein* occasionally chooses to "give" or "send" itself to Dasein but nowadays has mostly "withdrawn itself," even "hidden itself," thereby abandoning Dasein to the depredations of metaphysics, technology and calculative rationality. This crude but deadly serious mythologizing of Heidegger's work completely misses the irony of claiming it has reached "the end of philosophy".[13]

# 2    Transcendence and Intentionality

The a priori fact of our being "pulled" or "stretched" or "thrown" open as the field of intelligibility[14] is what Heidegger calls "transcendence". In turn, transcendence is what accounts for the fact that our conscious activities are necessarily intentional. Using scholastic terminology, Heidegger called transcendence the *ratio essendi* of intentionality, and intentionality the *ratio cognoscendi* of transcendence (*GA* 24: 91).[15] That is, our thrown-openness is the fundamental principle that accounts for the fact that our conscious acts are and must be *about* something, must make sense *of* something. In what follows, the word "intentionality" always means "transcendence-based intentionality," and I'll eventually term it "minding".

What is intentionality for Heidegger? When I discuss the mind-body problem with students, I sometimes ask them to close their eyes and point to their minds. Virtually always they point to their heads, i.e., their brains. (The occasional exception are Chinese students who, in the spirit of St. Augustine, point to their chest, i.e., their 心 or heart.) On this view, the mind is "inside," and consciousness is a matter of slipping out through the senses to grab some data and drag it back into the brain.

One might be reminded of Sartre's parody of "digestive epistemology," the nutritional model of knowledge where "to know is to eat". Hungry for nourishment, our minds force us to sally forth into the world to snatch prey (think of the chameleon's projectile tongue darting out to snare a bug), which we then drag back into the closet of consciousness as into a stomach, where we steep it in gastric juices and peristaltically reduce it to mental mulch that gets absorbed as nourishment into the muscles and sinews of our minds.[16]

For Heidegger, as for Aristotle, there is no "inside" to ex-sistence. We are always outside (*Draußensein*), exposed to what is other (*SZ* 62).[17] But paradoxically our outsideness is our condition of being *inside meaning*. In an early lecture course Heidegger translated the title of Aristotle's Περὶ ψυχῆς or *De anima* as "*Über das In-der-Welt-sein*". But being-in-the-world is not primarily a matter of living within the universe of space and time, or merely perceiving "stuff out there". It's the structural condition of being thrust into the *meaning* of things, into what and how we think they currently are. Ex-sistence is necessarily *Vertrautheit mit der Bedeutsamkeit* (*SZ* 87),[18] familiarity with both meaningfulness at all and the possible meanings of the specific things we encounter, with the result that we are always and ineluctably making sense of whatever we meet (*be-deuten*) (*SZ* 87).[19]

The human ψυχή is not a mental closet, but rather our power to contact what is *other* than ourselves—and to be in touch with *ourselves* as *related to* whatever. We do so not by magically transubstantiating "outside things" into "mental images" that get stored "inside our minds". Rather, we *assimilate ourselves to* the intelligible content (the εἶδος or *Gehaltsinn*) of the encountered other, conforming ourselves to how it is meaningfully present. The Greek verb ὁμοιόω means "to make something be similar to something else". In the middle voice, ὁμοιοῦμαι means to make *oneself* be similar to something else (as in Plato's ὁμοίωσις θεῷ, becoming like god: *Theaetetus* 176b1).[20] In *De interpretatione* 1, 16a6–8, a text that Heidegger frequently discussed, Aristotle says the mind has παθήματα of things, a word that Heidegger renders as *Erlebnisse* ("experiences") and glosses with the Greek word νοήματα, *Vorstellungen*. These παθήματα that we "undergo" (πάσχω, second aorist: παθεῖν) are "likenesses" (ὁμοιώματα) of things in the world—but not as "inner images" of things outside. Our experiences are directly of those things "outside" insofar as they are meaningfully present (*SZ* 214).[21] The παθήματα are the ways we are assimilated to, made like unto, the encountered things.

But how exactly are we "made like unto" what we encounter? In *SZ* Heidegger cites Aristotle's dictum that the human ψυχή is "somehow all things," which he follows with Aquinas's statement that the soul is *ens quod natum est convenire cum omni ente*: the nature of the soul is to "come together" with all things.[22] Heidegger takes those two statements as saying not that the soul (read: ex-sistence) becomes entitatively the same as what it encounters. Rather, our "assimilation to" what we encounter is our understanding of *how* and *as what* the thing is meaningfully disclosed within a specific world of significance.

Obviously the soul will be "all things" only with regard to the *Anwesen* of things, their meaningful presence; and that occurs because (1) the soul is determined by νοῦς ["minding"] and (2) νοῦς is determined by ἀληθεύειν ["making-sense-of"]. The soul is the place where things, of and by themselves, can come-to-appearance [i.e., come-to-εῖδος and thus have intelligible content]. Thus, the soul participates in *the meaningful presence* of whatever is meaningfully present.[23]

All of this comes with the important proviso that, even as we make sense of something, we may very well get it wrong. In other words, ἀληθεύειν as the bringing of something to meaningful presence is no guarantee of the *correctness* of the endeavor.

So again: What is intentionality? In its broadest and most inclusive sense intentionality is νοῦς-qua-νόησις (see the quotation above): it is the "minding" of things. And since things show up as νοήματα in correlation with νοῦς-as-minding, intentionality is "minding the meant". In saying there is no "inside" to ex-sistence we're saying that we are *never not* minding-the-meant.

In *SZ* Heidegger's cover-all term for "minding" is *Sorge*, usually translated as "care" but more suitably rendered as "concern" or better yet as "interest". Our concernful/interested minding has a double focus: (1) on meaningfulness, and (2) on the things that can be meaningful.

1. We hold open the field itself of possible meaning through

   * our "attunement" (*Befindlichkeit*) to that field, and
   * our "aheadness" (*Verstehen*) as possibility among the field's meaningful possibilities.

2. We relate to things *within* that field by being

   * meaningfully present to them (*Sein bei*), i.e., making sense of them in terms of the field of possible meaning.

As regards the first piece—the holding open of the clearing— Heidegger weaves the two distinguishable but inseparable moments of *Befindlichkeit* and *Verstehen* into one, which can be called either "attuned minding" of the clearing (*befindliches Verstehen*) or "mindful attunement" to the clearing (*verstehende Befindlichkeit*).

Our minding is not primarily an existentiel-psychological operation that we perform only occasionally; it is hard-wired into us as an existential structure that we cannot not be. Moreover, as an existential structure, it makes possible not just theoretical-cognitive activities (thematically understanding the meaning of something) but also includes such senses as "Do you mind if I smoke?" "Mind how you speak to her," "I'll mind the children while you're out," and (in the London tube) "Mind the gap!" It encompasses all the ways we relate to things, other persons, and ourselves.

Telling students to "point to your mind" is to be understood as: "Point to what you're minding right now and how you're minding it". The mind is not a "thing within," least of all within one's skull. Minding is the structure and the process of being ever-exteriorized, both as existential ability and existentiel activity.

***Existentielly-personally*** it is all the ways I relate-to-whatever (and relate to my relating-to-whatever) as

- interested in and concerned about things: *Besorgen*
- interested in and concerned for other people: *Fürsorge*
- interested in and concerned for myself: *Selbstsorge*.

***Existentially-structurally*** it is the fundamental way I ex-sist at all

- as a self-related relating to whatever (including myself)
- while holding open the field of possible intelligibility (*In-der-Welt-sein*)
- and having ex-sistence as mine-to-become (*Jemeinigkeit, Zu-sein, Seinkönnen*)
- with a penumbral awareness of my ever-present mortality.

## 3     Interlude: Phenomenology

For Aristotle, the study that crowns philosophy is called πρώτη φιλοσοφία, "first philosophy". But first philosophy has two moments, grounded in two distinct questions:

1. What counts as real? (τί τὸ ὂν ᾗ ὄν;)
2. What counts as the *realness* of whatever counts as real? (τίς ἡ οὐσία).[24]

The second question bumps the subject matter up a notch from the *onto*-logical to the *meta*-ontological: under examination now are not what we take as real but the very realness of those things. Moreover, by substituting the words "What *counts as?*" for Aristotle's simpler "What is?" I'm following Heidegger's lead in transforming these questions from Aristotle's direct-realist format, where the inquirer is left out of the picture, to a phenomenological one in which the questioner—the one for whom something might "count" or matter—is back in the picture, now in correlation with what's under discussion.

In Aristotle's straightforward realism the subject matter of the inquiry—whether it be the real (τὸ ὂν) or realness itself (οὐσία)—is considered in independence of the inquirer. Aristotle takes the real and its realness as "outside of and apart from" (ἔξω καὶ χωριστόν) the minding that raises the question.[25] That is, Aristotle's two questions ask for the *intrinsic* structure, the in-itself-ness ("inseity") of those two subject matters. For Heidegger, on the other hand, "the one who is philosophizing belongs together with the things under discussion" (*GA 9*: 42).[26] (I can't be aware of *what*-X-is, without being *aware* of what-X-is.) In Heidegger's phenomenological interpretation of Aristotle, τὸ ὂν becomes τὸ παρόν, and οὐσία becomes παρουσία, where in both cases the παρ- piece (= παρά = Latin *prae* or *coram*: "in the face of") indicates intelligible relatedness, i.e., significance, to ex-sistence.

Heidegger is not imposing phenomenology on ontology from without but simply rendering the Stagirite's implicit phenomenology explicit. Aristotle himself held to the convertibility of ὂν and ἀληθές: "Each thing has as much intelligibility as it has being" (*Metaphysics* 1, 993b).[27] Heidegger simply spells out the consequences of that principle: "Is" is convertible with "is-meaningful-as," *Wesen* comes out as *Anwesen*, *Sein* is read as *Sinn*, and to be = to be intelligible. Likewise, the two basic questions of Aristotle's metaphysics are transformed: (1) The inquiry into what something is becomes the question of what counts for us as real; and (2) the question of what realness–as–such is becomes the question of how realness is intelligible at all.

# 4   πάθος

Granted the correlation of thrown-open-ness and intelligibility, and given that intentionality is the phenomenological structure of minding-the-meant, what do these two have to do with πάθος? To answer the question, we turn to the lecture "What Is Philosophy?" that Heidegger gave in Cérisy-la-Salle (Normandy) on 28 August 1955 (*GA* 11: 7–26).[28]

Like the lecture "What Is Metaphysics?" which he had delivered a quarter-century earlier, Heidegger's "What Is Philosophy?" directs the audience to a *personal experience* of what's under discussion. In the earlier lecture (1929) he had told his listeners not to expect a talk *about* metaphysics but rather to let themselves be "transported *into* metaphysics" (*GA* 9: 103)[29] by way of a personal experience of "nothing," i.e., that which is not-a-thing, the clearing as *das Nichts*. Only with such an experience, he claimed, do we personally and responsibly answer the question "What is metaphysics?"—but again, only if we keep the experience alive and refuse to say anything about it that doesn't come from the claim that this "nothing" makes on us (*GA* 9: 113).[30]

So too, in the 1955 lecture: Heidegger says we will truly answer the question "What Is Philosophy?" only if what philosophy is *about*—the basic factum—"concerns us personally, touches us deeply, and affects us in the very core of our ex-sistence" (*GA* 11: 7).[31]—But doesn't that make philosophy a matter of affects, feelings, and emotions? Heidegger takes what André Gide said about literature—"Fine sentiments make for bad literature"—and suggests the same may apply to philosophy. If philosophy is a rational activity, it cannot be based on passions and emotions that well up from the irrational depths of the psyche.[32]

But maybe it's not that simple. If what we call "reason" (*ratio*, *Vernunft*) first got established as such *only within* the historical unfolding of philosophy, can we say with full confidence that philosophy is exclusively a matter of "reason"? Moreover, since philosophy *stricte dicta* arose among the Greeks, and since asking for the "essence" of something (e.g., "What is philosophy?") stems from Greek philosophy, shouldn't we first settle what φιλοσοφία meant for them?

The word φιλοσοφία does not occur in Heraclitus (fl. 500 BCE). Instead one finds only φιλόσοφος (in the plural) in fragment 35, where

Heraclitus says that only those who are "learned in a great many things" merit that title.[33] Heidegger claims that the φιλέω piece of Heraclitus' φιλόσοφος does not mean *striving* for σοφία, in the sense of an ὄρεξις or ἔρως. Rather, it refers to being *already attuned to* and *in harmony with* what σοφία is about. He bases this interpretation on fragments 50 and 51, specifically on the verb ὁμολογέω ("to be in accord with, to correspond to") and the noun ἁρμονίη.

50: οὐκ ἐμοῦ, ἀλλὰ τοῦ λόγου ἀκούσαντας ὁμολογεῖν σοφόν ἐστιν ἓν πάντα εἶναι.

51: … διαφερόμενον ἑωυτῷ ὁμολογέει· παλίντροπος ἁρμονίη ὅκωσπερ τόξου καὶ λύρης.

Roughly: If we have listened to the λόγος, we will understand that to be σοφός is to be attuned to the basic factum. Here that factum is called

- λόγος, in the sense of the ingathering,
- in which all that is borne apart (διαφερόμενον, τὰ πάντα),
- is gathered up and held in the unity (ἓν),
- of a tense harmony (παλίντροπος ἁρμονίη),
- that is like a tightly strung bow or lyre (ὅκωσπερ τόξου καὶ λύρης).

Heidegger argues that by the time of Plato and Aristotle, some two centuries later, the harmonious attunement that once defined Heraclitus' φιλόσοφος had devolved into a *striving* for σοφία. What is more, Plato declares that the source of such striving is πάθος. After Theaetetus has expressed his wonderment at matters related to becoming, Socrates responds:

μάλα γὰρ φιλοσόφου τοῦτο τὸ πάθος, τὸ θαυμάζειν· οὐ γὰρ ἄλλη ἀρχὴ φιλοσοφίας ἢ αὕτη. (*Theaetetus* 155d2–4)

This kind of πάθος—wondering, marveling—is the basic characteristic of the φιλόσοφος, the one who strives for wisdom. In fact, there is no other ἀρχή of philosophy than such wonder.

As the ἀρχή of philosophy, the πάθος of marveling or wondering is not just what gets philosophy going, only to be left behind. An ἀρχή is both the source and the sustaining, the origin and ordering, of something. Wonder not only kick-starts the philosophical life but also maintains it throughout.

But what is this πάθος? Is Plato saying philosophy is based on and sustained by feelings? Heidegger's discussion moves πάθος out of the psychological realm of existentiel emotions and into the existential structure of ex-sistence. As he had previously done with *Befindlichkeit* (*SZ* §29), here Heidegger interprets πάθος as the existential structure that he calls *Stimmung*: attunement to *Seyn*. But that very phrase ("attunement *to*…") harbors the possibility of a ruinous error, that of dividing ex-sistence from the factum by declaring "the one" (ex-sistence) to be *attuned to* "the other" (*Seyn*).

The transitive verb *stimmen* (whose first meaning is "to tune an instrument") can abet this error if we think of this existential *Stimmung* in terms of tuning in music. Before the symphony begins, the oboist sounds an A 440, and the other members of the orchestra reproduce that note at the same 440 cycles per second on their own instruments. The oboist and her instrument have thus "tuned" the orchestra. Likewise, when a tuning fork is struck, it can set another tuning fork vibrating at the same frequency. So analogously, doesn't *Seyn* "attune" our ex-sistence by sending out the ontological vibes that set us resonating in correspondence with *Seyn*?

Along with the "tuning" image, Heidegger employs a call-and-response metaphor. When he reads the factum in terms of the Heraclitean λόγος and says ex-sistence cor-responds to it (ὁμολογεῖν, *entsprechen*), he seems to imply there is a separate something *to* which ex-sistence responds and *by* which is attuned. He speaks of the *Stimme* and *Zuspruch des Seyns*—the voice of Being that calls and claims (*spricht zu*) ex-sistence. This trope—*Seyn* calling to Dasein (like Augustine's *abyssus abyssum invocat*) and Dasein responding to *Seyn*—reinforces the notion that there are indeed *two* moments within the factum rather than an undifferentiated singularity.

If that were the case, Heidegger's thought would devolve into one more iteration of the subject-object split, a crypto-metaphysics structured around a mysterious Super-*Seyn* that plays hide-and-seek, occasionally giving itself to Dasein, but lately (and disastrously) withholding itself.

We need to shift away from the images of tuning and cor-respondence and, along with that, radically revise our understanding of what Heidegger means by *Stimmung* and *Entsprechen*. In "What Is Philosophy?" he reads the single, undivided factum in terms of ex-sistence as *be-stimmt*. According to the brothers Grimm, the verb *bestimmen* corresponds to the Latin *constituere* and the Greek καθίστημι, both of which, as transitive, are causative verbs: "to set something in a place, to bring it into a certain condition, to establish it". Three remarks are in order here:

1. Ex-sistence's *Bestimmt-sein* is its condition of having been de-*fin*-ed or de-*term*-ined, i.e., brought to its *finis*/*terminus*/τέρμα/τέλος. Those terms refer *not* to the point where ex-sistence breaks off and is no more, but rather to the achieved and fulfilled state of ex-sistence, its proper way of being.
2. *Bestimmt-sein* is a reinscription of what the early Heidegger had called *Geworfenheit* and later termed *Ereignet-sein*. All three terms refer to the same single factum: ex-sistence as having always already been appropriated to its *proprium*, its τέλος, to what and how it essentially is: thrown open as the clearing.
3. Just as, with *Geworfenheit*/*Ereignetsein*, there is no agent that throws or appropriates ex-sistence into being the clearing, so too with *Bestimmt-sein:* there is no supervenient Being that "calls," "claims," or "attunes" (i.e., determines or defines) ex-sistence *ab extra*, the way an efficient cause *qua* ποιητικόν would effect a change in the patient *qua* παθητικόν. And yet πάθος lies at the heart of Heidegger's project, although it is now understood not in terms of passing emotions but as only another name for the existential structure of ex-sistence, the equivalent of *Geworfenheit* and *Ereignetsein*.

The crux of the matter lies in how Heidegger understands the word "relation" (*Bezug*), and for that we turn to the "Conversation with a Japanese Professor," where Heidegger defines what he means by the "hermeneutical *Bezug*" of ex-sistence and *Sprache*.

By *Sprache* he does not mean either the system or elements of human communication, whatever form that might take. Rather, *Sprache* refers to Heraclitean λόγος as found in fragment 50: the clearing as the possibility of intelligibility. And Heidegger radically redefines ex-sistence's *Bezug* or "relation to" the clearing. It is emphatically *not* about a connection between two things, and especially not a "two-sided" relation of the form "*Dasein* ⟵⟶ *Seyn*".

> Wohl dagegen möchte das Wort "Bezug" sagen, der Mensch sei in seinem Wesen gebraucht, gehöre als das Wesende, der er ist in einen Brauch, der ihn beansprucht. (*GA* 12: 119)[34]

That is: The word "*Bezug*" refers to our fate of being *needed and required* to sustain and in fact to *be* the clearing. This *Bezug* is not a relation between any "two," whatever they might be, but instead indicates the *one-sided* existential fact that without us there is no in-break into the solid fullness of things, no open region for synthesizing and distinguishing, and therefore no possibility of meaning.[35] Our thrown-openness *as* the clearing is here expressed as the "claim" on our ex-sistence, our "fatedness" to being needed for there to be intelligibility at all.

The clearing is not something other than ex-sistence, something we could "enter into" from outside or "relate to" as other than our ex-sistence, Heidegger insists that we stop talking about "relating *to*" the clearing ("Darum dürfen wir auch nicht mehr sagen: Bezug zur. ...") (*GA* 12: 119).[36] There's nothing to relate "to"—first of all because the clearing is not "something" and secondly because the clearing is nothing other than our own ex-sistence, understood in terms of "das Walten des Brauches," the powerful "needed-ness" that has always already defined and determined us to be thrown open as the clearing (*GA* 12: 119).[37]

In that sense, Heidegger says, our thrownness means we do not "belong to ourselves"[38] so much as we are at the service of, in thrall to, the possibility of meaning, which is—call it as you will—our *raison d'être*, our *Worumwillen*, our οὗ ἕνεκα, our τέλος, our essence, in short: what we cannot not be. In *SZ* Heidegger writes that "ex-sistence is thrown, [i.e.,] brought into its openness *not* of its own accord" (*SZ* 284).[39] Years later he wrote: "Geworfen—nicht aus sich. / Woher anders denn aus Seyn selber? / *Ereignis*" (*GA* 78: 335).[40] Both texts say the same thing. The condition of being thrown open or ap-propri-ated has always already been "done unto" us. By what? By the factum itself—but not as an agent *ab extra* (the hypostasized "Being" of Heideggerian mythology) but by our very facticity as πάθος.

Heidegger derives much of what he has to say about thrownness, appropriation, *Bestimmtsein* and the like from Aristotle's treatment of δύναμις τοῦ παθεῖν in *Metaphysics* IX (on δύναμις cf. ibid. V 12). The verb πάσχω and the noun πάθος bespeak a certain passivity (πάθησις) in a thing, in the sense of the ability to undergo, receive, or "suffer"—i.e., bear up under—some action or activity (ποίησις) that might be visited upon it.[41] Aristotle's treatment of the δύναμις τοῦ παθεῖν in *Metaphysics* IX is about the being of *things*, but Heidegger radically adapts that to the structure of human being itself, where πάθος now bespeaks the fundamental facticity of ex-sistence.

We have always already "suffered" the burden of thrown-openness as the clearing. No prior agent has acted upon ex-sistence, forced facticity upon us, thrown us into being-needed for the sake of intelligibility at all. To say that facticity has always already been "done unto us" is a round-about way of saying that it is the fundamental "given" of our ex-sistence, back behind which we cannot go. Finally, therefore, πάθος is our facticity, and our facticity is itself the factum.

## Notes

1. "When Sartre Talked to Crabs (It Was Mescaline)," *New York Times*, 14 November 2009, http://www.nytimes.com/2009/11/15/weekinreview/15grist.html, based on John Gerassi, ed. and trans., *Talking With Sartre: Conversations and Debates* (New Haven: Yale University Press, 2009), 62–63.

2. "Weil Dasein in seinem Sein selbst bedeutend ist...." On "having λόγος": cf. Aristotle, *De anima* III 9, 432a31, *Nicomachean Ethics* I 13, 1102b15, 1103a2; V 1, 1139a4; 1138b9; VI 1, 1139b22–23; etc.

3. *GA* 58: 104.19–24: "...sehen den Sinn, in dem das faktische Erfahren sein Erfahrenes erneut und immer im Charakter der Bedeutsamkeit hat. Auch das Trivialste ist bedeutsam, nur eben trivial; auch das Wertloseste ist bedeutsam." Also *GA* 61: 91.14: "erfahren in Bedeutsamkeit."

4. "Ich pflege seit langem diesen Seinscharakter des Daseins als *Bedeutsamkeit* zu bezeichnen. Dieser Seinscharakter ist das Primäre, in dem die Welt begegnet."

5. "Bedeutsamkeit als des primären Seinscharakters der Welt."

6. "[Ontologie als] das explizite Fragen nach dem Sinn des Seienden."

7. *GA* 7: 234.13–17: "nur das vorläufige Wort." *GA* 15: 20.8–9: "Obwohl ich dieses Wort nicht mehr gern gebrauche…."

8. *GA* 6.2, 304.11–12: "Herkunft von Anwesen." *GA* 73, 2: 984.2: "Wesensherkunft." *GA* 10: 131.19–20 and .28: "Wesensherkunft des Seins." *GA* 2: 53 n.: "Das Anwesen aus dieser Herkunft." *GA* 73, 1: 82.15–16: "das von woher und wodurch … das Sein west."

9. *GA* 58: 104.32–33: "bedeutsamkeitsgefangen," emphasized in the German.

10. *GA* 83: 69.4: "Exsistentia" and ibid., 72.23–24: "Das *sistere*—ex."

11. *SZ* 53.12–13: "ein *einheitliches* Phänomen. … Dieser primäre Befund muß im Ganzen gesehen werden."

12. *GA* 73.1: 790.2–8. The sentence that precedes these two reads: "Die Wahr-heit des Seyns ist das Höchste dessen, was den Menschen zu den-ken gegeben."

13. The standard-bearer of this position is Prof. Richard Capobianco.

14. Angezogen, erstreckt, geworfen: respectively, *GA* 8: 11.10; *SZ* 375.3; and *SZ* 144.12.

15. *GA* 24: 91.20–22. On ratio cognoscendi, cf. Thomas Aquinas, "Commentum in tertium sententiarum ['De incarnatione Verbi'] Magistri Petri Lombardi," distinctio 14 ("Si anima Christi habuerit sapientiam parem cum Deo, et si omnia scit quae Deus"), quaestio 1, articulus 1 ("Utrum in Christo sit aliqua scientia creata"), quaestiuncula 5, solutio 4: "Ratio autem cognoscendi est forma rei inquantum est cognita, quia per eam fit cognitio in actu; unde sicut ex materia et forma est unum esse; ita *ratio cognoscendi* et res cognita sunt unum cog-nitum: et propter hoc utriusque, inquantum huiusmodi, est una cog-nitio secundum habitum et secundum actum," in Thomas Aquinas, *Opera Omnia*, ed. Stanilaus Fretté and Paul Maré (Paris: Louis Vivès, 1873), IX, 215, column a, ad fin.

16. See Sartre, Jean-Paul, "Une idée fondamentale de la phénoménologie de Husserl: l'intentionnalité," in *Situations I* (Paris: Gallimard, 1947), 29–32. Also *SZ* 62.19–21: "das Vernehmen des Erkannten ist nicht ein Zurückkehren des erfassenden Hinausgehens mit der gewonnen

Beute in das 'Gehäuse' des Bewußtseins, sondern auch im Vernehmen, Bewahren und Behalten *bleibt* das erkennende Dasein *als Dasein draußen.*"

17. *SZ* 62.13, "immer schon 'draußen'"; ibid., 62.16–18 "auch in diesem 'Draußen-sein' beim Gegenstand ist das Dasein im rechtverstanden Sinne 'drinnen'... als In-der-Welt-sein"; ibid., 162.26–27: "als In-der-Welt-sein verstehend schon 'draußen' ist." *GA* 2: 216, n. glosses "Draußensein" as: "Das Da; Ausgesetztheit als offene Stelle."

18. *SZ* 87.19–20.

19. *SZ* 87.9 and 87.15; also above, Note 2.

20. *Theaetetus* 176b1. Plotinus went him one better by declaring that our concern is *to be* god (σπουδή ... θεὸν εἶναι): *Enneads* I 2, 6.3.

21. *SZ* 214.26–36.

22. Respectively *De anima* III 8, 431b21 (ἡ ψυχὴ τὰ ὄντα πώς ἐστι πάντα) at *SZ* 14.6, and Thomas Aquinas at *SZ* 14.20–21. In *SZ* Heidegger translated the Greek as: "Das Seele ist in gewisser Weise das Seiende alles," omitting by mistake the word πάντα. Twenty-five years later, in his lecture course *Übungen im Lesen* (13 February 1952, ms. 45.8–9) Heidegger noted the error: "Das πάντα ist in S.u.Z. aus Versehen herausgeblieben."

23. Heidegger, *Übungen im Lesen*, winter semesters 1950–1951 and 1951–1952, Stanford University, Green Library Archives, 13 February 1952, 45.16–45.20 (with my emphasis). The text is omitted at *GA* 83: 654.8. Gehaltsinn: *GA* 58: 261.5–12; *GA* 60: 90.1.

24. Respectively *Metaphysics* IV 1, 1003a21 and VII 1, 1028b4.

25. Combining *Metaphysics* VI 4, 1028a2 and XI 8, 1065a24.

26. *GA* 9: 42.24–27: "...weil in den Wissenschaften lediglich die Forderung der Sachlichkeit entscheident ist, zu den Sachen der Philosophie aber der Philosophierende selbst... mitgehört."

27. *Metaphysics* 1, 993 b 30–31: ὥσθ' ἕκαστον ὡς ἔχει τοῦ εἶναι, οὕτω καὶ τῆς ἀληθείας.

28. "Was ist das—die Philosophie?" *GA* 11: 7–26.

29. *GA* 9: 103.2–6.

30. *GA* 9: 113.2–10.

31. *GA* 11: 7.32–34: "... uns selbst angeht, uns berüht (nous touche), und zwar uns in unserem Wesen."

32. Gide made his comment—"C'est avec des beaux sentiments que l'on fait la mauvaise littérature"—en passant in remarks about William

Blake in the fifth of his six conférences delivered in 1922 at the Théâtre du Vieux-Colombier: André Gide, *Dostoïesky (Articles et causeries)* (Paris: Plon, 1923), 247.17–19.

33. Fragment 35: χρὴ γὰρ εὖ μάλα πολλῶν ἵστορας φιλοσόφους ἄνδρας εἶναι. The noun ἵστωρ (here in the accusative plural; it is the etymon of "history") is related to οἶδα, the perfect form of the presumed \*εἴδω, which means to know in the sense of "having seen," i.e., learned from experience.

34. *GA* 12: 119.8–10.

35. Re "in-break": *GA* 9: 105.7, "Einbruch."

36. *GA* 12: 119.25.

37. *GA* 12: 119.35.

38. Cf. *GA* 11:160.26–27.

39. *SZ* 284.11–12: "Seiend ist das Dasein geworfenes, *nicht* von ihm selbst in sein Da gebracht."

40. *GA* 78: 335.10–12.

41. Alternately it can also indicate the ability to *resist* a certain action or activity, but that sense is not front and center here.

# Reference

Gerassi, John, ed. and trans. 2009. *Talking with Sartre: Conversations and Debates*. New Haven: Yale University Press.

# 3

# The Affects of Rhetoric and Reconceiving the Nature of Possibility

## Niall Keane

The proto-phenomenological ballast that Aristotle lends to Heidegger's early analysis is surely a corrective to what Thomas Sheehan has called Heidegger's later "over-wrought" and "over-heated rhetoric" (Sheehan 2015, 263). In the concrete spirit of Aristotle's philosophy, in the following I will look at the genesis of Heidegger's reflections on affect, embodied speaking together, the nature of possibility and the critique of actuality, which form the soil in which the later existential analysis of *Being and Time* (*BT*) sinks its roots. These original reflections are to be found in the 1924 summer semester lecture course entitled *Basic Concepts of Aristotelian Philosophy* (*BCAP*). On the basis of this, I will show how the early lectures help us to understand what happens to Heidegger's reflections on affect, *dynamis*, and being together with others, shaping the development of his later critique of the metaphysics of actuality in both *BT* and in the *Contributions to Philosophy* (*CP*).

N. Keane (✉)
Mary Immaculate College, Limerick, Ireland

© The Author(s) 2019
C. Hadjioannou (ed.), *Heidegger on Affect*, Philosophers in Depth,
https://doi.org/10.1007/978-3-030-24639-6_3

**47**

From the beginning of this lecture course, Heidegger analyzes rhetoric with respect to the specific ground or soil (*Boden*) out of which the basic concepts of Aristotle's philosophy emerge, and more specifically with respect to how this ground is given and how it is disclosed to the understanding by way of speaking (*legein*). Heidegger sets himself this task in the name of "science" and in the name of taking absolute "responsibility" for conceptuality, which belongs, Heidegger tells us, to the *"possibility of the existence of human beings"* (*GA* 18: 6; *BCAP* 5). This amounts to the fundamental determination of the relation between the way of being of the human being and an understanding of being as such, which is carried out provisionally by calling "Aristotle himself as witness" (ibid.).

Yet in a provocative introductory remark to the 1924 summer semester course, Heidegger claims that this lecture has "no philosophical aim whatsoever [and] is [simply] interested in understanding basic concepts in their conceptuality" (*GA* 18: 5; *BCAP* 4). He then adds the following qualification, "the aim is philological in that it intends to bring the *reading* of philosophers somewhat more into practice" (*GA* 18: 5; *BCAP* 4–5). However, Heidegger's approach is de facto both philosophical and philological, which he defines as the *"passion for knowledge of what has been expressed"* (*GA* 18: 4; *BCAP* 4). And hence what he demonstrates in these lectures is an attentiveness to Aristotle's words in order to subsequently say something about the ground out of which these basic concepts have emerged and how they have emerged (ibid.). Yet, when following Heidegger's own advice when it comes to reading Aristotle, we should perhaps show less interest in what Heidegger said about his own lecture courses (for Heidegger, too, "was born at a certain time, he worked, and he died" [*GA* 18: 4; *BCAP* 5]), and instead follow the careful orientation of his analysis. With this in mind, let me begin by examining the nature of Heidegger's rehabilitation of rhetoric and its affective dimension in 1924, before moving on to see how his interpretation of affective rhetoric lays the foundations for his broader reassessment of the nature of speaking and the social, and his critique of the priority accorded to actuality over possibility by Aristotle in *Metaphysics* Theta (1049b13).

To examine Heidegger's analysis of the relation between rhetoric and speaking (*legein*), it is important to note the emphasis Heidegger places on rhetoric being more accurately definable in terms of a *dynamis*, a potentiality, than of a *techne*, a craft (*GA* 18: 114–115; *BCAP* 78–9).[1] Endorsing Aristotle's approach over the one found in Plato's *Gorgias* (463a6–465e1), the rhetorician is not the smooth talking technician of mere appearances, a skilled wand-waver who uses the right words to bring about the desired convictions, and is not engaged in mere contrivance or flattery. Instead, rhetoric is a capacity (*dynamis*) to concretize the diverse ways of speaking that disclose something substantive to someone, and not a persuasive means aiming only at the illusory or what is most expedient. Unlike other *technai*, such as medicine, geometry, and arithmetic, when it comes to rhetoric, Heidegger is clear that there is no "underlying matter", no "determinately demarcated region of beings", and no specific objects of study pertaining to this area beyond the expressible and conveyable (*GA* 18: 118; *BCAP* 81. Aristotle, *Rhetoric*, 355b27–1355b35). For this reason, rhetoric does not merely have the function of establishing new convictions about something, but rather identifies, through what Heidegger terms its "knowing-the-way-around" (*GA* 18: 118; *BCAP* 81), the most appropriate means of disclosing *something* persuasive to the listener, understood in terms of something that speaks for the matter and strikes at the heart of the matter. Heidegger's interpretation here emphasizes the existential dimension of rhetoric, which can be seen in its passion for listening to discourse and in being affected by what is said and what is experienced.

Thus rhetoric is not an improper form of speaking but is rather a passionate speaking about things in speaking together about things. Heidegger reads Aristotle's rhetoric then against the account found in Plato's *Gorgias*, as testifying to the power of expressivity in human existence as a mode of being outside of oneself and towards the world in relation to things or other human beings. Starting from here, rhetoric is defined in terms of seeing what "speaks for a matter", of cultivating through the act of speaking the "πιστεύειν with those to whom one speaks, specifically, about a concern that is up for debate at the time; to cultivate a δόξα" (ibid.). What this means is that rhetoric is not trying to bring about a determinate stance in the listener, it is not trying to convince unconditionally, but is instead opening up the affective nature of discourse in cultivating the capacity to see what speaks for a matter, of putting the listener in the right position to see it, in order for them to see what is at issue. It is precisely this that Heidegger wants to affirm when he writes that *"Rhetoric is nothing other than the interpretation of concrete being-there, the hermeneutic of being-there itself"* (*GA* 18: 110; *BCAP* 75).

Heidegger avers that the rhetorician is the one who can let the matters that speak for themselves be seen to speak for themselves by alerting the listener to those matters. Or as Mark Michalski puts it, "[rhetoric] is a question of making the thing evident in its substantive character" (Michalski 2005, 73). Moreover, it is the very notion of possibility, *dynamis*, in this case "the possibility of seeing, at each moment, what speaks for a matter" (*GA* 18: 118; *BCAP* 81), which allows one to distinguish rhetoric from sophistry. This means that rhetoric embodies a form of moving possibility which is not reducible to the yet to be actualized, and at the same time rhetoric's possibility is the hermeneutic possibility of alerting the listener to something that enlightens their understanding of the matter at issue, without coercing that understanding.

One the other hand, sophistry focuses not on the possibility of letting the matter speak for itself, or of orienting a listener towards the matter to be deliberated on and understood, but more on the unqualified intention to "conquer the other without knowledge of the matter discussed" (*GA* 18: 109; *BCAP* 75) and the self-absorbed efficacy of the given discourse. The efficacy of this type of discourse would have its end in the political assembly where rigorous logical demonstration was not the priority. Referring to the sophists, Heidegger sees this form of distorting speech in terms of being "taken in a peculiar direction and [becoming] absorbed in the immediate, in fashions, in babble. For the Greeks themselves, this process of living in the world, *to be absorbed* in what is ordinary, *to fall* into the world in which it lives, became, through language, the *basic danger of their being-there.* The proof of this fact is the existence of *sophistry*" (ibid.).[2] Heidegger is with Aristotle here, and arguably with the Plato (or better the Socrates) of the *Phaedrus*, in claiming that rhetoric need not be viewed as sophistical rhetoric and should be seen as the possibility of guiding someone towards substantive issues by means of the word. This means that rhetoric, like dialectic, has a psychagogic capacity and aims at arriving at what is at stake together in discussion (Plato, *Phaedrus* 276e5–6).[3]

# 1    Aristotle's *Rhetoric*

What Aristotle calls the endoxic character of rhetoric, how it takes its start from established belief or conviction, is thus represented in the proper use of *pisteis*, the case being made or means of persuasion, which in the parallel field of dialectic are termed syllogisms. *Pistis*, then, is not simply concerned with conviction or belief, but is a form of demonstration or exhibiting (*apodeixis tis*), one "that goes directly to the heart (*en-thymos*)" (Kisiel 2005, 137) of the matter and is "taken more to heart" by the listener (*GA* 18: 133; *BCAP* 90). This means that while an expert in syllogistic logic is distinct from an expert in rhetoric, the two share something in common, allowing one in principle to be an expert in both. In the end, understanding the counterpart (*antistrophos*) nature of these two fields of *logos*, rhetoric and dialectic, hinges on grasping their parallel and yet distinctly contrasting approaches to the question of demonstrable truth and how it is disclosed, either by the logical back and forth of refutation and counter-refutation, or by affective demonstration. Thus one could speak here in terms of logical in the narrow and in the broad sense of the term. The narrowly logical refers to demonstrably sound reasoning or syllogistic deduction, which is found in rigorously scientific discourse. Logical in the broad sense, i.e. those making use of rhetorical logic, is the so-called *enthymema* or demonstrative rhetorical syllogism which provides proof of something by orienting the listener to a shared and affective evidential reality or "body of proof" (*soma tes pisteos*) (Aristotle, *Rhetoric*, 1354a15; 1356a37–1356b26). Aristotle is thus concerned with how rhetoric serves to explain or clarify something by helping listeners to arrive at a certain insight by providing them with both concrete arguments and illustrative examples.

As mentioned, Heidegger focuses on Aristotle's claim that rhetoric is not a *techne* in the narrow sense and is instead the art of persuasion (*ars persuadendi*), understood as a way of being-affected and oriented by the matter under discussion thanks to the indicative guidance of the rhetorician. What is central for Heidegger is that Aristotle provides a descriptive access point to the domain of persuasion possibility, viewing rhetoric not so much as a persuasion skill, but rather as the *capacity* to detect the necessary features that would contribute to the process of persuading and being persuaded, or of the capacity to draw inferences from the given facts about something and allowing others to see those inferences as compelling. Aristotle thus examines the means, circumstances, and possibilities for genuinely persuading each other of something and of taking what shows itself to heart. In order to harness this capacity to persuade, one must reason cogently, understand character and virtue, and have a good knowledge of the emotional life of those who are listening. The latter requires the insight into what touches people and what goes on in the hearts and minds of people (Aristotle, *Rhetoric*, 1356a22–1356136).

The above mentioned capacity is connected to how rhetorical *logos* is bound up with highlighting the means of persuasion, the available means of coming to be persuaded by the evidential reality of the world which, even if we are not aware, makes a claim on us. It is for this reason, Heidegger claims, that *logos* is the fundamental mode of our being in the world, which does not simply mean that the world is grasped conceptually or by means of apodeictic propositions, but that the world is the space of appearances that corresponds to speaking in the world and speaking to others in the world. It is from this that Heidegger claims, with Aristotle, that *logos* constitutes the ontological ground of our affectively engaged and understandingly concerned being-together with others. As Heidegger has it:

> Every speaking is, […] a speaking *to someone* or *with others, with oneself* or *to oneself.* Speaking is in concrete being-there, where one does not exist alone, speaking *with others about something.* Speaking with others about something is, in each case, a *speaking out of oneself.* In speaking about something with others, I express myself [*spreche ich mich aus*], whether explicitly or not. (*GA* 18: 17; *BCAP* 14)

It is in our being affected by others in speaking in and of the world, in expressing myself in the world, that the concrete world becomes an abiding concern for us and not just for me.

Heidegger's interest in Aristotle's *Rhetoric* is therefore exclusively concerned with a manner of speaking that gives us access to the constitutive phenomenon of our speaking and embodied being with others in the world. As such, rhetoric says something about something, discloses something in a situated context, and allows one to see and understand the difference between something uncovered, something experienced objectively, and its generative ontological source in the world of reciprocal speaking with others that discloses this situated objectivity affectively. Rhetoric allows us to catch sight of the available means of coming to be persuaded by a speaking that discloses, contributing to the formation and vetting of our shared convictions about the world in discerning the truth of that world.

## 2    Heidegger's Appropriation of Rhetoric

This 1924 lecture attests unequivocally to Heidegger's attempts to interpret Aristotle as a proto-phenomenologist, one who equips contemporary phenomenology with the means of examining the connection between the being-true of a being or entity, i.e. that something uncovered shows itself as true, and the manner of its being disclosed to the understanding *as* true. This is what *BT* highlights in terms of originary "disclosedness" (*Erschlossenheit*) as opposed to the founded mode of "uncoveredness" (*Entdecktheit*) (*SZ* 220–221). In fact, Heidegger's 1924–1925 lecture course on Plato's *Sophist*, which took place in the winter semester following his lectures on Aristotle's *Rhetoric*, puts forward the same connection between the manifestation of truth and the essence of human understanding: truth is a determination of the essence of Dasein, understood as an affected and responsive discloser, and truth is uncovered in a determinate way by speaking. As Heidegger puts it, promising much, "Ἀληθεύειν is a mode of being-in-the-world, such that one has unconcealed it there just as it is. This ἀληθεύειν is the basic phenomenon toward which we are headed" (*GA* 18: 119; *BCAP* 81).

Hence, every manner of truth disclosing occurs by way of speaking which is concerned with what it is speaking of or about (*GA* 19: 82; *PS* 57). It is a speaking "right in the midst of" what concerns it, *meta-logou* (*GA* 18: 61; *BCAP* 43). In sum, thoughtful rhetoric, for Heidegger, is one that allows us to distinguish what is uncovered, 'objectivity', and what allows it to manifest its shared sense and become intelligible.

Now *pisteis*, the demonstrative means of persuasion or capacity to provide proofs, are in fact divisible into two categories: non-technical and technical, *pisteis atechnoi* and *pisteis entechnoi* (Aristotle, *Rhetoric*, 1355b36–1356a1). The *pisteis entechnoi*, the creative or artistic side of rhetoric, is broken down into three types: (1) Speaking that manifests the credibility (*axiopistia*) and character (*ethos*) of the speaker: his/her integrity, capability, and reliability; (2) Speaking that disposes the listener in a certain way, a self-expressing that elicits a determinate and affective response (*pathos*); and (3) Speaking (*logos*) that demonstrates disclosively the true nature of something or matter at hand. Now the merit of type three, for Heidegger, the demonstrating offered by *logos*, is that "λέγειν itself is πίστις as the basic function of being-there itself" (*GA* 18: 120; *BCAP* 82). Pre-empting the discussion that would emerge in *BT*, this means that the being of Dasein is both understandingly discursive and affectively disclosive, making a shared concern visible to someone else in a specific context in which the speaker is credible or committed.

While Heidegger's approach is often exegetical and philological, what defines the philosophical originality of his interpretation is the insistence with which he claims that Aristotle's *Rhetoric* is the expression of a sensitive and dynamic thinking-together, which allows us to make a distinction between the field of uncovering (ontology and ontological content) and the disclosive origin and access point of this uncovering (the phenomenological hermeneutics of Dasein). As Heidegger puts it:

> Speaking-with-one-another is… the clue to the uncovering of the basic phenomenon of the discoveredness of being-there itself as being-in-a-world. We take *rhetoric* as a *concrete guide* insofar as it is nothing other than the *interpretation of being-there with regard to the basic possibility of speaking-with-one-another*. (*GA* 18: 139; *BCAP* 95)

Therefore, in many ways, Heidegger is finding ample alternative resources within the metaphysical tradition to counter-balance what he sees as an excessively one-sided dialectical tendency to posit premises (found in Aristotle's *Prior Analytics* and in the *Topics*, for instance) to prioritize scientific truths which are true necessarily, that is true in the absolute and unqualified sense. He is doing this to emphasise the fundamental and arguably overlooked role of historical existence and shared historical experience as the enabling condition of arriving at truth which is not the truth of the universally, actually, or necessarily true. I will return to this in Sect. 4.

And yet in these early lectures Heidegger insists that rhetoric and dialectic are fundamentally discursive capacities (*dynameis*), while scientific thinking strives for a knowledge of real things (*pragmata*). What makes rhetoric unique, however, is that it exhibits a *poietic* character, a productive element, and simultaneously a demonstratively scientific character: it facilitates knowledge of real things which have been disclosed or rendered thematic productively. Rhetoric exhibits a specific form of *logos*, or knowing, parallel to, but distinct from, scientific knowing, insofar as it structures arguments differently and persuasively or indicatively draws attention to the evidential nature of truth, what Heidegger calls the "thoroughgoing trust in that which initially shows itself" (*GA* 18: 150; *BCAP* 102). Hence, a good rhetorician, in Heidegger's view, can see and understand what speaks for the matter, and as a *phronimos* the rhetorician can subsequently lead the listener to an appropriate conviction regarding the matter up for discussion. This is primarily and importantly because they have inspired trust in their listeners by means of their continual, or better their credibly insistent, self-expression.

Therefore, the intellectual virtues (*techne, episteme, sophia, nous* and *phronesis*), these disclosive and excellent *hexeis*, facilitate the capacities of rhetoric and dialectic differently, in that *logos* is given with different degrees of rigor and proof, but always with demonstrative force. *Logos* is the fundamental determination of the moved and expressive life of the human being, and finds in rhetoric a degree of demonstrative force, namely *pistis*, which discloses the modal character of truth, which is tied to historical context, responsive listener, and affect.

# 3     Being with Others and Speaking with Others

It is the great merit of Heidegger to have drawn our attention to an approach to evidential truth which has perhaps been downplayed in the history of philosophy, indicating a fidelity towards a truth which is compelling but not absolute, and he has done so by reflecting on a form of affectivity which has arguably fallen out of favor philosophically in the twentieth and twenty-first centuries. Prior to Arendt and Gadamer, it is Heidegger who drew our attention to the hermeneutical core of rhetoric and to the fact that we are genuinely human only insofar as we exist with others in the midst of matters disclosed and made interpretatively intelligible in conversation. And it is at this point that 'pure phenomenology' becomes 'phenomenological hermeneutics', understood as "genuine hermeneutical ontological science" (*GA* 18: 351; *BCAP* 238) which is at the service of "working out the conditions on which the possibility of any ontological investigation depends" (*SZ* 37). The upshot here is that prior to a theoretical-metaphysical reflection on actuality and necessity, the practical life of "speaking-with-one-another where others are themselves speaking" is what establishes the possibility of understanding *koinonia*, understanding the possibility of the being in common of things (*GA* 18: 50; *BCAP* 36). Unlike the over-wrought rhetoric of the later Heidegger, in 1924, under the guidance of Aristotle, he insists that the most fundamental issues of philosophy, on what there is and how it is given or rendered intelligible, is essentially tied to our embodied and affective being-together. Let me say a little more about this below and how Heidegger connects the issue of being with others to the issue of disposedness and self-understanding in terms of *hedone*.

While the body-world relationship was never explicit or front and center in Heidegger's analyses, he is quite clear in these lectures that affects are not simply states of mind, as the infelicitous translation of *Befindlichkeit* perpetuates, but are concerned with the disposedness and disclosive bearing of embodied beings in their world. In these lectures he is concerned with our being understandingly turned towards the world, drawn out by the world, in allowing a matter to matter to us. What is more, the affects or dispositions of life play a determining role when it comes to our embodied being-in-the-world and of our embodied being-with-and-toward-others in being turned towards this world.

The above is developed in Heidegger's 1924 analysis of *hedone*, usually translated as pleasure, but translated by Heidegger as *Befindlichkeit*, understood as modality of "the self-having" of Dasein, which at first sight appears to collapse Aristotle's distinction between *hexis* and *pathos*, something that I *have* versus something I *undergo*. However, ever fearful of it being interpreted in terms of the "average feeling of the crowd" or "the interpretation of the being-there of the many", when Heidegger uses the term "self-having" to define the disposedness of *hedone*, he is in fact alluding to the transformative potential which lies in my being attuned, the possibility of breaking with the everyday in "feeling oneself" in a genuine manner, of being awakened to the possibility of an "*originary interpretedness*" of life by life in "the moment" of the rousing disposedness of *hedone* (*GA* 18: 277; *BCAP* 188).

What is most compelling and arguably most relevant about Heidegger's reading of Aristotle's *Rhetoric*, prefiguring the existential analytic in *BT*, is the move to cast thinking and the embodied movement of thought as the concerned making present to itself of the world and of others in the world, and his insistence that the human being is determined as an embodied being-in-the-world with other embodied speakers and listeners. While it would be naïve to claim that Heidegger is at this point a champion of the everybody in the public realm (*die Öffentlichkeit*), what we do see, perhaps even more clearly than in *BT*, is that these speakers and listeners are simultaneously both the condition of the human being achieving a genuine *ethos*, i.e. having an apprehended interpretation and understanding of itself and the world in becoming visible to others, and the possibility of the human being losing itself in being taken hold of by the many in the world.[4] And yet this genuine *ethos* achievement is not simply character or comportment driven, it is not simply Dasein-centered, but is fundamentally bound up with the possibilities the human being both embodies and stretches out towards when encountering a world that is constitutively with others and for others.

Championing phenomenological method and what he terms its radical breakthrough, Heidegger claims that there is "No division between 'psychic' and 'bodily acts' [...] and that the primary [...] function of embodiment secures the ground for the full being of human beings" (*GA* 18: 199; *BCAP* 134). And yet later in the lecture Heidegger is quick to qualify his position, claiming that affects are not reducible to psycho-physical processes, emphasizing instead that affects primarily constitute the soil from which speaking and being-together emerge. He writes:

> Insofar as the πάθη are not merely an annex of psychical processes, but are rather *the ground [Boden] out of which speaking arises, and what is expressed grows back into*, the πάθη, for their part, are *the basic possibilities in which being-there itself is primarily oriented toward itself*, finds itself. The primary being-oriented, the illumination of its being-in-the-world is not a *knowing*, but rather a *finding-oneself* that can be determined differently, according to the mode of being-there of a being. Only within the thus characterized finding-oneself and being-in-the-world is it possible to speak about things, insofar as they are stripped of the look they have in immediate relations. (*GA* 18: 262; *BCAP* 176)

Affects, then, are how the embodied human being is turned toward itself but not as an object of knowledge and, perhaps more importantly, how the human being *finds itself* precisely in *finding itself* turned *towards* others, towards other embodied and attuned human beings in the world. Yet this turning towards itself, this *Sichbefinden*, is not a mere procedural self-apprehension or wilful reflection carried out by an 'I can', but rather a fundamental and embodied finding-oneself *with* and affected *by* others, both drawn to and repelled by others, which is delimited and negotiated continually in speaking together of what is common in the 'feeling' together of what is common.

In 1924, Heidegger sees in rhetoric a hermeneutic of concrete human existence and praises the Greeks for recognizing that the transformative back-and-forth of discursiveness is first a characteristic of human life and that philosophical conceptuality sinks its roots into the soil of everyday conversation in developing its elaborate metaphysical systems.

Yet Heidegger also claims that philosophy has lost touch with this same soil. His aim, however is not to praise the traditional Greek notion of possibility, as "bringing-forth" (*poeisis*) over against *techne*. Rather, he is suggesting that metaphysical thinking, as a fundamental approach to beings as actualized, structurally inhibits reflection on other modes of disclosing and, most crucially, reflection on disclosing as such. But I will return to this later.

For Heidegger, Aristotle's thought provides what he terms a "jolt to the present, or better put, to the future" (*GA* 18: 6; *BCAP* 5). Rhetoric allows us to comprehend the foundations of scientific thinking and philosophical knowing in lived speech, which takes its start from being-affected by what is other, both within and without. It is because of this insight, contained in rhetoric, that Heidegger decides to develop a fundamental ontology of lived and possibilizing *pathos* as opposed to an ontology of the actual. He does so because we are primarily embodied self-expressing and self-disclosing beings attuned to one another, to what is common, and to the world in different yet analogous ways. This means that we can be moved and guided by the right words that make a matter evident substantively.

Without the *koinon*, what is common and communal, we would be, as Heidegger puts it, "fish […] caught in the stream" (*GA* 18: 266; *BCAP* 178). We would be unable to come to this authentic self-understanding or project and realize possibilities as *our* own possibilities. Affects are therefore bound up with living-with-one-another and are considered insofar as they are determinations of the being together of speaker and hearer, what Heidegger terms the attuned and comprehending being in the world. However, it is a truism to state that everyone is necessarily with others in the world. Hence, that the affects participate in the doxastic formation grounded in "*being-with-one-another*", and not merely "being situated alongside one another" (*GA* 18: 47; *BCAP* 33), is characterized by Heidegger as living in an average and everyday way by *doxa* but also, interestingly, as the fundamental possibility of arriving at an authentic self-understanding or self-projecting, "in the sense of *being-as-speaking-with-one-another* through communicating, refuting, confronting…" (ibid.). This is understood as addressing and responding to one another and by doing so coming to an authentic self-understanding of my being as world disclosing, which is, as he tells is in *BT*, the most fundamental "truth of existence" (*SZ* 221).

Being given to one another, understood as speaking with one another reciprocally, is hence the very condition of deciding something genuine for oneself and of swimming against the above-mentioned "stream" when the time is right. And as early as 1924, Heidegger is clearly grappling with the oscillating and constitutively productive tension that exists between authenticity and inauthenticity, non-relationality and relationality, speaking and the distortions of speaking. The claim being made in these lectures is quite explicit, namely: the human being is not primarily understandable in terms of its autonomous self-relatedness, but nonetheless has the non-substitutable possibility of deciding something for itself authentically, of expressing the "genuine drive" (*GA* 18: 20; *BCAP* 16) of the being of humanity, a drive towards what Heidegger terms in 1924 the "ἕξις with respect to the uncoveredness of its being" (*GA* 18: 264; *BCAP* 176). It is explicit in these lectures that Heidegger, following Aristotle, is deliberating on the manner of our constitutive being towards others and towards oneself which is at one's disposal. And he is also analyzing the nature of appearing in such a way that one's appearing *with* others need not be a distorted or deceptive appearing, but a genuinely open and affective being in common.

Thanks to Heidegger's interpretation of Aristotle's *Rhetoric*, he finds in *doxa* not what is epistemically impoverished, but the very source of being-together, namely the constitutive phenomenon of 'everydayness' outlined in *BT*. It is out of this context that he writes in *BT* that Aristotle's *Rhetoric* must be understood "as the first systematic hermeneutic of the everydayness of being with one another" (*SZ* 138). What this means is that the surrounding world appears for us as co-disclosed doxastically and this means we experience the common world with others (*GA* 18: 34, 39–40; *BCAP* 101). Thus, *doxa* is both the ground and impetus of the open-ended speaking-with-one-another, in the relationality of our communicative being together, both authentically and inauthentically.

# 4      On Actuality and Possibility

One thing that I have only touched on thus far, and it is highlighted throughout the 1924 Aristotle lecture course, is how Heidegger's analysis of rhetoric and affect is tied to his attempts to offer a critique of the metaphysical concept of actuality. And it is only by going back to these early Aristotle lectures that the notion of "possibility" being "higher" than "actuality" can be made sense of. In spite of the obvious importance of "possibility" in *BT*, first as an existential and futural sense, it would nevertheless have been quite difficult, if not impossible, for its first readers to appreciate the breadth of the critique of actuality that Heidegger lays out, but which seems in retrospect to have been contained within the claim as to the priority of possibility and possibilizing ways of being in the early lectures on Aristotle. *BT* does not make sense unless it is read in the light of Heidegger's reading of Aristotle and the metaphysics of actuality and possibility.

*BT* was an attempt to reconceive the nature of the human being as Dasein and to examine its way of being as the original possibility of the appearance and understandability of reality and actuality. Heidegger is clear then that Dasein displays an ontological constitution which is distinct from all other types of real, extant, or actual entities in the world and that the 'what is it?' question is unsuitable to Dasein, and in fact acts as an impediment when it comes to interrogating the manner of being of Dasein. Over against the what-question, Heidegger prioritizes the 'who is it?' question, focusing on its discrete manner of existence as possibililizing and self-possibilizing. This is all to point to the fact that the manner of existence that belongs to Dasein is such that it cannot be defined in terms of an available and actualized presence, or as a produced and determined reality. The ontological constitution of Dasein is such that it requires a different articulation of essence and existence in the direction of a fundamental possibility that articulates itself in terms of the restless movement of the understanding of being that determines the being of Dasein. This movement does not consist in objectifying itself but rather in making itself aware of its distinctly possibilizing way of being in the world. As such, Heidegger writes, "the thematizing of entities within-the-world presupposes being-in-the-world as the basic state [or fundamental constitution] of Dasein" (*SZ* 363–364). What is at stake here is the specific entity who is identified as the affective dis-closer of manifold possibilities and of possibility as such, of being constitutively ahead of itself as being in the world, and yet liberated from the traditional reference to an autonomous, self-grounded, and self-determined thinking subject which subsequently connects itself to the world.

It is important to note that the disclosive way of being of Dasein, whose essence is contained in this way of existing, is the space which opens up or exists in the performance of the difference between being and beings (*GA* 24: 454; *BP* 319). It is the being that understands both tacitly or explicitly what it means for something to 'be' and this understanding is pre-ontologically latent in Dasein's existence. The ontological difference, then, is a possibility only because the being of Dasein possibilizes and performs this difference in disclosing the excess of being's sense with respect to beings which are simply there as determined and available. Yet Heidegger is not simply aiming at a further determination of the being of Dasein but is rather pointing to Dasein as the very *possibility* of understanding the difference between being and beings, which is irreducible to the possibility of this or that actual being or entity. It is only within this frame of reference that one can provide an answer to, or better phrase a question about, the meaning of the 'who' of the human being. This question concerns an entity that is ontically-ontologically possibilizing like no other entity and whose possibility is no longer a possibility belonging to a subject, i.e. no longer belonging to the 'I' or the experience of an 'I can' (*SZ* 116). Thus in *BT* Heidegger was attempting to identify a different way of thinking about actuality and possibility and how the nature of possibility must be reconceived starting from the being that makes the distinction *possible* in the first place.

As early as 1924, Heidegger was drawing on Aristotle's *Rhetoric* in order to indicate a blocked possibility, or an unheeded or submerged *dynamis*, when it comes to the re-conception of the human being as an affective, communicative, and comprehending exemplar of possibility and communal sense. This means a fundamental metaphysical perspective on beings, along with its interpretation of actuality and attendant possibilities, has blocked or suppressed another affectively grounded understanding of possibility as the possibility of the being in common of things. This understanding is one which is primarily undergone and performed, and not just brought about or actualized, the aim of which is to let what shows itself be seen from itself.

But the historical configuration of beings suggests something more, namely, that the submerged or blocked possibility in question is not just one possibility among others (e.g. the possibility of a better philosophical understanding of beings), but a more original possibility that is of an entirely different order, incompatible with the modalities of metaphysical actuality. Indeed, for Heidegger, this incompatibility extends to any interpretation of being in terms of beings that are ultimately understood as given, present and actualized entities.

Thus, on the one hand, metaphysical thinking (i.e. the interpretation of being in terms of beings understood as unconcealed, present entities) is not a banal danger that can be sidestepped with ease. On the other hand, the blockage is not so total that the transition between the first and the other way is fantastical or impossible. In fact, the danger that metaphysics represents also indirectly transmits specific knowledge both of the shortcomings of erroneous interpretations of being and of the nature and shape of the other way. This danger appears first of all in the importance accorded to actuality in the metaphysical tradition, which skews possibility and necessity in relation to an actuality too narrowly conceived as the mere unconcealedness of beings along with all their interrelations and properties.

Heidegger's attack on metaphysical conceptions of modality thereby takes as its first target the traditional priority of actuality over possibility. As Heidegger puts it in *CP*: "The origin and dominance of the 'modalities' are *even more* questionworthy than the interpretation of beings in terms of *idea*," (*GA* 65: 281; *CP* 221) which for Heidegger stands at the origin of the first, Greek beginning of philosophy. But in order to understand this origin and dominance, he adds, "what is important is the priority of 'actuality' (cf. also *existentia* as what preeminently stands in distinction to *essentia*): actuality as *energeia*, with possibility and necessity as—so to speak—its two horns" (ibid.).

The problem here seems first and foremost to be the way in which the metaphysical tradition has, almost without exception, defined possibility and necessity in terms of actuality, which functions as the sole point of reference for these "modalities". One version of this priority of actuality, stemming from Aristotle, although importantly not the Aristotle of the *Rhetoric*, is that to any possibility there must correspond an existing, active or passive power of actualization. Another view, also traceable to Aristotle, is that possibility can be defined in terms of what is at least *sometimes* actual, while necessity corresponds to what is *always* actual. In this way, actuality holds first rank in the metaphysical order of things, not only by virtue of its intrinsic priority—which is largely conceded as soon as truth is understood as unconcealment and unconcealment is understood as presence, but also in the relative extensions of its subordinate terms: possibility and necessity constitute the total range of actuality, running from the sometimes actual to the always and necessarily (*ex anankes*) actual. They guarantee, as it were, that the logic of actuality exhausts all being, up to and including what *is not* in the form of the non-being of the possible (i.e. the not-yet-actual). Everything, even what is not yet (i.e. what is possible), is thereby reduced to the order of actuality, like points on a scale running from remote possibility through general possibility up to fullest actuality, from *dynamis* to *energeia* or *entelecheia*. As Heidegger puts it, metaphysically speaking the word "being" (i.e. entity, *das Seiende*) "names *not* only the actual [*das Wirkliche*] (and certainly not if this is taken as the present at hand and the latter merely as the object of knowledge), not only the actual of any sort, but at the same time the possible, the necessary, and the accidental, everything that stands in beyng in any way whatever, even including negativity and nothingness" (*GA* 65: 74; *CP* 59). Simply put, Heidegger sets himself the task of dismantling and examining the unquestioned presence and actuality of objects to subjects, as well as the subject's self-presence to itself as object, its standing before itself as the very power of representation. How is it that *there are* objects and subjects "for each other" at all? What is the origin of the "there–ness" that lies at the basis of objective knowledge and of the fundamental experience of the exteriority of things? And in the same questioning, Heidegger takes aim at the unhelpful (and unexplained) differentiation between beings and the being (beingness, presence, actuality, etc.) that metaphysics has always claimed to be their foundation.

In conclusion, the long-running attack on metaphysical modality in the name of a deeper and more essential blocked possibility traverses Heidegger's writings and is easy enough to spot once we know what to look for. Heidegger's reading of the *Rhetoric*, the world negotiating exercise of speaking and hearing together,[5] a fundamental mode of "perceiving" (*GA* 18: 44; *BCAP* 32) together, and his analysis of conversational *pathos* as "coming-to-an-understanding in being-with-one-another" and in "being-trusted" by others, are just splendid examples of this (*GA* 18: 154; *BCAP* 104). In short, *pathos* is a disclosive activity which is receptive to and concerned with something, it is "a *disposition of living things in their world* [*Befindlichkeit des Lebenden in seiner Welt*], in the mode of being positioned toward something, allowing a matter to matter to it" (*GA* 18: 122; *BCAP* 83). The experience being outlined in the movement of *pathos* is the experience of something striking or touching us, and yet this striking or touching is simultaneously bound up with my letting something which has been voiced to matter to me and my responsive position or comportment (*verhalten*) towards what touches me as mattering (Withy 2015, 24).

Of course, for Heidegger, the near-total dominance of metaphysical thinking in the last two-and-a-half millennia, evidenced by the marginal status of Aristotle's *Rhetoric* and *Poetics* in the history of philosophy, poses certain problems, among which is the fact that there is absolutely no guarantee that what is possible will ever come to pass. In this regard, the fragility of thinking and the provisional nature of philosophical questioning, still under the determining influence of metaphysics, are common themes in Heidegger's work. What is striking, however, is the configuration of something that Heidegger holds to be distinctly possible and in some sense hidden or supressed within the history of metaphysics, alive within Aristotle's *Rhetoric* perhaps—namely, the possibility of reconceiving the essence of possibility starting with a reflection on speaking, listening, and being-affected.

Yet, this reconceiving is also inhibited or blocked, possibly to the point of its perpetual repression. On the one hand, such a possibility is clearly a real possibility, in Heidegger's view, insofar as "real" is opposed to "logical," "formal," "metaphysical," "fantastical," and so forth; and yet, on the other hand, insofar as it is structurally inhibited by metaphysical thinking, it remains unreal, in the specific sense that the conditions of its realization or possibilization are by and large unavailable. Such is the nature of blocked possibility that defines Heidegger's work from the beginning to end. His interpretations of Aristotle's *Rhetoric* and the affects of rhetoric are precisely an early attempt to draw our attention to blocked possibilities and, where and when possible, to unblock them.

## Notes

1. It is ironic that in the following winter semester course on Plato's *Sophist*, Heidegger would define rhetoric as a *techne*, when he writes: "In the *Phaedrus*, Plato's attitude toward rhetoric is quite different [than in the *Gorgias*]. There it is positive, but not such that Plato recognized in rhetoric a proper τέχνη, as Aristotle later did" (*GA* 19: 310; *PS* 215).

2. Or as Heidegger puts it in the *Sophist* course: "Plato shows indirectly what the philosopher is by displaying what the sophist is. And he does not show this by setting up an empty program, i.e., by saying what one would have to do to be a philosopher, but he shows it by actually philosophizing" (*GA* 19: 12; *PS* 8).

3. It should be said that Plato's judgements on rhetoric are still quite negative. In the *Phaedrus*, Plato emphasizes the centrality of discursiveness or dialogue over the seeming monologue of rhetorical persuasion. And naturally, he continues to ascribe an absolute priority to philosophy over rhetoric, and for rhetoric to be viewed more positively it must become rhetorical dialectic or dialectic rhetoric. Rhetoric and sophistry are the recurring themes of Plato's corpus of dialogues and one could even claim that Platonic philosophy is a product of this polemic. For Plato, there will always exist a tension between the good word, which orients the speaker to the "upward way", and the deceptive word, which leads one astray.

4. Charles Bambach has referred to Heidegger's early *Rhetoric* inspired move towards authentic or proper self-understanding as an attempt to outline "an appropriate *ethos*– an *ethos* that authentically serves as a way to connect ones factical life to the hidden dimension of being covered over by habitual routine and familiarity". See Charles Bambach, *Thinking the Poetic Measure of Justice: Heidegger—Hölderlin—Celan* (Albany: SUNY Press, 2014), 118.

5. On the very interesting claim that Heidegger is nonetheless guilty of the "de-acoustification" or "de-vocalization" of speaking and listening against the backdrop of "publicness" and "fallenness", see P. Christopher Smith, "The Uses and Abuses of Aristotle's Rhetoric in Heidegger's Fundamental Ontology: The Lecture Course, Summer, 1924," in *From Phenomenology to Thought, Errancy, and Desire: Essays in Honor of William J. Richardson*, ed. Babette Babich (Boston: Kluwer Academic Publishers, 1995), 329.

# References

Kisiel, Theodore. 2005. "Rhetorical Protopolitics in Heidegger and Arendt." In *Heidegger and Rhetoric*, edited by Daniel M. Gross and Ansgar Kemmann. Albany: State University of New York.

Michalski, Mark. 2005. "Hermeneutic Phenomenology as Philology." In *Heidegger and Rhetoric*, edited by Daniel M. Gross and Ansgar Kemmann. Albany: State University of New York.

Sheehan, Thomas. 2015. *Making Sense of Heidegger: A Paradigm Shift*. London: Rowman & Littlefield.

Withy, Katherine. 2015. "Owned Emotions: Affective Excellence in Heidegger on Aristotle." In *Heidegger, Authenticity and the Self: Themes from Division Two of* Being and Time, edited by Denis McManus. Oxon: Routledge.

# 4

# Angst as Evidence: Shifting Phenomenology's Measure

## Christos Hadjioannou

# 1    Introduction

*Being and Time* (*BT*) is meant to radically revise the basic concepts of traditional ontology and metaphysics, but it is also intended to shake the foundations of the phenomenological science envisioned by Heidegger's teacher, Edmund Husserl. As Heidegger writes:

> The real 'movement' of the sciences takes place when their basic concepts undergo a more or less radical revision which is transparent to itself. The level which a science has reached is determined by how far it is *capable* of a crisis in its basic concepts. [...] Basic concepts determine the way in which we get an understanding beforehand of the area of subject-matter underlying all the objects a science takes as its theme, and all positive investigation is guided by this understanding. Only after the area itself has been explored beforehand in a corresponding manner do these concepts become genuinely demonstrated and 'grounded'. (*SZ* 9–10)

C. Hadjioannou (✉)
Sofia University, Sofia, Bulgaria

© The Author(s) 2019
C. Hadjioannou (ed.), *Heidegger on Affect*, Philosophers in Depth,
https://doi.org/10.1007/978-3-030-24639-6_4

While explicitly Heidegger's aim here is to convince the reader of the exigency of a radicalization of ontology and its basic concepts, implicitly *BT* is about a crisis in the very science of phenomenology—its methods and epistemological foundations: *BT* is meant to lay the foundations of phenomenology anew. This helps to explain why Heidegger dedicated the book to Husserl.[1] *BT* not only shifts attention of the theme of phenomenological research from the theme of intentionality to the meaning of Being, and from the transcendental ego to the factical structure of Dasein; it also shifts the *measure* of what counts as epistemic justification.

Indeed, Heidegger's project is incompatible with epistemology and its basic concepts such as "epistemic justification", for reasons that will become clearer later on. Strictly speaking, *BT* is not about epistemic justification: it is not a treatise that yields justified "knowledge" in the theoretical sense, but rather it is an interpretive text that formally indicates the provisional results of a phenomenology of Dasein and its structural make-up.[2] However, even a hermeneutic treatise makes philosophical claims that have *the status of knowledge*, in the sense that they are grounded in and phenomenologically justified by evidence. Insofar as this is the case, and for the purpose of making this chapter more engaging to analytic readers, we can assume that *BT* offers something *like* epistemic justification.

Both Heidegger and Husserl embark on a project of laying bare the ground upon which meaning is made possible, and in the process offer new categories which conceptually grasp meaning. The two philosophical projects share the transcendental aim of identifying a priori conditions of meaning. However, while Husserl's transcendental project conceptualizes meaning in terms of intentionality and theoretical *knowledge*, i.e. ideal intentional structures that comprise scientific knowledge, Heidegger is interested in more primordial structures that ground meaning in the sense of *understanding*. Husserl tries to lay bare the ground of knowing the world, Heidegger tries to lay bare the ground of understanding the world. For Heidegger, meaning is the achievement of understanding. What is more, understanding, for Heidegger, is hermeneutic. As Taylor Carman argues, *BT* aims to analyze the phenomenon of interpretation, which is "the express or explicit (*ausdrücklich*) understanding of something *as* something" (Carman 2003, 5). In sum, *BT* is a treatise that aims to uncover the horizon, i.e. the a priori structures, that allow for understanding and interpretation to emerge.

In order to achieve such a foundationalist project, both Husserl and Heidegger must clarify the conditions of possibility of meaning, and this inevitably includes developing the criteria for justificatory evidence. Phenomenology is, after all, a project that aims to ground its findings in phenomenological *evidence*, so as to counter dogmatic/speculative metaphysics. As I hope to show, an important aspect of *BT* is that, through this work, Heidegger radicalizes the basic concept of "evidence" that is operative in Husserlian phenomenology, which commits Husserl to mentalist evidentialism. Thus, Heidegger overcomes mentalist evidentialism and relaunches phenomenology on the basis of a different "epistemic" measure.

In this chapter, I will analyze the fundamental mood of angst in terms of evidence and certainty, so as to better illustrate the methodological role it plays in *BT*. As I will show, angst serves as the hermeneutic equivalent to what analytic epistemologists call "justifier of knowledge", that is, it takes on the function of *evidence* that phenomenologically grounds the interpretation of the basic structures of Dasein, as these are disclosed in authentic existence. Angst is evidence for the factical, temporal truth of Dasein—it is evidence for the encounter of death as the possibility of impossibility, which holds open the deep temporal structure of Dasein. It is in angst that Dasein finds itself face to face with the "nothing"—the ultimate possibility-for-Being.

The role of angst in *BT* marks an epistemological shift, in which Heidegger radicalizes Husserl's conception of experiential justification and the associated notion of evidence, which commits him (Husserl) to mentalist evidentialism.[3] I will argue that Heidegger's position (in *BT*) is a phenomenological conception of experiential justification that, while still committing him to quasi-evidentialist principles, makes his position incompatible with either internalism or mentalism.

While Husserl, in *Ideas I*, establishes phenomenological inquiry on the evidence provided by *originary intuition*, Heidegger wants to overthrow this reflective beginning which anchors evidence on perceptual experience in which the content is presented as bodily present, so as to allow epistemic justification to arise from *"owned feelings"*, specifically the existential feeling of angst. The latter does not disclose by presentifying something (as clear and distinct presence), but rather discloses the structural whole of Dasein, pre-reflectively, pre-conceptually, and in an indeterminate manner.

The chapter comprises four sections and a concluding remark. In Sect. 2, entitled "Phenomenology as a Foundationalist Project: Grounding Knowledge/Interpretation in Evidence", I argue that the primary tendencies in phenomenology (both Husserlian and Heideggerian) are foundationalist in nature, its aims being to ground knowledge/interpretation in evidence. In Sect. 3, entitled "Husserl's Conception of Evidence", I provide an overview of Husserl's conception of evidence as Apodictic Certainty. Then, borrowing from Philipp Berghofer's recent work, I analyze Husserl's *phenomenological* conception of experiential justification, focusing on its self-giving character and finally explaining why Husserl's position is mentalist evidentialist. In Sect. 4, entitled "The Critique of Husserl and Evidence in *Being and Time*", I show how Heidegger redeveloped the notion of evidence in critical contrast to Husserl's. I then sketch out the notion of evidence operative in *BT*, with specific focus on angst as evidence. Finally, in Sect. 5, entitled "Angst and Mentalist Evidentialism", I analyze how angst as evidence makes Heidegger's position in *BT* incompatible with the basic tenets of Husserl's mentalist evidentialism.

## 2    Phenomenology as a Foundationalist Project: Grounding Knowledge/ Interpretation in Evidence

Insofar as the idea of evidence is integral to the idea of scientific grounding, we must firstly look at the idea of "grounding" itself and the way in which it operates in phenomenology. Husserl's phenomenology is a project of grounding knowledge in *evidence*. In a sense, the Husserlian project is a modern philosophical one whose aim is to offer a foundation for cognitive knowledge, in line with the general idea of science. As such, it is a continuation of the Cartesian project of discovering a safe starting point that can serve as the foundation upon which to build the philosophical edifice. This grounding character permeates the entire Husserlian corpus, from the early to the later works. It is, I think, safe to say that Husserlian phenomenology is a type of foundationalist exercise with the overarching aim of achieving a version of epistemological foundationalism.[4] And if phenomenology claims to be a presuppositionless science, then it must offer the evidence upon which the epistemic edifice rests. "Evidence" is therefore the rationale for the development of his scientific transcendental phenomenology; it is "the hidden spring of phenomenology" (Öktem 2009, 5).

As Philipp Berghofer argues, Husserl makes clear that "there is more to knowledge than true belief/judgment. Not every true belief is knowledge. This more that is required is *evidence*" (Berghofer 2018, 1). Science demands that cognition (*Erkenntnis*) has to be based on *real grounding* (*Begründung*), which is grounding on "pure evidence" (Berghofer 2018, 3), and without the notion of evidence, science itself, as Husserl understands it, would not make sense! (Berghofer 2018, 2)

In this context, insofar as phenomenology is about grounding transcendental knowledge in intuitive evidence, it is useful to think of both Heidegger and Husserl as belonging to the Kantian tradition. *BT* is a transcendental project, one that aims to uncover the horizon for the interpretation of meaning (of being in general). It is a treatise that uncovers transcendental structures (*existentials*). As Carman notes, Kant was interested in "epistemic conditions", and Heidegger was interested in "conditions of interpretation or explicit understanding" (Carman 2003, 12). While Heidegger's project of fundamental ontology is indeed irreducible to Kant's transcendental idealism, I agree with Carman that there is a useful analogy to be drawn between what Henry Allison called Kant's "epistemic conditions" and Heidegger's "hermeneutic conditions" (ibid.).

Insofar as Husserl's aim was to ensure that the findings of phenomenology amount to justified knowledge, he puts the epoché in place and devises the Principle of All Principles, which determines the golden epistemological standard of apodictic certainty. In effect, the Principle of All Principles purifies consciousness and guarantees that phenomenological reflection, i.e. originary intuition, provides *evidence* for transcendental knowledge. Husserl had to develop a method that would deem philosophy autonomous and self-responsible. In this context,

> Husserl developed the method of the reductions in order to do justice to what he took to be the fundamental norm governing philosophy, namely, the norm of "ultimate philosophical self-responsibility." Because philosophical inquiry can take nothing for granted—neither from the sciences nor from previous philosophies—it must be radically first-personal. Only what I can validate on the basis of my own evidential insight can stand as actual philosophical knowledge; the assertions of others are initially merely "empty," mere truth-claims that I must demonstrate for myself against the things that "fulfill" them. To take responsibility for evidential fulfillment defines the *practice* of philosophizing. The various reductions, then—including the reduction of one's own being to transcendental consciousness—are meant to stake out the kind of *Evidenz* that measures up to the norm, the first-person experience within which any possible claim to meaning and being must be assessed. (Crowell 2013, 76)

But the demand for evidential self-responsibility is also a basic tendency in Heidegger's early phenomenology, culminating in *BT*. As Crowell rightly argues, this demand is actually *built into* the structure of *BT*, beginning from the "everyday lostness in the anonymity of *das Man* to that point where Dasein can genuinely say 'I,' that is, recover its 'ownmost' self and so be responsible to itself. This is the methodological significance of the chapters on death, conscience, and authenticity as resoluteness" (Crowell 2013, 76–77).

Division II of *BT* has as a purpose to clarify how Dasein is able to authentically understand itself from the first person perspective and achieve transparency as to the foundational structures of being-in-the-world. This is not to say that *BT* is based on a projected ideal of total self-realization, or self-actualization, or completion. I agree with Carman here that such a totalizing prospect is incoherent and in principle impossible for Dasein (Carman 2003, 226). Heideggerian authenticity is the achievement of "resoluteness" (*Entschlossenheit*) and of such self-responsibility. Resoluteness is a comportment that is as much about a way of existence as it is about a way of relating to the being of the world and its ontological structures, i.e. a way of understanding how the meaning of Being is constituted. It is, in other words, a primordial understanding of the grounding (transcendental) structures of the meaning of Being. Resoluteness, therefore, has a methodological function: it is a normative criterion that, once brought into view, enables the *reinterpretation* of Dasein and the meaning of Being, much like the epoché in Husserl enables the reinterpretation of phenomena. We ought to think of Heidegger's notion of resoluteness in *BT* as analogous to Husserl's Principle of Evidence and the Apodictic Reduction inasmuch as they all ground transcendental knowledge in evidence. The difference between them lies in their definitions of evidence and the way they close down or open up the limits of self-knowledge/self-understanding. In Husserl's case, evidence is attached to the self-certainty of a transcendental ego that *knows* itself absolutely, whereas in Heidegger's, evidence is attached to a thrown Dasein that finitely *understands* itself in unresolvable tension with its own facticity.

# 3   Husserl's Conception of Evidence

## 3.1   Originary Intuition and Apodictic Certainty

The very "discovery" of the notion of "evidence" is associated with the process of "genuine grounding," as Husserl himself says in *Cartesian Meditations* (*CM*), in which he argues that in "explicating more precisely the sense of a grounding or that of a cognition, we come forthwith to the idea of *evidence*" (Husserl 1982, 10). In *CM*, Husserl lays down the so-called "first methodological principle," which organizes his scientific project and postulates that "genuine science, must neither make or go on accepting any judgment as scientific *that I have not derived from evidence*, from 'experiences' in which the affairs and affair-complexes in question are present to me as 'they themselves'" (Husserl 1982, 14). But a similar version of this principle was already in operation earlier in *Ideas I*. There, Husserl referred to the "Principle of All Principles," which stipulates that

*every originary presentive intuition is a legitimizing source of cognition,*
that *everything originarily* [...] *offered* to us *in "intuition" is to be accepted
simply as what it is presented as being,* but also *only within the limits in
which it is presented there.* We see indeed that each <theory> can only
again draw its truth itself from originiary [sic] data. Every statement [...]
conforming to them is [...] actually an *absolute beginning* called upon
to serve as foundation, a *principium* in the genuine sense of the word.
(Husserl 1983, 44)

"Evidence" is therefore implicit in the notion of laying a foundation for
legitimizing knowledge, and this laying serves as a principled *beginning*
for the entire philosophical endeavor. It is, in other words, associated
with the very act of *beginning to philosophize.* In *CM*, Husserl explicitly connects apodictic evidence with the beginning of philosophy. As
he writes:

> In accordance with what has already been said, we now formulate, as an
> initial definite question of beginning philosophy, the question whether
> it is possible for us to bring out evidences that, on the one hand, carry
> with them—as we now must say: apodictically—the insight that, as
> "first in themselves," they precede all other imaginable evidences and, on
> the other hand, can be seen to be themselves apodictic. If they should
> turn out to be inadequate, they would have to possess at least a recog-
> nizable apodictic content, they would have to give us some being that is
> firmly secured "once for all," or absolutely, by virtue of their apodicticity.
> (Husserl 1982, 16)

In his 2001 article "Apodictic Evidence," Hans Bernhard Schmid
divides Husserl's work from 1900 to 1936 into five major stages, and
claims that "Husserl's concern with 'evidence' remains more or less on
the same level of intensity throughout his work" (Schmid 2001, 223).
In this context, "apodicticity" becomes more important in the course
of the development of Husserl's thought, its role peaking in the *CM*.
Indeed, in his later works, after the 1920s, Husserl distances himself
from his earlier thinking on "evidence," which was based on the ideal of
adequation, and accords primacy to "apodicticity," a notion he had not
paid attention to earlier.

Husserl's analysis of "evidence" in *CM* typifies his revised position on evidence and his shift from adequation to apodicticity. In §5, entitled "Evidence and the Idea of Genuine Science," Husserl defines evidence thus: "Evidence is, in an *extremely broad sense* […] a mental seeing of something itself" (Husserl 1982, 12). And: "*Perfect evidence* and its correlate, *pure and genuine truth*, are given as ideas lodged in the striving for knowledge, for fulfilment of one's meaning intention" (ibid.). Further on, in §6, he clarifies that the idea of "perfection" corresponds to that of "*adequate evidence*," and so it is the idea that replaces the older normative notion of adequacy, which is no longer an achievable ideal. On the contrary, this "perfection," called "apodicticity," can occur even in evidence that is inadequate. Apodictic evidence, according to Husserl, "is not merely certainty of the affairs or affair-complexes (states-of-affairs) evident in it; rather it [has the] peculiarity of being *at the same time the absolute unimaginableness* (inconceivability) of their *non-being*, and thus excluding in advance every doubt as 'objectless,' empty" (Husserl 1982, 15–16).

## 3.2    Husserl's Mentalist Evidentialism

Philipp Berghofer argues that insofar as Husserl's phenomenology is a project of "first philosophy," of "ultimate justification" (*Letztbegründung*), its basic epistemological character can and ought to be analyzed also in contemporary epistemology terms. Berghofer argues that Husserl's epistemological position, the way he conceives of the systematic role of evidence, makes him a *mentalist evidentialist* (Berghofer 2018). For Husserl, evidence is the criterion by virtue of which the subject distinguishes the reasonable from the unreasonable, and the better justified from the worse justified. Ultimately, evidence is coextensive with scientificity: "all scientific knowledge […] rests on evidence: as far as such evidence extends, the concept of knowledge extends also" (Berghofer 2018, 2). In other words, evidence determines epistemic justification (Berghofer 2018, 11).

Evidence is a mode of givenness: it is a quality of the intuitive mode, in which "the object is presented as 'bodily present' and is given in a 'fleshed out manner'" (Berghofer 2018, 4). But intuitiveness, and hence evidence, for Husserl, does not only refer to sensuous intuition (i.e. sense experience of objects); it can also broadly refer to "categorial intuitions of states of affairs, essential intuitions of logical or mathematical or phenomenological truths, [as well as] introspective intuitions of one's own mental states" (ibid.). In this respect, then, according to Berghofer, the current analytic epistemology that exhibits crucial similarities to Husserl's theory of evidence is mentalist evidentialism (Berghofer 2018, 12).

The basic tenets of mentalist evidentialism, as determined by Conee and Feldman, are that "epistemic justification of a belief is determined by the quality of the believer's evidence for the belief" and that "evidence determines justification" (as cited in Berghofer 2018, 12–13). At the same time, Conee and Feldman's evidentialism is internalist because the ultimate justifier for beliefs, the evidence that justifies beliefs, is "internal to the person's mental life" (Berghofer 2018, 13). More specifically, the nature of evidence consists in "mental states."

This does not mean that *all* mental states are justifiers (i.e. count as evidence); rather, it means that all justifiers are mental states. For example, writes Berghofer, some "*unconscious, indeterminate state of anxiety may be a mental state, but it may not be a justifier*" (Berghofer 2018, 14; my emphasis).

In sum, what Husserl shares with Conee and Feldman's mentalist evidentialism is the following: Husserl, like them, "holds that (a) evidence determines justification, (b) evidence consists of mental states [which, for Husserl, are originary presentive intuitions], and (c) one's ultimate evidence consists of one's experiences" (ibid.). Hence, mentalist evidentialism perfectly captures Husserl's position on the systematic role of evidence—in modern epistemological parlance, Husserl is a mentalist evidentialist.

# 4     Heidegger's Critique of Husserl and the Notion of Evidence in *Being and Time*

## 4.1     Heidegger's Alternative Beginning: Affective Evidence vs. Intuitive Evidence

Heidegger's ontological rehabilitation of affects involves a radicalization of the very notion of evidence, of what counts as evidence. His claim that moods are ontological evidence involves a methodological radicalization of phenomenology itself, *contra* Husserl. In particular, Heidegger's rehabilitation of moods involves a—sometimes tacit, sometimes explicit—juxtaposition of affective evidence with the Cartesian/Husserlian criteria of *clarity and distinction*, the certainty of reflection and originary intuition, which determine the Husserlian notion of evidence.

The Cartesian/Husserlian epistemological criteria delimit ontological discoveries; hence, a breakthrough involving those criteria would radicalize ontological findings, enable the question of the meaning of Being to be posed and allow ontology to move beyond "Being as presence." For example, in *BT*, Heidegger argues that "the absolute 'Being-certain' [*Gewissen*] of the *cogito* exempted [Descartes] from raising the question of the meaning of the Being which [Dasein] possesses" (*SZ* 24). If the idea of evidence is coterminous with the ideas of certainty and clarity, it goes without saying that the findings of an ontological inquiry that takes said idea of evidence as a measure, will be in a position to only discover an epistemic ground that resembles these ideas.

It is with these ideas that Heidegger takes issue. Heidegger held that Husserl's phenomenology, just like Descartes' inquiry, was "*guided by the predominance of an empty and thereby fantastic idea of certainty and evidence*" (*IPR* 33). What remains absent and undiscovered in Husserlian phenomenology is precisely the *factical* ground of knowledge, which cannot be grasped by the epistemic criteria that he adopts. Such criteria hold the key to ensuing discoveries.

Phenomenology must strive to make manifest the ground which normally remains hidden. "Every inquiry," Heidegger argues, "is a seeking [*Suchen*]. Every seeking gets guided beforehand by what is sought" (*IPR* 24). Phenomenology lets us see

> something that proximally and for the most part does *not* show itself at all: it is something that lies *hidden*, in contrast to that which proximally and for the most part does show itself. [...] Yet that which remains *hidden* in an egregious sense, or which relapses and gets *covered up* again, or which shows itself only "*in disguise*," is not just this entity or that, but rather the *Being* of entities, as our previous observations have shown. (*IPR* 59)

Unlike in Husserl, Heidegger's phenomenology allows moods, existential feelings, to count as evidence for Dasein's facticity—the ground of the understanding of the meaning of Being.

In *Ideas I*, Husserl establishes phenomenological inquiry on the evidence provided by originary intuition, following the epoché. Heidegger wants to overthrow this reflective beginning (see Hadjioannou 2018); he wants another methodological beginning, one that takes the pre-reflective evidence supplied by moods as a vantage point, and that allows the phenomenologist to *see past the objects of intuition* and take affective movement as evidence of ontological understanding. The affective beginning on the basis of evidence supplied by *angst* is *analogous* to the Husserlian departure from originary intuition, because it serves the same methodological function. As Heidegger writes:

> The way in which Being and its structures are encountered in the mode of phenomenon is one which must first of all be *wrested* from the objects of phenomenology. Thus the very *point of departure* [*Ausgang*] for our analysis requires that it be secured by the proper method, just as much as does our *access* [*Zugang*] to the phenomenon, or our *passage* [*Durchgang*] through whatever is prevalently covering it up. The idea of grasping and explicating phenomena in a way which is "original" and "intuitive" [*originären* and *intuitiven*] is directly opposed to the *naïveté* of a haphazard, "immediate," and unreflective "beholding" [*Schauen*]. (*IPR* 61)

Heidegger repeatedly juxtaposes the kind of evidence supplied by angst with the kind of evidence supplied by the apodictic certainty of theoretical cognition—a clear, albeit implicit, reference to Husserl's apodictic certainty of phenomenological reflection. For example, Heidegger writes: "From the existential-ontological point of view, there is not the slightest justification for minimizing what is 'evident' in dispositions, by measuring it against the apodictic certainty of a theoretical cognition of something which is purely present-at-hand" (*SZ* 136; translation modified).

As mentioned above, the problem of evidence amounts to a methodological problem of beginning: it is about discovering an acceptable vantage point from which the science of phenomenology can begin.

In other words, what is sought is a point from which one becomes a proper phenomenologist, one "switches" from being inauthentic to being authentic. Husserl discovers this measure in originary intuition, which is discovered after the epoché—the reflective bracketing of the natural attitude. Can Heidegger then "discover" within facticity the phenomenological structure that enables Dasein to overcome its inauthenticity, that is, to exist either inauthentically or authentically, which is Dasein's existentiality? As Heidegger says:

> If the existential analytic of Dasein is to retain clarity in principle as to its function in fundamental ontology, then in order to master its provisional task of exhibiting Dasein's Being, it must seek for one of the *most far-reaching* and *most primordial* possibilities of disclosure—one that lies in Dasein itself. The way of disclosure in which Dasein brings itself before itself must be such that in it Dasein becomes accessible as *simplified* in a certain manner. With what is thus disclosed, the structural totality of the Being we seek must then come to light in an elemental way. (*SZ* 182)

Heidegger then points out that the phenomenon that satisfies these methodological requirements is *the fundamental mood of anxiety*: "As one of Dasein's possibilities of Being, anxiety—together with Dasein itself as disclosed in it—provides the phenomenal basis for explicitly grasping Dasein's primordial totality of Being" (ibid.). Hence, Heidegger identifies a particular aspect of the existential constitution of Being-in-the-World, i.e. a disposition, which enables Dasein to *become authentic* and reveal the unity of existentiality and facticity.[5]

Moods are pre-reflective, and hence what they disclose and the way they disclose it *precedes* the range of disclosure of "cognition" and "volition": "ontologically mood is a primordial kind of Being for Dasein, in which Dasein is disclosed to itself *prior* to all cognition and volition, and *beyond* their range of disclosure" (*SZ 136*). In a sense, then, *one needs to set the bar "lower" in order to enable the pre-reflective, affective, understanding of Being to become evident.* Moods are normally taken to *distort* understanding rather than to be constitutive of it; they are seen as leading one to err, as factors of instability and uncertainty, and therefore they are taken not to count as evidence for understanding, since knowledge is associated with justified certainty. What is missed is the positive evidentiary capacity of moods, since the Husserlian/Cartesian principle—apodictic certainty—is associated with indisputable, clear and distinct presence. At the same time, this attachment to justified certainty covers up the ontological value of delusion, since truth is an issue of universal validity and permanent presence, instead of a hermeneutic interplay of presence and absence. As Heidegger writes:

> The fact that, even though dispositions are primarily disclosive, everyday circumspection goes wrong and to a large extent succumbs to delusion because of them, is a μὴ ὄν [non-being] when measured against the idea of knowing the "world" absolutely. But if we make evaluations which are so unjustified ontologically, we shall completely fail to recognize the existentially positive character of the capacity for delusion. It is precisely when we see the "world" unsteadily and fitfully in accordance with our moods, that the ready-to-hand shows itself in its specific worldhood, which is never the same from day to day. (*SZ* 138)

## 4.2 Heidegger's Critique of Husserlian Evidence

Heidegger's most sustained and systematic critique of Husserl's conception of the notion of "evidence" is found in his lecture course *IPR*, delivered in the winter semester 1923/1924. In this lecture course, Heidegger compares and contrasts Husserlian phenomenology with Cartesian philosophy and zeroes in on the basic differences, but also—crucially—what he sees as the common tendency in their philosophical endeavors, what Heidegger calls the "care for certainty." This tendency, which Husserl inherits from Descartes, is responsible for an array of characteristics that influence Husserl's transcendental phenomenology vis-à-vis the conception of phenomenology as a science and connected methodological considerations. Specifically, the "care for certainty," which organizes both Descartes' and Husserl's work, is responsible for the normative ideals of "certainty" and "evidence" operative in Husserl's phenomenology.

In what immediately follows, I will set out Heidegger's critique of Husserl's conception of "evidence" in three parts, proceeding from the general to the particular. I will explain how, according to Heidegger, Husserl's phenomenology inherits the Cartesian vision of science, the essence of which is the "care for certainty." As a consequence, the ideal of science is that of *security*. This stems from a care for already known knowledge, which imposes a need for purification that weeds out the uncertain in order to achieve certainty. I will then explain how the aforementioned scientific ideal results in the respective themes of the "cogito" and "consciousness" as the areas of being that remain available after the criteria of truth (clarity and distinctness) are put in place.[6] I will explain how, according to Heidegger, care for certainty results in Husserl mangling the notion of "evidence."

### 4.2.1 Care for Certainty: Science, Knowledge and Purification

*IPR* is a lecture course ultimately dedicated to identifying what went wrong in Husserl's "transcendental turn," in Heidegger's eyes, and to preparing the ground for Heidegger's own transcendental project, which has the existential analytic of Dasein as its centerpiece. Ultimately, Heidegger will want to change the thematic field of phenomenology: from consciousness to the meaning of Being. It is in this context that he says that the course is "supposed to be nothing less than a *proper preparation for the critical encounter with what is set forth as the thematic field in present-day phenomenology*" (*IPR* 198–199). Heidegger analyzes the ways in which the Husserlian promise of a phenomenological *science* ultimately succumbs to the Cartesian ideal of certainty, and shows that Husserl betrays his initial phenomenological discoveries as laid down in *Logical Investigations*. Heidegger's critical analysis is here mainly focused on *Ideas I* and on "Philosophy as a Rigorous Science."

Heidegger is quite careful not to conflate Husserlian terms with Cartesian notions, and he repeats several times that, for example, Husserlian "consciousness" should not be conflated with the Cartesian "cogito" (ibid.). However, "a common character obtains in spite of the difference in decisive connections, a common character such that it becomes apparent how Husserl, in spite of the difference, stands within the uniform, basic tendency of Cartesian research, in such a way that in him the care of knowledge is ultimately at work as *care about certainty*" (ibid.).

Science, as an expression of the care for certainty, has the task of *securing* not just knowledge but, as Heidegger argues, existence and culture (*IPR* 44). It is this care for security that turns the care about absolute knowledge into epistemological security, that is, justified knowledge (*gerechtfertigte Erkenntnis*) (*IPR* 73). According to Heidegger, the care for certainty means there is no tolerance for uncertainty, and this allows for the prioritization of methodology over the matter itself, and the reverse: the idea of a definite sort of knowledge determines the theme, rather than vice versa (*IPR* 34). In this way, consciousness becomes the theme of phenomenological research. Yet consciousness is, in Husserl's project, still in need of a further *purification* (*Reinigung*) (*IPR* 38). As mentioned earlier, the rigorousness of the natural sciences serves as the ultimate example of rigorousness. But Husserl wants consciousness, which is the theme of his philosophy, to be further purified, so as to "bring the scientific bias to natural science radically to end," (*IPR* 53) because the scientific bias may make the acquisition of absolute certainty impossible (since all the claims of *natural* science may be doubted). It is this purification that the transcendental reduction achieves (*IPR* 58).

For Heidegger, the purification process enacted by the transcendental reduction (and the epoché) leaves out human existence (Dasein) and temporality, and his own existential analytic of Dasein, which thematizes Dasein's *facticity* and *thrownness*, tries to remedy this. In Heidegger's own words: "The question remains: What, then, is neglected? In this care about the absolute certitude of the norm and, at the same time, about elaborating a genuine lawfulness, the task of examining human existence itself does not come up at all. [...] *What is neglected is what is the genuine object of concern: human existence*" (*IPR* 66).

### 4.2.2 Criteria for Truth: Clarity and Distinctness

According to Heidegger, the "method in connection with the care for certitude is [...] taken in a completely determined sense: as the path to the acquisition of the greatest possible *evidence*" (*IPR* 92). But how is evidence defined? As mentioned earlier, Descartes' justification of the criterion of knowledge is connected to his definition of truth as *clear and distinct perception*. So how does Descartes determine *clarity* and *distinctness*, which are the characteristics by virtue of which one encounters the truth (*verum*)?

Perception must firstly be clear and then distinct. As Heidegger says, the "perceptum is such that it is grasped by a manner of *grasping explicitly* aimed at it, by a *mens attendens* [mind attending] to the sort of grasping that is at work where the aim is to get a hold of what is to be grasped in itself" (*IPR* 154–155). The perceptum must be there *present* and *exposed* (ibid.). Heidegger interprets it thus: the perceptum must in any case be "*lying there in the open*, the entity existing there in itself, such that it is in no way concealed, is not indirectly given itself" (ibid.). In other words: it must be there fully present. Remember that this is how Husserl also defined evidence in *Ideas I*. According to the Principle of All Principles, in *originary intuition* thought and thing coincide, and this coincidence is what constitutes evidence, what constitutes fulfillment and presence, what guarantees presence.

But clarity is not enough on its own for true perception—we also need distinctness, which is an added condition: while there are some clear perceptions that are not distinct, there are no distinct perceptions that are not clear, since "distinctness is a factor founded on the clarity" (*IPR* 156). Heidegger recalls Descartes' example of a clear but non-distinct perception: non-localized pain. "If someone feels a great pain, then he has the pain as existing and has it in an absolutely clear but not always distinct way. […] Here, to be sure, the pain is given in an absolutely clear way, but it is not given distinctly" (ibid.). It is important to take note of this example, because it shows that Heideggerian moods (*Stimmungen*) would not fulfill the Cartesian (and Husserlian) criteria for evidence, since moods, like pain, are not distinct entities.

### 4.2.3  The Mangling of Evidence

Despite the differences between Husserl and Descartes, Heidegger argues, their philosophies share the same tendency: the care for certainty.

In trying to fight historicism and achieve his transcendental turn, Husserl adopts the Cartesian tendency (the care for certainty) and betrays his most important phenomenological discoveries. Heidegger becomes very critical of the transcendental turn, as he believes it mangles Husserl's earlier fundamental phenomenological discoveries. According to Heidegger, Husserl mangles the notion of evidence. For the purposes of this chapter, in order to understand what Heidegger means in saying that Husserl mangles the notion of evidence, it is best to consider it in relation to two other connected phenomena Heidegger thinks Husserl distorts: intentionality and affective life.

As regards intentionality, Husserl's care for certainty distorts his initial discovery of intentionality in the following way. Intentionality is always—either explicitly or implicitly—construed as a specific *theoretical* behavior, and it is characteristically translated as meaning: intending something (*Meinen*), i.e. *theoretically knowing* something (*IPR* 209). This way of interpreting intentionality distorts the intentional *life* of a subject; for example, it obscures the way intentionality itself is infused with feeling. Husserl's reflective method devivifies intentional life, posing the problem of the constitution of intentional life in a way that suppresses (and distorts) the vital grounds of this life. Heidegger is interested in showing how intentional life—intentionality in all its forms and variations—is grounded in the affective. It is in this context that Heidegger begins his analysis of intentional life, by prioritizing the enactment (*Vollzug*) of life. Intentional life *is* enactment, a praxis that is affectively determined.

Husserl's care for certainty fixes his gaze in such a way that his analysis prefigures intentionality as theoretical knowing. As Heidegger writes:

> Through this fixing of usage, a definite prefiguration of perspective creeps into every intentional analysis. This is explicitly evident from the fact that it is expressly claimed that for every intentional context of a complicated sort, theoretically meaning something forms the foundation, that each judgment, each instance of wanting, each instance of loving is founded upon a presenting [*Vorstellen*] that provides in advance what can be wanted, what is detestable and loveable. This transformation lies in the fact that the prevailing study of intentionality is itself oriented to the intentional in knowing. (ibid.)

As a consequence, Husserl's analysis also distorts emotional acts themselves (for example, an act of loving), which are reduced to acts of theoretical knowing and taken to be founded on presenting (*Vorstellen*). According to Heidegger, however, it is "a methodical misunderstanding to make the investigation of emotional experiences simply analogous to knowing" (ibid.). The distortion that takes place here, a distortion that is a basic phenomenon of the care for certainty, is a phenomenon determined as *reflection*. Recall that for Husserl, it is phenomenological reflection that is the secure source of evidence. Following the epoché, the source of authority for knowledge is, according to the Principle of All Principles, *originary intuition*, in which thought and thing coincide, and this coincidence is what constitutes evidence, fulfillment and presence. But for Heidegger, it is precisely reflection that *distorts*; it distorts affective phenomena such as anxiety, joy, terror, etc. In Heidegger's words:

> This basic phenomenon of distorting, a basic phenomenon that has long been determined as reflection, is seen here concretely and, indeed, in terms of a preview of the structure of existence's being as such. For us this phenomenon has the character of a methodic clue, insofar as, viewed from its vantage point, the basic character of consciousness, the *intentionality*, is cut down to size and led back to its limits, to the *limits of its interpretative function*. At the same time this phenomenon is the structural ground on which such phenomena as joy, terror, sadness, anxiety can be explicated— phenomena that are overlooked if they are determined as intentionality. I cannot grasp the phenomenon of anxiety as a manner of being-related-to-something; it is instead a phenomenon of existence itself. (*IPR* 220)

This distortion of affective phenomena is key to understanding why, for Heidegger, they provide evidence for truth, whereas Husserl suppresses, ignores, or entirely dismisses their evidentiary value. As a result, Husserl mangles the notion of *evidence*.

Heidegger notes that evidence plays a fundamental role in phenomenology and that what Husserl says about evidence "is far superior to everything else that has ever been said about it and that he has placed the matter on a suitable basis for the first time" (*IPR* 210).

Evidence is interpreted as coincidence of what is meant and what is grasped in itself, and "evidence itself is normatively determined by indisputability and disputability, analogous to the way the cogito sum is normatively determined by the principle of contradiction" (ibid.).

Evidence is therefore "a *specific sort of evidence for grasping and determining*, a specific sort of evidence that is transposed, by way of analogy, to the remaining manners of behavior and their evidence. It is transposed in such a way that Husserl sees that each object-domain, corresponding to its inherent content, has a specific sort of evidence" (ibid.). According to Heidegger, Husserl's phenomenology, just like Descartes' philosophy, "has also been *guided by the predominance of an empty and thereby fantastic idea of certainty and evidence*. This predominance of a specific idea of evidence predominates *over* every *genuine effort to free up the possibility of encountering the genuine matters of philosophy. Care about* a specific, *absolute knowledge*, taken purely as an idea, predominates over every question about the matters that are decisive" (*IPR* 33).

## 4.3   Evidence in *Being and Time*

In *BT*, affective phenomena are manifested in the notions of disposition (*Befindlichkeit*) and mood (*Stimmung*). Moods constitute a distinct faculty of existence; they are *necessary conditions* for the constitution of understanding and the capacity to judge. It is via moods that the world is meaningful for us. Hence, moods are essential to any normative notion of "authenticity."

In *BT*, "authenticity" (*Eigentlichkeit*) is the achievement of resolute self-transparency, a comportment that embraces existential anxiety (Angst) and reveals the deep temporal essence of Dasein. But anxiety also serves a crucial methodological function: in revealing the deeper structures of Dasein, anxiety is *evidence* for ontological understanding.[7] Ascribing to moods such an "epistemic role" means that Heidegger's phenomenology is in tension with Husserl's when it comes to the problem of evidence. For Husserl, phenomenology cannot be methodologically grounded in any sort of feeling, because feeling cannot count as evidence for knowledge; in fact, when Husserl elaborates on his conception of "evidence," he explicitly develops his own definition in opposition to the notion of the "feeling of evidence" (*Evidenzgefühl*).

In *BT*, Heidegger provides an "existential analytic of Dasein," in which he describes and interprets the constitutive states of Dasein qua Being-in-the-world. The ultimate aim of the book is to lay open the horizon of Dasein's understanding of Being. Heidegger analyzes how Dasein understands Being and how Dasein is the site of the truth of Being. Heidegger sees Dasein as *in* truth—Dasein understands the truth of Being, even though most of the time it covers up this understanding with inauthentic misinterpretation. Insofar as Dasein is in truth, this means that Dasein's own way of being must "have" evidence of truth, even amid the inauthentic edifices—hence, the evidentiary operation of Dasein's basic existential structure must be analyzed.

In this context, Heidegger identifies two equiprimordial ways in which the "there" of Dasein is constituted: "disposition" (*Befindlichkeit*) and "understanding" (*Verstehen*).[8] Equiprimordiality means that disposition always has its understanding, even if it merely keeps it suppressed, and understanding always has its mood (*SZ* 142–143). Disposition refers to the affective character of Dasein, the way it finds itself thrown in the world, which is manifested in moods.

Heidegger's twofold description of Being-In (-the-world) goes against traditional cognitive-mentalist interpretations of human knowing/understanding. According to Heidegger, "the phenomenon of Being-in has for the most part been represented exclusively by a single exemplar—knowing the world," (*SZ* 59) which is a derivative mode of Being-in-the-world. Here, Heidegger is going against not only Descartes but also the Husserlian mentalist approach to knowledge.

To begin with, Heidegger dismisses the idea that Dasein is ever without a mood. As he says, even the "pallid, evenly balanced lack of mood [*Ungestimmtheit*], which is often persistent and which is not to be mistaken for a bad mood, is far from nothing at all" (*SZ* 134). Even in this seeming "lack of mood," its being-there has already been disclosed in a particular way: as a burden. The "lack of mood" discloses the burdensome character of Dasein's facticity, which is a basic character of its being that "we cannot come across by beholding it [*Anschauen*]." Mood is therefore that by virtue of which facticity is revealed (*SZ* 135).

Mood "brings Dasein before itself," and through mood Dasein "finds itself" in a peculiar way, which extends beyond the scope or capacities of perception: mood discloses not in the way of "looking" but in "turning towards or turning away" (*An- und Ab- kehr*) (ibid.). In other words, mood reveals the truth of Dasein's being not in the way perception grasps a phenomenon that is present-at-hand, or in the way a valid judgment reveals something true, but rather as one directs oneself either toward or away from something as either pleasing or displeasing.

Disposition, for Heidegger, discloses Being-in-the-world as a whole, because it discloses significance itself; it discloses the way the world *matters*, the way the world is organized as a meaningful whole. Because of disposition's power to disclose, Heidegger's analytic takes affects very seriously: disposition is, in his own words, "methodologically significant in principle for the existential analytic" (*SZ* 139). Disposition discloses the world qua world—that is, it discloses the world as possibility. Specifically, it discloses the "world" as "a totality of involvements," a "categorial whole of a *possible* interconnection of the ready-to-hand" (*SZ* 144).

## 4.4    Angst: The Authentic Certainty of Resoluteness

Throughout this chapter, I have depicted both Husserl's and Heidegger's projects as seeking to establish a firm footing for phenomenological findings by setting normative standards according to which their phenomenological findings will be grounded in evidence. Their aim is to ensure that their phenomenological findings are justified. Husserl devises the Principle of All Principles, which purifies consciousness and guarantees that phenomenological reflection provides *evidence* for transcendental knowledge. Here, evidence is identified with self-givenness, with clarity and distinction, which can supply the necessary (apodictic) certainty. Heidegger rejects Husserl's methodological position. His own normative criterion is "resoluteness." The notion of resoluteness provides a different answer to the question of what can provide certainty and evidence, and in this context, Heidegger argues that angst, which is an existential feeling, provides the ultimate evidence that justifies, even if tentatively, ontological understanding and the formally indicative interpretation of *BT*.

For Heidegger, *resoluteness* is an existential ("*existentiell*") possibility for Dasein that attests to Dasein's authentic potentiality-for-Being (*SZ* 301–302). Dasein's authentic potentiality-for-Being is a phenomenon grounded in *anticipation*, which amounts to Dasein's authentic potentiality-for-Being-a-whole, i.e. Dasein's authentic Being-towards-death. In being resolute, Dasein authentically anticipates its own death: Dasein is authentically *anxious*. What is the significance of death? What is achieved by anticipating death, and why is it important? Heidegger defines death thus: "*death, as the end of Dasein, is Dasein's ownmost possibility—non-relational, certain and as such indefinite, not to be outstripped. Death is, as Dasein's* end, in the Being of this entity *towards* its end" (*SZ* 258–259). What does resoluteness therefore achieve? On the one hand, in anticipatory resoluteness "[t]emporality *gets experienced in a phenomenally primordial way*" (*SZ* 304) and is a distinctive mode of temporality that brings Dasein "before the primordial *truth* of existence" (*SZ* 307). On the other hand, it achieves *certainty*. The attainment of certainty is crucial here and as such it calls for further analysis.

How does resoluteness achieve certainty? Resoluteness involves the reticent "projecting oneself upon one's ownmost Being-guilty, and *exacting anxiety of oneself*" (*SZ* 305; my emphasis). Insofar as resoluteness involves the attainment of certainty, and this certainty is achieved by "exacting anxiety," *it follows that anxiety is the evidence that grounds the understanding involved in the truth of resoluteness*. What remains to be answered, now, is the question of how this certainty differs from Husserlian apodictic certainty, and what counts as evidence for it.

In *BT*, Heidegger distinguishes between authentic certainty and inauthentic certainty, each of which involves maintaining oneself in the truth that has been revealed. The immediate truth that has been revealed in Being-towards-death is the death of Dasein: Dasein is certain of its own death. Inauthentic certainty of death involves an inauthentic way of encountering the event of death, which involves the expectation of a future event as a *matter of fact*. This is inauthentic certainty because it maintains itself in the truth of an event present-at-hand in an indifferent, "purely objective" manner—much like the empirical certainty of apodictic evidence, whereby a truth is disclosed as certain because its opposite is logically inconceivable. Authentic certainty, on the other hand, is another kind of certainty, the certainty of

*Being-certain*, which is more primordial, and for which angst is the primary evidence. In Heidegger's own words:

> To maintain oneself in this truth—that is, to be certain of what has been disclosed—demands all the more that one should anticipate. We cannot compute the certainty of death by ascertaining how many cases of death we encounter. This certainty is by no means of the kind which maintains itself in the truth of the present-at-hand. When something present-at-hand has been uncovered, it is encountered most purely if we just look at the entity and let it be encountered in itself. Dasein must first have lost itself in the factual circumstances [*Sachverhalte*] (this can be one of care's own tasks and possibilities) if it is to obtain the pure objectivity—that is to say, the indifference—of apodictic evidence. If Being-certain in relation to death does not have this character, this does not mean that it is of a lower grade, but that *it does not belong at all to the graded order of the kinds of evidence we can have about the present-at-hand.* (SZ 264–265)

To maintain oneself in the truth of authentic certainty, therefore—what Heidegger calls "Being-certain"—Dasein ought to rely on a different sort of evidence, rather than rely on the reflection of the apodictic reduction: it must rely on angst. Angst is evidence for the understanding of death as a possibility, which is the "possibility of impossibility of existence" (*SZ* 262).

It takes a lot of courage to accept the evidence of angst—a courage that "they" will not let Dasein have. In fact, the "'they' concerns itself with transforming this anxiety into fear in the face of an oncoming event. In addition, the anxiety which has been made ambiguous as fear, is passed off as a weakness with which no self-assured Dasein may have any acquaintance" (*SZ* 254) and is thus banished from the "epistemological frame".

Heidegger's rehabilitation of moods, of existential feeling, radicalizes not only the notion of certainty, but also the notion of evidence. In *BT*, angst is the ultimate evidence of the authentic understanding of the meaning of Being. In Heidegger's words:

> All understanding is accompanied by a disposition. Dasein's mood brings it face to face with the thrownness of its "that it is there." *But the disposition which can hold open the utter and constant threat to itself arising*

*from Dasein's ownmost individualized Being, is anxiety.* In this disposition, Dasein finds itself *face to face* with the "nothing" of the possible impossibility of its existence. Anxiety is anxious *about* the potentiality-for-Being of the entity so destined [*des so bestimmten Seienden*], and in this way it discloses the uttermost possibility. (*SZ* 265–256)

# 5 Angst and Mentalist Evidentialism

As I have been arguing, the specific role that angst plays in *BT* marks an epistemic shift in phenomenology, in which Heidegger radicalizes Husserl's phenomenology, which is committed to mentalist evidentialism.[9] In this final section, I will explain why Heidegger's position in *BT* commits him to a sort of quasi-evidentialism that is incompatible with mentalism and internalism. It is beyond the scope of this chapter to provide a positive definition of Heidegger's own position in contemporary epistemological terms (if that's even possible). However, I hope to have paved the way for more work to be done on this issue in the near future.

*BT*, while being a quasi-evidentialist project, moves phenomenology away from (Husserlian) mentalist evidentialism. The epistemic principles of phenomenology are shifted away from mentalist evidentialism insofar as: (a) Heidegger lambasts Husserl's phenomenology for prioritizing epistemology over ontology and rejects his epistemological notion of "certainty"; (b) angst, which serves the role of "evidence" in *BT*, is not a "mental state", unlike Husserlian originary intuition; and (c) angst is not "internal" to Dasein (unlike originary intuition to the subject). Insofar as mentalist evidentialism is an internalist theory of justification (because mental states are internal to the subject), *BT* is incompatible with mentalist evidentialism.

As regards (a), *BT*'s quasi-evidentialism, it is useful to recall what was mentioned in Sect. 2 of this chapter: Heideggerian phenomenology is indeed a foundationalist project, which tries to ground transcendental interpretation in evidence. In this context, resoluteness and authenticity respond to the demand for evidential responsibility. Ultimately, Dasein needs phenomenological evidence in order to justify ontological insights about its own structure and the meaning of Being. Having

said that, as mentioned earlier, Heidegger remains critical of any prioritization of methodology over matter, indeed of epistemology itself (and
of the idea of "justified knowledge") and specifically of Husserl's and
Descartes' fixation on certainty, insofar as certainty guarantees indisputability of knowledge. This principle of certainty is fantastical, according to Heidegger. In *BT*, Heidegger identifies this sort of certainty as
inauthentic, because it relies on the objectivity of presence-at-hand. For
this reason, it is difficult to call Heidegger an evidentialist, in any standard understanding of the term. However, he needs to retain a positive
use of the notions of certainty and evidence in what he calls "authentic
certainty", which is more primordial, incomputable and non-apodictic.
Without this commitment to evidence and certainty, Heidegger's project would collapse because it would lose its phenomenological coher-
ence. For these reasons, I call Heidegger a quasi-evidentialist.

As regards (b), the fact that angst is not a mental state. While
Macquarrie and Robinson translate *Befindlichkeit* as "state-of-mind"
in their 1962 translation of *BT*, *Befindlichkeit* is neither a "state", nor
does it refer to a "mind" (or anything "mental"). "Disposition" is a more
appropriate translation as this concept conveys the sense of situatedness
in an environing world, and also has the sense of findingness (being
disposed is how one finds oneself "available"). What *Befindlichkeit*
(and *Stimmung*) are, and why they do not refer to "mental states", will
become clearer once we see what phenomena they indicate. Moods disclose Dasein's *thrownness* (*Geworfenheit*). Heidegger elaborates on the
phenomenon of thrownness by referring to the phenomenon of *facticity*
(*Faktizität*).[10] As he says: "The expression 'thrownness' is meant to suggest the *facticity of its being delivered over*" (*SZ* 135). But what is facticity? It is not the "state-of-affairs" or "matters of fact"—these are ontic
phenomena, which can indeed be grasped by intuition. As Heidegger
says in §29 in *BT*, thrownness is "the 'that-it-is' of facticity [which]
never becomes something that we can come across by beholding it" (*SZ*
135).[11] Disposition discloses facticity in a manner whereby it remains
an "inexorable enigma," which cannot be measured against the "apodictic certainty of a theoretical cognition of something" (*SZ* 136).[12]

How does disposition disclose the facticity of being-there?
Dispositions disclose mostly in the manner of evasive "turning away"

(ibid.). In Heidegger's own words: "the *first* essential characteristic of dis-positions [is] that *they disclose Dasein in its thrownness, and—proximally and for the most part—in the manner of an evasive turning-away*" (ibid.; translation modified). Dasein's thrownness can only be revealed in a par-ticular way: it is a *finding* of one's "there", not through a direct percep-tive seeking, but rather primarily through the movement of "fleeing" (*SZ* 135). The way mood discloses the "there" of Dasein is not through "beholding" (*Anschauen*)[13]; rather, it discloses being-there as kinesis, in a dynamic and pre-conceptual way: the "there" is disclosed as a "turning towards" or "turning away" from something (*An- und Abkehr*).[14] Facticity is therefore the *becoming* of Da-Sein, the *being* of *becoming*, which is inherently transient and "unsettled." For these reasons, mood, which is the primary manifestation of facticity and thrownness, is not a state of mind because it is neither a "state" (since it is not something that is pres-ent and actual), nor is it part of the "mind" since it is precognitive and "felt" by the moving body, barely grasped by the faculty of the mind.

As regards (c), angst is not internal to a subject (nor is it internal to Dasein, for that matter). Angst is a mood (*Stimmung*), and moods are the basic way in which disposition (*Befindlichkeit*) is manifested. It is crucial to understand why *Befindlichkeit* is neither a mental state nor a phenomenon internal to a subject. Disposition and fundamental moods are neither subjective nor objective, but rather are "in-between" the sub-ject and the object, between the internal and the external. Fundamental mood is neither about the subject nor about an object—it reveals the "there" in a pre-intentional way. As Heidegger says, mood is something that *assails* us but it comes *neither from the "inside" nor from the "out-side"* (*SZ* 136). Heidegger's phenomenology of mood therefore is cru-cial for his rejection of the subject-object model of understanding the relationship between human and world (see Freeman 2014). As Stephen Mulhall aptly puts it, "[m]oods are an aspect of Dasein's existence and hence an aspect of Being-in-the-world, and so they are revelatory of the world as they are of Dasein" (Mulhall 1996, 194). A mood arises out of Being-in-the-World, and this is why it cannot be said to come either from the "outside" or from the "inside" (*SZ* 136).

Angst reveals self and world in their togetherness: it reveals the thrownness of Dasein into the world. Angst is therefore evidence for

Being-in-the-world as a whole, and that refers to not just that in the face *of* which the anxious person is anxious, but also that *for* which he or she is anxious: itself. Angst is part and parcel of Heidegger's response to, as Stephen Crowell notes, "Husserl's residual individualism, rationalism (theoretism), and internalism" (Crowell 2013, 67). The appeal to affective evidence is a way of capturing Dasein's openness to the world in a non-representationalist manner that undercuts consciousness as the ground of intentionality, since it construes knowledge (openness) "as a kind of *forum internum*" (Crowell 2013, 69). As Crowell says, "Heidegger's analysis of affectedness—of the passivity and finitude of being-in-the-world—would seem to contest such internalism" (Crowell 2013, 71).

# 6     Concluding Remark

I have argued that while *BT* continues Husserl's modernist project that aims to ground ontological interpretation in phenomenological evidence, Heidegger radicalizes the basic concept of "evidence" operative in Husserlian phenomenology.

For Husserl, it is *originary intuition* that serves as *apodictically certain evidence*. Husserl's position is akin to mentalist evidentialism, complying with its basic tenets, namely that justification is determined by the quality of the believer's evidence, and that evidence is internal to the person's mental life (in other words: evidence consists in mental states).

Heidegger criticizes Husserl's phenomenology precisely on account of the fact that it was guided by an empty and fantastic idea of certainty and evidence. In *BT*, it is angst that plays the crucial methodological function of evidence upon which the ontological interpretation gained by the existential analytic of Dasein is grounded. Heidegger repeatedly juxtaposes the kind of evidence supplied by angst with the kind of evidence supplied by the apodictic certainty of originary intuition. This makes Heidegger's own epistemic principles incompatible with Husserl's. While Heidegger remains committed to a sort of quasi-evidentialism, his position is fundamentally incompatible with Husserl's mentalist evidentialism: angst cannot be reduced to an internal condition, and it cannot be reduced to a mental state either.

What is more, it is precisely through fundamental moods, such as angst, that Heidegger's phenomenology in *BT* indicates a phenomenon that overcomes the internal-external dualism, and also overcomes the mentalism characteristic of Husserl's phenomenology.

**Acknowledgements**  Work on this chapter was part of the research activities in the context of my Irish Research Council Postdoctoral Fellowship at University College Dublin, under the mentorship of Professor Dermot Moran. I would like to thank Lukas Makovicky and an anonymous reviewer for helpful comments on past versions of this chapter. I would also to thank Bence Marosan for recommending key literature on Husserl's notion of evidence, during a conversation we had in Warsaw in 2017.

# Notes

1. While Heidegger's relationship with Husserl was complex and not as straightforward as one of loyalty, respect and admiration, with Heidegger praising Husserl in his presence but lambasting him in his absence (i.e. behind his back), I still think that there is a certain discursive and intellectual honesty in the dedication, precisely because he knew that Husserl would have been surprised by the ways in which *BT* departs from his own method.
2. I would like to thank an anonymous reviewer for useful feedback on this issue.
3. For Husserl's mentalism, see Philipp Berghofer's recent articles: Philipp Berghofer, "Husserl's Conception of Experiential Justification: What It Is and Why It Matters," *Husserl Studies* 34 (2018): 145–170; Philipp Berghofer, "Towards a Phenomenological Conception of Experiential Justification," *Synthese* (2018), https://doi.org/10.1007/s11229-018-1744-5; and Philipp Berghofer, "On the Nature and Systematic Role of Evidence: Husserl as a Proponent of Mentalist Evidentialism?" *European Journal of Philosophy* (2018): 1–20, https://doi.org/10.1111/ejop.12405.
4. For a critical discussion of Husserl's (non-)foundationalism, see Walter Hopp, "Husserl, Phenomenology, and Foundationalism," *Inquiry* 51, no. 2 (2008): 194–216; Dagfinn Føllesdal, "Husserl on Evidence and Justification," in *Edmund Husserl and the Phenomenological Tradition,*

ed. Robert Sokolowski (Washington, DC: The Catholic University of America Press, 1988), 107–129; and Philipp Berghofer, "Why Husserl Is a Moderate Foundationalist," *Husserl Studies* 34 (2018): 1–23, https://doi.org/10.1007/s10743-017-9213-4.

5. In §40 of *BT*, Heidegger says that disposition and understanding enable Dasein to disclose to itself "information" about itself as an entity. Anxiety is a distinctive mood because in anxiety Dasein gets brought before its own Being; Anxiety reveals the Being of the totality of the structural whole (*SZ* 184).

6. *clara et distincta perception.*

7. In her article, "The Methodological Role of Angst in *Being and Time*," *Journal of the British Society for Phenomenology* 43, no. 2 (2012): 195–211, Katherine Withy argues that while angst is usually understood as part of an ontological story about the fragility of meaning and the pertinent ontological risk involved, specifically connecting to an ethical-existential dimension of *BT*, it would be more helpful to approach angst from a methodological perspective, namely from the perspective of the methodological role (Heidegger says) it plays. As Withy writes: "We analyse angst because it has to do not with how we lead our lives generally, but specifically with how we do philosophy" (ibid., 195). Thus, we are enabled to see the positive valence angst has: "Angst is an experience within a life that provides genuine ontological insight into what it takes to lead a life" thus revealing "something that we cannot access otherwise, and which is crucial for Heidegger's phenomenological project" (ibid., 196). What angst does, then, is to resolve a serious methodological problem that Heidegger faces: to phenomenologically *reveal* the structural unity of our being (ibid., 199).

8. While Macquarrie and Robinson translate *Befindlichkeit* as "state-of-mind," I opt for "disposition." (See Hadjioannou 2015). In their article "Affectivity in Heidegger I," *Philosophy Compass* 10, no. 10 (2015): 661–671, Andreas Elpidorou and Lauren Freeman provide a comprehensive account of how *Befindlichkeit* has been translated into English by various scholars, and rightly argue that no translation is really *adequate* to the German notion. Hence, they opt to leave *Befindlichkeit* untranslated.

   Whilst I agree that the safest option is to leave the word untranslated, I still think that we can translate it as "disposition." Elpidorou and Freeman are right in saying that Macquarrie and Robinson's (1962) use of the phrase "state-of-mind" is problematic since *Befindlichkeit* is philosophically neither a "state", nor does it refer to a "mind"; this is the most misleading translation of all, from a *literal* point of view. However, "state-of-mind" is an actual expression in everyday English that would be semantically equivalent to *Befindlichkeit*. Hence, if we are to stick to the phenomenological principle of starting from expressions used in everydayness, and use words said from οἱ πολλοί, as well as the hermeneutic principle of starting from the more familiar and moving to the least familiar, then "state-of-mind" is not such an inappropriate term. But it does introduce significant problems once the ontological analysis proceeds. (See Mahon O'Brien's Chapter 1 in this volume for a noteworthy defense of "state-of-mind".)

Haugeland uses "findingness," whilst he had also used "sofindingness" (2013), without noting the drawbacks of these renderings. I think that whilst "findingness" is indeed the most linguistically accurate translation into English, since it is constructed from the same root verb *finden*, it is psychologically dry and relays a neutral spatiality, and is also too static. It does reveal the factical aspect though (the sense of "inheritance"). In addition, it sounds awkward in English. Elpidorou and Freeman then note how Guignon (1984) uses "situatedness," dismissing it because it lacks the important sense of *finden* in *Befindlichkeit*. I would add that whilst "situatedness" as a category is indeed linked to *Befindlichkeit*, translating the latter as "situatedness" risks conflating *Befindlichkeit* with another notion, that of *Situation*. *Situation* (as well as *Lage*) are not basic existentiales of Being-in-the-World; they are closed-off for the inauthentic Dasein, but they are disclosed to the resolute Dasein. *Situation* has its foundations in resoluteness (*Entschlossenheit*) (see *BT* §60), which may or may not be enacted, whereas *Befindlichkeit* is a basic existentiale that is always already there since it is a condition of possibility of Dasein. In sum, translating *Befindlichkeit* as "situatedness" is too close to committing a categorical mistake, according to the inner logic of *BT*.

Elpidorou and Freeman then note how Dreyfus (1991), Blattner (2007), and Crowell (2013) all translate *Befindlichkeit* as "affectedness" or "affectivity." They rightly argue that this captures the notion that Dasein is always already affected by and feels things, which is an important element of *Befindlichkeit*. The drawback of these notions though, they argue, is that they call to mind Kant's notion of "receptivity" and thus import the very subject/object distinction that Heidegger attempts to overturn. Whilst they are right in their sensitivity to any notion that imports the subject/object distinction which *Befindlichkeit* is meant to overcome, I cannot see why the issue of receptivity is particularly reminiscent of Kant and not, say, Plato's πάσχειν. In any case, whilst *Befindlichkeit* is indeed, from a historical perspective, Heidegger's way of making sense of what have been historically termed as "affective phenomena", he himself does not want to reduce *Befindlichkeit* to *Affekt*. In fact, in *BT* Heidegger explicitly writes that these "phenomena [associated with *Befindlichkeit*] have long been well-known ontically under the terms 'affects' and 'feelings' and have always been under consideration in philosophy" (§29), and then goes on to mention Plato and Aristotle on πάθη, the Scholastics, as well as volition and other accounts that take affects to be of epiphenomenal character. So "affectivity" is indeed inadequate, as Elpidorou and Freeman argue, but for more reasons than the ones they invoke. What is more, *Befindlichkeit* is indeed something more than affect, precisely because *Befindlichkeit* is, philosophically speaking, more than a *passive being affected*: it is also about *having a comportment*, in the sense that it requires a certain, even minimal, (relational) enactment that *relates* to an other. For this reason, "disposition" is, in my opinion, the best option for translating *Befindlichkeit*. Elpidorou and Freeman note that Carman (2003), Dahlstrom (2001), and Wrathall (2001) all use "disposition" or "disposedness", but they think that this is not a good word because it suggests more of an ontic state than an ontological structure, and thus fails to adequately convey *Befindlichkeit's* ontological depth. In this context, they invoke Haugeland's (2013) argument that "disposition" risks implying subjectivity as well as conflicts with an established philosophical usage of the term, and carries behavioral connotations.

Whilst I share these concerns to a certain extent, I still think that "disposition" is a suitable translation of *Befindlichkeit*. I cannot see why "disposition" (and its cognates) fails to render ontological depth. In principle, any notion whatsoever can be ontologically reduced and convey ontological depth. The fact that "disposition" is an already established philosophical term is not a sufficient reason for avoiding the word, since phenomenology in general offers the potential for appropriation and radicalization of any given notion, in a way that could free it from its baggage, based on phenomenological evidence. After all, if we are to accept Haugeland's argument, then even the very word *Dasein* already has an established philosophical usage in the German Idealist tradition, but that did not stop Heidegger from using it and offering a phenomenological ontology *of Dasein*. As regards the behavioral connotations of "disposition", again, as long as an ontological reduction is in place, then that should not be a problem. Besides, the very same issue of "behaviorism" can be raised for other pertinent notions as well, for example the notion of *Verhalten*, which in everyday German means "behavior", or *Haltung*, which would normally be translated as "attitude" or "posture", or *Verfassung*, which would normally be translated as "state" or "condition", but that did not stop Heidegger from using these words. Granted, the notion of *Befindlichkeit* did fall prey to an anthropological interpretation, along with other notions used in *BT*, and that might have contributed to Heidegger's favoring of *Stimmung* in his future work. But still, the behavioral connotations of *Befindlichkeit* cannot constitute a sufficient reason for Heidegger's general replacement of *Befindlichkeit* with *Stimmung* (and *Gestimmtheit*) since if that were the case he should have also minimized the usage of several other notions, such as the notions of *Verhalten* and *Haltung*. So the behavioral connotations of a notion in themselves should not be a reason for avoiding such a notion. "Disposition" is an appropriate translation of *Befindlichkeit*, as it is a word that can account for the foundation of "affective phenomena", it conveys the sense of situatedness in an environing world, and it also has the sense of findingness (being disposed is how one find themselves "available"), without reducing it to sheer passivity but seeing it as a kind of comportment. It is a word that conveys how Dasein is "positioned" in the world, and how it is oriented in it. In addition, it is a word in everyday English that precisely refers to what *Befindlichkeit* also refers to in everyday German. Another reason why we should translate *Befindlichkeit* as "disposition" is that Heidegger himself on a couple of occasions uses the French word *Disposition*, in order to refer to the same phenomenon. Finally, a genealogical account of the notion of *Befindlichkeit* in *BT* makes it clear that this is how he rendered the Aristotelian category of διάθεσις, a word whose best translation in English is indeed "disposition." If one accepts the "Aristotelian reading" of *BT*, then one has to accept the homology between *Befindlichkeit* and διάθεσις (see Hadjioannou 2013).

Elpidorou and Freeman finally note how Stambaugh (1996) translates *Befindlichkeit* as "attunement" and note that the problem with this translation is that this is how *Stimmung* is often translated, and this introduces confusion as regards their distinction. Indeed, if one were going to use "attunement", then it would have to be a translation for *Stimmung*. Even though Heidegger is not entirely clear and consistent in a philosophical distinction between *Stimmung* and *Befindlichkeit* in *BT*, something that contributes to the extinction of the word *Befindlichkeit* in his post-*BT* analyses, we would still need to translate the two words (*Befindlichkeit* and *Stimmung*) differently, and "attunement", if it is to be used at all, is much closer to the word *Stimmung* (or *Gestimmtheit*) than *Befindlichkeit*.

9. For Husserl's mentalist internalism, see Philipp Berghofer's recent articles, as detailed in Note 4.

10. Thrownness is a formal indication that Heidegger uses to refer to what others have called facticity. Whilst this indicates that Heidegger is trying to offer his own phenomenological description without becoming entangled in the traditional vocabulary, it seems to me that here he *makes sense* of thrownness *in terms* of facticity, and thus reverts to the language of German Idealism. I do not think this is a problem though, because we can think of this the other way round: Heidegger tries to rethink facticity in a new way, making sense of facticity in terms of moods and thrownness.

11. I take it that the critical reference to *seeing* (*Anschauen*) is primarily directed at Husserl's phenomenology. Disposition and mood discloses being in a way that a phenomenology based on *Anschauen cannot* grasp.

12. According to my reading, Heidegger does not want moods to be understood as simply the binary opposite of rationality, i.e. as that which is irrational and remains completely *absent*. In my opinion, whilst Heidegger wants to clearly retain, to some extent, an irreducible incompatibility between moods and rationality, his hermeneutic position does to a certain extent overlap with linguistic realism, arguing for a quasi-organic relationship between moods and concepts; moods are, after all, definitively involved in concept formation. Moods are recalcitrant to rational understanding, but they can also be said to be "logos-like", and in a way "present" in rational understanding. This is why, in *What is Metaphysics?* Heidegger can argue that Angst enables us to speak about the Nothing. In a sense, Heidegger is consistent with Aristotle's

position in *Peri Hermeneias*, where in Chapter 1 he says that spoken sounds are symbols of affections in the soul. [Ἔστι μὲν οὖν τὰ ἐν τῇ φωνῇ τῶν ἐν τῇ ψυχῇ παθημάτων σύμβολα, καὶ τὰ γραφόμενα τῶν ἐν τῇ φωνῇ. καὶ ὥσπερ οὐδὲ γράμματα πᾶσι τὰ αὐτά, οὐδὲ φωναὶ αἱ αὐταί· ὧν μέντοι ταῦτα σημεῖα πρώτων, ταὐτὰ πᾶσι παθήματα τῆς ψυχῆς, καὶ ὧν ταῦτα ὁμοιώματα πράγματα ἤδη ταὐτά.]

13. Here, Heidegger clearly moves beyond Husserl's phenomenology, which is based on "beholding" (*Anschauen*) [I would have rather translated *Anschauen* as "seeing" or "viewing"]. I believe that in this sentence Heidegger is tacitly criticizing Husserl, whose phenomenology failed to take moods as anything other than a "founded" level of intentionality.

14. This is very close to Aristotle's notion of movement as μεταβολή, and Aristotle's account of πάθη in the *Rhetoric*, as συμφέρον or βλαβερόν, and as ἡδύ or λυπηρόν.

# References

Berghofer, Philipp. 2018. "On the Nature and Systematic Role of Evidence: Husserl as a Proponent of Mentalist Evidentialism?" *European Journal of Philosophy* 1–20. https://doi.org/10.1111/ejop.12405.

Blattner, William. 2007. *Heidegger's 'Being and Time': A Reader's Guide*. London: Bloomsbury Academic Publishers.

Carman, Taylor. 2003. *Heidegger's Analytic*. New York: Cambridge University Press.

Crowell, Steven. 2013. *Normativity and Phenomenology in Husserl and Heidegger*. New York: Columbia University Press.

Dahlstrom, Daniel. 2001. *Heidegger's Concept of Truth*. Cambridge: Cambridge University Press.

Dreyfus, Hubert. 1991. *Being-in-the-World: A Commentary on Heidegger's Being and Time Division I*. Cambridge, MA: MIT Press.

Freeman, Lauren. 2014. "Toward a Phenomenology of Mood." *The Southern Journal of Philosophy* 55 (4): 445–476.

Guignon, Charles. 1984. *"Moods in Heidegger's Being and Time." What is an Emotion? Classic and Contemporary Readings*. Edited by R. Solomon and C. Calhoun. Oxford: Oxford University Press.

Hadjioannou, Christos. 2013. Befindlichkeit as retrieval of Aristotelian διάθεσις. Heidegger reading Aristotle in the Marburg years. In *Heideggers Marburger Zeit: Themen, Argumente, Konstellationen*. Edited by Tobias Keiling. Frankfurt am Main: Vittorio Klostermann.

Hadjioannou, Christos. 2015. *The emergence of mood in Heidegger's phenomenology*. PhD doctoral thesis. University of Sussex.

Hadjioannou, Christos. 2018. Heidegger's Critique of Techno-science as a Critique of Husserl's Reductive Method. In *Heidegger on Technology*. Edited by Aaron James Wendland, Christopher Merwin, and Christos Hadjioannou. New York: Routledge.

Haugeland, John. 2013. *Dasein Disclosed: John Haugeland's Heidegger*. Edited by Joseph Rouse. Cambridge, MA: Harvard University Press.

Heidegger, Martin. 1962. *Being and Time*. Translated by John Macquarrie & Edward Robinson. New York: Harper & Row Publishers.

Heidegger, Martin. 1996. *Being and Time*. A Translation of "Sein und Zeit" (7th ed.). Translated by Joan Stambaugh. Albany, NY: SUNY Press.

Husserl, Edmund. 1982. *Cartesian Meditations: An Introduction to Phenomenology*. Translated by Dorion Cairns. The Hague: Martinus Nijhoff Publishers.

Husserl, Edmund. 1983. *Ideas Pertaining to a Pure Phenomenology and to a Phenomenological Philosophy*. Translated by F. Kersten. The Hague: Martinus Nijhoff Publishers.

Öktem, Ülker. 2009. "Husserl's Evidence Problem." *Indo-Pacific Journal of Phenomenology* 9 (1): 1–14.

Schmid, Hans Bernard. 2001. "Apodictic Evidence." *Husserl Studies* 17 (3): 217–237.

Stephen, Mulhall. 1996. "Can There Be an Epistemology of Moods?" *Royal Institute of Philosophy Supplement* 41: 191–210 (194). https://doi.org/10.1017/s1358246100006111.

Wrathall, Mark. 2001. "Background Practices, Capacities, and Heideggerian Disclosure." *Heidegger, Coping, and Cognitive Science: A Festschrift for Hubert Dreyfus*, vol. 2. Cambridge: MIT Press.

# 5

# Missing in Action: Affectivity in *Being and Time*

## Daniel O. Dahlstrom

*Ich glaube auch, dass nichts ohne musik im geist*
*bestehen kann, und dass nur der geist sich*
*frei empfindet, dem die stimmung treu bleibt.*
Bettina von Arnim (1840, 15)

## 1    The Essentialness of Affectivity

There is a lot to like about Heidegger's existential analysis of *Befindlichkeit* and *Stimmung*, here translated as 'disposedness' and 'attunement' or 'mood' respectively.[1] By treating *Befindlichkeit* before any other basic existential, he effectively assigns it a certain priority. Under certain descriptions at least, this priority seems perfectly justified, as does his contention that Dasein's disposedness first discloses that it is and has to be. As for moods, they tell us, he rightly observes, how we are; indeed, they disclose us to ourselves in ways that outstrip

D. O. Dahlstrom (✉)
Boston University, Boston, MA, USA
e-mail: dahlstro@bu.edu

© The Author(s) 2019
C. Hadjioannou (ed.), *Heidegger on Affect*, Philosophers in Depth,
https://doi.org/10.1007/978-3-030-24639-6_5

possibilities of disclosure through knowing or even belief (though they can also close us off from ourselves all the more stubbornly). We find ourselves always already attuned ("attuned through mood," as Lauren Freeman puts it [Freeman 2016, 248])[2], already pre-reflectively moving towards or away from some aspect of our human condition, when we come to perceive ourselves. In an "ontologically fundamental sense," Heidegger writes, we have to leave the primary discovery of the world to moods. Following a tradition with roots in the eighteenth and nineteenth centuries (Mendelssohn, Kant, and William Hamilton) and continued by Scheler, he asserts the irreducibility of affectivity to any knowing or willing (*SZ* 136).[3] He may be overreaching with his claims that we are always attuned, always in some mood or other (after all, what is the evidence of that?), but he is certainly right to stress the pervasiveness of moods (*SZ* 134–138).[4]

The overriding strength of Heidegger's analysis of being disposed is undoubtedly his sure-handed demonstration of what and how it discloses. It discloses, in the first place, our thrownness into the factical situations that make up our worlds. This "first essential character" of being disposed, as he puts it, taps into a traditional insight that, far from creating moods and emotions, we typically find ourselves swept up into them and the worlds enveloped by them. Like the Greek πάθη and πάθος and other variants presumably stemming from πάσχω and implying something suffered or undergone, 'passion' (a cognate of 'mood' and 'emotion') signifies a passiveness, the opposite of an activeness (πρᾶξις). In a similar way, there is something about the way we are disposed (and the affectivity accompanying it) that we chance upon or, better, that chances upon us. On an existential level, we do not and did not ourselves put ourselves into the situation, into the world in which we exist; instead we find ourselves (*sich befinden*) in it. Finding ourselves in it is part of what it means existentially to be disposed.

Finding our selves in a situation and finding ourselves in a mood coincide; they coincide because they are both aspects of the disclosiveness of being disposed. Enlarging on this point, Heidegger introduces the "second essential character" of being disposed, namely, the way it discloses at once our own existence, that of others, and the world, thereby making possible any orientation to something within that entire complex. Being disposed is "an existentially basic sort [*Grundart*] of the equiprimordial disclosedness of world, others who are here [Mitdasein], and existence since this is itself essentially being-in-the-world" (*SZ* 137). The experience of being disposed brings with it a sense of our dependency upon the world and our ability to be affected by what we encounter within-the-world. The fact that things matter to us, that we can be "touched" by them, that they can be threatening and fearful or not—all this is grounded in the way we are disposed. Herein lies what Heidegger dubs the "third essential character" of being disposed, namely, how through various moods it "existentially constitutes being-here's openness to the world" (*SZ* 137).[5]

The ways we find ourselves to be disposed take the form of feelings and emotions as well as moods—in general, the sorts of experiences that have been traditionally grouped under the heading of affectivity (*SZ* 138–139; *GA* 20: 353). This specification of the general sense of finding ourselves disposed corresponds to what Heidegger dubs the existentiel correlate to the basic existential of being disposed. This disposedness is felt in a mood but, unlike traditional conceptions of feelings and moods, neither the disposedness nor the mood (feeling, emotion) is by any means a feature of an internal mental state, separate from the world (like arguably some interoceptive phenomena such as a sore throat or a ringing in the ear). To the contrary, disposedness is nothing less, as noted, than a way of disclosing the world and disclosing our being-in-the-world.

These disclosures, Heidegger contends, are "equiprimordial," making up a "unitary phenomenon" (*einheitliches Phänomen*) (*GA* 20: 348, 350). The phenomenon is existential, a way of being that is disclosive; accordingly, in a qualified sense, there is a cognitive dimension to being disposed. Yet, as Heidegger puts it in the summer semester of 1925 (lectures given a year before the completion of *SZ*), far from being "a particularly thematic knowing [*Wissen*] of the world or even a determinate knowing of itself," being disposed discloses tacitly but no less fundamentally and authentically "the structure of being that is distinctive of being-here itself" (*GA* 20: 349).[6] This "here-character," Heidegger adds, is what enables (*ermöglicht*) us to encounter the world and ourselves.[7]

The role of being disposed in this process—together with all its affective components—is wrapped up in our worldliness or, better, our "openness to the world" (the above-mentioned third essential feature of being disposed) and its meaningfulness for us. How we are disposed and the moods we find ourselves in coincide with our dependence upon and immersion in our respective and shared worlds as well as our concerns for what is and what is not facilitating and threatening therein. "In every transaction with the world," Heidegger observes, "being-here as being-in is in some manner approached and summoned" and the respective manner is, he adds parenthetically, a manner of disposedness (*Weise der Befindlichkeit*) (*GA* 20: 351).[8] *Angegangen* (the word in the 1925 lectures translated 'approached' here and repeated in the *SZ* gloss on being disposed) is the counterpart to our active concerns and cares about what the world affords us, how it *matters* to us, how we are affected (*betroffen*) by it—for good and for ill. Our dependency upon and active engagement in the world (forcing ourselves on it, welcoming it, enduring it, etc.) is matched by the world's engagement of us (forcing itself on us, threatening us, meeting or not our needs, etc.).[9] Accordingly, the translation 'approached' fails to get at the force of the term *angegangen* that runs a gamut of connotations from being 'enticed' by the world, being 'enthralled,' or 'solicited' by it (Kisiel's translation[10]) to being 'bothered,' 'hounded,' 'badgered' by it and the like. In any event, we invariably find ourselves (*befinden sich*)[11] in this or that mood, and 'disposedness' (*Befindlichkeit*) designates the "basic form" (*Grundform*) of this co-discovery of the world and being-in-the-world. This co-discovery (i.e., the second essential character of being disposed) runs in tandem with being approached enthralled, hounded, etc. by the world (the third essential character) (*GA* 20: 352).[12]

Heidegger's elaboration of the second and third essential features of being disposed amounts to the contention that finding oneself in a mood—as a way that we are *here* (*da*)—is at once disclosive and enabling. In the process of disclosing the world and our being *in* it,[13] our experience of finding ourselves in a mood enables our encounter of the world and what it affords us. That is to say, the disclosive and enabling characters coincide; one is not prior to the other, temporally or otherwise.

This unitary yet twofold character (disclosive enabling, enabling disclosure) points to a complexity common to the relation between existential and existentiel dimensions. This complexity is easily misunderstood, threatening the collapse of the two levels, e.g., the reduction of being disposed to a mood. Yet, as if to forestall the tendency to overlook that complexity, Heidegger states that a mood is "an exponent of disposedness" (*GA* 20: 353). This metaphor aptly preserves the difference between them as well as the nature of a mood's groundedness in a disposedness. Far from disappearing into a respective mood, disposedness is partly constitutive of the mood and experienced as such (just as the presence of $x$ is undeniable in $x^2$).

To be sure, the experience of being disposed and its three essential characters is typically hidden or occluded, indeed, often by the mood itself. Just as moods can be transparent, i.e., just as we can be in a mood without knowing that we are, so we can be oblivious to the disposedness underlying and co-constituting the mood. But the task of the existential phenomenologist is precisely to bring out the hidden structures of the experience of existing, in this case a structure instantiated by a mood but thereby not identical to it. Whereas moods and emotions show up first and for the most part, the existential phenomenologist is charged with making explicit what, while not showing up in this way, is essential to those moods and emotions, making up the "sense and ground" of them (*SZ* 35).[14] To put the matter in Aristotelian terms congenial to Heidegger, while moods are first for us, disposedness is first by nature; and, for this reason, the existential-ontological analysis of the latter is ultimately rooted in the existentiel-ontic analysis of the former (*SZ* 13).

In all the aforementioned ways, Heidegger provides a masterful analysis of the existential dimension of being disposed and finding oneself in a mood. But along with his general treatment of dispositions and moods, the robustness of his structural analyses of fear and angst should not be overlooked. By discriminating what is fearful, the fearing itself, and that on account of which we fear, he gives an illuminating sketch of fear and its variations, from alarm and misgivings to dread and terror. We fear what is threatening, as long as it is close enough to threaten, fearing for ourselves or others in the process.

Heidegger follows a similar path in charting the structure of angst, only now the object is nothing and nowhere in the world, but rather the world itself. In angst an experience of the meaninglessness of anything we might encounter within the world and, thereby, of the world itself brings with it a sense of the meaninglessness of our individual being-in-the-world as such. At the same time, angst comes over Dasein on account of its being-in-the-world, precisely as its unique possibility, something that it is free to choose and take hold of. The experience of angst (the parallel to fearing itself) brings Dasein face-to-face with itself as this freedom. The operative mood in the experience of anxiety is a certain uncanniness, an eerie sense of not being-at-home in the public world of average everydayness, by virtue of the experience of being free for a potential to be that is uniquely our own.[15] Heidegger uses the gloss of its three dimensions and their unity to hone in on how Dasein can be defined as care (*SZ* 185–188).

Heidegger augments these similarities and dissimilarities in fear and angst with accounts of parallels and differences in their temporal character. One parallel (exemplifying the first essential character of being disposed) consists in the ways that in both fear and angst we come back to ourselves—we find ourselves (*wir befinden uns*)—as something that has been thrown into the world and, thus, as something constituted by already and foreseeably having been (*Gewesenheit*). We do so, to be sure, as is true in every case, in tandem with what we are projecting (what we understand). In the case of fear, for example, we come back to ourselves insofar as we fear for ourselves by awaiting some impending threat from something within-the-world. But to do so, he emphasizes, is to forget our authentic selves, since the fear assimilates us quite inauthentically to something handy that is an object of manageable concern. Fear thus stands in sharp contrast to an experience of the authentic future, i.e., an experience, not of awaiting something threatening, but of resolutely "running ahead" toward the possibility of the end of our possibilities. Through this projection, i.e., a resolute anticipation, we come back in an authentic way to our mortal thrownness, the pre-eminent possibility of having been that we always are already. As the experience of the irrelevance—in a certain sense—of everything encountered in the surrounding world, angst has the character neither of expecting nor of awaiting the arrival of some entity. The object of angst is instead already here, namely, Dasein itself, together with the disclosure and the sense of being, the timeliness, that defines it. By bringing to light Dasein's authentic potential-to-be, angst brings it back to its thrownness as something that it can retrieve and repeat.[16]

# 2    Missing Modes of Affectivity

The first part of this paper sketches various ways in which Heidegger foregrounds affectivity (my umbrella term for disposedness, moods, and emotions). He gives pride of place to disposedness as a basic existential that first discloses to us that and how we are. He demonstrates, more particularly, the sense in which affectivity is co-extensive with being-in-the-world, disclosing our worlds to us in ways that matter to us. In addition to providing structural analyses of fear and angst that highlight their similarities and differences, he demonstrates the distinctive timeliness of the experiences.

For all these reasons (and they could be supplemented[17]), it is easy to conclude, when it comes to the importance of dispositions and moods, that Heidegger talks the talk. But does he walk the walk? Does he follow through with his insistence upon their importance? Does he incorporate affectivity effectively and sufficiently into his existential analysis? My aim is to suggest ways that affectivity is missing in action, in some cases conspicuously, perhaps even egregiously, from Heidegger's existential analysis in *Being and Time*. I say 'egregiously' because the absence of an account of the relevant affectivity imperils, by his own account, the integrity of the analysis.

## 2.1    Gleichursprünglichkeit (Equiprimordiality)

Let me begin by drawing attention to Heidegger's insistence upon the equiprimordiality of disposedness and understanding as basic existentials. He underscores and ultimately gives a firm basis for the claim of this equiprimordiality by way of his alignment of each basic existential with a different ecstasis of time, where time is always also a matter of the unity of three ecstases. To appreciate this aspect of Heidegger's analysis, it is important to offset construing understanding in some Kantian or post-Kantian sense as a deployment of concepts. The understanding, as Heidegger construes it, can take that form, but it is first and foremost a projection (the root sense of futurity) of possibilities of the world into which it has already been thrown and which is part of who it already is (the root sense of having been). Disposedness is precisely the affective disclosure of having been or, better, already being in one sense or the other. There is no projecting without the possibilities that come with Dasein's thrownness, just as there is no thrownness without some projecting of the possibilities it provides. If this internal unity of thrownness and projecting—what Heidegger sometimes dubs the 'thrown projection'—is kept in view, then the equiprimordiality of disposedness, the disclosing of thrownness, and understanding, the disclosing that comes with projecting possibilities, is relatively uncontroversial.[18]

Heidegger constantly iterates this point. Dasein's potential-to-be (its *Seinkönnen*) is, he observes, essentially disposed (*wesenhaft befindliches*) and he concludes §31 on understanding with the claim that, as existentials, Dasein's disposedness and understanding characterize "the primordial disclosedness of being-in-the-world."[19] When he introduces §34 on discourse, he stresses that disposedness and understanding are not only both "fundamental" existentials, but "equiprimordial" (*SZ* 160).[20]

But here's the rub. Heidegger's choice of locutions tends to privilege the understanding. For example, he speaks repeatedly of 'disposed understanding' (*befindliches Verstehen*); in fact, the expression surfaces at least fourteen times in *SZ*.[21] By contrast, on only four occasions does he flip the word order such that 'understanding' modifies 'disposedness' (*verstehende Befindlichkeit*).[22] The problem is that putting 'understanding' in the place of the noun and 'disposed' in the place of the adjective can signal the priority of the modified over the modifier.

But this priority is also evidenced from the beginning of the work. Heidegger distinguishes Dasein as the entity who has an understanding of being. "Dasein understands itself in some sort of way and with some sort of explicitness in his being…An understanding of being is itself a determination of the being of Dasein" (*SZ* 12). This *Seinsverständnis* (an understanding of being) is a go-to expression for practically every analysis in the text (such that it would be tedious to enumerate the instances) but there is no comparable talk of a disposedness or attunement to being (*Seinsbefindlichkeit, Seinsstimmung*). To be sure, at the outset of *SZ* Heidegger stresses that *Seinsverständnis* is inherent to Dasein precisely insofar as being is at *issue* or *matters* to it (*SZ* 12). Yet, while this expression can be reasonably read as flagging an affective dimension, he also states unambiguously that "*Verständnis* has its being in a *Verstehen*" (*SZ* 85).

## 2.2   Begleitphänomenen (Accompanying Phenomena)

Mention has already been made of how Heidegger continues a tradition of rescuing affectivity from its amalgamation into cognition or volition. Not that he sees matters in this way. He faults everyone since Aristotle and before Scheler with failing to give an ontological interpretation of affectivity. Instead, he observes (probably with Kant and Brentano in mind) that emotions and feelings have been traditionally classified as mental phenomena, falling under a third class of such phenomena, next to presenting and willing. He then adds that, in the process, instances of affectivity sink to the status of "accompanying phenomena" (*Begleitphänomenen*) (*SZ* 139; *GA* 20: 353).

Yet his analyses of several existential phenomena contain in fact no mention of the sort of affectivity involved at all or, if there is mention of it, it is presented precisely as an accompaniment to understanding. It is perhaps unfair to point to the sections in *BT* before he explicitly treats disposedness (§29). Still, it is noteworthy that the analyses of concern (*Besorgen*), the use of tools, the particular kind of seeing involved therein (*Umsicht*), signs, relevance, and significance include little if any allusion to the sorts of affectivity involved in these ways of being-in. It is perhaps possible to tease out some sense of affectivity from the disturbances create by the breakdowns described in §16, but Heidegger hardly highlights any such sense. It is notable that, on one occasion, in the course of glossing significance (*Bedeutsamkeit*), he looks ahead to the treatment of the basic existentials, but when he does, he appeals, not to being disposed, but to understanding (*SZ* 87). Yet when we consider the meaning or significance of the purposeful referential totality and the trust we have in it, including, as he puts it, the way that we are captivated (*benommen*) by it (*SZ* 76) as well as the suitability and unsuitability of certain things (*SZ* 83) within it, not to speak of the inherent prospects for success and failure, it hardly seems like a matter of understanding alone. Presumably there is—and, based upon his account of their equiprimordiality, there should be—affective dimensions of the experience of this entire complex of phenomena.[23]

When Heidegger turns to Descartes' bloodless determination of the world as *res extensa*, affectivity is, perhaps understandably, absent. But Heidegger's treatment of the spatiality of Dasein is also free of any allusions to affectivity (he in fact pans an appeal to feeling to get at the experience of direction) (*SZ* 109). So, too, when Heidegger turns to the phenomenon of others being-here-with us, with the insistence upon "making it, in its most proximate everydayness, phenomenally apparent and interpreting it in an ontologically adequate manner," he relies largely on encounters within economic settings where a kind of anonymity reigns (thus, the breeding ground of *das Man*). It is in these settings, Heidegger stresses, that "Dasein first finds herself" and others are encountered as being-here-with her, but only because Dasein is essentially being-with (*SZ* 119f). Yet he makes no mention of any affective dimension in this regard. To be sure, as a means of underscoring that others are not simply also on hand (*vorhanden*), he notes how being alone and lacking others as well as modes of indifference and alienness are modes of being-here-with others, but there is no elaboration of how it feels to have those experiences (*SZ* 121). The same holds for this account of the two positive modes of solicitude or caring for others, leaping in and leaping ahead. What he rightly sees as the mistrust and the trust inherent in inauthentic and authentic unions respectively are plainly highly emotional experiences, as are the ways that considerateness, inconsiderateness, and indifference differently animate acts of solicitude. But there is nary a word about how fundamentally emotional these experiences are (*SZ* 122f).

Also telling is the fact that, once again, in a section prior to the analysis of the basic existentials, he appeals to the understanding alone. Thus, after acknowledging that Dasein's understanding of being (*Seinsverständnis*) entails the understanding of others, he underscores that this understanding—and here he shifts from *Verständnis* to *Verstehen*—is "a primordially existential sort of being" that makes knowledge of others and acquaintance with them possible; indeed, even self-acquaintance, he adds, is grounded in "the being-with that understands in a primordial way" (*SZ* 123f). Reference to any affective component is conspicuously—indeed, here I would say 'egregiously'—absent, as he exclusively invokes understanding to account for being-with. Nor does his argument against empathy (*Einfühlung*) get him off the hook here, since he explicitly says that the latter is "not a primordial, existential phenomenon"; that it to say, it is not on the level of a basic existential like *Befindlichkeit* (*SZ* 124f).

The only place where Heidegger alludes to affective dimensions in his analysis (prior to the discussion of the basic existentials) is his interpretation of *das Man*. There he speaks of how disturbing our care about overcoming or maintaining the distance between ourselves and others can be, how the ways we feel and evaluate become assimilated and leveled off into the all-accommodating averageness of a public profile, and how these processes provide a relief from the burden of being. Anticipating his discussion of angst, he describes the experience of being lost, strewn among the many, an experience he attributes to the inauthenticity of *das Man*, the self of everyday existence (*SZ* 126–130).[24]

Following the discussion of the basic existentials, Heidegger returns to the phenomenon of everyday existence with the aim, as he puts it, of looking for the affectivity specific to *das Man*. Yet the results are mixed. In the discussion of idle talk, a discussion that is, once again, dominated by understanding, mention of affectivity is largely an afterthought (though he registers that the dominance of public interpretations has already decided on the possible ways of being attuned; the crowd "pre-figures" the disposedness) (*SZ* 169f).[25] Although the phenomenon of ambiguity is rife with layers of moods and emotions, he is similarly inattentive to them. By contrast, Heidegger is explicit about the affective dimensions of curiosity. He stresses the restlessness and excitement, the distracted and uprooted character of only being concerned about the next new thing.

We would expect to find this same attentiveness to the affective dimensions in his treatment of fallenness and thrownness. We are not disappointed, even though his account, too, is principally structural. Dasein is itself the source of the seductiveness of the inauthenticity of falling prey to the 'world.' While the point is structural, succumbing to that seductiveness does yield a certain sedating tranquility. This tranquility, one might justly contend, is clearly a mood or attunement. Still, it is the tranquility of mindless absorption in the world that is itself alienating, a self-ensnaring movement that conceals from Dasein its ownmost potential-to-be. Once again, structural features dominate the analysis—but not completely, as Heidegger introduces the notion of a whirl-wind (*Wirbel*) to capture this movement, this dizzying plunge into nothingness. Weatherman that he was, Heidegger clearly appreciates the way this metaphor captures an affective dimension, something of how it feels to be inauthentic.

## 3    Angst-Bereit (Angst-Preparedness)

Have I talked myself out of my main thesis? Don't these descriptions, particularly when coupled with the enormous significance of the experience of Angst for his existential analysis, offset the apparent overreliance upon understanding that we otherwise flagged in the first half of *BT*? Indeed, Heidegger stresses the importance of affectivity even more, one might argue, when it comes to his account of authentic existence. For example, after glossing that what it means to understand the call of conscience authentically (one's ownmost guilt) amounts to "wanting-to-have-a-conscience," Heidegger explicitly asks what mood corresponds to this understanding (*SZ* 288, 295). Once again a form of understanding takes the lead, but there can be no doubt of the importance that Heidegger attaches to the affective dimensions of existential guilt and conscience. The operative mood, he tells us, is the uncanniness of conscience—uncanny because it places matters so utterly on the shoulders of the individual. He then follows up with the observation that this uncanniness—"the uncanniness co-revealed in the understanding"—is genuinely disclosed by finding oneself in a mood of angst, i.e., it is disclosed through the disposedness of angst (*die Befindlichkeit der Angst*) inherent to that understanding. In understanding the call of conscience Dasein is brought before the uncanniness of itself, above all the uncanniness of both a potential-to-be that is uniquely its own and a freedom for it, the freedom to choose itself (*SZ* 296).

One might question whether this uncanninness of angst, the affectivity of conscience, is not importantly different from the experience of angst described more generically in the first half of *BT*. But I see no reason to fault Heidegger seriously on this score. Even if there are experiences of the uncanniness of angst that do not in fact rise to the level of existential guilt and the existential call of conscience, there is no reason to think that they cannot.[26]

Nevertheless, the affective dimension of heeding the call of conscience is, I submit, underdetermined to a fault. Moods and emotions remain missing in action in important ways at this crucial juncture in the existential analysis. Directly after stating that "wanting-to-have-a-conscience" is constituted, not only by understanding the call of conscience, but also by the uncanniness disclosed by angst, Heidegger adds that this "wanting-to-have-a-conscience becomes a preparedness for angst," a feature that he subsequently builds into his formal description of resoluteness as "the reticent, angst-ready projecting of oneself onto the ownmost guiltiness" (*SZ* 296f, 301). But what then is the difference between the uncanny angst co-constitutive of wanting-to-have-a-conscience and the angst-preparedness of resoluteness? Heidegger slides without warning or explanation from the former to the latter. Are they importantly different? If they are, what sort of experience is the move from angst to the preparedness for angst? What does it feel like? It cannot be the same experience of angst or uncanniness, but Heidegger leaves us high and dry as to what the affective character of the experience (that of being prepared for angst) is. We could claim that the move is immediate. But then we are still left wondering what it is like—what's the mood, what it feels like—to be prepared for angst. An elaboration of the affective component of resoluteness is missing from his first pass at it (§60).[27]

The situation improves albeit only marginally, I suggest, when, "thinking it through to the end," he argues that resoluteness "authentically becomes what it can be," when it anticipates death (*SZ* 305, 309). Instead of using the expression 'reticent, angst-ready' to characterize resoluteness, he begins this discussion (§62) by saying that "resoluteness was characterized as reticent, exacting angst [*sich-Angst-zumutende*]" (*SZ* 305). Being ready for angst and exacting it from ourselves are arguably different but, in any case, neither characterization explains how someone is disposed or attuned when she is resolute.[28]

To be sure, Heidegger is not completely silent on this score. His lone comment in the context of his analysis of anticipatory resoluteness comes in the wake of insisting that it stems not from some high-flying "idealistic" expectation but instead from "the more sober understanding of Dasein's basic, factical possibilities." Applying the same adjective to the corresponding angst, he then observes:

> Going together with the sober angst that brings up the individualized potential-to-be is the armed joy at this possibility. (*SZ* 310)

Theses allusions to sober angst and joyful anticipation are certainly telling but also meager to a fault, given the fundamental importance of both the theme of being disposed and that of authenticity for the existential analysis as a whole. The brevity of the allusions corroborates more than it mitigates the thesis that I have been advancing in this paper. More than a passing account of the corresponding moods and emotions is conspicuously missing from the analysis.

As if anticipating this line of criticism, Heidegger immediately adds that the analysis of "basic moods" like joy oversteps the boundaries of his interpretation, set as it is on the question of fundamental ontology. The observation is consistent with remarks, repeated throughout *Being and Time*, that differentiate between his ontological investigation and a philosophical anthropology, despite the latter's need for the former (*SZ* 17, 49f, 131, 183, 194, 200, 301). But it is difficult not to see the observation as a dodge or diversion, particularly when it comes to the analysis of authenticity which is, it bears recalling, the alleged key to the analysis of temporality (*SZ* 323–329). After all, Heidegger is not shy about enlisting moods—from curiosity's restless distractedness and the alienating tranquility of absorption in *das Man* to dimensions of the uncanniness of angst—and incorporating them into his ontological investigations when it suits his purposes.

The last paragraph of §62, following the passage just cited, seems to confirm these critical misgivings. In that concluding paragraph Heidegger acknowledges that "a definite ontic conception of authentic existence, a factical ideal" underlies the ontological interpretation (*SZ* 310). That is as it should be, to be sure; indeed, it is inescapable, he goes on to say. The point conforms to another commitment of the entire investigation, flagged earlier in connection with the relation between moods and being disposed, namely, "the ultimately *existentiel, i.e., ontic* rooting of the existential analysis" (*SZ* 13). But then how rooted in ontic phenomena can the existential analysis of authentic existence be if an adequate account of the mood of resoluteness is missing from the analysis?[29]

## 4    Concluding Remark

In this paper I have been arguing that discussions of affectivity are conspicuously underdeveloped if not absent from several analyses in *Being and Time*. While this absence can perhaps be excused in some cases, it is particularly hard to excuse its absence in the context of the analysis of existing authentically, precisely where Heidegger specifically—but, as it turns out, all too indeterminately—lays claim to the role of various affective dimensions (angst, uncanniness, soberness, joy) in being authentic.

Whether Heidegger's lack of attention to these matters proves debilitating for his existential analysis remains to be seen. But it may be of a piece with another aspect of *Being and Time*, namely, the lack of an expression of the mood that corresponds to the existential analysis itself. Why, we might wonder, is it missing? If it is, for some reason, too much to ask—or impertinent to ask—what the fundamental ontologist's mood is, why is that?

# Notes

1. 'Disposedness,' as a translation of *Befindlichkeit*, is not ideal, but there are several reasons to prefer it over the alternatives. 'State of mind' can suggest a contrast with the state of the body and, in particular, its orientation to the surrounding world, that being-in-the-world does not. As Eugene Gendlin would put it, *Befindlichkeit* is both inward and outward but prior to their differentiation (Gendlin 1978/1979). Unlike 'disposition,' 'disposedness' often clearly captures an affective component, without necessarily being a mood (*Stimmung*) or emotion. Formed from the passive of a verb of placement, 'disposedness' also has the advantage of signaling something akin to the thrownness, the experience of a state of always finding ourselves (*sich befinden*) already in a situation. Like the French *se trouver*, some uses of *sich befinden* merely indicate where someone happens to reside or that something happens to be the case (*sie befindet sich in Berlin, es befindet sich kein Hindernis inzwischen*). But it also frequently signals a state or condition one happens to be in or to find oneself in. See, for example, the following uses, all taken from Schleiermacher's correspondence: "zu meiner und anderer Freude, befinde ich mich nach meiner Art recht wol"; "ich befinde mich in einer besonderen Lage"; "in einer sehr traurrigen Gemüthszerrüttung"; "in engen Verhältnissen" (Schleiermacher 1988, 199, 289, 441, 446). 'Mood' is perhaps a more obvious translation for *Stimmung*, but 'attunement' preserves the aural and vocal reference of the roots *Stimme* and *stimmen*, nicely captured by the line *die schönste Stimmung ist, die nach der Liebe kling*t (von Hoffmannswaldau 1695, 160; see, too, the opening quotation from Bettina von Arnim). For a clear overview of advantages and disadvantages of possible translations of *Befindlichkeit* and *Stimmung*, see Elpidorou and Freeman (2015a), 4 note 4 and 5 note 5.
2. Freeman ably demonstrates the promise of Heidegger's account of moods, notwithstanding serious problems facing it.
3. In the eighteenth century, in contrast to Christian Wolff's doctrine that all the capacities of the mind were reducible to one "basic force" (*Grundkraft*) of representation, Tetens distinguished three "basic capabilities: (*Grundvermögen*): feeling, understanding, and will; and Mendelssohn alike differentiated the three irreducible capacities of knowing, feeling, and desiring; see Johannes Tetens, *Philosophische Versuche über die menschliche Natur und ihre Entwickelung*,

Band I (Leipzig: Weidmann, 1777), 625; Moses Mendelssohn, "*Ueber das Erkenntnis-, das Empfindungs- und das Begehrungsvermögen*" (1776) in *Gesammelte Schriften*, Band 3.1, hrsg. Fritz Bamberger und Leo Strauss (Berlin: Akademie, 1932), 276–277. Kant adopts a similar differentiation, corresponding to his three *Critiques*. In the nineteenth century Sir William Hamilton adopts a similar approach, later criticized by Brentano in a passage and text quite familiar to Heidegger; Sir William Hamilton, *Lectures on Metaphysics and Logic*, Vol. 1 (London: Blackwood, 1859), 182–189 and volume 2, second edition (London: Blackwood, 1861), 431–434; Franz Brentano, *Psychologie vom empirischen Standpunkte*, erster Band (Leipzig: Duncker und Humblot, 1874), 115–118.

4. Heidegger appeals to indifference to buttress his claim that we are always in some mood or other; see *SZ* 134. His thinking seems to be that a person may be neither angry nor happy but simply indifferent to these and other moods. Since, however, such indifference is presumably felt, it leaves the possibility of experiencing an absence of mood on the table. Heidegger's strong claim for the invariability of being in one mood or another can be salvaged by insisting (a) that, even if there be momentary absences of mood (where we feel nothing), we have no experience of going for very long without experiencing an affective component of one sort or another (feeling, emotion, mood) and (b) that certain moods override others, persisting and dominating our comportment across momentary episodes. That he has something of this sort in mind is suggested by his reference to characteristics of utter indifference—e.g., "emptiness and staleness" (*Leere und Schalheit*)—"that in the *most fleeting moment* of being-here are always constitutive for the absorption in the world" (*GA* 20: 352–353; emphasis added).

5. "Die Gestimmtheit der Befindlichkeit konstituiert existenzial die Weltoffenheit des Daseins."

6. This tacit dimension, together with the way a mood is said to disclose "being-in-the-world as a whole" (*SZ* 137), may explain why Heidegger favors moods over emotions or feelings in his elaboration of disposedness, i.e., as the ontic (existentiel) dimension that chiefly pairs with the existential. A mood is more indeterminate, global, and transparent (in G. E. Moore's sense) than an emotion. Being in a romantic mood is different from the emotion of love; so, too, being in a feisty mood

is different from a feeling of anger. Whereas a mood is like a fog that envelops us, an emotion can be as clear as the sound of thunder or a flash of lightning. A parallel can be found in studies of the difference between shame and guilt. Shame is often considered to concern a person diffusely as a whole; by contrast, guilt seems to point to someone's specific actions (transgressions). In this way, a mood of shame differs from a feeling of guilt. With this distinction in mind, it is worth noting that Heidegger describes *Angst* as both a *Grundbefindlichkeit* and a *Grundstimmung*; see *SZ* 188–190, 310.

7. 'Here' (da) is Heidegger's term, not for a place nearby in contrast to a yonder there, but for the very co-disclosure (of the world and being-in-the-world) peculiar to what is also called 'a human being' (*GA* 20: 349; see, too, *SZ* 139: "Die Befindlichkeit ist eine existenziale Grundart, in der das Dasein sein Da ist.") Psychology's failure to appreciate this dimension of the structure of being-here accounts, Heidegger contends, for its inability to discern the genuine phenomena of affectivity. A similar obtuseness explains, he adds, traditional anthropology's treatment of affectivity as bothersome accompaniments of knowing and willing; see *GA* 20: 353.

8. In these 1925 lectures it is clear that Heidegger has not yet settled on his terminology. In particular, the uses of 'uncoveredness' and 'disclosedness' are the opposite of their uses in *SZ* (where entities are uncovered and being is disclosed). But the general account given in the lectures of *Befindlichkeit* as the "a priori" of both uncoveredness and disclosedness—mutatis mutandis—carries over into *SZ*; see *GA* 20: 354.

9. There are, in effect, something like two directions or vectors of presence or self-presentation disclosed in being disposed, that of the movement of being-here towards the world and that of the world toward being-here. Since these directions entail withdrawal as well, one might speculate that a full analysis of being disposed anticipates the dual U-turns making up the structure of the *Kehre*.

10. Martin Heidegger, *History of the Concept of Time: Prolegomena*, trans. Theodore Kisiel (Bloomington, IN: Indiana University Press, 1992).

11. The 'selves' we find, Heidegger is quick to add, are more likely to be anonymous selves of the everyday crowd (*das Man*) than "a developed and thematically conscious I" (*GA* 20: 352).

12. On Heidegger's use of the term 'co-discovery' (*Mitentdecktheit*) here, see n. 8 above. In the same context Heidegger also employs the

expression "bei all dem, was uns ... in irgendeinem Sinne 'zumute' ist," i.e., "in regard to everything that in any sort of sense makes us feel something." It is worth noting that, according to the OED, the root *mut* and its variants in various Old German dialects gives rise to the English *mood*.

13. *GA* 20: 352: "Befindlichkeit ist ... eine Grundart des Seins des Daseins, seines In-seins."

14. The point expressed in this paragraph applies mutatis mutandis to other analyses in *SZ*. To the extent that *SZ* has the trappings of a transcendental phenomenology, it is necessary to guard against treating basic existentials purely as transcendental structures that enable existentiel phenomena but are not themselves experienced as such. Whereas basic existentials are phenomena hidden from ordinary approaches that focus on ready-made categories, the task of the phenomenologist is to indicate how they are themselves experienced. So while it is true that the emotions and moods are the ways we typically experience being disposed, there is an experience of being disposed that is constitutive of them.

15. My son seemed to have an analogous experience when we were driving in the car one day and he started to ask what different things were for. I told him that the dials were for the radio, the knobs for the heater, the buttons for the lights, the levers for the wipers and turn signals, and so on. Everything had a purpose because it was an artifact, made by human hands for some purpose. But then he paused and asked: "What about me?"

16. For a clear exposition of Heidegger's account of the temporal dimensions of affectivity, see Elpidorou and Freeman (2015b, 7–12).

17. See, for example, Heidegger's remarks about the temporal grounding of various moods (hope, enthusiasm, cheerfulness, weariness, sadness, melancholy, and despair) in *SZ* 345f.

18. Still, a problem does surface here inasmuch as we can sometimes clearly distinguish being disposed in the sense of finding ourselves in a mood-and-situation from being disposed to project/understand certain possibilities as well as from the dispositions that accompany/modify the projecting. In this respect at least a finer-grained analysis seems to be warranted.

19. *SZ* 148, 260; see, too, *GA* 20: 356: "*Verstehen...ist...ein erschließendes Sichbefinden.*"

20. *SZ* 220: "Erschlossenheit wird durch Befindlichkeit, Verstehen und Rede konstituiert und betrifft gleichursprünglich die Welt, das In-Sein und das Selbst." See, too, *GA* 20: 363: "In jeder Rede…wird immer das Dasein selbst und seine Befindlichkeit mitentdeckt."

21. *SZ* 143, 144, 148, 161, 162, 168 (zugehörig), 177, 185, 252 (gestimmtes), 260, 265f, 335, 339, 409.

22. *SZ* 179, 182, 270, 335.

23. I am grateful to Robert Engelmann for bringing the question of the *Befindlichkeit* and *Stimmungen* involved in the use of tools and tool-complexes to my attention.

24. As noted (see n. 11), his 1925 gloss on being disposed places it squarely in the context of absorption into the indeterminate, everyday self of the crowd (*GA* 20: 352).

25. The uncanniness of floating along in mid-air, ungrounded, as it were, remains hidden (*SZ* 170).

26. One might question, however, the extent to which the *Faktum* of *Gewissensangst* corroborates his interpretation, as he contends without further explanation (*SZ* 296).

27. Along the way, one finds, to be sure, some revealing comments about the potential of resoluteness, e.g., an authentic way of being-with-one-another that stands in contrast to jealous relations (*SZ* 298).

28. Further complicating matters is Heidegger's remark, after noting that death's indeterminacy discloses itself primordially in angst, that "this primordial angst endeavors to exact resoluteness" (*trachtet die Entschlossenheit sich zuzumuten*) (*SZ* 308).

29. One might want to argue that Heidegger does supply something of a clue to the mood (or is it 'moods' of authenticity?), when he observes in passing—earlier in the text, to be sure—that *das Man* does not allow "the courage for angst in the face of death" to come about (*SZ* 254). But Heidegger refrains from any further comment in this regard. Moreover, he knows his Aristotle far too well to confuse the ἕξις of courage with a πάθος or ἡδονή (which he characterizes as *Befindlichkeit* at several junctures in his 1924 summer semester lectures on *Grundbegriffe der aristotelischen Philosophie*; see *GA* 18: 242–248).

# References

Elpidorou, Andreas, and Lauren Freeman. 2015a. "Affectivity in Heidegger I: Moods and Emotions in *Being and Time*." *Philosophy Compass* 1–17.

Elpidorou, Andreas, and Lauren Freeman. 2015b. "Affectivity in Heidegger II: Temporality, Boredom, and Beyond." *Philosophy Compass* 1–20.

Freeman, Lauren. 2016. "Defending a Heideggerian Account of Mood." In *Philosophy of Mind and Phenomenology*, edited by D. Dahlstrom, A. Elpidorou, and W. Hopp, 247–267. New York: Routledge.

Friedrich, Schleiermacher. 1988. *Kritische Gesamtausgabe*. Fünfte Abteilung: Briefwechsel und biographische Dokumente, edited by Hans-Joachim Birkner et al. Band 2. Berlin: de Gruyter.

Gendlin, Eugene T. 1978/1979. "Befindlichkeit: Heidegger and the Philosophy of Psychology." *Review of Existential Psychology & Psychiatry* 16 (1–3): 43–71.

von Arnim, Bettina. 1840. *Günderode*. Band I. Leipzig: Levysohn.

von Hoffmannswaldau, Christian. 1695. *Begräbnis Gedichte in Herrn von Hoffmanswaldau und anderer Deutschen auserlesene und bißher ungedruckte Gedichte*. Band 1. Leipzig: Fritsch.

# 6

# Affect and Authenticity: Three Heideggerian Models of Owned Emotion

## Denis McManus

This chapter will examine three ways in which Heidegger's work might shed light on the notion of authenticity in our affective lives.[1] That work poses many challenges and that notion is itself difficult to pin down, eliciting different intuitions or perhaps different notions of "authenticity." Authentic emotions are sometimes seen as those that reflect how one truly thinks of something or someone; these are one's "true" or "real" feelings in contrast with those that one adopts or cultivates—for example, when we succumb to sentimentality, or "manage" our emotions in order to fit with a particular social circle or role. Concerns about such management can lead to the celebration of spontaneous emotion as distinctively authentic. But such reactions can also be disavowed as inauthentic—as inexpressive of how one "really" or "truly feels"—if they are the legacy of indoctrination or a prejudice-instilling upbringing.[2] So the notion of affective authenticity is complex, an elusive moving target or set of targets.

D. McManus (✉)
University of Southampton, Southampton, UK
e-mail: mcmanus@soton.ac.uk

© The Author(s) 2019
C. Hadjioannou (ed.), *Heidegger on Affect*, Philosophers in Depth,
https://doi.org/10.1007/978-3-030-24639-6_6

Seeking to illuminate this notion by drawing on Heidegger's reflections faces further complications because, in one sense, authenticity is not a topic he discusses: he discusses *Eigentlichkeit*. This term is typically translated as "authenticity" but the adequacy of this translation has been challenged. For example, the adjective "*eigen*" means "own"—as in having a room or a mind of one's own—and contrasts with "*fremd*"—meaning "alien" or "another's"; thus, it has often been proposed that a more literal translation of "*Eigentlichkeit*" would be "own-ness" or "owned-ness."[3] But that choice comes with costs too. For example, in ordinary—non-Heideggerian—German, "*eigentlich*" means "real," "actual" or "genuine," a feature that the standard translation of *Eigentlichkeit* captures—consider, for example, the authentic works of art that we distinguish from fakes—and rivals like "ownedness" do not. Having noted these complexities, I will use the standard translation in what follows, not least because it is standard; but I also invite the reader to listen out for the other resonances that *Eigentlichkeit* carries.

Of the three models of Heideggerian authenticity that I will consider, the first, which I call the "decisionist model," will be most familiar to the reader. The second, which I call the "standpoint model," can be seen at work in a variety of readings of Heidegger and I have myself defended versions of it elsewhere.[4] More recently though, I have come to question this model and this has prompted me to explore another, which I will call the "All Things Considered Judgment Model."[5] Each of these models suggests a distinctive notion of what authenticity in one's affective life might be.

# 1     Heidegger on Affect—I: *Befindlichkeit* and *Stimmung*

As Kate Withy has recently observed, "[m]ost interpretations of [his] account of authenticity … follow Heidegger in focusing on owned understanding" (2015, 21), and there is no explicitly articulated account in Heidegger of owned or authentic emotion. But this is a little incongruous as emotion is key to his discussion of two concepts that are central to his existential analytic of Dasein: "*Befindlichkeit*" and "*Stimmung*."

There is a broad consensus that Macquarrie and Robinson's translation of the former in their version of *Sein und Zeit* as "state-of-mind" is not one of their better choices, not least because it suggests an internal state of a thinker, when Heidegger invokes the notion of *Befindlichkeit* precisely to stress that we always already find ourselves in, and exposed to, a world.[6] Consequently, other commentators have offered as alternative translations, "situatedness," "findingness," "affectedness" and "disposedness." Heidegger stresses the affective dimension of our *Befindlichkeit* through his notion of "*Stimmung.*" Macquarrie and Robinson render this as "mood," while also noting its original use to refer to the "tuning" of a musical instrument.[7] Heidegger himself exploits this connection in arguing that our engagement with the world around is characterized by an affective "tuning" to what comes to pass there. For example, the life of a gardener is not only one in which she engages in particular activities and deploys particular concepts but also one in which she is moved by particular kinds of events: she takes pleasure in a good harvest, worries over the first signs of blight, and despairs over a drought.

Heidegger's 1924 *Basic Concepts of Aristotelian Philosophy* lectures—in which the concept of "*Befindlichkeit*" first becomes prominent[8]—give us further striking articulations of this point. So, to stick with my example, gardeners as gardeners "carry the possibility of something occurring to them within their constitution" (*BCAP* 131). Such occurrences "happen to," "befall" and "strike" such individuals; through the former, the latter too "become-otherwise" (*BCAP* 131, 312). Emotion is a "*being-taken* of Dasein ... *from without*" (*BCAP* 132–133): we are "attuned," one might say, to such "external" events. But a proper appreciation of this vulnerability lies in seeing that Dasein is being-in-the-world—that this "without" is where we as Dasein exist: Dasein is taken "from without *in the sense of the world as the wherein of my being*" (*BCAP* 133).[9]

Thus, Heidegger insists that "[a]ttunement [*Stimmung*] is ... *the fundamental way in which Dasein is as Dasein*" (*FCM* 67). Alongside our *In-der-Welt-sein*—and our *Mitsein*, our being-with-others—our condition is also one of *Gestimmtsein*, of "being-attuned," "which constantly and from the ground up penetrates [*durchstimmt*] our Dasein" (*ET* 158, cf. *WM* 87). As we will see in what follows, this parallel runs further in that—as with those other better-known existentiales—our inescapable "being-attuned" can also seem to make authenticity difficult to understand. A long-standing problem for readers of Heidegger has been to distinguish being-in-the-world and being-with-others from the "absorption in the world" and the "dispersal in *das Man*" (*SZ* 129) that he identifies with inauthenticity: what can authenticity's radical "individualizing" of Dasein (*SZ* 190–191) be other than—as David Cooper puts it—a "Promethean" "standing apart from or above" conditions that Heidegger elsewhere labels essential, structural features of Dasein's existence (Cooper 1997, 112, 110)? As we will see as we turn to consider our first model, what is perhaps the most influential interpretation of Heideggerian authenticity also seems to rest affective authenticity on a "Promethean" liberation from *Gestimmtsein*, from the fact that "we are never free of moods" (*SZ* 136).

## 2    The Decisionist Model

According to that interpretation, Heideggerian authenticity is the recognition and embracing of a radical choice. We grow up within, and normally unthinkingly comply with, a set of values and concerns that the social and historical context in which we find ourselves endorses; but when authentic, we come to see this compliance as expressing a choice on our part which we may take back and remake for ourselves. As Michael Friedman has recently expressed this view, when authentic,

> *Dasein* recognizes … that its normal or everyday practical context is simply one possibility among others, *one which is thereby subject to its own free choice*. This context need not be taken up unquestioningly from tradition or society, or even from the past choices that *Dasein* itself has already made. [This recognition] thus opens up the possibility of a very particular kind of liberation—the possibility of a truly 'authentic' existence in which *Dasein*'s own choices and decisions rest on no taken for granted background framework at all. (Friedman 2000, 51)

The authentic make then "a 'resolute' and thoroughgoing decision, a decision that goes all the way down, as it were" (Friedman 2000, 51–52).

The authentic faces up to—and "own"—the need for such decision and thereby—in some deep and radical sense—take on responsibility for themselves and the course their lives then take. Rather than fall back on accepted ways of behaving, authentic Dasein can then be said to "let[] its ownmost Self *take action in itself*" (*SZ* 288), to "take action in itself of its own accord" (*SZ* 295), indeed to "exist of [its] own accord [*von ihm selbst her sein*]" (*CT* 44). The authentic make themselves "answerable [*verantwortlich*]" for their actions,[10] whereas, when inauthentic, Dasein is "relieves[d] of its choice, its formation of judgments, and its estimation of values" (*HCT* 247), all of which it "out-sources" to *das Man*.

What then would authenticity in one's affective life look like according to this model? It would seem to present a radical but seemingly straight-forward account. Our having "taken up unquestioningly" the concerns and values of our "normal or everyday practical context" has dictated to us—has "managed"—how we have cared about—and been moved by—the world around us. In this sense, our emotions have not been our own; rather we have simply learned to feel as *das Man* feels. This thought seems to be confirmed when Heidegger insists that "[t]he dominance of the public way in which things have been interpreted" is "decisive even for the possibilities of having a mood": "*das Man* prescribes one's *Befindlichkeit*" (*SZ* 169–170, cf. *CT* 28). According to our first, decisionist model, we can remedy this dependency only by freely choosing for ourselves the concerns and values by which we will live: we will thereby choose for ourselves how to be moved by the world.[11]

Though popular and still—I think—subtly influential on the discussion of Heideggerian authenticity, this view has been widely criticized and reflection on the vision of owned affect that it presents offers us an interesting perspective on—and reinforces—those criticisms.

## 3  Heidegger on Affect—II: Disclosive Submission to a World That Matters

It is a commonplace that Western philosophy has tended to downplay or denigrate emotion; but there is also—as Susan Bordo puts it—a "recessive" tradition that resists that tendency (Bordo 1987, 114–118) and in which, along with Aristotle, Hume, and Nietzsche, Heidegger clearly stands. He rejects the depiction of "affects and feelings" as mere "third class" "psychical phenomena"—"fleeting Experiences which 'colour' one's 'psychical condition'," merely "accompanying" "representation and volition" (*SZ* 139, 340).[12] For such a depiction, emotion is at best "merely a radiance and shimmer," "the adornment of our thinking and willing"; and at worst, it is "something that obfuscates and inhibits these" (*FCM* 64), "something which hamper[s] or impair[s] rationality" (*HCT* 256). Against such a view, Heidegger argues that affect represents "a primordial kind of Being for Dasein," through which "Dasein is disclosed to itself *prior to* all cognition and volition," "outlin[ing] in advance" how Dasein, as Being-in-the-world, has "already submitted itself [*sich schon angewiesen*] to having entities within-the-world '*matter*' *to* it,"[13] something that could not be disclosed to a "subject which merely beholds" (*SZ* 136, 137, 341).[14]

Such remarks sit uncomfortably alongside the decisionist account of owned affect as freely chosen affect. Instead Dasein must always already have "submitted itself to having entities within-the-world '*matter*' *to* it": our *Befindlichkeit* "*implies a disclosive submission to the world, out of which we can encounter something that matters to us*," "this *submission* belong[ing] essentially to [Dasein's] Being" (*SZ* 137, 88).[15] Similarly, "[i]n being-attuned [*Gestimmtheit*], Dasein is always disclosed through mood [*stimmungsmäßig*] as that entity to which it has been delivered over [*überantwortet*] in its Being" (*SZ* 134)[16]; Dasein finds itself "constantly being summoned [*aufgerufen*]" by the world around it (*HCT* 254).

Such thoughts are supported by—and the decisionist model must push against—the familiar phenomenological fact that emotion is characteristically not subject to our control. It would be wrong to insist that we lack any such control; but we exercise what control we have in response to other emotions to which we are subject—with a view to attaining some other end that matters to us, that "summons" us. So Heidegger too recognizes that we have some such control:

> Factically, Dasein can, should, and must, through knowledge and will, become master of its moods; in certain possible ways of existing, this may signify a priority of volition and cognition. (*SZ* 136)[17]

But he stresses the limited nature of this "mastery" and our capacity to misunderstand its significance. So the above passage continues:

> Only we must not be misled by this into denying that ontologically mood is a primordial kind of Being for Dasein, in which Dasein is disclosed to itself *prior to* all cognition and volition, and *beyond* their range of disclosure. And furthermore, when we master a mood, we do so by way of a counter-mood; we are never free of moods. (*SZ* 136)[18]

# 4    Criticism of the Decisionist Model Reframed

I mentioned earlier that the decisionist model has been subject to much criticism and key to that criticism is doubt about whether the kind of radical choice that it envisages makes sense, because its radicalism—its "going all the way down"—seems to deprive the chooser of any basis on which this choice might be made. Hence, as Iris Murdoch was amongst the first to ask, "are we really choosing [here] at all?" (1970, 36).

This point has typically been made by saying that the decisionist model deprives the chooser of reasons on the basis of which she might choose. "A choice ... that is not made in the light of reasons," Tugendhat has argued, "is a choice in which I leave how I choose to accident" (Tugendhat 1986, 216).[19] The "liberation" that makes possible this "pure choice," in which I might be thought to "stand alone, in total responsibility and freedom," renders that choice one over which "I may as well toss a coin" (Murdoch 1970, 8, 30, 91). Here "we have to say that it was not I who chose" (Tugendhat 1986, 216). But Heidegger's remarks on affect give another perspective on the "very particular kind of liberation" that seems necessary for the decisionist's choice that "goes all the way down."

"If the will is to be totally free," Murdoch proposes, "the world it moves in must be devoid of normative characteristics" (1970, 42); but equally, if we are to be free to choose how to feel—how to be moved—Heidegger's remarks above suggest we must also be stripped of any sense of things mattering. In seeking to step away from any "taken for granted background framework," we seek to step away from any given way in which the world might touch us, might call for a response. Such a condition is sometimes attacked as one in which Dasein would be paralyzed.[20] But this charge is misleading if it suggests a thwarted desire to move; when we consider decisionist "liberation" through the lens of Dasein's attunement to its world, we see it as instead a condition of stasis: when Dasein becomes free in this sense, one might say it shuts down.

When Heidegger says that entities that matter to us could not be disclosed to a "subject which merely beholds" (*SZ* 341), this may suggest that only through affect are certain features of the world revealed to us—"the unserviceable, resistant, or threatening character [*Bedrohlichkeit*] of that which is ready-to-hand" (*SZ* 137). But his more considered view would seem to be that affect is a fundamental precondition of intentionality as such: it "*makes it possible first of all to direct oneself towards something*" (*SZ* 137). It is not the case that "man is in the first place the rational living being … [who] thinks and wills"; attunement "is not—is never—simply a consequence or side-effect of our thinking, doing and acting"; rather "[i]t is—to put it crudely—the presupposition for such things, the 'medium' within which such things happen" (*FCM* 64, 67–68). "Dasein as Dasein is always already attuned in its very ground" (*FCM* 68, cf. *BCAP* 176); and, hence, "even the purest *theoria* [theory] has not left all moods behind it" (*SZ* 138, cf. *BCAP* 166).[21] In this sense, there is no "subject which merely beholds": such a "subject" wouldn't look in any particular direction or with any particular interest.

So decisionist liberation is not one of a thwarted will or—as Murdoch sometimes puts it—the "wild leap[ing]" of a "giddy" "point of pure will" (Murdoch 1970, 16, 27, 36). Rather as she puts it at other points, such a will is "empty," "substanceless" (Murdoch 1970, 16, 27). In place of unfettered, self-determining subjectivity, we find silence, stasis. Such a Promethean "subject" is free from—has stepped out of—the "medium" within which our thinking, doing and acting happen. But if authenticity in one's affective life is not to be understood through the decisionist's impossible voluntarism "*prior to* all cognition and volition," how else might we understand it? In the rest of the paper, I will sketch two Heideggerian alternatives that instead embrace Dasein's essential *Gestimmtsein*.

# 5 The Standpoint Model

The second model we will consider understands authenticity as the owning of a standpoint. The model comes in a variety of forms, different understandings of what such a "standpoint" is combining with different understandings of what it is to own one.[22] Some envisage authenticity as our making our own particular vocations or life-projects: for example, Somogy Varga has recently depicted "authenticity" as our "integrating our lives by projects that we wholeheartedly endorse" (Varga 2013, 7).[23] Others envisage it as a weddedness to particular roles, commitments or norms.[24] So, for example, the actions of the inauthentic are ruled by different norms as they move from one context to the next, while the actions of the authentic are governed by a set of norms to which they are wedded—which they "own"—which we can then identify as their own.

We find these thoughts at work outside of the Heideggerian literature too. For example, R. M. Hare proposes that "[i]f we were to ask of a person 'What are *his* moral principles?' the way in which we could be most sure of a true answer would be by studying what he *did*" (first emphasis added): "[i]t would be when … he was faced with choices or decisions between alternative courses of action, between alternative answers to the question 'What shall I do?,' that he would reveal in what principles of conduct he really believed" (Hare 1952, 1). Similarly, Christine Korsgaard proposes that "[i]f you choose to run in order to escape your predator, to stand your ground in order to protect your offspring, or to dance for the sheer joy of dancing, then those are your principles, your conception of what is worth doing for what" (2009, 127). What gives sense to the notion that there is such a thing as "*your* conception of what is worth doing for what" and of a person having "*his* moral principles" would then be—at least in part—a consistency in one's "choices or decisions between alternative courses of action." Such a person does not "fall apart," "drop[ping their] projects in the face of the slightest temptation or distraction" (Korsgaard 2009, 177, 175); instead, as Paul Katsafanas has put it, such a person is characterized by "*having commitments*" and "a kind of *diachronic stability*" (2013, 94, 93).

Understandings of authenticity as the owning of a narrative or life-story could also be seen as to some extent instantiating what I am here calling the standpoint model. Charles Guignon contrasts an inauthentic "tumbling into the frenzy and preoccupations of day-to-day existence," with an authentic "life-course" of "continuity and constancy," "a coherent, cumulative narrative" (Guignon 1992, 135; 2000, 89), which we can see as the story of an identifiable "character" with "personality traits, life-styles, roles, or attitudes" that are "definitive of [her] identity" (Guignon 1993, 225).[25] In treating these views—about projects, norms and narratives—as instances of a single model, I set aside differences between them. But I hope that identifying the commonality that this model represents is, nonetheless, of value.

Such a model gives sense to familiar notions mentioned above. For simplicity's sake, I will express these in the idiom of norms. So in acting on its own norms, authentic Dasein can then be said to be "letting its ownmost Self *take action in itself*" and to be acting "of its own accord." It can also be held answerable for its actions in that it sees the same normative considerations as having force across contexts, whereas the inauthentic don't; they cannot be expected to regard an action performed in one context as having normative implications for—say, requiring consistency with—actions performed in others.[26] Rather than impose upon their lives what can be seen as their own standpoint on how to act, the inauthentic fall into line with ways of acting endorsed in the various contexts in which they find themselves; in this way, inauthentic Dasein is "relieve[d] of its choice, its formation of judgments, and its estimation of values."

What then of authentic emotion? In light of our discussion of the first, decisionist model, the second model conspicuously embraces our *Gestimmtsein*. What distinguishes the authentic person would seem to be that the world moves her in a consistent manner: in as much as she owns certain norms, commitments, or projects, she is subject to certain characteristic emotions. To adapt an example from Varga (2011, 72), her readiness for righteous indignation "outlines in advance" that the principle of social injustice matters to her. Similarly, the "certain constancy" that Anthony Rudd's narrativist account of the "serious ethical agent" depicts her as distinctively exhibiting is recognizably an affective one:

Someone who possesses the virtues of e.g. generosity and compassion in private life cannot simply turn them off on entering the office, and put on the "virtues" of competitiveness, ruthlessness, efficiency etc. Someone who could ... would be someone hollow at the core, or a mere chameleon, changing to fit in with any social situation. (2009, 69)

Now there may be some truth in this, but it can't be the whole truth.[27] Consider the following situation. A student comes to see me because he didn't get the mark for which he'd hoped for an essay. Now I'm no mere chameleon: I don't turn off my well-known generosity and compassion on entering the office. So, moved by my characteristic generosity, I say "Go on, have a few extra marks!" Or moved by my characteristic compassion, I say "Oh, the mark really upset you, didn't it? Go on then, have a few extra marks!" But this doesn't seem right, and the reason is that I ought to be moved by a few other things here, including professionalism and a sense of fairness. The second model does not have the faults of the first model: there is no Promethean standing apart from or above our *Gestimmsein*. Instead the model very much embraces the fact that "Dasein as Dasein is always already attuned in its very ground"; it identifies the distinction between authenticity and inauthenticity as one between constant and inconstant attunement. But there may be a subtler form of Prometheanism at work here, a standing apart from or above another essential feature of the life of creatures like us.

# 6    Normative and Emotional Pluralism

That feature is that real human lives are subject to multiple norms interacting in complex ways. Some trump others in some situations and are trumped in others by others. From this perspective, our predicament is one in which we are attuned to multiple, competing normative demands, which we must weigh in each situation in which we find ourselves to establish which matters most *here*. The world matters to us and summons us in multiple ways and if the standpoint model requires that we somehow silence all but a few of those emotions if we are to be authentic it seems to offer neither an appealing nor a very realistic picture. *Some* individuals may be particularly given to particular emotions—anger, contempt, mirth, et cetera. But they aren't subject to *only* those emotions; and nor do such individuals seem distinctively exemplary of the characteristics ascribed to the *Eigentlich*—"answerability," for example.

It is unfair to suggest that accounts such as Rudd's and Varga's have no appreciation of this pluralist intuition. For instance, Varga insists that authenticity also requires that we be "open to eventual changes" in the projects to which we are wholeheartedly wedded (2011, 72).[28] But as I have argued elsewhere,[29] Varga's view still clashes with our pluralist intuition in thinking that this openness should be openness to the possibility that we might need to replace our wholeheartedly endorsed "projects" with others—a "reemplotment" of one's "life as a whole" and "an essential modification of [one's] basic commitments" (2013, 117–118).

The multi-dimensionality that I have in mind is that of my being a son, a father, a husband, a brother, a friend, a neighbor, a colleague, a teacher, a philosopher, a member of a team, a supporter of a team, a member of a political party, a believer in freedom, in justice, in beneficence, and in manners, a lover of nature and of art, et cetera, et cetera, et cetera. From this perspective, there is something fundamentally fanciful about the idea that I might—and authenticity might require me to—wholeheartedly embrace one or two of these normative commitments and renounce all the rest. That does not mean—equally fancifully—that I must see them as all generally equally important. Generally speaking, I may well think that the obligations that go with being a father are more important than those that go with being a member of a team. But in particular situations, the latter may outweigh the former—such as if the cup final clashes with my son's desire to see the Lego Movie for the fifth time.[30] So when obligations $x$, $y$ and $z$ clash, the answer to the question of which I should strive to meet is not "$x$, because I am wholeheartedly committed to $x$" but "It depends," followed by an attempt to evaluate which matters most *here*.

Our third model explores whether Heideggerian authenticity might have less to do with a constant narrative or owned projects or roles and more with addressing the need to evaluate and weigh together the multiple normative demands to which we as human beings are subject. I mentioned above that Rudd acknowledges the pluralist intuition: he does so when he insists that "[a] typical life narrative will not be a story of the pursuit of one single goal, but the story of how the protagonist attempts … to coordinate his/her different projects and goals with one another" (2009, 65). The thought behind the third model is that what Rudd here adds to a standpoint model of authenticity might itself come closer to capturing Heideggerian authenticity—not as a supplement to a standpoint model but in its place. The penultimate section of the paper will sketch this third model, which understands emotional conflict not as an inauthentic failure of wholeheartedness but as a fact of life, one which the authentic address and the inauthentic do not.[31]

# 7 The All-Things-Considered Judgment Model

A concept I have used elsewhere in articulating the third model is that of all-things-considered judgment. Our third model understands Heideggerian authenticity as a responsiveness not just to the particular aspect of my situation that would strike a holder of office *a*, the pursuer of goal *b*, the adherent of norm *c* or project *d*, but instead a responsiveness to all of those aspects at once and to the need to adjudicate between them. Such responsiveness is demanded of me because I may be the holder of office *a, and* the pursuer of *b, as well as* the adherent of *c and* of *d*; and the response for which this normative plurality calls is an all-things-considered judgment (ATCJ).

But why think of such a judgment as *self*-expression, of judging and acting on one's own behalf? Consider a judgment that falls short of being all-things-considered:

1. From the point of view of someone pursuing goal *w* or an occupant of role *x*, what ought to be done here is *y*.

In response to my uttering (1), I can be asked "Yes, but what do *you* think ought to be done?" The same question does not seem to make sense, however, when made in response to my uttering instead

2. All things considered, what ought to be done here is $y$.

Something akin to Moore's paradox arises if I follow my uttering of (2) with "… though *I* think that what ought to be done is $z$." (1) does not take into account—is not true to—some of what I think or value, which might then intelligibly find expression in a subsequent endorsement of $z$. There is no room for such an endorsement with (2), in which, one might say, I have already expressed *myself*, as I do not with (1).[32]

Dasein that acts on judgments of the form of (2) thus "let[s] its ownmost Self *take action in itself*" and acts "of its own accord." It also makes itself "answerable" in that, were it instead merely to utter (1), it would take no stand on what it thinks ought to be done but only on what one ought to do *if* one pursues goal $w$ or occupies role $x$. In light of uttering (2), however, there will be a manifest incongruity for which I can reasonably be held accountable if I fail then to perform $y$. The call on me to perform y to which my uttering (1) gives rise is mediated precisely in that *all things considered* I may not believe that act best; and what sets in place determinate implications for how I can be expected to act is only the latter—ATC—judgment.

Like commentators who have turned to talk of "narratives," "norms," "vocations" or "commitments," I turn here to a concept that Heidegger does not use in any explicit fashion; I do so—as they do—because I believe that using it helps us understand Heidegger's texts, where simply reusing Heidegger's terms does not. As with the other models, I won't attempt here to make a proper case for its interpretive plausibility; instead I have attempted to do so elsewhere.[33] But I will mention briefly two elements of that case here.

One focus is Heidegger's discussion of "guilt" and another is his detailed and extended readings of perhaps the most important discussion of ATCJ in the history of philosophy, Aristotle's discussion of *phronesis*.[34] There we see Heidegger propose that, for a person to "*himself* bear witness"—to "speak *with his person* [*mit seiner Person*]"— he must not merely "recommend something as profitable"—for the pursuit of goal $x$ or the fulfilment of role $y$—but instead must "say what is best" (*BCAP* 112); only on the basis of a judgment of "the full situation within which [he] act[s]"—of "what is best among the possible actions" that that situation makes available (*PS* 95, 101)—does a person "act from out of himself" (*BCAP* 123), does "the acting person as such" "burst forth" (*PS* 103).

Key to Heidegger's notion of "guilt," on the other hand, is that Dasein, which "always stands in one possibility or another," "constantly is *not*"—and has "waived"—"other possibilities": "[f]reedom ... *is* only in the choice of *one* possibility—that is, in tolerating one's not having chosen the others and one's not being able to choose them" (*SZ* 285). For a finite creature,

> Every action is at the same time something marked by guilt. For the possibilities of action are limited in comparison with the demands of conscience, so that every action that is successfully carried out produces conflicts. To choose self-responsibility, then, is to become guilty in an absolute sense. Insofar as I am at all, I become guilty whenever I act in any sense. (*WDR* 169)

Here too we see the ATCJM's guiding pluralist intuition. Our lives are normatively multi-dimensional and, as finite creatures, we need, nonetheless, to resolve that plurality into a unity in the moment of action: "[e]very action is ... marked by guilt" because the "demands of conscience" outstrip "the possibilities of action."

## 8   Owning Emotions and All Things Considered

But what then—for the ATCJM—is authentic emotion? I will address that question by considering an objection that the model invites. There are all sorts of worries one might have about the model exegetically— for example, what story does it then tell about authenticity's temporality and its place in the broader *Being and Time* project[35]—but also about the very idea of ATCJ: for example, just how does one responsibly might make such a judgment, when—as normative pluralism seems to require—there is no decision procedure that one might follow?[36] But I will consider here only one such worry, which will lead us back to the notion of authentic affect, and bring into play a theme from Heidegger's discussion of emotion that we have so far overlooked and that lacks an obvious construal through the first and second model. As well as revealing how the world matters to us, Heidegger proposes that "it is just as everyday a matter for Dasein not to 'give in' ['*nachgibt*'] to such moods—in other words, not to follow up [*nachgeht*] their disclosure and allow itself to be brought before that which is disclosed": "Dasein for the most part evades the Being which is disclosed in [such a] mood" (*SZ* 134–135).

The objection I will consider is: doesn't the ATCJM make authentic existence too deliberative, too intellectualized? Where else can all this talk of "judgment" and "consideration" lead us, one might ask; and isn't Bill Blattner right to insist that "[d]eliberation is a decidedly secondary phenomenon for Heidegger, ... rather than a basic form of Dasein's activity" (2013, 332)? I think Blattner is right: a key aim of Heidegger's is to reveal preconditions on our being able to adopt propositional attitudes, deliberate, et cetera, preconditions that the philosophical tradition has generally overlooked in focusing instead on those conditioned phenomena. But I think that the ATCJM accommodates such an outlook as long as we do not adopt an overly intellectualized vision of *it*.

Inasmuch as ATCJ is deliberative, it is *how* the authentic deliberate that makes them authentic. Fundamental here is, so to speak, the breadth of one's horizon; to use an expression from the mood discussion, it is one's "range of disclosure," one's capacity to look at one's situation in all its multi-dimensional concretion rather than myopically assimilating it to how it manifests itself to the occupant of role $x$ or the pursuer of goal $y$. So, in a sense, deliberation and consideration indeed are "decidedly secondary phenomena" for Heidegger, as indeed is "judgment," because he is focused on *how* we deliberate—consider—and how that makes ATC judgment possible.[37] More "basic forms of Dasein's activity" here are its drawing together into one (perhaps deliberative) conversation the many aspects of its concrete situation, a meeting that the inauthentic never convene. But the thought on which I wish to focus here is that talk of "judgment" and "consideration" ought not to blind us to the possibility that the openness to our situation that ATCJ requires of us is also an *emotional* openness.[38]

Let's recall Heidegger's proposal that, through affect, "Dasein is disclosed to itself *prior to* all cognition and volition," "outlin[ing] in advance" how Dasein, as Being-in-the-world, has "already submitted itself to having entities within-the-world 'matter' to it", something that could not be disclosed to a "subject which merely beholds." From this perspective, ATCJ is challenging because it requires me to acknowledge the full range of emotions that my situation elicits from me, corresponding as they do to the many ways in which it matters to me. ATCJ would require that I "own" these (potentially many) feelings and what they tell me about the normative demands that my situation makes. The need to act in the face of distinctly mixed feelings—tracking the plurality of ways in which we have "already submitted" ourselves to the world mattering to us—is not the fate of the inauthentic and less-than-wholehearted but is instead a need that the authentic are distinctively ready to meet. For our third model, we express ourselves not when all of our emotions happily happen to fall into alignment, but instead when we make ATCJs about which we may then have plenty of misgivings.[39]

To put flesh on these bare bones, consider what inauthenticity might look like for this third model. Rather than listen to my friend's worries, I head home to drive my son to rugby practice, on the grounds—when challenged—that "I've got to take care of my family!" And, of course, I do have to take care of my family; so, on a superficial level, I am beyond reproach: I am acting in line with a norm that is generally accepted in my society, by myself and indeed by my friend. But in fact I am seeking here to be "relieve[d]"—"disburdened"—"of [my] choice, [my] formation of judgments, and [my] estimation of values" (*HCT* 247) by falling back on this background general acceptance that one indeed ought to take care of one's family. Such a background acceptance cannot, in fact, bear this burden because our society generally accepts a plurality of norms, including that one ought to take care of one's friends. In my inattention to the other demands that my situation places upon me, and that we all generally agree we should meet, I resist the need to resolve those many demands into an ATCJ, and my invocation of a generally-accepted norm of my society only disguises that fact rather than providing such a resolution. To use expressions from Heidegger's discussions of *phronesis*, I here embrace the role of "a slave of circumstances and of everyday importunities" (*PS* 89); I "take easy refuge" in the "supposedly indispensable resolution" of some "mundane task or other" (*PIA* 92); and what this requires of me is, I suggest, an evasion of my full range of emotions—here, a "closing off" or a "managing" into marginality of my awareness that my friend's worries matter. Were I to make an ATCJ, I might conclude that these matter less than my son's needs; but when inauthentic, I close myself off from the emotions through which I appreciate those needs and, with them, the need for an ATCJ.[40]

Authenticity requires then that "the dominance" of some "public way in which things have been interpreted"—the general acceptance that one must indeed take care of one's family (or one's friends, or one's work, etc.)—must not be allowed to "prescribe[] one's *Befindlichkeit*"; to allow such a way to be "decisive ... for the possibilities of attunement [*die Möglichkeiten des Gestimmtseins*]—that is, for the basic way in which [I] let[] the world 'matter' to" me (*SZ* 169–170)—is to close off the multiple "demands of conscience" that outstrip "the possibilities of action," and thus to close off the need for ATCJ. That, in turn, is to "close [my]self off from"—refuse to be "*summon[ed]* to—my 'ownmost Being-guilty'" (*SZ* 269, 286) and the need for *myself* to be "decisive." Instead I allow myself to be dominated—"enslaved" by that which is "supposedly indispensable" rather than acting for "what is best."

The openness upon which ATCJ rests requires then that I resist the temptation merely to feel about my situation as "one feels" about "such situations" and its capacity to blind me to the normative multi-dimensionality of my concrete situation—of the *many* things that "one must do."[41] To resist the temptation to be "relieved" by *das Man* "of its choice, its formation of judgments, and its estimation of values," Dasein must then remain open to the full range of ways in which its situation "summons" it: "when we master a mood"—here a generally-accepted and exculpatory public sentiment about "how one must act"—"we do so by way of a counter-mood," by openness to the other "demands of conscience" of which my emotional life speaks.[42] In this light, and in contrast with an intellectualized vision of ATCJ, such judgment requires that I be open to my situation in its concretion in allowing my many emotions a voice in my deliberations, acknowledging rather than evading the full range of ways in which I am already attuned—tuned—to my situation, the many ways my situation already matters to me, touches me and moves me, whether I wish to acknowledge that or not. According to our third model then, inauthenticity is precisely "*an evasive turning-away*" (*SZ* 136) from the fullness of our affective life and the "guilt"-laden normative pluralism that it—only in its fullness—discloses.[43]

# Notes

1. References to works by Heidegger use acronyms given in the Abbreviations section, followed by page numbers. References to *Being and Time* use the pagination of the German original (*SZ*), given in both available English translations. Although I give references to their locations in published translations, I will often use my own translations of passages from Heidegger.
2. See Salmela (2005) for an overview of some of this literature.
3. Cf. Macquarrie and Robinson's note to *SZ* 43, Guignon (2004, 169) and Inwood (1997, 21–22).
4. See McManus (2015a, forthcoming-b).
5. See McManus (forthcoming-a).
6. See *HCT* 255: "We must ... totally give up any attempt to interpret *Befindlichkeit* as a finding of inner lived experiences or any sort of apprehension of an inner something." Similarly, Heidegger insists that *Stimmung* "is *not* at all '*inside*' in some interiority," "in some sort of soul" (*FCM* 66). Cf. *HCT* 255, *SZ* 136–137, and *BCAP* 119–120 and 133: "the *pathe* are not 'psychic experiences', are not 'in consciousness', but are a being-taken of human beings in their full being-in-the-world."
7. See Macquarrie and Robinson's Note 3 on p. 172 of their translation of *Sein and Zeit*.
8. See also, from the same year, *CT*, and, in particular, 26–28.
9. Cf. *CT* 27: "Dasein Is Its *There* [Da]."
10. See, e.g., *SZ* 127 and 288.
11. The popularity of this reading of Heidegger is surely based to some extent on its assimilation of his thought to that of Sartre, whose work was translated earlier and—at least until recently—has been read more widely. See, e.g., Sartre's notion of "an original choice which originally creates all values and all motives which can guide us" (1969, 465).
12. Cf. *CT* 26–27, 29, *HCT* 256 and *FCM* 64 and 283.

13. Similar thoughts can be seen at work in Rorty (1980), de Sousa (1987), and Ridley (1997). Heidegger's anticipation of a number of themes in the current literature is probably traceable in part to his Aristotelianism (to an aspect of which I return briefly below). This anticipated the "revivification of the Aristotelian approach that rescued [analytic] philosophy of emotion from a dark age" (Ridley 1997, 165).

14. In its *Befindlichkeit*, "Dasein is always brought before itself, and has always found itself, not in the sense of coming across itself by perceiving itself, but in the sense of finding itself in the mood that it has [*nicht als wahrnehmendes Sich-vor-finden, sondern als gestimmtes Sichbefinde*]" (*SZ* 135).

15. Cf. *SZ* 139, 161, 297, 348, 383, and 412 and *HCT* 254.

16. Cf. *SZ* 135, 144, 148, and 188.

17. Cf. *SZ* 139 on the orator's need to "understand the possibilities of moods in order to rouse them and guide them aright."

18. Cf. *FCM* 68 and *SZ* 134: "in every case Dasein always has some mood [*gestimmt ist*]."

19. Cf. *MFL* 116: "We know possibilities of preference only in areas where there are decisions about value or lack of value, higher or lower value."

20. See, e.g., Dreyfus (2005, xx).

21. There are different ways in which one might understand this claim which draw on different themes in Heidegger's depiction of science. One theme is that "when we look theoretically at what is just present-at-hand, it does not show itself purely as it looks unless this *theoria* lets it come towards us in a *tranquil* tarrying alongside" (*SZ* 138). But another is that "theoretical research is not without a *praxis* of its own" (*SZ* 358), a mode of behaving and responding to the world illustrated, for example, by a concern that experimental techniques and methods of measurement be properly applied; to adapt John Haugeland's memorable words, "[n]o one who simply did not give a damn ... could be a proper scientist" (2013, 204).

22. For example, if one owns it through a "thoroughgoing" "pure choice," this second model arguably collapses into the first. Another option is illustrated by Rebecca Kukla's view that we own norms "in virtue of our recognition of their force," their "legitimacy" (Kukla 2002, 4, 15). (Cf. John Haugeland's proposal in his early work that an authentic person's standpoint is "critically realized" by her "find[ing] and root[ing] out ... inconsistenc[ies] in [her] overall self-understanding" [Haugeland 2013, 14–15].) The version of the model I have defended previously and sketch

further here focuses instead on the notion of a standpoint being owned by virtue of its consistently informing one's life. But I won't consider the strengths and weaknesses of these different views of ownership here.

23. Cf. Crowe (2006, 10, 188) and Flynn (2006, 122–123).

24. The "owning of norms" is an important theme in the work of Steven Galt Crowell; see, e.g., the essays collected in his 2013.

25. It may be worth noting that another familiar theme from the work of Rorty and de Sousa is that emotions possess distinctive narrative structures (see de Sousa 1987; Rorty 1980). But Guignon's concern with the "continuity and constancy" of a life as a whole seems to address a broader structure.

26. Cf. the view that David Velleman ascribes to Kant, for which "a unified, persisting point of-view [is] defined by a constant framework of reasons": "In order to be a person, you must have an approach to the world that is sufficiently coherent and constant to qualify as a single, continuing point-of-view. And part of what gives you a single, continuing point-of-view is your acceptance of particular considerations as having the force of reasons whenever they are true" (Velleman 2006, 22, 23).

27. Another respect in which this model cannot be the whole truth emerges when we consider constancy that results from brainwashing or other forms of manipulation. The model would seem to need at least supplementation with a version of the kind of "historical" condition that is familiar from the philosophy of action literature, stipulating that knowledge of how one came to be moved by a standpoint must not undermine one's being so moved. See, e.g., Fischer and Ravizza's "mechanism ownership" (1998, ch. 8), Katsafanas' "equilibrium" (2013, ch. 5), and—for an application directly to affective authenticity—Salmela (2005, 212–214).

28. Cf. Salmela's "integrity view of emotional authenticity," according to which "authentic emotions are congruent with, or integral to one's *self*, not just passing episodes that occur in one's body and mind," but for which "it is [also] essential that one's coherent patterns of emotions, beliefs, and values remain open to revision and change" (2005, 210, 217, 224).

29. See McManus (forthcoming-a).

30. Cf. Chang's 'nominal-notable comparisons' (1997, 14–15) and the Extreme Comparison Argument of Lord and Maguire (2016, 5–6).

31. Although I won't pursue further here the virtues or vices of standpoint models or—what are with respect to the typology presented

here—hybrid models like Rudd's and Varga's, McManus (forthcoming-a) presents interpretive worries about their plausibility as readings of Heidegger.

32. Compare the role that the notion of ATC judgment plays in the philosophical literature on self-control. An agent lacks that control when she performs "uncompelled intentional action that, as [he himself] recognizes, is contrary to a decisive better judgment that he consciously holds" (Mele 1995, 16), such a judgment being one "based on ... a consideration of the totality of the agent's pertinent beliefs and values," an "*all things considered*" judgment (Mele 1998, 5–6). Only if an agent acts contrary to such a judgment can the lack of *self*-control over which this literature puzzles emerge.

33. See McManus (forthcoming-a), upon which this section draws.

34. See *PICA* 129–130 and 134–136, *BCAP* 111–115, 123–130, 169, and *PS* 33–41, 93–120.

35. For an examination of the latter worry, see McManus (2015b). Another obvious lacuna in my discussion here is how the different models discussed would understand anxiety, a *Grundstimmung* that obviously has a crucial part to play in Heidegger's discussions of authenticity. McManus (2015a) shows how the first model understands this notion and presents one way in which our second model might. I believe that the third model would draw on parts of that account (those discussed in that paper's sects. 5–8) but a full account of the third model's understanding of anxiety is a topic for another day.

36. For a brief consideration of this worry, see McManus (forthcoming-a, sect. 11).

37. Heidegger certainly does associate the natural German equivalent for "judgment"—"*Urteil*"—with that tip of the iceberg upon which philosophers have unwisely focused in taking propositional attitudes to be fundamental to Dasein's intentionality (see, e.g., *SZ* 32–33, 214); and my use of "judgment" in articulating the ATCJM might be seen as threatening to undo Heidegger's good work. But, as I argue above, a proper appreciation of ATCJ also depends on appreciating what lies below the water-line. According to the case that McManus (2012) presents, this is in line with Heidegger's broader attitude towards the concept of "*Urteil*".

38. Cf. *CT* 26–27 on how *Befindlichkeit* is not a "theoretical act of understanding" but something that "holds Dasein's particular situation in its entirety in the there [*hält gerade die volle jeweilige Lage des Daseins im Da*]."

39. A rival interpretation of what the ATCJM should understand as owned affect would be a Frankfurtian vision according to which we "own" the emotion that corresponds to the particular "demand of conscience" upon which we do decide to act. "Through his action in deciding," the emotion indicative of the demand acted upon *being* such a demand—of its mattering to the agent—"has become his own in a way in which it was not unequivocally his own before"; the agent "dissociates himself from" those emotions that correspond to the "demands" upon which he chooses not to act: he determines the latter to be "external to his will" (Frankfurt 1988, 170, 174; 1999, 99). But this strikes me as an odd, forced conclusion. It seems more natural to me to say that the emotions upon which one does not act are still very much one's own; instead I suggest that "emotions from which we dissociate ourselves" is a label much more naturally applied to those we refuse to acknowledge by refusing to make ATCJs; and that this is inauthenticity in our affective lives. From this perspective, the account of owned affect that the ATCJM yields is more naturally seen not as identifying which of one's emotions are one's authentic emotions, but rather what it is to have an authentic affective life.

40. Cf. Heidegger's discussion of the need to "awaken" attunements and of our capacity to allow them instead to "sleep". See, e.g., *FCM* 60, 62–63, and cf. *BCAP* 68–69.

41. This vision differs from, but—I believe—is compatible with, a stress on openness to what Alison Jaggar calls "outlaw emotions," emotions which are possible if "the hegemony that our society exercises over people's emotional constitution is not total" and which perhaps "may provide the first indications"—"preced[ing] our conscious recognition"—"that something is wrong with … accepted understandings of how things are" (1989, 166–167). (Frankfurt too talks of our "extruding entirely" an affect "as an outlaw" (1988, 170) but Jaggar would seem to be calling for an extra level of caution in our doing so.)

42. Such an account also echoes the account of "owned affectivity" that Withy has extracted from Heidegger's 1924 Aristotle lectures, lectures that also—as noted above—interestingly examine *phronesis*. Withy characterizes our "owning affectivity" as a condition in which we "resist averageness" and instead "hold[] ourselves open and let[] ourselves be moved": "In closing ourselves to the pull of averageness and holding ourselves open to the situation, we set ourselves *out for* being touched

and *against* the customary ways of being so. We choose or resolve to be open" (2015, 29–30).

43. Earlier versions of this paper were presented at the "Heidegger on Affect" conference held at University College Dublin in May 2017 and the "Owning our Emotions" conference hosted by the Open University and the Institute of Philosophy in September 2016. For helpful comments, I would like to thank Lilian Alweiss, Sophie-Grace Chappell, Darshan Cowles, Dan Dahlstrom, Manuel Dries, Christos Hadjioannou, Niall Keane, Kristján Kristjánsson, Irene McMullin, Nikola Mirkovic, Dermot Moran, Mahon O'Brien, Carolyn Price, Thomas Sheehan, Jonathan Webber, and other audience members.

# References

Blattner, W. 2013. "Authenticity and Resoluteness." In *The Cambridge Companion to Being and Time*, edited by M. Wrathall, 320–337. Cambridge: Cambridge University Press.

Bordo, S. R. 1987. *The Flight to Objectivity: Essays on Cartesianism and Culture.* Albany, NY: State University of New York Press.

Chang, R. 1997. "Introduction." In *Incommensurability, Incomparability, and Practical Reason*, edited by R. Chang. Cambridge, MA: Harvard University Press.

Cooper, D. E. 1997. "Wittgenstein, Heidegger and Humility," *Philosophy* 72: 105–123.

Crowe, B. D. 2006. *Heidegger's Religious Origins: Destruction and Authenticity.* Indianapolis: Indiana University Press.

Crowell, S. G. 2013. *Normativity and Phenomenology in Husserl and Heidegger.* Cambridge: Cambridge University Press.

de Sousa, R. 1987. *The Rationality of Emotion.* Cambridge: MIT Press.

Dreyfus, H. L. 2005. "Foreword." In *Time and Death*, edited by H. White. Aldershot: Ashgate.

Fischer, J. M., and Ravizza, M. 1998. *Responsibility and Control: A Theory of Moral Responsibility.* Cambridge: Cambridge University Press.

Flynn, T. R. 2006. *Existentialism: A Very Short Introduction.* Oxford: Oxford University Press.

Frankfurt, H. 1988. *The Importance of What We Care About.* Cambridge: Cambridge University Press.

Frankfurt, H. 1999. *Necessity, Volition and Love.* Cambridge: Cambridge University Press.

Friedman, M. 2000. *A Parting of the Ways: Carnap, Cassirer, and Heidegger.* Peru, Il: Open Court Publishing.

Guignon, C. 1992. "History and Commitment in Early Heidegger." In *Heidegger, a Critical Reader,* edited by H. L. Dreyfus and H. Hall. Oxford: Blackwell.

Guignon, C. 1993. "Authenticity, Moral Values, and Psychotherapy." In *The Cambridge Companion to Heidegger,* edited by C. Guignon. Cambridge: Cambridge University Press.

Guignon, C. 2000. "Philosophy and Authenticity: Heidegger's Search for a Ground for Philosophizing." In *Heidegger, Authenticity, and Modernity, Essays in Honour of Hubert L. Dreyfus,* Vol. 1, edited by M. Wrathall and J. Malpas. Cambridge: MIT Press.

Guignon, C. 2004. *On Being Authentic.* London: Routledge.

Hare, R. M. 1952. *The Language of Morals.* Oxford: Clarendon Press.

Haugeland, J. 2013. *Dasein Disclosed.* Edited by J. Rouse. Cambridge, MA: Harvard University Press.

Inwood, M. 1997. *Heidegger.* Oxford: Oxford University Press.

Jaggar, A. M. 1989. "Love and Knowledge: Emotion in Feminist Epistemology." *Inquiry* 32: 151–176.

Katsafanas, P. 2013. *Agency and the Foundations of Ethics: Nietzschean Constitutivism.* Oxford: Oxford University Press.

Korsgaard C. M. 2009. *Self-Constitution: Agency, Identity, and Integrity.* Oxford: Oxford University Press.

Kukla, R. 2002. "The Ontology and Temporality of Conscience." *Continental Philosophy Review* 35: 1–34.

Lord, E., and B. Maguire. 2016. "An Opinionated Guide to the Weight of Reasons." In *Weighing Reasons,* edited by E. Lord and B. Maguire. Oxford: Oxford University Press.

McManus, D. 2012. *Heidegger and the Measure of Truth.* Oxford: Oxford University Press.

McManus D. 2015a. "Anxiety, Choice and Responsibility in Heidegger's Account of Authenticity." In *Heidegger, Authenticity and the Self: Themes from Division Two of Being and Time,* edited by D. McManus. London: Routledge.

McManus D. 2015b. "On Being as a Whole and Being-a-Whole." In *Division III of Being and Time: Heidegger's Unanswered Question of Being,* edited by L. Braver. Cambridge, MA: MIT Press.

McManus D. Forthcoming-a. "On a Judgment of One's Own: Heideggerian Authenticity, Standpoints, and All Things Considered." *Mind*.

McManus D. Forthcoming-b. "Vision, Norm and Openness: Some Themes in Heidegger and Murdoch." In *Novelty and Seeing-As*, edited by M. Beaney, B. Harrington, and D. Shaw. London: Routledge.

Mele, A. 1995. *Autonomous Agents*. Oxford: Oxford University Press.

Mele, A. 1998. *Irrationality*. Oxford: Oxford University Press.

Murdoch, I. 1970. *The Sovereignty of Good*. London: Routledge.

Ridley, A. 1997. "Emotion and Feeling." *Aristotelian Society Supplementary Volume* 71: 163–176.

Rorty, A. 1980. *Explaining Emotions*. Berkeley: University of California Press.

Rudd, A. 2009. "In Defence of Narrative." *European Journal of Philosophy* 17: 60–75.

Salmela, M. 2005. "What Is Emotional Authenticity?" *Journal for the Theory of Social Behaviour* 35: 209–230.

Sartre, J. P. 1969. *Being and Nothingness*. Translated by H. Barnes. London: Methuen.

Tugendhat, E. 1986. *Self-Consciousness and Self-Determination*. Translated by P. Stern. Cambridge, MA: MIT Press.

Varga, S. 2011. "Existential Choices: To What Degree Is Who We Are a Matter of Choice?" *Continental Philosophy Review* 44: 65–79.

Varga, S. 2013. *Authenticity as an Ethical Ideal*. London: Routledge.

Velleman, J. D. 2006. *Self to Self*. Cambridge: Cambridge University Press.

Withy, K. 2015. "Owned Emotions: Affective Excellence in Heidegger on Aristotle." In *Heidegger, Authenticity and the Self*, edited by D. McManus. London: Routledge.

# 7

# Finding Oneself, Called

## Katherine Withy

"*Wie befinden Sie sich?*" -- "How are you doing?" -- "How do you find [*befinden*] yourself?"

To *find oneself* is, colloquially, to be open to "'how one is, and how one is faring'" (*SZ* 134).[1] One might be *going great!*, *savoring the cool breeze*, or *desperate to return to sleep*. Being open to how one is faring belongs to the aspect of our being that Heidegger calls *Befindlichkeit*, findingness. I will call it *Befinden*, finding.[2] 'Finding' is Heidegger's successor to 'affectivity', and it belongs to his successor to 'consciousness': being open, or disclosing. Along with finding, disclosing is also understanding (*Verstehen*) and discoursing (*Reden*) (or, sometimes, falling [*Verfallen*]). Although finding, understanding, and discoursing are equiprimordial, Heidegger tends to sideline discoursing and to privilege understanding, which is the projective and futural aspect of our being open. By projecting ourselves forward into some identity, we take a stand on who we are and open up a world of meaning.

K. Withy (✉)
Georgetown University, Washington, DC, USA
e-mail: kaw84@georgetown.edu

© The Author(s) 2019
C. Hadjioannou (ed.), *Heidegger on Affect*, Philosophers in Depth,
https://doi.org/10.1007/978-3-030-24639-6_7

Finding, in contrast, is associated with passivity, affectivity, and the past. Although Heidegger discusses at some length modes of finding such as angst, boredom, and fear, his account of finding as such is relatively underdeveloped.

Both Heidegger and his readers typically approach finding through the phenomenon of mood (*Stimmung*). Mood is an ontic expression or manifestation of our finding being-open, and many readers (more or less explicitly) take Heidegger's claim that "[w]hat we indicate *ontologically* by the term 'finding' is *ontically* [...] our mood" (*SZ* 134) to mean that mood is the *only* ontic expression of finding, or at least that the two always travel together. But to approach finding exclusively or even primarily through mood is problematic, since it diminishes the fact that there are modes of finding other than mood. Heidegger mentions sensing (*SZ* 137), and there might in principle be others. To think finding solely in terms of mood thus offers a restricted view on it that might lead us to miss the full scope of the phenomenon or to import features of mood illegitimately into the characterization of finding. Lacking a full and clear view of the nature of finding, we also risk a distorted perspective on mood, since we lack its proper context. Thus, for example, Heidegger's account of mood has been criticized for not tracking the folk-psychological distinction between emotion and mood and for not elaborating on the necessary role of the body in mood.[3] But while centring the body and tracking folk psychology might be desiderata of a theory of moods as affects, are they also desiderata of a theory of moods as modes of finding? The answer is not obvious.

To understand Heidegger's analysis of finding and how to think moods and other modes of it (§5), I analyze the nature of finding as a dimension of disclosing—one which, in principle, may express itself ontically in different ways. I identify one reason that something like finding must be present in Heidegger's account (§1), and I outline how finding opens us up to ourselves (§§1–2), to the world (§4), and to entities (§3). I argue that to be finding is to find ourselves called by both vocations and the solicitings of entities, and I show how these are related through the disclosing of understanding.

# 1    Existentiell Self-Disclosing: Finding Myself Called to Be Me

Heidegger analyzes both finding and understanding by considering how they open us (i) to ourselves (self-disclosing), (ii) to the world as a space of possible intelligibility (world-disclosing), and (iii) to entities, intelligible as that and what they are (discovering). In brief, his account of understanding is this: (i) we project ourselves onto, or take up, some identity—such as entrepreneur, grandparent, or coffee drinker. This identity (ii) serves as a 'for-the-sake-of-which' (*Worumwillen*, cf. Aristotle's *hou heneka*) that determines and organizes all the possible ways in which entities can be (meaningful to us)—as useful for, detrimental to, irrelevant to, etc., living out our particular identity. On the basis of these possible ways of being (meaningful), we (iii) make sense of particular things as useful, detrimental, irrelevant and so on. Thus, for example, if I take up the identity of *entrepreneur*, the world of entrepreneurship opens up for me, in terms of which I can discover (among other things) venture capital, lines of credit, and public relations disasters.

But why do I take up the project of being an entrepreneur in the first place? Why not that of office worker, or stay-at-home parent, or backyard tinkerer? Obviously, my talents and aptitude suit me to some identities and not others—and some identities might be ruled out by other identities I have already taken up. But why did I take up *those* identities in the first place? And why do I pick *this* identity from the suite of those to which I am suited? I do so because I am *called* to. Our identities are vocations (L. *vocāre*, to call, to summon)—not necessarily in the sense that they are our deepest, truest callings, but at least in the sense that they 'speak' to us. (If, for example, my profession or my socially-given gender does not speak to me in this way, then it is merely a social role that I inhabit and not an identity onto which I project). Finding myself called to a vocation is necessary for me to project myself onto that way of being me. Otherwise, there would be no reason for my projecting to seize upon one identity rather than another.

The call to a vocation is delivered by the call of conscience. Conscience is introduced in Division II of *BT* to show that it is existentielly possible to relate to death authentically. As an instance of disclosing, conscience involves finding, understanding, and discoursing. It is discoursing insofar as it is a *call*—although one that speaks silently and without determinate words or content. It does not chide us for some infraction but summons us to ourselves: it calls us *from* our authentic being *to* some possible way of being us, upon which we resolve. Resolutely projecting onto this possibility of being is hearing the summons of conscience and is the understanding moment of conscience's disclosing. Heidegger argues that when this projecting is carried out in anticipation of death, it is most fully itself and the case of Dasein projecting is authentic.

There are many possibilities of being, or identities, available to take up from the public world. How is it decided which of these we are to resolve upon? Despite Heidegger's voluntaristic language in this chapter, the identity that we take up is not chosen but given, and so found: "On what is it [sc. Dasein] to resolve? *Only* the resolution itself can give the answer" (*SZ* 298). What we resolve upon is given—and given in the resolution itself. It is given as that which has already made a claim on us, that which has already called us to resolve upon it. Even, and perhaps especially, when we go through a long deliberative period about who to be and which identities to take up, what we describe as the final moment of choice is (to a greater or lesser degree) experienced as a moment of being chosen—of receiving a call that "comes *from* me and yet *from beyond me*" (*SZ* 275).

To receive a call like that of a vocation is to hearken (*horchen*) to it (cf. *SZ* 163). While to hear is to understand (*SZ* 163) (and this is why hearing the call of conscience is resolute projecting), to hearken is to listen, to receive, to prick one's ears up at the call and allow oneself to be addressed. I suggest that this hearkening is the finding moment in conscience. As hearkening, finding is our being open to being addressed, called, summoned. We can also think it as a tuning or attuning (*Gestimmen*): hearkening to the call of our vocation is a matter of becoming in tune (*richtig gestimmt*) with ourselves. By tuning (*stimmen*) us to our vocation, finding is self-disclosing.

But what about the fact that we find ourselves not only called to take up a particular identity but already stuck with identities? Some of these are identities we are already projecting upon, and some of these (such as gender, race, and social standing) are or can be identities that we find thrust upon us by our community. Indeed, we find ourselves already having been issued not only some of our identities but also our aptitudes and talents, as well as our bodies, our histories, our time and place, and so on. Is this a different type of finding—not finding ourselves called, but finding ourselves stuck with something? No; it is a variety of finding ourselves called. For what we find ourselves stuck with is what Heidegger calls our 'facticity' (*SZ* 56). Whereas present-at-hand objects are simply possessed of facts (*Tatsachen*), such as their dimensions, weight, and spatial location, we—as cases of Dasein—are possessed of Facts (*Fakten*) (*SZ* 56), such as being short, being over-weight, and being in Chicago—as well as being good at math, being a woman, and having gone to boarding school. *Fakten* are different from *Tatsachen* in that the former figure in our self-interpreting. This means that they are identities or vocations that we are given and that we must take up—that we must *be*—in one way or another.[4] If we do not find something as such a calling, then it is a mere fact rather than a Fact and so irrelevant to our lives. It follows that, for self-interpreting entities like us, what we find given to us to deal with is a species of what we find called to take up. Thus we can say generally that to be self-finding is to find ourselves called to a vocation, in the broadest possible sense.

## 2 Existential Self-Disclosing: Finding Oneself Called to Be Dasein

According to Heidegger's official story, however, the finding dimension of conscience is not its call to a vocation but its being attuned by angst (*SZ* 277). The call is anxious because it speaks from our authentic self, which "*finds itself in the very depths of its being uncanny*" (*SZ* 276)— and "being uncanny reveals itself authentically in the basic finding [*Grundbefindlichkeit*] of angst" (*SZ* 276). By unpacking this argument and its concepts, I will show that its conclusion is consistent with my claim in the previous section.

I begin with being uncanny. Dasein is uncanny insofar as it is "thrown being-in-the-world, which has been delivered over to itself in its being" (*SZ* 189; cf. *SZ* 276). To be so delivered is for Dasein to be stuck with its being as a fact (*that it is*) and to be called to take that being up, as what it *has to be*. Having-been-thrown is thus "the fact 'that it is, and that it has to be something with an ability-to-be as the entity which it is'" (*SZ* 276). If being uncanny belongs to *this* phenomenon, then it cannot be feeling unsettled or estranged. Instead, as I have argued elsewhere (2014, 2015), Dasein is uncanny in that the whence or ground of its 'that it is' is obscure to it: "the 'that-it-is' of its 'there' [...] stares it in the face with the inexorability of an enigma" (*SZ* 136). Why it *is*—as the entity that discloses being and discovers entities—is "incomprehensible" (*SZ* 228). So, Dasein is open—just not to the 'why' of that being open. As such, it "never comes back behind its having-been-thrown" (*SZ* 284, 383) to its ground and so is fundamentally estranged from itself as open. This makes it uncanny (*unheimlich*) or unhomely.

And yet, Dasein is called to take up the obscure Fact that it is and has to be. This is what conscience most fundamentally discloses (which Heidegger calls 'guilt'). The call reveals that Dasein has not laid its own basis, and so is not its own ground, and that it cannot get its thrown ground into its sense-making power (*SZ* 284). Still, Dasein is stuck with this obscure Fact of itself: "To this entity it has been delivered over, and as such it can exist solely as the entity which it is; and *as this entity* to which it has been thus delivered over, it *is*, *in its existing*, the basis of its ability-to-be" (*SZ* 284). Being this basis is a "burden" or a "weight" (*SZ* 284)—"the manifest burden of being" (*SZ* 134)—since it is a Fact that calls to Dasein as a vocation that it must take up as its own: "it must take over being-a-basis" (*SZ* 284). In sum: in conscience, Dasein is called to take up the fact that it is, and to project upon its being as Dasein, without being able to make sense of *why* it is such—and indeed, it must take up this very non-openness to its thrown ground not merely as a contingent limitation but as constitutive for what it is. Dasein must take up its own self-alienation as part of what it is called to be.

Thus to say that conscience calls from Dasein's being-uncanny is to say that it opens Dasein to the task of taking over its finite being.

Dasein's being open to its being-uncanny is its being open to the voca-tion of being the entity that it is. The call "calls Dasein *back* to its having-been-thrown so as to understand this having-been-thrown as the null basis which it has to take up into existence" (*SZ* 287). In thus calling Dasein to take over the being into which it is thrown, finding "*discloses Dasein in its having-been-thrown*" (*SZ* 136). This is the first essential feature of finding that Heidegger identifies in §29.

Such a finding being-open is a *Grundbefinden*, a ground-finding—both because it opens Dasein to the obscure ground of its having-been-thrown into being and because it is the foundational being-open that makes for there being Dasein rather than not. For there to be Dasein is for Dasein to find itself called to take over its being and to do so. Such projecting is Dasein's foundational self-understanding: its pre-ontological understanding of its own being (and the being of other entities, as we will see in §4). Thus the call (discoursing) to take over (in understanding) its own being as a vocation (hearkened to in find-ing) is the first opening of the *da* (or 'there') that Dasein is. As such, it is a condition of possibility of the phenomena discussed in Division I. Specifically, the finding dimension of conscience is the condition of possibility of the fact that any instance of finding will "*disclose Dasein in its having-been-thrown, and – proximally and for the most part – in the manner of an evasive turning-away*" (*SZ* 136).

All modes of finding open Dasein to its *that it is and has to be* in one way or another, and this is possible because Dasein is originally open, in conscience, to its having-been-thrown. As Heidegger puts it: "to be thus closed off [from its thrown being, in inauthentic falling] is merely the *privation* of a disclosing", since "[o]nly to the extent that Dasein has been brought before itself in an ontologically essential manner through whatever disclosing belongs to it, *can* it flee *in the face of* that in the face of which it flees" (*SZ* 184). If in any instance of finding we face up to or flee from our having-been-thrown, then all instances of finding presup-pose an original opening to having-been-thrown. This original opening, I have argued, is the finding dimension of conscience.

Heidegger also calls it 'angst'. While I cannot rehearse the full argu-ment for this interpretation of angst, I can note a few compelling points.[5] First, the passage I just quoted about inauthentic flight from Dasein's having-been-thrown comes from §40, where it introduces and motivates Heidegger's analysis of angst. This is because, second, what Heidegger needs methodologically from the analysis of angst in §40 is access to a ground-level opening to Dasein's being that will help the existential analytic to circumvent the distortions of fallen everydayness. Thus, third, angst cannot be an ordinary mood or other mode of finding. It is a *Grundbefindlichkeit* or ground-finding (*SZ* 276)—indeed, one which "always already latently determines being-in-the-world" (*SZ* 189), such that "Dasein is anxious in the very ground of its being" (*SZ* 190). But, fourth, it does not merely 'occur' deep in Dasein's being, as a repressed or all-pervasive mood might; instead, "as finding, angst is a basic kind [*Grundart*] of being-in-the-world" (*SZ* 188). Heidegger is actually entitled to a stronger claim. He holds that angst is distinctive because its three structural moments (*that in the face of which* it is anxious, *that about which* it is anxious, and *the angst itself*) coincide as being-in-the-world (*SZ* 188). It follows from this that angst is anxious *in the face of* being-in-the-world, that it is anxious *about* being-in-the-world, and that angst itself *is* being-in-the-world, *qua* the being-open of Dasein's *da*.

Thus 'angst' is the name for Dasein's foundational hearkening to the call of its being, and it is the finding dimension of conscience. This does not mean that being called to take over our being involves sweaty palms or a feeling of dread. Indeed, we could just as easily call it 'boredom'— as Heidegger does in *FCM*. There, he analyses profound boredom as the "*calling*" (*Anrufen*) (*FCM* 143) that announces "the most extreme demand": "*that Dasein as such is demanded of man, that it is given to him – to be there*" (*FCM* 165) (see my [2013]). Just as angst is, boredom is the call to the vocation of being Dasein.

At this level of analysis, conscience is not something experienced but a foundational structure that is constitutive for Dasein's being open. Yet this is not all that it is. Since "[t]he question of existence never gets straightened out except through existing itself" (*SZ* 12), the existential call to be Dasein always takes place as an existentiell call to a particular identity. In turn, this is always 'heard' authentically or inauthentically— and always in some determinate mode of finding, and always in relation to oneself as an entity and to other entities in the circumspective environment. As with several other phenomena in *BT*, then, conscience operates simultaneously on multiple levels. At the existentiell level, the relevant phenomenon of finding is Dasein's being open to the call of some particular identity, and at the existential level, it is Dasein's being open to the call of its own being.

## 3    Discovering: Finding Myself Called by Solicitings

Finding is not typically associated in the literature with a vocational call. It is, however, frequently associated with another type of call: that of entities, calling us to engage with them. This brings us to the third respect in which we are findingly open: in discovering entities. (I address the second, world-disclosing, in the next section). As entity-discovering, finding is our being open to the call or 'summons' (*HCT* 254) of the 'mattering' (*SZ* 137) or 'soliciting' (*HCT* 254) of entities.

Solicitations are typically taken to be a special class of what the psychologist James J. Gibson (1986) dubbed 'affordances'. Cups afford *picking up and drinking from*, venture capital affords *seeking* or *investing*, and gloves afford *wearing for warmth*. What entities afford constitutes *what* they are (i.e., their what-being), and their affording is their being *there* rather than not (i.e., their that-being). When we encounter entities in their being, then, we encounter not inert objects with properties or essences but fields of affordances. Further, these fields are sometimes especially charged. When we are undercaffeinated, underfunded, or underclad, the coffee cup, venture capital, or gloves do not merely afford drinking from, seeking, or wearing but solicit these. In soliciting, entities call us to engage with them. As a way of being open to entities, finding is our being open to this call: our hearkening to or being 'addressed by' (*HCT* 254) solicitings or matterings.

There is a rich variety of distinctions to be drawn within the category of affordances and solicitings. Gibson distinguishes affordances that "offer benefit or injury, life or death" (1986, 143), just as Heidegger typically contrasts entities that are useful and those that are detrimental (e.g. *SZ* 83). We can distinguish various intensities of soliciting (producing, perhaps, addiction and revulsion), as well as different modalities: "things can appear pressing, urgent, or required" (Ratcliffe 2015, 45). Some solicitings will be practical but others will call for other sorts of engaging, such as curious inspecting, artistic representing, or hypothesis-formulating. Further, different sorts of entities may solicit in distinctively different ways. The way that a deadline solicits meeting it differs from how a transitive verb solicits providing a direct object, which differs from how bereavement solicits condolences. Other sorts of distinctions within the category are surely possible.

Importantly, entities do not matter to or solicit us independently of our finding ourselves called by them. Finding does not 'tune' us into solicitings as a radio tunes into some independent frequency. Rather, our finding being-open and the solicitings of entities are 'attuned' together, in concert with one another. Things matter only *for* and *in* the finding that is open to such mattering. Thus we cannot say that solicitings are revealed, responded to, or discovered. Although the phenomenology of being solicited involves finding things as *already* mattering to us (just as we experience ourselves as *already* called to a vocation), this temporal index indicates not that the mattering predates our being open to it but that it is experienced as a *fait accompli*.

Some readers, however, may think that finding *reveals* solicitings because they take solicitings to be produced by understanding: projecting onto our identities opens a normative space within which things matter in relation to our projects, and finding tunes us into that. But this reading posits understanding as world-disclosing and finding as entity-discovering, whereas I have claimed that each discloses the self, discloses the world, and discovers entities. Having seen how finding opens us to the calls of our vocations and of soliciting entities, then, it remains to explore how finding is world-disclosing.

## 4    World-Disclosing: Finding the World as a Possibility Space[6]

Heidegger identifies the world-disclosing moment of finding as its disclosing of being-in-the-world (note: not the world) as a whole (*SZ* 137). He points out that this insight into finding's disclosing arises from the contrast between finding ourselves in some way and introspectively discovering ourselves. The latter does not capture how moods are findingly disclosive because moods, as modes of finding, "come[] neither from 'outside' nor from 'inside', but arise[] out of being-in-the-world" (*SZ* 136). But what does this have to do with the disclosing of being-in-the-world as a whole? And what, in turn, does that have to do with finding as world-disclosing?

Consider the following passage. Heidegger has moved on from the world-disclosing aspect of finding to how it discovers entities as mattering, which I discussed in the previous section:

> [T]o be affected by the unserviceable, resistant, or threatening character of that which is ready-to-hand, becomes ontologically possible only in so far as being-in as such has been determined existentially beforehand in such a manner that what it encounters within-the-world **can** '*matter*' *to* it in this way. The fact that this sort of thing can 'matter' to it is grounded in one's finding; and as finding it has already **disclosed the world** – as something by which it can be threatened, for instance. Only something which is in the finding of fearing (or fearlessness) can discover that what is environmentally ready-to-hand is threatening. (*SZ* 137, Heidegger's italics, my bold)

Heidegger is explaining not how we find entities as mattering but how we *can* do so. We can do so because we open up a realm of possible ways in which entities *can* matter: possibilities of soliciting. This opening, I suggest, is the world-disclosing moment of finding. If this is right, then when Heidegger identifies the third, discovering dimension of finding, he is actually speaking of its second, world-disclosing dimension: "*Existentially, finding implies a disclosive 'submission' to the world, out of which we can encounter something that matters to us*" (*SZ* 137). 'Can encounter' shows that at issue is not discovering particular entities as mattering but opening the world as a space of possibilities of mattering.

The world is opened up as a possibility space primarily by and in understanding. As we have seen, understanding is a self-disclosing in that it amounts to projecting oneself onto some identity, which (as a for-the-sake-of-which) shapes and structures the world as a possibility space. A possibility space is a network of possible ways in which entities can be: a "categorial whole of a *possible* interconnection of the ready-to-hand" and other modes of being (*SZ* 144). In particular, understanding opens up possible ways in which entities can be *coordinated with our projects*. To be coordinated with our projects is to *afford* certain types of engagement. Thus these possible ways to be are all possible ways of affording. (That the possibilities opened by understanding are possibilities of affording is further guaranteed by the fact that projecting ourselves onto an identity is a matter of being skilled in or competent at living out that identity [*SZ* 143], and [as many have argued] affordances are opened up by our skills).

Insofar as our project is being a case of Dasein as existing being-in-the-world, the possible ways for entities to be will be quite general. Entities can be ready-to-hand (affording circumspective engagement), (perhaps) present-at-hand (affording disinterested engagement), or Dasein-with (affording solicitous engagement). Within each of these categories, there will be relatively more fine-grained possible ways to be. For example, within the category of the ready-to-hand, entities might be usable for, serviceable in, or detrimental to our projects (*SZ* 83, 144). Insofar as our project is existentiell, the world opened up will be populated by even more specific possible ways in which things can be, or possible ways of affording. Thus if I am an office worker, entities could be cubicle-mates, performance reviews, or TGIF stops at the bar. Presumably, there will be for-the-sakes-of-which intermediate between being a case of Dasein and being an office worker—all the way from being spatially embodied, to being mathematical, to being a coffee drinker. These sorts of intermediate projects will (in some cases separately, in some cases together) generate other possible ways for things to be, such as being-an-obstacle, being-an-easy-sum, or being-a-flat-white. Heidegger's examples are more mundane: being-a-table, being-a-door, being-a-carriage, and being-a-bridge (*SZ* 149).

But, as we have seen, entities can be more than *coordinated with our projects*. They can also be demanding, important, or irrelevant—as well as delightful, exhilarating, or threatening. To possibilities of affording, then, there must correspond possibilities of soliciting. These will be different ways in which ways of being coordinated with my projects can strike me, speak to me, or resonate with me. Heidegger distinguishes possibilities of affording from possibilities of soliciting or mattering whenever he distinguishes the detrimental from the fearsome (*SZ* 140, 185–186, 341). That the two come apart is clear from the fact that we can fear things that are not detrimental (as is the case in most phobias) and we do not necessarily fear things that are detrimental (e.g., college students typically do not fear binge drinking). Being detrimental is a possible way of being related to our projects: when we project upon an identity (such as being a case of Dasein, being embodied, or being an entrepreneur), the possibility is opened up that entities (including other cases of Dasein) may inhibit, undermine, or destroy our ability to live out that identity (by treating us as ready-to-hand, by injuring us, or by not investing in our venture). These are possibilities of detrimentality. Being fearsome is something different; it is the possibility of being *threatened* by what is detrimental. What makes for this difference?

It may seem that the difference is that between an objective threat and a subjective threat, or between the fact of detrimentality and the negative value that I place upon it. If this were the case, then understanding would open us to the objective and/or facts, and finding would open us to the subjective and/or values. But neither the fact/value distinction nor the objective/subjective distinction quite gets at the phenomenon. On the one hand, affordings and possibilities of affording are not objective facts that are independent of us since they have to do precisely with our projects and how entities can be coordinated with them. On the other hand, solicitings and possibilities of soliciting are not 'merely' subjective values or reactions since they track reality in important ways. Gibson himself recognized that affordings, including solicitings, escape and undermine any subjective/objective distinction (1986, 129, 138): an affording is "something that refers to both the environment and the animal in a way that no existing term does. It implies the complementarity of the animal and the environment" (1986, 127). We have seen Heidegger make the same point: modes of finding—and so, possibilities of soliciting—do not arise from the inner sphere of a subject; they "come[] neither from 'outside' nor from 'inside' but arise[] out of being-in-the-world" (*SZ* 136).

Specifically, they arise out of "a disclosive 'submission' to the world" (*SZ* 137, original italicized), a "world which is already disclosed with its [sc. Dasein's] own being" (*SZ* 139). The world in question is not the sum totality of entities but the context of affordings that is 'already' opened up in understanding, by projecting forward onto some identity (where the 'already' is logical rather than temporal).[7] To submit to the world *qua* a space of possible affordings is to surrender ourselves as subject to it and so to let it touch us. The detrimental, for example, is so because of its relationship to my projects. It becomes fearsome only when it *draws close* (*SZ* 140, 185) in the sense that it "reaches what is threatened [...] with definite regard to a special factical ability-to-be" (*SZ* 186): "that which threatens [...is] awaited *right back to* the entity which I myself am; only so can my Dasein be threatened" (*SZ* 341). We can now see why "the existentially basic character of moods lies in *bringing* one *back to* something" (*SZ* 340). To be threatened and so fear, I must 'bring back' what is detrimental to me carrying out my project so as to put at stake the very facts *that I am* (someone with that project) and *have* (such a person) *to be*—that is, to put at stake my thrown, factical ability-to-be. Thus while an entrepreneur's first attempts to secure venture capital might fail and so be detrimental to her *project* of being an entrepreneur, she does not find herself threatened until one failed attempt 'hits home': until she experiences her *vocation* of being an entrepreneur as at stake.

So, when affordings implicate our vocation, they become solicitings. This differs slightly from the usual story about how affordings become solicitings—namely, by offering possibilities of engagement that correspond specifically to our needs. I said earlier that the coffee cup solicits us to drink coffee from it when we are undercaffeinated; otherwise, it merely affords that. But Heidegger does not understand us as either organisms with biological imperatives (cf. *FCM*) or as volitional creatures with desires and needs. Instead, we are entities that are called to take up and live out, amidst other entities, particular ways of being us. But as vocational entities of this sort, we are in a condition that resembles need: we "understand [ourselves] as bound up in

[our] 'destiny' with the being of those entities which [we] encounter[] within [our] own world" (*SZ* 56). Heidegger says that this is 'implied by' our facticity (*SZ* 56). To be bound up with the destiny of the possible ways in which entities can *be* is to have brought those possibilities of affording back to our having-been-thrown—as possibilities of affording that impact our *that we are* (*x*) *and have to be* (*x*). As so brought back, these possibilities of affording (or affordings) become possibilities *that are and have to be dealt with*. They are possible ways in which entities *demand* to be engaged with, and so possibilities of soliciting. My being becomes an issue—not in the sense that I must take a stand on who I am (in understanding), but in the sense that my taking such a stand and being called to do so are vulnerable to the impacts of other entities.

By allowing our thrown vocation to be at stake, finding *qua* world-disclosing brings Dasein back its having-been-thrown. It is in this sense that finding's world-disclosing is always at the same time a self-disclosing (*HCT* 257). We can now understand why Heidegger characterizes the world-disclosing aspect of finding as its disclosing of being-in-the-world as a whole (*SZ* 137). Projecting first opens the world as a network of possibilities of affording. Finding brings those possibilities back to Dasein's having-been-thrown so that they become possibilities of soliciting. In doing so, finding contributes to world-disclosing, since it contributes possibilities to the possibility space. But these possible ways of being are parasitic upon the possibilities that projecting opens up. Being so parasitic expands the scope of finding's world disclosing, since in bringing back to having-been-thrown possible ways in which entities can be coordinated with our projects, finding opens Dasein to its being thrown, its projecting, and its being open to entities. Finding, as world-disclosing, thus opens Dasein to its own being as thrown projecting amidst entities: to being-in-the-world as a whole (*SZ* 137).

We now have a more complete picture of how understanding and finding are (each and equiprimordially) disclosing (Table 1).[8]

**Table 1** Understanding and finding as self-disclosing, world-disclosing, and entity discovering

| Self-disclosing | I find myself called to a vocation | Finding |
|---|---|---|
| | projecting upon which | Understanding |
| World-disclosing | opens up a space of possible afford-ings, which are | Understanding |
| | brought back to my having-been-thrown, implicating my vocation and opening up a space of possible solicitings | Finding |
| Discovering entities | thus allowing me to find things as mattering/soliciting | Finding |
| | as I project them onto that and what they are, by grasping them as afford-ing circumspective/solicitous/etc. engagement | Understanding |

# 5     Modes of Finding

Finding always takes a definite form—a 'mode'. Since finding is either soliciting or vocational, so too will be its modes. First, we find our-selves vocationally called in two ways: we are called existentially to be Dasein, and we are called existentielly to particular projects (Table 2). The modes of existentiell vocational calls remain to be investigated; they might be internally- or externally-sounded, deep passions or passing interests, talent-developing or transformational, and so on. The modes of being called to be Dasein are ground-moods (*Grundstimmungen*) or ground-findings (*Grundbefinden*), such as angst or boredom.

Second, we find ourselves called by soliciting entities in modes such as mood and sensing (Table 3).

In this final section, I show how to analyze mood and sensing in terms of this framework, and I suggest a few further modes of solicitous finding.

Let me start with fear (Table 4).

Notice that 'the mood of fear' could refer to either fear as world-disclosing or fear as discovering entities. Heidegger calls the former 'fearfulness' or 'fearing': "[f]earing, as a slumbering possibility of find-ing being-in-the-world (we call this possibility 'fearfulness') has already

**Table 2**  Finding oneself called to a vocation

| Self-disclosing | I find myself called to a vocation | | |
|---|---|---|---|
| | existentially, in ground-finding: being called to the project of being Dasein. Modes: angst, boredom, etc.(?) | existentielly, in being called to some existentiell project. Modes: ... | = Vocational finding |

**Table 3**  Finding oneself solicited by entities

| | Projecting upon my vocation | Understanding |
|---|---|---|
| World-disclosing | opens up a space of possible affordings, which are | Understanding |
| | brought back to my having-been-thrown, implicating my vocation and opening up a space of possible solicitings. Modes: moods (fearing, etc.), sensing (tasting, etc.), etc. | Solicitous finding |
| Discovering entities | thus allowing me to find things as mattering/soliciting. Modes: moods (fearing, etc.), sensing (tasting, etc.), etc. | Solicitous finding |
| | as I project them onto that and what they are, by grasping them as affording circumspective/solicitous/ etc. engagement | Understanding |

disclosed the world, in that out of it something like the fearsome may come close" (*SZ* 141). With 'slumbering possibility', Heidegger indicates that such fearing is the possibility of being solicited by something threatening and so of being afraid of things. This possibility helps to constitute our suite of affective possibilities, and a person who lacked it would be 'fearless' not in the sense that they did not fear but in the sense that they could not.

Since Heidegger's moods must be grasped as both discovering and world-disclosing, they depart significantly from moods as understood folk-psychologically. Folk psychology does not acknowledge the world-disclosing dimension of mood. It does distinguish moods

**Table 4**  The mood of fear as a mode of finding

| | | |
|---|---|---|
| Self-disclosing | I find myself called to a vocation | Finding |
| | projecting upon which | Understanding |
| World-disclosing | opens up (among others) the possibility of **being-ready-to-hand in the mode of detrimentality,** which is | Understanding |
| | brought back to my having-been-thrown, implicating my vocation and opening up **the possibility of being fearsome** | Finding |
| Discovering entities | thus allowing me to find things as **fearsome/to fear** | Finding |
| | as I project them onto that and what they are, by grasping them as affording circumspective/solicitous/etc. engagement | Understanding |

and emotions, taking the former to be 'bigger' (in their duration) and 'deeper' (in their lack of a definite intentional object). But this is not the same distinction. And since neither temporal duration nor the question of an intentional object has a role in Heidegger's analysis of finding, the distinction between emotion and mood will have no bearing on or authority over his account.[9]

What *is* relevant to Heidegger's account is Dasein's projects and the possibilities of affording they open up, since bringing the latter back to Dasein's thrown vocation is what opens possibilities of soliciting. Notice, in particular, that which entities (can) solicit me depends on which projects I am called to and do take up. What I (can) find fearsome will depend on what is detrimental, which in turn depends on my projects. If I am a pillar of the community, then damage to my reputation will be detrimental and so could be fearsome to me—but not to the eccentric recluse. Thus Aristotle is right to say in the *Nicomachean Ethics* that "what is frightening is not the same for everyone" (1115b), since the appropriate object and degree of fear is "relative to us, not in the object" (1106b) (Aristotle 1999). It is relative not to our physical strength or to our military prowess but to our skills generally—that is, to our projecting, *qua* being competent at living our identity.

If there are things that are frightening to everyone, they will be so because we each take up the same project. Since we each take up the existential project of being Dasein, death threatens each of us. And if 'we' each take up the existentiell project of being a coffee drinker, then the declining supply of coffee beans as a result of climate change would be fearsome to each of us. Of course, not everyone is a coffee drinker. Are there any existentiell projects that are common to all cases of Dasein? Embodiment is a plausible candidate, since it is necessary as an "organizing factor" for producing distinct cases of Dasein (*MFL* 138). If embodiment is an existentiell project that all cases of Dasein each take up, then anything detrimental to the project of embodiment will be potentially fearsome to all cases of Dasein.

Notice that the body has entered the account as a project and not as part of what it is to be finding per se. It seems that the body plays no essential role in the way that modes of finding are self-disclosing, world-disclosing, and discovering. It is possible that the role of the body permeates the account of disclosing and discovering as a whole—as a requirement for taking up any existentiell project, perhaps, or as a presupposition of circumspection. Or, it may be that bodily skills are essential correlates of all affordings, and so are implicated indirectly in the account of solicitings.[10] These possibilities—and others—deserve careful scrutiny.[11] But neither gives support to the idea that the account of finding must make special reference to the body. As far as the account of finding goes, Heidegger's 'neglect' of the body is no neglect at all.

The body may yet be an essential *ontic* condition of some modes of solicitous finding, such as being mooded and sensing. But there are modes of solicitous finding that do not obviously involve the body at all. How are we to know this? Modes of solicitous finding may be deduced from the possible existential and existentiell projects that we might or must take up, via their correlated affordings. It would be impractical to deduce all such modes of finding, but let me note a few central ones that arise from the fact that we take up existentiell projects at all, as well as from the fact that we take up the project of being embodied.

First, the very fact that we project onto existentiell possibilities produces a special class of entity: normative requirements and prohibitions.

That is, when I take up an identity, there are things that I *must* (not) or *ought* (not) to do, as the sort of person that I am. (E.g., a grandparent *ought* to spoil their grandchildren a little and *ought not* to favor one grandchild over the others). To be such a normative requirement is to afford meeting it, violating it, policing it, and so on. The possibility of things having such normative valence is thus a possibility of affording opened up by the fact that we take up identities. Further, to take this possibility back to one's thrown vocation as a projector is to place oneself under the normative demands of the identity and to hold oneself to them. In this way, finding opens the possibility of normative calls soliciting us: what is required is *necessary*, what is prohibited is *impossible*, and infractions are *to be sanctioned*. Correspondingly, one finds oneself solicited: *bound* to the normative demands, *compelled* by what is required, and *repelled* by what is forbidden. Being normatively responsive is thus a mode of finding.

Second, because we take up the project of being Dasein by carrying out existentiell projects, entities can be *usable in our projects*. Bringing this possibility of affording back to our having-been-thrown opens the possibility of being *practically useful*. The distinction between the affording and soliciting is difficult to express in this case, but it is something like the difference between being merely usable and being the right tool for the job.[12] It is clearer when the two come apart—as in, for example, extreme anxiety. Sufferers of such anxiety report an overwhelming, general sense of impossibility and incapacity. They are open to what entities afford and so are, but they do not feel capable of *doing* anything with those entities. In contrast, when entities present themselves as the right tools for the job, we feel capable and confident—able to do things in the world.

What about when entities are *not* so usable? While such 'unaffording' puts semantic strain on the language of affording and soliciting, recall that Heidegger—like Gibson—allows affordings and solicitings to be both positive and negative, attractive and repelling. In the case of entities affording unusability, taking this possibility back to our having-been-thrown allows entities to be distracting, impeding, and/or irrelevant. Correspondingly, we can be distracted, frustrated, or indifferent.

We see the same positive/negative duality in the possibilities of soliciting belonging to other cases of Dasein. In taking up the project of being Dasein, we take up the project of being-with other cases of Dasein (*SZ* 114). According to Heidegger, other cases of Dasein afford either leaping-in-for-them or leaping-ahead-of-them (*SZ* 122). Bringing these back to our having-been-thrown allows others to solicit either being-supported or being-manipulated. Correspondingly, we are solicited as either loving or domineering.

Finally, the project of being embodied will produce (among others) sensing, and its modalities, as modes of solicitous finding. As sensorially embodied, we find our bodies with their particular sensory organs (proximally and typically: eyes, skin, ears, tongues, and noses) as Facts or vocations that we are called to take up.[13] We take up the task of sensing in specific ways (typically: seeing, touching, hearing, tasting, and smelling) by being skilled at sensing the world in those ways. This sensory project opens a range of possible affordings, or possible ways for entities to be: being visible, tangible, audible, tastable, and olfactible. There will be further possibilities within each of these categories, depending on the precise configuration of our sensory organs, such as being bright, being smooth, and being sweet.

But things being tasted, and tasting sweet, is not the same as their being appetizing or unappetizing—and their being visible and bright is not the same as their being glowing or glaring. The latter possibilities are produced by bringing the possibilities of affording back to the vocation of being embodied, so as to put it at stake. The details of this will have to be sourced from the sciences, but here is a simplified example. We have taste buds that register different tastes, such as 'sweet', and being skilled at tasting opens the possibility of things affording taste, including tasting sweet. Grant that something that tastes sweet to us is a food rich in nutrients that support our particular bodies and so is conducive to the project of embodiment. When our bodies 'know' this (in whatever way(s) bodies 'know' what is good for them), that knowing is the bringing back of the possibility of being sweet to the thrown project of being embodied. This opens the possibility of things being (un)appetizingly sweet—which is the possibility of being (un)solicited by the sweet.

Thus we see how sensing, like being mooded, is a mode of solicitous finding—as is loving others or dominating them, finding entities practically useful, and being normatively responsive.

There are many other modes of solicitous finding to be identified. The modes of existentiell-vocational finding have also yet to be explored. Finally, the unity of finding as being called to a vocation and finding as being solicited has yet to be established. Are these really the same kind of being-open or are they two distinct phenomena?

We may not know if they are unified, but we do know that vocational and solicitous findings are both essential parts of the story of disclosing and discovering. We find ourselves called to vocations—to take up projects. Taking up a project opens possibilities of affording, and bringing these possibilities back to implicate our vocation allows us to be called by soliciting entities. To be finding is thus to be called to carry out a vocational project in the midst of entities that put that vocation at stake. How this carrying out is going is how we are faring as being-in-the-world—and this is precisely what we ask after when we ask, "*Wie befinden Sie sich?*".

## Notes

1. Page references to *BT* are to the pagination of the eighth German edition of *Sein und Zeit* (*SZ*), which is provided in the margins of all current English translations. I quote Macquarrie and Robinson's translation of *BT* but frequently modify it. To reflect the point in footnote 2, I also interpretively alter some of Heidegger's key terms in the process of translation.
2. For my argument as to why Heidegger's terms for aspects of the being of an entity (including Dasein) must be (nouns formed from) present participles, see my (2017a, b).
3. E.g. Freeman (2016, 249, 253), and Ratcliffe (2013, 171).
4. I was helped in understanding this point by Blattner (2006, 44–45).
5. For the full argument, see Chapter 2 of my (2015), and my (2012).
6. My interpretation of finding as world-disclosing departs significantly from Ratcliffe's (2013, 2015) but is inspired by and indebted to it.

7. This claim of Heidegger's sits uneasily with his claim that *"from the ontological point of view* we must [...] leave the primary discovery of the world to 'bare mood'" (*SZ* 138).

8. More needs to be said about how understanding, grasped in this way, is self-understanding, and about how others and *das Man* are implicated in understanding. For more about each, see Rousse (2018).

9. One might object that Heidegger stresses the fact that angst lacks an intentional object. But while angst does lack an *ontic* intentional object (*SZ* 186), it possesses an *ontological* intentional object: being-in-the-world.

10. Ratcliffe argues along these lines (2015, 59). But while possibilities of affording are plausibly constituted by skills, these need not all be bodily skills.

11. I thank Mark Okrent and Joe Rouse for discussion on this point.

12. Thus I disagree with Ratcliffe, who takes finding to open us to practical utility *qua* the affording rather than the soliciting (2015, 45).

13. Unfortunately, this is contrary to Heidegger's claim that "[w]e are not able to 'see' because we have eyes; rather, we can only have eyes because, according to our basic nature, we are beings who can see" (*Zo* 232; cf. *FCM* 218).

# References

Aristotle. 1999. *Nicomachean Ethics*. Second Edition. Translated by Terence Irwin. Indianapolis: Hackett.

Blattner, William. 2006. *Heidegger's* Being and Time: *A Reader's Guide*. New York: Continuum.

Freeman, Lauren. 2016. "Defending Heideggerian Mood." In *Philosophy of Mind and Phenomenology: Conceptual and Empirical Approaches*, edited by Daniel O. Dahlstrom, Andreas Elpidorou, and Walter Hopp. New York: Routledge.

Gibson, James J. 1986. "The Theory of Affordances." In *The Ecological Approach to Visual Perception*. Mahwah, NJ: Lawrence Erlbaum Associates Inc.

Ratcliffe, Matthew. 2013. "Why Mood Matters." In *The Cambridge Companion to Heidegger's* Being and Time, edited by Mark Wrathall. New York: Cambridge University Press.

Ratcliffe, Matthew. 2015. *Experiences of Depression: A Study in Phenomenology.* New York: Oxford University Press.

Rousse, B. Scot. 2018. "Self-Awareness and Self-Understanding." *European Journal of Philosophy.* https://onlinelibrary.wiley.com/doi/10.1111/ejop.12377.

Withy, Katherine. 2012. "The Methodological Role of Angst in *Being and Time.*" *The Journal of the British Society for Phenomenology* 43 (2): 195–211.

Withy, Katherine. 2013. "The Strategic Unity of Heidegger's The Fundamental Concepts of Metaphysics." *The Southern Journal of Philosophy* 51 (2): 161–178.

Withy, Katherine. 2014. "Situation and Limitation: Making Sense of Heidegger on Thrownness." *European Journal of Philosophy* 22 (1): 61–81.

Withy, Katherine. 2015. *Heidegger on Being Uncanny.* Cambridge, MA: Harvard University Press.

Withy, Katherine. 2017a. "Haugeland's Heidegger and the Metaphysics of Normativity." *European Journal of Philosophy* 25 (2): 463–484.

Withy, Katherine. 2017b. "Still, the Unrest of the Question of Being." In *After Heidegger?* edited by Richard Polt and Gregory Fried. London: Rowman & Littlefield.

# 8

# Is Profound Boredom Boredom?

## Andreas Elpidorou and Lauren Freeman

Martin Heidegger is credited as having offered one of the most thorough phenomenological investigations of the nature of boredom in the history of philosophy. Indeed, in his 1929–1930 lecture course, *The Fundamental Concepts of Metaphysics: World, Finitude, Solitude* (*FCM*), Heidegger goes to great lengths to distinguish between different types of boredom and to explicate their respective characters. Moreover, Heidegger, at least within the context of his discussion of profound boredom (*tiefe Langeweile*), opposes much of the philosophical and literary tradition on boredom insofar as he articulates how the experience of boredom, though disorienting, can be existentially beneficial to us. Yet despite the many insights that Heidegger's discussion of boredom offers, it is difficult to make sense of profound boredom within the context of contemporary psychological and philosophical research on

A. Elpidorou (✉) · L. Freeman
Department of Philosophy, University of Louisville, Louisville, KY, USA
e-mail: andreas.elpidorou@louisville.edu

L. Freeman
e-mail: lauren.freeman@louisville.edu

© The Author(s) 2019
C. Hadjioannou (ed.), *Heidegger on Affect*, Philosophers in Depth,
https://doi.org/10.1007/978-3-030-24639-6_8

boredom. That is because profound boredom does not map neatly onto either our pre-theoretical understanding of boredom or extant psychological accounts of boredom.

In this chapter, we undertake a study of the nature of profound boredom with the aim of investigating its place within contemporary psychological and philosophical research on boredom. Although boredom used to be a neglected emotional state, that is no longer the case. In recent years, boredom's causal antecedents, effects and concomitants, experiential profile, and neurophysiological correlates have become topics of active, rigorous study. The same goes for boredom's influence on behavior, its relationship to self-regulation, and its connection to other related affective states. Such a situation provides a ripe opportunity to scrutinize Heidegger's claims and to try to understand them both on their own terms and in light of our contemporary understanding of boredom.

The structure of this chapter is as follows. In Sect. 1, we offer a concise overview of the psychology of boredom. There, we distinguish between the constructs of *state* boredom and *trait* boredom; describe their respective natures; and briefly discuss their effects on behavior, cognition, and other affective states. In Sect. 2, we turn to Heidegger's account of boredom. Although we discuss the nature of all three kinds of boredom, we focus primarily on profound boredom and consider the existential and philosophical value that Heidegger ascribes to it. In Sect. 3, we address the question of whether profound boredom is indeed boredom by comparing it to the ways in which boredom has been understood in contemporary psychology and in philosophy. We argue that although profound boredom shares some features with such understandings, it cannot be seamlessly assimilated to any known category of boredom. Such a finding is important. It cannot be assumed that Heidegger's (profound) boredom is identical to either our colloquial or scientific understanding of boredom. Nor can one use Heidegger's account of this type of boredom to make general claims about the phenomenon of boredom. All the same, we offer an interpretation of profound boredom that retains the characteristics that Heidegger assigns to it and allows for a meaningful comparison both to our common experience of boredom and to our scientific understanding of it.

# 1   Boredom: A Primer

One obstacle that the study of boredom faces, but certainly not the only one, is the unfortunate fact that the term "boredom" is polysemic: depending on the context, the term both denotes and connotes different things (Fenichel 1951, 349; Vodanovich 2003, 589). As such, one can draw different, and sometimes even conflicting, conclusions about the nature of boredom. For the present purposes, we utilize the distinction between *state* boredom (a transitory affective experience) and *trait* boredom (a lasting personality trait). Empirically, the distinction has been both confirmed and proven to be exceptionally useful. Conceptually, the distinction is capable of capturing much of our pre-theoretical grasp of boredom—it accounts, *inter alia*, for the various principles governing the application of the concept *boredom*.[1]

Consider, first, how the term "boredom" is usually used in everyday situations, such as when a child becomes bored with a toy, when you find a movie boring, or when patients are bored by having to wait at the dentist's office. In such situations, boredom is understood to be a *state*: namely, a short-lived (i.e., transitory), aversive experience. State boredom is characterized by feelings of dissatisfaction, a perception of lack of meaning, attentional difficulties, and even an altered perception of the passage of time. While bored, one is disengaged with one's current situation and experiences a strong desire to escape from it. In terms of its physiological character, boredom is characterized by a decrease in arousal, although an increase may also occur. As a low arousal state, boredom is disengaging; whereas as a high arousal state, it prepares one for action or change.[2] All in all, boredom is an unpleasant state from which one seeks escape and solace.

Whereas "state boredom" refers to a transitory experience, "trait boredom" is meant to capture a characteristic of agents that persists through situational change and which is predictive of one's behavior. Trait boredom is variously described as the "tendency," "propensity," "disposition," or "susceptibility" to experience boredom often and in a wide range of situations. It is thought to be a lasting personality trait and is assessed by multi-item, self-report scales. Several measures of trait boredom exist in the literature. However, the only two existing measures of trait boredom that are neither limited in scope nor lacking in reliability and validity (Vodanovich 2003), are the Boredom Proneness Scale (BPS) (Farmer and Sundberg 1986) and the Boredom Susceptibility Scale (ZBS) (Zuckerman 1979). Of these two scales, only BPS is a full-scale measure of boredom. As such, we restrict our attention primarily to findings that involve the use of BPS.

Research on the correlates of trait boredom has demonstrated that the propensity to experience boredom is associated with numerous harms (for reviews see Elpidorou 2017; Vodanovich 2003; Vodanovich and Watt 2016). Boredom proneness (i.e., the construct that BPS operationalizes and measures and which is thought to correspond to trait boredom) has been positively correlated to poor social relationships, lower life and job satisfaction, difficulty in finding meaning in one's life, depression, anger and aggression, anxiety, loneliness, and apathy. Individuals prone to boredom experience impulse control deficits, are more likely to engage in risk-taking behavior, and are prone to drug and alcohol abuse. It has also been suggested that boredom proneness is morally significant insofar as it hinders one's ability to live a flourishing life (Elpidorou 2017). And if all of the above were not enough, there is even evidence suggesting that too much boredom can be an indication of early death (Britton and Shipley 2010). Understood as a lasting personality trait, boredom is a pervasive existential condition. It changes our world, our selves, and our relationships to others. It is no surprise then that (trait) boredom has the (poor) reputation that it does.

## 2     Heidegger's Boredom

Heidegger's account of boredom appears in the first part of *FCM*, a lecture course delivered in 1929–1930. Prior to the lecture course, the only fundamental attunement that Heidegger discussed was anxiety (*Angst*), which played a key role both in *Being and Time* (*BT*) (1927) and in "What Is Metaphysics?" (1929). One aim of *FCM* was to delineate his conception of philosophy and metaphysics, already evolving from the one presented in *BT*. Another aim was to develop his account of the fundamental attunement (*Grundstimmung*) of boredom in order to grasp the fundamental meaning of our being. Importantly, he set out to do this *not* by developing an anthropology or philosophy of culture (*Kulturphilosophie*) (*FCM* §18c) but rather by considering the ways in which profound boredom is a key step in opening up the proper questioning of philosophizing for us.[3]

On Heidegger's account, there are three types of boredom, each of which corresponds to a distinctive way in which we experience the passage of time[4] and each of which we describe below. They are: (1) becoming bored *by* something (*Gelangweiltwerden von etwas*); (2) being bored *with* something (*Sichlangweilen bei etwas*); and (3) profound boredom (*tiefe Langeweile*), which is expressed by the impersonal phrase "it is boring for one" (*es ist einem langweilig*).[5] Within this third form of boredom, Heidegger makes a distinction between "profound boredom" and "contemporary boredom" but he does not flesh it out systematically or with much clarity.[6] Crucially, each form of boredom manifests in relation to how time passes (*die Zeit vertreiben*) in that within each form, there are two related structural moments: being left empty (*Leergelassenheit*) and being held in limbo (*Hingehaltenheit*). Only by understanding how each form of boredom relates to the passage of time and what role each of the two structural moments play in the experience of boredom, can we fully grasp what boredom is for Heidegger.

## 2.1   Becoming Bored by Something

Though the first form of boredom is the most familiar to us, it is also, according to Heidegger, the most superficial. This form of boredom is the experience of being bored *by* something—person, object, or state of affairs—a phenomenon that we all know well. For example, waiting for our delayed fight to depart, with no departure time in sight; waiting to see a doctor who is running far behind schedule; trying to get off the phone with someone who will not stop talking to us; these are all instances of becoming bored by something. Here, boredom is unpleasant and we do whatever we can to try to get rid of it. In terms of the two structural moments of boredom, we are *held in limbo* insofar as our situation does not let us do what we intend to do, namely, board our flight, see our doctor, and get on with our day. At the same time, we are also *left empty* insofar as our situation does not fulfill us; it is not what we want to be doing.

## 2.2    Being Bored with Something

With the second form of boredom, things become slightly more complicated and slightly more interesting. Whereas with the first form, the object of boredom is clear to the one experiencing it, with the second form, it is not immediately clear precisely *what* it is that is boring—it is also not clear that one is, in the moment, bored. In order to explain this form of boredom, Heidegger develops an example of going to a dinner party at which neither the company, conversation, food, nor the ambiance is perceived by us, while at the party, to be boring. However, upon returning home, we come to the realization that the evening itself was boring. Here "boring" does not denote a subjectively obvious aversive experience; rather, "boring" means something like casualness (viz., one of the same, what others do), the inauthentic following of a social ideal (*FCM* 111–112).

In order to fully comprehend the depth of Heidegger's account of the second form of boredom, it is crucial to understand the structural moment of being *held in limbo*, which requires us to return to the example. That evening, we made the decision to attend the dinner party and in so doing, we transformed our relationship to time: both by leaving time for ourselves and by taking this time for ourselves. But, according to Heidegger, during the party, the time that we have given to ourselves comes to stand still and we become trapped in a standing present (*stehendes Jetzt*). That has happened because our choice of activity disconnected us from our past and future projects. Stuck in this standing present, our comportment to originary temporality changes and the significance of the full temporal horizon is lost (*FCM* 124). By not pursuing an activity that is meaningful to us, we are *held in limbo*.

Furthermore, by immersing ourselves in activities that are not our own, we are *left empty*. But the emptiness is not directly caused by something in the surrounding; rather, it arises as a result of having left behind (*Sichzurücklassen*) our authentic, temporal, existential self. Our situation does not fulfill us; it does not contribute to the completion of our projects, nor does it relate to our having-been. We spend our time; give it up; and in doing so, we make it stand.

## 2.3   Profound Boredom

Whereas with the first form of boredom, a determinate object or situation is the source of our boredom, with the second form, boredom arises both from the particular situation and from ourselves. There is an additional form of boredom which is the most profound of all. According to Heidegger, it is also the most perplexing.

The reason why the third form of boredom is both the most profound and the most perplexing is because in it, there is nothing in particular that is boring, nor is there a determinate cause of or reason why one is bored. And yet still, everything bores us, even ourselves. The impersonal construction "it is boring for one"—where "it" (*es*) is the same subject found in expressions such as "it is raining" or "it is hot"—is Heidegger's way of expressing the ubiquity of profound boredom. It is limitless and depersonalized. It is neither me, nor you who experiences this form of boredom; rather, Dasein becomes an "undifferentiated no one" (*FCM* 135). We stand without any concerns and interests. All identifying characteristics, history, and projects are stripped away. Profound boredom is unconditioned, overpowering, and extreme. In it, the passing of time is altogether missing. That is to say, all three temporal dimensions (past, present, future) merge into a unified temporality and beings as a whole withdraw. In their withdrawal, they lose all significance which means not only that everything around and alongside us is drained of meaning; it also means that nothing carries any future prospects for us and that nothing relates to or gives meaning to our past (having-been). One thus grows indifferent to who and what one was, is, and will be. And yet, contrary to the first form of boredom which one actively tries to escape, in this third form of boredom, one does not respond by trying to distract oneself or to escape from it. There is simply no point in resisting profound boredom. No thing, no being, no situation matters to us. In the midst of profound boredom, we stand entirely indifferent to everything and everyone.

Because nothing matters to us and we are unable to become involved in anything, profound boredom *leaves us empty*. Because one's possibilities are foreclosed, profound boredom *holds us in limbo*. Yet counter-intuitively, these two structural moments do not lead to despair. Rather, in withdrawing and thereby losing their significance—a kind of concealing—entities in the world and Dasein's own unexploited possibilities suddenly and paradoxically reveal themselves to Dasein. "All telling refusal [*Versagen*]," Heidegger writes, "is in itself a telling [*Sagen*], i.e., a making manifest" (*FCM* 140). When the pressing world of everyday concern fades into indifference, the world is made present to us anew. In that moment of totalizing boredom, we can come to understand what projects carry proper significance to us—that is, we can discern the projects that are related to our past and that define us, both in the present and in the future. In doing so, we come to understand not only that we are the type of being for whom existence is an issue, but also that we can take up and appropriate (at least to a certain extent) our own existence. As such, profound boredom drives Dasein to enact its ownmost possibilities in what Heidegger calls the "*Augenblick*," the instant or "moment of vision" in which Dasein faces itself as the kind of being it is—a power to take over its ground and to choose what it will be (*FCM* 149). The revelatory moment of profound boredom is Dasein's being called toward its authentic self-disclosure wherein it is brought face to face with itself and its temporal freedom. That is, in profound boredom, Dasein has the opportunity to become authentic.

## 3    Understanding Profound Boredom

How well does Heidegger's discussion of boredom align with what we know about boredom from psychology? We can make two quick observations. First, the first form of boredom (*becoming bored by something*) appears to be akin to state boredom, although Heidegger would not call it a "state" (*BT* §29; *FCM* 63–68; Elpidorou and Freeman 2015). In other words, what Heidegger describes as the most superficial kind of boredom is our ordinary experience of boredom. For both Heidegger and psychological accounts, this form of boredom is an aversive experience that signifies a failure to engage with or to be engaged by one's environment in a desired manner despite one's desire to do so. In this kind of boredom, we want to be doing something other than what we are currently doing. We feel trapped or are *held in limbo* in a situation that does not provide us with meaningful possibilities. And precisely because of this unavailability of meaningful possibilities, we are *left empty*.

Second, the second form of boredom (*being bored with something*) does not appear to be an affective experience proper. That is, it is not an experience that is primarily characterized by an affective or qualitative character. As Heidegger tells us, "There is nothing at all to be found that might have been boring about this evening, neither the conversation, nor the people, nor the rooms" (*FCM* 109). Instead, the second form of boredom appears to be a type of cognitive attitude: the retroactive realization that we wasted our time. During the experience of this boredom, we are given hints that we are bored ("[j]ust as we are on the verge of playing with our watch chain or a button, cigars are passed around again" [*FCM* 11–12]), but those hints are not recognized by us at the time as symptoms of the presence of an unsatisfactory activity. Instead, we carry on with the activity that we had chosen to pursue and only after the activity concludes do we realize that what we had done was a waste of time. It was, for Heidegger, literally a waste of *our* time, the time that is Dasein. By agreeing to go to the party, to continue with Heidegger's example, we have immersed ourselves in an activity that is not our own—we decided to go along, to embrace "casualness" as Heidegger puts it, and thus, to do as others do (*FCM* 114). We have allowed ourselves to be fully absorbed by a present that is disconnected from our past and future. The party neither promotes our projects nor meaningfully stems from or relates to our past. As such, it is not an authentic activity. Thus, the party was boring but not because it felt boring. It was boring because we came to realize that it was not meaningful to us. The psychology of boredom does not study this retroactive experience of boredom that Heidegger highlights, at least not by this name. All the same, given the intimate relationship that boredom bears to the perception of meaninglessness (Van Tilburg and Igou 2011, 2012), the second form of boredom can be recognized as boredom, even if it is not the typical (self-luminous)[7] form of boredom and even if it is predicated on our attitudes regarding what is valuable, meaningful, or fulfilling to us.

Matters become much more complicated, however, when we turn our attention to profound boredom. Is profound boredom state boredom, trait boredom, or something else, perhaps a distinctive kind of experience that is captured neither by our ordinary nor by the scientific understanding of boredom? In what follows, we consider these three possibilities in order.

## 3.1    State Boredom Is Not Profound Enough

The differences between state boredom and profound boredom are both important and numerous. To begin with, state boredom is thought to be an emotion: a relatively short-lived, flexible, multi-dimensional response to specific physical and social situations. Emotions are typically initiated by an individual's appraisal of an event that bears some personal significance to the individual. Such an appraisal can be either conscious or unconscious and it gives rise to a set of interrelated responses in the individual—such as changes in felt experiences, physiology, facial expressions, perception, cognition, and action. But Heidegger is quite clear that profound boredom is not an emotion but a fundamental mood (*Grundstimmung*). As a mood (*Stimmung*), boredom is the ontic manifestation of *Befindlichkeit*—a basic structure of Dasein's existence that makes engagement with the world possible (*BT* §29; Elpidorou and Freeman 2015; Ratcliffe 2013; Slaby 2015). Moods are the various, specific, and pre-reflective ways in which the world is disclosed to us and the background horizon or context through which we understand and make sense of the world and of ourselves. Importantly, they reveal the world as mattering to us and in doing so, they are the necessary conditions for our emotional existence (Freeman 2014). As understood in psychology, boredom would then be that which arises on account of the fact that as human beings we are already mooded.

The psychology of boredom studies, one might say, the symptoms of our affective existence. Heidegger's discussion of boredom as a *Stimmung* attempts to explicate what makes such an affective existence possible (Freeman 2014).

But boredom is not just one *Stimmung* among others; it is a *Grund*stimmung, a fundamental or grounding mood. Indeed, it is fundamental in at least two senses. First, it is fundamentally revealing of the nature of our human existence. In profound boredom, we stand disconnected from our world of concerns and we 'see' ourselves for what we really are—as a power or potentiality to seize our own existence in a way that is meaningful to us. Second, profound boredom is distinctive insofar as it is a preparatory mood for philosophical inquiry. Only once this mood has been awakened in us, will we be in a position to study and understand the fundamental concepts of metaphysics (world, finitude, and solicitude).

State boredom lacks the features that make profound boredom a *Grundstimmung*. This is not say that state boredom is not revealing of anything; it is (Elpidorou 2018a). Nevertheless, state boredom does not appear to be 'deep' in any sense. State boredom arises often and in various contexts without revealing anything about the ground (or lack thereof) of our existence, our being, or our temporality. If one is made to wait long enough, one's dentist appointment can be a lesson in patience or frustration, but not in ontology. Relatedly, state boredom does not have the philosophical significance that profound boredom is thought to have. We find nothing in our common everyday experience of boredom that is necessary, preparatory, or even congenial to metaphysical thinking. The existential and philosophical functions of profound boredom are related. Metaphysics is not a theoretical enterprise but "a fundamental way of Da-sein" (*FCM* 23). The questioning that metaphysics involves and requires is comprehensive. We too fall under its scope and as such we are affected by it (*FCM* 24). Insofar as state boredom fails to disclose to us the nature of our being, it fails to affect us in this profound way. Insofar as it fails to affect us in any profound way, it fails to prepare us for metaphysical inquiry, which is after all the explicit aim of Heidegger's lecture course.[8]

The realization that state boredom does not seem capable of doing the philosophical work that Heidegger wants profound boredom to do is underscored by yet another difference between the two. Profound boredom is totalizing. It affects every aspect of our existence. It makes every characteristic of our existence (present, past, or future) irrelevant to us and in so doing, renders us an "undifferentiated no one" (*FCM* 135). State boredom does none of those things. On the contrary, state boredom typically depends on our situation and as a consequence, can be easily alleviated by a change in situation, action, or even way of thinking. Precisely because state boredom lacks the comprehensive scope of profound boredom, it fails to have profound boredom's existential and philosophical import. Simply put, state boredom is not profound enough. It does not shake us up. It does not reveal ourselves as potentiality or as a power to choose. It does not motivate us to take up our lives anew.

## 3.2    Trait Boredom Is Too Negative, Too Personal

A comparison between state boredom and profound boredom quickly revealed that state boredom is not profound enough to be profound boredom. Such a realization suggests that if profound boredom is to be identified with a different type of boredom, then that type of boredom must be more extreme. Trait boredom meets this requirement. First, individuals who are thought to possess the trait of boredom often and easily find themselves to be bored, even in situations that others typically find interesting and stimulating. Second, trait boredom can affect one's existence in profound ways. For instance, it can affect one's habits and actions. And it can render one's personal, professional, and inter-personal life uninteresting. As such, trait boredom carries the potential to be existentially or ontologically informative, insofar as it can reveal to us both the various ways in which we relate to the world and how such relations may languish. Third, and most importantly, trait boredom, just like profound boredom, is totalizing. Individuals possessing the trait of boredom can experience the totality of their world as boring. Such a feature of trait boredom is not only corroborated by the way in which trait boredom is assessed, but also by testimonies from individuals who experience their lives and worlds as boring. Consider, for example, the following first-personal testimonies reported by Bargdill in his phenomenological study of life boredom.

> Presently, I am bored with my whole life. None of the old things I used to do bring enjoyment to me anymore. Nothing. [Boredom] covers my social life. It covers school. It covers work. It covers going to the grocery store . . . It covers a lot of things. My hair. (Bargdill 2000, 198)

> I might think that I would become bored with whatever activity I'm look-ing at. I project boredom. I'm looking ahead and saying 'Oh boy, it looks like it's going to be boring after all.' So I don't even start it. (ibid.)

Although Bargdill does not describe these individuals as ones who possess the personality trait of boredom, it is very plausible, given how trait boredom is assessed, that these individuals would be categorized as boredom prone individuals by the Boredom Proneness Scale (Farmer and Sundberg 1986). In other words, although Bardgill's focus is on what he calls "life boredom," this notion can be understood to be a a proxy for trait boredom.

Trait boredom appears to be totalizing. It is thus profound. But is it profound in Heidegger's sense of profound boredom? The answer to this question is no. First, trait boredom is related to the frequent experience of state boredom. In other words, one is said to be prone to boredom (i.e., one possesses the trait of boredom) only if one experiences state boredom frequently and in a wide range of situations. When we turn to Heidegger's account, we find no discernible relationship between pro-found boredom and how frequently one experiences boredom (state or otherwise). If anything, it seems that profound boredom, given its existential import and effects, is a rare occurrence. Although one might argue that in order to experience the whole world as boring, one needs to experience boredom often and in all situations, this is not how Heidegger describes profound boredom. Profound boredom "can occur out of the blue, and precisely whenever we do not expect it at all" (*FCM* 135). Profound boredom comes with no warnings and it is not causally related to the first form of boredom. But assuming that the first type of boredom is, as we argued, state boredom, then even though profound boredom does not require state boredom, trait boredom does. After all, trait boredom is predicated on the frequent experience of state boredom. Thus, whereas trait boredom is both conceptually and causally dependent on state boredom, profound boredom is not.

Second, trait boredom is understood to be a lasting personality trait. As a personality trait, trait boredom is grounded in one's psychological or biological characteristics and is used to account for differences between individuals that cannot be accounted for in terms of situational factors. Precisely because trait boredom is a personality trait, the task of showing how it can have the ontological 'weight' of profound boredom becomes extremely difficult. Not every individual possesses this personality trait, yet profound boredom is something that can be experienced by everyone. After all, profound boredom "is rooted in time — in the time that we ourselves are" (*FCM* 133). Profound boredom arises out of the most fundamental features of human existence—namely, our care structure (our thrown and situated projection). Consequently, any attempt to assimilate profound boredom into trait boredom runs the risk of conflating two levels that Heidegger wants to keep separate: the psychological/biological and the ontological.[9]

Third, trait boredom is pathological: it is related to a host of issues that are incongruent with Heidegger's contention that profound boredom can lead one to an authentic existence. This feature of trait boredom becomes most clear when we turn again to first-person descriptions by individuals who experience chronic or life boredom. Consider the following testimonies:

> I feel I lack a sense of purpose, and completeness. Most of all I feel extremely bored. Bored of everything—work, friends, hobbies, relationships, music, reading, movies, bored all the time. I do things [merely] to occupy my time, to distract myself from trying to discover the meaning of my existence, and I would gladly cease to do anything if the opportunity arose. *No matter what the activity is it leaves me feeling unfulfilled [....] What possible difference does it ultimately make whatever I do? What difference does anything make?* (Maltsberger 2000, 84; emphasis added)

When I lose my vision, I lose any idea or projection of what I want to do in the future. I don't have any distinct plans, or even an idea of what I want to do and so I wanted to immerse myself more in the present rather than projecting myself in the future… (Bargdill 2000, 199)

Being in the disillusioned state I didn't have the will power to be disciplined. I knew what I was getting into, but I just didn't care. (Bargdill 2000, 200)

Trait boredom may bring about a totalizing experience of boredom: everything and everyone is boring to one. Yet precisely because of its totalizing nature, this form of boredom has the opposite result of profound boredom. The experience of totalizing boredom that can come about as a result of constant and pervasive boredom is accompanied not by a will to reaffirm authentically one's existence, but by an inability both to project possibilities for oneself and to act. The Dasein who is characterized by trait boredom might experience the total withdrawal of beings described by Heidegger. It would, in that case, be *held in limbo* and *left empty* by the world. Nothing would interest Dasein; nothing would seem as significant or meaningful to it. Yet, unlike profound boredom, such boredom is not motivating but incapacitating. It does not lead to resoluteness or authentic existence. In fact, given the host of physical, psychological, and social harms that are correlated with its presence, the truth is very much the opposite. Thus, profound boredom cannot be trait boredom. It cannot serve its existential function.

## 3.3   Profound Boredom as Sui Generis

A third possibility is that profound boredom is something entirely different from both our ordinary experience of boredom and our psychological conceptions of it: namely, it is *sui generis*. *Prima facie*, there seem to be at least two reasons in support of this reading and such reasons are not affected by the fact that Heidegger calls profound boredom "boredom"—after all, in the mid-to-late 1920s, Heidegger is known for claiming that though he is using ordinary words and concepts in his thinking (e.g., "care," "guilt"), the meaning of these terms is importantly different from our ordinary understanding of them (given their place and role in fundamental ontology).

First, as Heidegger makes clear throughout the mid-to-late 1920s and then again at the end of his career in the *Zollikon Seminars* (*Zo*), the empirical sciences in general and psychology in particular do not engage with the same questions that he is asking; they tell us nothing about fundamental attunement or ontological modes of being. Rather, the empirical sciences study the psychological states of a subject. But Dasein is neither a subject (in any traditional sense of the term "subject") nor the subject *of* psychology. Moreover, fundamental attunement is not a psychological state but rather, the condition for the possibility of such states. On Heidegger's account, to focus on the psychological states of a subject is to miss the disclosive capacities of attunement—both as an ontological structure (*Befindlichkeit*) and in its various concrete manifestations (moods [*Stimmungen*]). And it is precisely this character of attunement that interests Heidegger insofar as his thinking in the mid-to-late 1920s aims to interrogate the nature and structure of Dasein in the service of answering the question of the meaning of being. Studying psychological states get us nowhere on the path to answering this question.

Second, Heidegger's main question in the context of which his account of boredom arises is not "what is boredom and why do we experience it?" Rather, it is "what is metaphysics (or philosophy) and what is the condition for the possibility of philosophizing?" His answer to this question is that boredom is the experience which catalyzes our capacity to do metaphysics and in the end, to become our authentic selves. Consequently, his account of boredom is instrumental to understanding the real question that interests him—"what is metaphysics (or philosophy) and how and in what mood can we best pursue it?" This question can only be understood through the lens of his underlying philosophical undertaking. Psychological states as understood by psychologists are not studied in terms of their relationship with the project of philosophizing or of doing metaphysics.

These two reasons can be brought together by considering Heidegger's notion of formal indication (*formale Anzeige*), characteristic of his phenomenological method from that period.[10] It was Heidegger's contention that theoretical and objectifying discourse tends to misrepresent or distort its own content primarily because it treats its subject matter as something present-at-hand (*PIA* 21). In order to avoid this misinterpretation or distortion, Heidegger deems it necessary to treat phenomenological concepts as formal indications. Unlike the objectifying concepts that are found in the positive sciences and in philosophy, phenomenological concepts as formal indications do not fully communicate or determine their content. Formal indications are indicative insofar as they furnish us with a sense of direction and allow us to undertake our phenomenological investigation (*GA* 63, 80; *PIA* 25). At the same time, they are also formal insofar as they do not specify or predetermine the object of investigation. As Heidegger states, "the formal indication functions both…to guide as well as to deter in various ways" (*PIA* 105). With respect to its "deterring" or "prohibiting" function, the method of formal indication

> prevents every drifting off into autonomous, blind, dogmatic attempts to fix the categorial sense, attempts which would be detached from the presupposition of the interpretation, from its preconception, its nexus, and its time, and which would then purport to determine an objectivity in itself, apart from a thorough discussion of its ontological sense. (ibid.)

Indeed, the sense of a formally indicative concept is not something that can be theoretically given or retrieved, since the very point of formally indicating something is to get at a truth rooted in a more fundamental concealment that is central to our existence (see also Polt 1999). Rather than capture the essence of a thing and give an account of it with perfect accuracy, formally indicative concepts nudge us to pay more attention to things; they bring to the fore something more basic than what science can reveal, namely, they underscore the very fact that we find ourselves in a meaningful world. For Heidegger, what we cannot speak about theoretically, we must indicate formally. But doing so involves more than a saying or pointing: we can come to terms with the phenomena under investigation only by undertaking a type of enactment or performance (see Dahlstrom 1994; Granberg 2003). Properly understood, philosophy is a type of comportment (*PIA* 41–42, 46–47) and formal indication is a call to philosophize by taking anew the question of being. Thus, what "boredom" as a phenomenological concept formally indicates is something that is both distinct from scientific and ordinary conceptions of boredom and ultimately connected to philosophizing.

There are thus reasons to support the position that profound boredom is something entirely other than both our everyday experience of boredom and the psychological state or trait revealed by the methods of the empirical sciences. Still, we cannot unqualifiedly agree with such a reading of profound boredom. Even though such a reading highlights the distinctive ways in which Heidegger is conceiving of boredom, it runs into important philosophical and interpretative difficulties.

First, if profound boredom is *sui generis*, then the text is rendered methodologically problematic: why would Heidegger consider the first two forms of boredom that *do* in some way resemble our ordinary experience of the phenomenon before addressing profound boredom if profound boredom has no relation to them and to our experience of boredom? The "methodological" issue that we are raising here is not a concern with Heidegger's use of formal indication.[11] Instead, it is a worry of how to understand the third form of boredom if not through some kind of understanding of or familiarity with the first two forms of boredom. In other words, even if Heidegger's method of formal indication allows him to treat profound boredom as something different than ordinary boredom, it still does not allow him to treat it as an entirely alien form of boredom, completely disconnected from the everyday experience of boredom (*SZ* 310). In its formally indicative guise, "boredom" would still share something in common with our everyday usage of the term and it is precisely because of this commonality and familiarity that it is capable of serving its indicative function. In fact, formal indications are not typically neologisms or terms of art (Dahlstrom 1994, 785), but concepts that are closely related to and derived from ordinary experiences and linguistic practices. Moreover, if profound boredom were *sui generis*, then the intricate structure of the part of the lecture course that discusses the character of each type of boredom would fall apart. That is because Heidegger understands all three forms of boredom in terms of their relationship to time and in terms of their two-fold structure (being *held in limbo* and being *left empty*). Insofar as all three forms of boredom are related in this double manner, it is hard to insist that profound boredom is a *sui generis* experience, entirely unrelated from the first two types of boredom.

Second, there is an ontological (or an *in virtue of*) relationship between the first type of boredom and profound boredom. Though the first form of boredom is not the causal antecedent of profound boredom, the latter is the condition for the possibility of the former:

> The first form of boredom as such can indeed never pass over into the third, yet conversely, the first is itself presumably still rooted in the possibility of the third, and comes from the third form of boredom with respect to its possibility in general. (*FCM* 156)

But if profound boredom is the condition for the possibility of the first, and the first is our ordinary experience of boredom, then the two cannot be unrelated.

Third, although profound boredom might not be identical to state and trait boredom, there are still important and undeniable similarities between them. Heidegger is quite clear that he is not concerned with psychological states (qua psychological states) (*FCM* 63–68); rather, his philosophical enterprise—phenomenology and fundamental ontology—aims to ask questions that are fundamental to our experiences in the world and to understand and underscore the condition for their possibility. All the same, it is incorrect to hold that Heidegger completely rejects the sciences—this is especially the case with regard to the second part of *FCM* where he uses biology to support ontological claims. Most importantly, elements of profound boredom seem to be present in experiences of boredom ordinarily understood and in scientific, empirical accounts of them. For example, profound boredom is constituted by a lack of meaning, disengagement from one's goals and projects, and an altered perception of time. But these elements are also present in varying degrees in both trait boredom and state boredom, as discussed above. If profound boredom were in fact *sui generis*, then we would not be able to recognize elements of it in the other types of boredom.

Finally, to claim that profound boredom is *sui generis* raises a pressing metaphilosophical concern: namely, if it is *sui generis*, then Heidegger's account of profound boredom loses part of its significance, both as a phenomenological study of the (common) experience of boredom and as a philosophical contribution to the study of boredom. If profound boredom were not an experience that bore any relationship to our ordinary experience of boredom, then what would be the point of studying it? Would it even be something that we could ever experience or understand? And if it were something completely other, what could it ever teach us about ordinary boredom? On account of these four reasons, the claim that profound boredom is *sui generis* should not be accepted.

# 4    Locating Profound Boredom

Profound boredom is equivalent neither to our ordinary conception of boredom nor to any of the scientific constructs that carry the name "boredom." For those who are familiar with Heidegger's thinking, such a conclusion will not be surprising. Ontology or fundamental ontology for Heidegger is not science. The latter could never unearth the truths of the former. And although Heidegger employs ordinary, everyday concepts in his thinking, he appropriates them (at least in the late 1920s and afterwards) and shows that there is much more to them than initially meets the eye. Our conclusion then is not surprising. But that does not mean that it is not important. Indeed, as we have also shown, understanding profound boredom as something completely distinct from our everyday and scientific notions of boredom yields a position that is replete with difficulties. It threatens to make parts of Heidegger's lecture course methodologically otiose and runs the risk of rendering Heidegger's view a mere historical curiosity—one that is endemic to Heidegger and which stands disconnected from both ordinary human experience and other philosophical accounts of boredom. Heidegger's account of boredom thus occupies a precarious position: it can neither be assimilated to what we know about boredom nor can it be taken to be describing a *sui generis* kind of boredom. How, then, should one proceed?

We offer a conciliatory reading. We acknowledge both that profound boredom is neither state boredom nor trait boredom, and yet that profound boredom is also not *sui generis*. Still, such a conclusion is not entirely negative. Our comparative analysis of profound boredom, state boredom, and trait boredom reveals important features of profound boredom that can be understood in light of our more familiar types of boredom.

We mentioned above that despite its severity, profound boredom is not an incapacitating experience. When one experiences profound boredom, though one becomes disconnected from one's own being or self (Dasein), one also comes to realize one's authentic being anew. In this way, profound boredom is motivational. It propels us to become the author of our own lives, to choose what is proper to us. State boredom does something similar, albeit less drastic. A variety of theoretical and empirical considerations on the nature of state boredom strongly suggest that it is a regulatory state that aims to keep one in line with one's projects (Elpidorou 2014, 2018a, b). The experience of boredom motivates one to cease to be engaged with one's current situation and instead to pursue an alternative situation that is more satisfactory, attractive, or meaningful. Just like profound boredom, state boredom is capable of bringing us closer to situations and activities that are in line with our own interests, goals, and desires.

Furthermore, the onset of boredom has been shown to be capable of triggering meaning reestablishment strategies that affect an individual's behavior and cognition (Van Tilburg and Igou 2011, 2012). Clearly, the desire to find meaning that arises out of the experience of boredom and in an attempt to alleviate its experience could be a useful attitude to have while philosophizing. State boredom is not necessarily anathema to philosophizing. Indeed, it seems that in some cases it could be precisely what gets us there.

Though these similarities between state boredom and profound are important, they are not perfect (e.g., the motivating effect of profound boredom does not compare to that of state boredom) nor are they sufficient to render the two one and the same. Furthermore, as we discussed above, state boredom is not profound enough. It is not totalizing nor is it necessarily existentially meaningful. Still, those features of profound boredom are found in trait boredom, even if trait boredom is not profound boredom. The situation thus appears to be as follows. Profound boredom is not state boredom nor is it trait boredom. Yet, profound boredom could be understood as involving features of both types or conceptions of boredom. Just like state boredom, profound boredom is motivating and capable of promoting authentic existence. Just like trait boredom, it is severe, totalizing, and existentially revealing (see Table 1).

To suggest that it is fruitful to understand profound boredom as involving features of both state and trait boredom is not to reduce profound boredom to either state or trait boredom. Our proposed interpretation of profound boredom aims to help us understand both its nature and its relationship to our common experience and scientific conception of boredom. As such, our interpretation highlights the ways in which Heidegger's account of profound boredom offers a distinctive, but not alien, kind of human experience. Given what we know from our empirical sciences of boredom, the co-existence of the features from trait boredom and state boredom that we have highlighted as important for profound boredom is probably rare. Profound boredom appears to be a peculiar mode of existence: one that combines the severity of trait boredom with the benefits of state boredom. In the grip of profound boredom, it is as if one experiences trait boredom but only for a moment. Because of the severity of this experience, its existential use would require us to know how to use it or deal with it. From the perspective of human psychology, the occurrence of profound boredom is extraordinary; and its successful implementation as a catalyst to propel us toward what is authentically ours is extremely difficult. But that does not make profound boredom less real. And in no way does it

**Table 1** A comparison of profound boredom, state boredom, and trait boredom. Shaded cells indicate the features of trait and state boredom that we suggest can help us understand profound boredom

| Features of profound boredom | Totalizing | Ontologically/ existentially revealing | Renders one an undifferentiated no one | Promotes authentic existence | Relates to philosophizing |
|---|---|---|---|---|---|
| Trait boredom | Yes | Yes | Yes | No | No |
| State boredom | No | No | No | Yes | Perhaps |

vitiate its philosophical and existential significance. "All things excellent are as difficult as they are rare," Spinoza reminds us at the end of his *Ethics* (Spinoza, Vp42s). The same fact holds, it seems, for fundamental attunements.

## Notes

1. The distinction between state boredom and trait boredom also allows us to make sense of various discussions of boredom in the history of philosophy. For instance, *acedia*, ennui, and *tedium vitae* can be usefully and perspicuously explicated in terms of those two constructs.

2. Space in the present chapter does not permit us to offer a comprehensive review of the empirical literature on boredom. For recent reviews on the nature of state boredom, see Eastwood et al. (2012), Elpidorou (2018a), and Westgate and Wilson (2018).

3. For a comprehensive and extraordinarily helpful account of the way in which this lecture course is a radicalization of fundamental ontology, see de Beistegui (2003).

4. It is worth noting that already in his 1924 lecture course *The Concept of Time* (*CT*), Heidegger raises the possibility of understanding boredom in terms of the lengthening of time. See *CT* 14–17.

5. Some of the following discussion is an expansion of Freeman's (forthcoming) discussion of boredom. Heidegger's account of boredom is also discussed in Freeman and Elpidorou (2015) and Slaby (2014).

6. With regards to contemporary boredom, Heidegger does not say a whole lot. His brief discussion occurs in *FCM* §18c, §§37–38. Nevertheless, what he does say is interesting on many levels (if not problematic, politically), insofar as it gestures toward an important shift in his thinking that occurs in the 1930s, namely, away from being focused on fundamental ontology through an interrogation of Dasein and toward a focus on history and on the co-respondence with the truth of being in its epochal unfolding (de Beistegui 2003, 63). Given that Heidegger's discussion of contemporary boredom is quite short, we can at most speculate as to what he might mean. A comprehensive and compelling reconstruction and interpretation of contemporary boredom can be found in de Beistegui (2003, 68–80). There, he problematizes Heidegger's account of

contemporary boredom vis-à-vis Heidegger's account of Dasein's attunement (in both *BT* and in *FCM*), fleshes it out within the context of Heidegger's critique of *Kulturphilosophie* (in *FCM*) and also in terms of how, collectively, profound boredom announces the great historical *Grundstimmung* that will both identify and define Heidegger's thought in the 1930s. De Beistegui shows how Heidegger's discussion of contemporary boredom bears a direct relation to the reprehensible and unforgivable political ideas and ideals that Heidegger held in the 1920s and 1930s. When de Beistegui was writing, the gravity of Heidegger's commitment to these ideas and ideals was less certain than it is now in the aftermath of the publication of the Black Notebooks.

7. An affective phenomenon (or affect) is self-luminous if the tokening of that phenomenon (or affect) is transparent to the agent. That is to say, an affect is self-luminous if the having of that affect guarantees that we are aware of having it. Not every affect is self-luminous—we might experience jealousy or guilt without knowing it. Furthermore, not every token of a type of affect that is typically self-luminous (e.g., anger) is necessarily self-luminous. Using this notion of self-luminosity, one could hold that boredom as a type is typically self-luminous even if not every concrete experience of boredom is.

8. One could add that there is an additional reason why state boredom cannot be profound boredom: the latter is historical whereas the former is ahistorical. Although this is one possible reading of state boredom, it is not the only one. Indeed, there are those who maintain that boredom is a state or experience that is historical insofar as it distinctive of modernity. See, e.g., Spacks (1995).

9. Perhaps one could argue that trait boredom is the symptom of something more fundamental—an ontological feature or aspect of human existence. Trait boredom is thus grounded in ontology even if it itself is not ontological; moreover, profound boredom should be identified not with trait boredom but with its ground. Whatever one makes of such a proposal, it is not one that corresponds to either a traditional understanding of boredom or to a scientific one. Neither commonsense nor the psychology of boredom talks of the ontological ground of boredom.

10. Heidegger's most extensive discussion of formal indication can be found in his WS 1921–1922 lectures (*PIA*). The topic of formal indication and its relationship to philosophy also arises in *PRL*, *GA* 63, and "Comments on Karl Jaspers's *Psychology of Worldviews*" in *PM*. Among

others, Crowell (2001), Dahlstrom (1994), Kiesel (1993), MacAvoy (2010), and Streeter (1997) offer insightful and helpful presentations of Heidegger's understanding and use of formal indication.

11. We would like to thank an anonymous reviewer for asking us to relate our discussion to the notion and use of formal indication.

# References

Bargdill, Richard W. 2000. "The Study of Life Boredom." *Journal of Phenomenological Psychology* 31 (2): 188–219.

Britton, Annie, and Martin J. Shipley. 2010. "Bored to Death?" *International Journal of Epidemiology* 39 (2): 370–371.

Crowell, Steven Galt. 2001. *Husserl, Heidegger, and the Space of Meaning: Paths Toward Transcendental Phenomenology*. Evanston, IL: Northwestern University Press.

Dahlstrom, Daniel O. 1994. "Heidegger's Method: Philosophical Concepts as Formal Indications." *The Review of Metaphysics*, 47 (4): 775–795.

de Beistegui, Miguel. 2003. *Thinking with Heidegger: Displacements*. Bloomington: Indiana University Press.

Eastwood, John D., Alexandra Frischen, Mark J. Fenske, and Daniel Smilek. 2012. "The Unengaged Mind: Defining Boredom in Terms of Attention." *Perspectives on Psychological Science* 7 (5): 482–495.

Elpidorou, Andreas. 2014. "The Bright Side of Boredom." *Frontiers in Psychology* 5. https://doi.org/10.3389/fpsyg.2014.01245.

Elpidorou, Andreas. 2017. "The Moral Dimensions of Boredom: A Call for Research." *Review of General Psychology* 21 (1): 30–48.

Elpidorou, Andreas. 2018a. "The Bored Mind Is a Guiding Mind: Toward a Regulatory Theory of Boredom." *Phenomenology and the Cognitive Sciences* 17 (3): 455–484.

Elpidorou, Andreas. 2018b. "The Good of Boredom." *Philosophical Psychology* 31 (3): 323–351.

Elpidorou, Andreas, and Lauren Freeman. 2015. "Affectivity in Heidegger I: Moods and Emotions in *Being and Time*." *Philosophy Compass* 10 (10): 661–671.

Farmer, Richard, and Norman D. Sundberg. 1986. "Boredom Proneness—The Development and Correlates of a New Scale." *Journal of Personality Assessment* 50 (1): 4–17.

Fenichel, Otto. 1951. "On the Psychology of Boredom." In *Organization and Pathology of Thought: Selected Sources*, edited by David Rapaport, 349–361. New York: Columbia University Press.

Freeman, Lauren. 2019. "Boredom." In *The Heidegger Lexicon*, edited by Mark Wrathall. Cambridge: Cambridge University Press.

Freeman, Lauren. 2014. "Toward a Phenomenology of Mood." *The Southern Journal of Philosophy* 52 (4): 445–476.

Freeman, Lauren, and Andreas Elpidorou. 2015. "Affectivity in Heidegger II: Temporality, Boredom, and Beyond." *Philosophy Compass* 10 (10): 672–684.

Granberg, Anne. 2003. "Mood and Method in Heidegger's *Sein und Zeit*." In *Metaphysics, Facticity, Interpretation*, edited by Dan Zahavi, Sara Heinämaa, and Hans Ruin, 91–113. Dordrecht: Kluver Academic.

Kisiel, Theodore. 1993. *The Genesis of Heidegger's* Being & Time. Berkeley, CA: University of California Press.

MacAvoy, Leslie. 2010. "Formal Indication and the Hermeneutics of Facticity." *Philosophy Today* 54 (SPEP Suppl.): 84–90.

Maltsberger, John T. 2000. "Mansur Zaskar: A Man Almost Bored to Death." *Suicide and Life-Threatening Behavior* 30 (1): 83–90.

Polt, Richard. 1999. *Heidegger: An Introduction*. Ithaca: Cornell University Press.

Ratcliffe, Matthew. 2013. "Why Moods Matter." In *The Cambridge Companion to Heidegger's* Being and Time, edited by Mark Wrathall, 157–176. Cambridge: Cambridge University Press.

Slaby, Jan. 2014. "The Other Side of Existence: Heidegger on Boredom." In *Habitus in Habitat II: Other Sides of Cognition*, edited by Sabine Flach and Jan Söffner, 101–120. Bern: Peter Lang.

Slaby, Jan. 2015. "Affectivity and Temporality in Heidegger." In *Feeling and Value, Willing and Action: Phaenomenologica 216*, edited by Marta Ubiali and Maren Wehrle, 183–206. Dordrecht: Springer.

Spacks, Patricia Meyer. 1995. *Boredom: The Literary History of a State of Mind*. Chicago: University of Chicago Press.

Spinoza, Benedictus. 1985. *The Collected Works of Spinoza*. Vol. 1. Edited and translated by Edwin Curley. Princeton: Princeton University Press.

Streeter, Ryan. 1997. "Heidegger's Formal Indication: A Question of Method in *Being and Time*." *Man and World* 30 (4): 413–430.

Van Tilburg, Wijnand A. P., and Eric R. Igou. 2011. "On Boredom and Social Identity: A Pragmatic Meaning-Regulation Approach." *Personality and Social Psychology Bulletin* 37 (12): 1679–1691.

Van Tilburg, Wijnand A. P, and Eric R. Igou. 2012. "On Boredom: Lack of Challenge and Meaning as Distinct Boredom Experiences." *Motivation and Emotion* 36 (2): 181–194.

Vodanovich, Stephen J. 2003. "Psychometric Measures of Boredom: A Review of the Literature." *The Journal of Psychology* 137 (6): 569–595.

Vodanovich, Stephen J., and John D. Watt. 2016. "Self-Report Measures of Boredom: An Updated Review of the Literature." *The Journal of Psychology* 150 (2): 196–228.

Westgate Erin C., and Timothy D. Wilson. 2018. "Boring Thoughts and Bored Minds: The MAC Model of Boredom and Cognitive Engagement." *Psychological Review* 125 (5): 689–713.

Zuckerman, Marvin. 1979. *Sensation Seeking: Beyond the Optimal Level of Arousal.* Hillsdale: Erlbaum.

# 9

# Truth, Errancy, and Bodily Dispositions in Heidegger's Thought

Daniela Vallega-Neu

The disclosive power of what Heidegger calls *Stimmung* has not only been a topic in his writings but becomes manifest as guiding his thinking and writing especially after the thirties. The word *Stimmung* (that in *Being and Time* [*BT*] he addresses interchangeably with the notion of *Befindlichkeit*) has been translated into English as mood, attunement, or disposition (I will use "attunement"), and exemplified through especially *Grundstimmungen*, i.e. grounding or basic attunements, such as *Angst*, deep boredom, restraint, presentiment, wonder, and others. That Heidegger focused more on grounding attunements and never undertook a more differentiated analysis of what I will address as non-grounding attunements (such as fear or curiosity), that he furthermore did not undertake the task of rethinking the phenomenological differentiations between different feelings and emotions, has to do with the fact that his focus had always been to think being (*Sein*) as such and

D. Vallega-Neu (✉)
University of Oregon, Eugene, OR, USA
e-mail: dneu@uoregon.edu

© The Author(s) 2019
C. Hadjioannou (ed.), *Heidegger on Affect*, Philosophers in Depth,
https://doi.org/10.1007/978-3-030-24639-6_9

**205**

not this or that relation to this or that thing or event (i.e. to beings, *Seiendes*). His aim was never to think the truth about this or that being but to think and reawaken a sense of truth (unconcealing and conceal-ing) as such, which is always the truth of being. Being is the event of presencing and withdrawal that always occurs in its unconcealing and concealing, i.e. in its truth. The power of grounding attunements is that they unsettle or dislodge us from being concerned with things, into experiencing the occurrence of being as such. Such an experience is, however, by no means undifferentiated, since being discloses and with-draws differently, for instance in Angst or wonder; furthermore, at least since the 1929/1930 lecture course *Fundamental Concepts of Metaphysics* (*FCM*), in which he discusses deep boredom as a grounding attunement determining "our Dasein" (*GA* 29/30: 238), for Heidegger, grounding attunements are historical in a way that determines how being discloses in certain epochs of Western philosophy for a people.

That Heidegger's focus is on the truth of *being* and not on the truth of *beings* and that especially since the thirties (when he began working on his non-public writings on the event)[1] he always sought to let his thinking be attuned by a historical grounding attunement, may be part of the reason why he did not question the relation between attunements and errancy despite the fact that since his famous 1930 essay "On the Essence of Truth" he always maintained that there is no event of truth without errancy (*Irre*), which means that there is not pure disclosure of truth as such without relation to beings that tend to cover over the occurrence of unconcealing-concealing of being, i.e. the truth of being.

The question of the relation between attunements and errancy thus addresses the difference and relation between grounding and non-grounding attunements; we may use the language of *BT*, and call this also the difference and relation between authentic and inauthentic (or more neutrally understood non-authentic) attunements, depending on whether attunements disclose being as such or dispose our relation to this or that being (thing or event).

I believe that questioning the relation between attunements and errancy and between grounding and non-grounding attunements requires as well consideration of the body, understood with Heidegger in terms of *Leib* (lived body) since it is through our lived body that we are concretely situated both in relation to being and to beings. In fact I concur, for instance with Stolorow (2014), that the primary role Heidegger attributes to attunement implicitly places the body at the core of Heidegger's thinking. I will introduce a differentiation between *Befindlichkeit* and *Stimmung*, words Heidegger uses interchangeably in *BT*, and use *Befindlichkeit* (that I will translate with "disposition")[2] when addressing specifically how attunements are bodily such that we find ourselves to be bodily disposed and accordingly "take place" (Heidegger related *Leib* especially to the spatiality of Dasein) in relation to things and event. I will continue to translate *Stimmung* with "attunement" (and not with "mood") mainly because of its close relationship with language, which we need to take into consideration as well. My emphasis on bodily dispositions will lead in the end to question the very differentiation between grounding attunements and bodily dispositions and between grounding and non-grounding attunements, a questioning that seems important to me precisely in order to be vigilant with respect to attunements or moods we might consider to be disclosive and thus "true" but that ultimately have an intrinsic complexity to which belongs always also errancy. It is my belief that Heidegger, too, failed to be vigilant precisely in this respect.

My essay is divided into three parts. I will begin with a discussion of Heidegger's notion of truth and errancy and how truth relates to attunements. For this discussion I will refer especially to Heidegger's essay "On the Essence of Truth."[3] Second, I will bring in the notion of the lived body and its *Leiben*, that is, its occurrence as a "bodying-forth" as he discusses them especially in the *Zollikon Seminars*. Lastly, I will bring together the two previous sections and rethink the relation between truth, errancy, and bodily being.

# 1    Truth, Errancy, and Attunements

In "On the Essence of Truth" Heidegger paves the way for his readers toward thinking the truth of being by departing from the traditional understanding of truth as the accordance between thing and intellect. This accordance makes possible "propositional truth," i.e. the correspondence between a statement and what it is about, for example, between a statement "The sun is shining" and the fact that the sun is actually shining. Pursuing the question of how such an accord (and the German work here is *Übereinstimmung*) between two very different things (statement and thing) is possible and how we ought to understand their relation, leads Heidegger to the notion of openness. Both the thing needs to be open for a relation to it and the relation to the disclosed thing needs to stand in an open comportment (*offenständiges Verhalten*) toward the thing so that the comportment may take the directive for a statement from the disclosed thing and "accord" with it.[4] Only thus can a proposition be *richtig* (right or correct) or *stimmt*, as one would commonly say in German. Although Heidegger makes no reference to attunements such as fear or curiosity, he makes evident that he hears in *Stimmen* not only the notion of "accord" between assertion and thing but also a verbal sense that lets resonate for the German ear the notion of attunement that he will highlight again in section 5. Thus he begins the third section of the essay with the questions: "Whence does the representative statement receive the directive to conform to the object and to accord by way of correctness? Why does this accord codetermine [*mitbestimmen*; note that the German word for determining, *Bestimmen*, has the same root 'stimmen'] the essence of truth? How alone can something like the achievement of the pre-giving of a directive and a directing into an accord occur?" (*GA* 9: 185; *PM* 142. My translation).

It seems clear to me that here already Heidegger alludes to the role attunements play in what some people like to take as rational truth-assertions that have nothing to do with feelings or emotions. Such so called rational assertions thus are grounded, according to what Heidegger tells us, in an open comportment that is attuning and attuned. We may say in a less Heideggerian language that our relation to things is affectively predisposed prior to us making "rational judgments" and that we can be right about something only because of a prior attunement to that which we can be "right" about. However, even the differentiation between an "us" and things is put into question through Heidegger's notion of an open comportment that he sees grounded in what he calls freedom, namely "*being free* toward what is opened up in an openness" (*GA* 9: 186; *PM* 142). In section 4 of his essay, Heidegger elucidates this freedom as a "letting beings be" (*GA* 9: 188; *PM* 144). This letting-beings-be should not be understood as an activity performed by a subject. Heidegger would never write that humans let beings be; he rather attributes freedom to Da-sein (Heidegger writes it with a hyphen here), that is (literally translated), to "there-being" that occurs in such a way that beings are let be. This freedom of Da-sein "possesses human beings," Heidegger writes, it is what grants to humans the relatedness to beings as a whole (*GA* 9: 190; *PM* 145). We are not the ones who let beings be but rather find ourselves exposed to and ek-sisting in the openness in which the letting be of beings occurs.

One can see how in "On the Essence of Truth" the notion of Da-sein is on the way to being rethought the way we find it in *Contributions to Philosophy (Of the Event)* (*CP*), i.e. not as designating primarily human being but rather as the being of the openness that also determines human being (indeed "historical" human being) together with the being of beings as a whole. Da-sein is rethought as a middle voice occurrence,[5] i.e. neither in terms of activity nor passivity but as the way the being of the openness, i.e. the truth of being, takes place.

As I announced above, in section 5 of his essay, Heidegger will highlight the notion of *Gestimmtheit* (being attuned), which he now differentiates from the notions of "lived experience" (*Erlebnis*) and "feeling" (*Gefühl*) in relation to the "letting be of beings" as which freedom (Da-sein) occurs: "As letting into the disclosure of beings as a whole as such, freedom has already attuned all comportment in relation to beings as a whole" (*GA* 9: 192; *PM* 147). I would like to draw the reader's attention to the fact that the attunement of which Heidegger writes here, concerns not beings but prior to these our relation to beings as a whole: "All comportment of historical human beings is, whether emphatically or not, whether grasped or not, attuned and carried into beings as a whole through this attunement" (*GA* 9: 192; *PM* 147). Only thus can we "experience" or "feel" our being exposed into beings as a whole.

At the end of section 5 Heidegger transitions into discussing a double concealment belonging to the occurrence of truth. The attuning letting be of beings is now said to be at the same time the concealment of beings as a whole, indeed a double concealment differentiated into the "mystery" and "errancy." What attunes (*das Stimmende*) is furthermore undetermined (*unbestimmt*); it is the concealment of beings as a whole. Since truth had been addressed as openness and disclosure, he speaks of this concealment as non-truth. For Heidegger this non-truth is constitutive of truth, indeed it is "older than any disclosedness of this or that being. It is older also than the letting be itself" (*GA* 9: 193f; *PM* 148). There happens, then, an almost unnoticeable shift in section 6 when Heidegger begins to address a dimension of truth that precedes the disclosure of the letting be of beings.[6] He points into the "not yet experienced realm of the truth of being (not first of beings)" (*GA* 9: 194; *PM* 149). And if we add to this what he writes at the end of section 5, we can assume that the attunement or the attuning that remains mostly unnoticed and that attunes us in relation to beings as a whole (and not in relation to this or that thing that may threaten us or draw our curiosity), occurs out of the mystery of being. It is a grounding or basic attunement (*Grundstimmung*) that carries with it a historical determination of the being of being as a whole. One may reinforce and further elaborate this interpretation by referring back to *BT* and ahead to *CP* and the non-public writings of the event following it.

What Heidegger addresses as the mystery of being, relates to the notion of *death* in *BT*. It is an originary concealment out of which possibilities of being as such emerge. Just as Heidegger thought how in authentic being-toward-death not only the possibility of the impossibility of being but also possibilities of being as such emerge, he thought that sustaining the abyssal disclosure of the originary concealment of being would allow for originary possibilities of historical being for a people ("the other beginning"). In *Contributions* he writes of death as being a mirroring (*Widerschein*) of the nothing belonging to being (*GA* 65: 282; *CP* 222). Death is the originary "away" (*das Weg*) that belongs to the "there" (*das Da*) of Da-sein (*GA* 65: 325; *CP* 257).

In *Contributions* Heidegger will think that being itself in our epoch does not occur as presencing (which was the case for the Greeks who experienced being as *physis*, as arising into being) but as withdrawal that leaves beings abandoned, deprived of truth in the domination of what he calls machination. The grounding attunement of thinking Heidegger evokes in *Contributions* is related to this withdrawal, i.e.

to the concealment of being. It is a complex grounding attunement comprising schock (*Erschrecken*), restraint (*Verhaltenheit*), and diffidence (*Scheu*). Just as according to *BT* Angst removes Dasein from everydayness, shock unsettles thinking "from the familiarity of customary behavior and into the openness of the pressing forth of what is self-concealing" (*GA* 65: 15; *CP* 14). This shock is "joined from within" by restraint in which "there reigns (although one is still taken aback) a turn toward the hesitant self-withholding as the essential occurrence of being" (*GA* 65: 15; *CP* 14). (This reminds of the notion of *Entschlossenheit* in *BT*, that is, the resolute opening that is ready for Angst and projects itself onto the ownmost being guilty, that means, onto being without ground.) Finally diffidence "is the way of drawing near and remaining near to what is most remote as such" (*GA* 65: 16; *CP* 15), which concerns the divine (the beckoning of the last God), and out of it arises the necessity of "reticence." For now, what I would like to indicate here is that Heidegger's thinking path will develop into the attempt of thinking more and more what he addressed in the truth essay as the mystery of being, the originary concealment of truth that remains removed from the customary (everyday and historically prevalent) mode of relating to beings. Such thinking attempts to hold itself in grounding attunements, to let itself be attuned and determined (*bestimmt*) by the originary concealment of the truth of being and to find words poietically (in reference to the Greek *poiesis*, bringing forth) that may hold open this originary experience of the truth of being.[7]

Yet the originary concealment is only one aspect of truth and one form of concealment at play in the essence (*Wesen* for Heidegger has a verbal sense and thus may be translated also as "essencing" or "essential occurrence") of truth. The other form of concealment is the concealment of the originary concealment, the forgottenness of the mystery. In "On the Essence of Truth" Heidegger describes it the following way: Although freedom as the letting be of beings grounds all comportment and the modes in which beings disclose, "this relation (*Verhältnis*) to the concealment thereby conceals itself" (*GA* 9: 195; *PM* 149). Note again that it is not humans who conceal concealment; they rather find themselves directed into a relation to beings in which they forget the original concealment: "By refusing itself into forgottenness and for it [forgottenness], the mystery leaves historical human beings with their dealings in the sphere of what is readily available to them" (*GA* 9: 195; *PM* 149). Consequently humans follow needs (*Bedürfnisse*) and goals (*Absichten*) from which they take their standards in oblivion of beings as a whole, in the forgottenness of the mystery of being. Human beings "go wrong with respect to the essential genuineness of their standards" (*GA* 9: 196; *PM* 149) and take themselves as the standards for all beings. They *insist* on securing themselves with what is readily available, hold fast to what is offered by beings. Human beings err.

Errancy names the way human beings are driven around, away from the mystery and toward what is readily available (beings), then on from one available thing to the next while passing by the mystery (the truth of being). "Errancy belongs to the inner constitution of the Da-sein into which historical human beings are admitted" (*GA* 9: 196; *PM* 150), i.e. it cannot be removed. If, however, errancy is experienced as such, then, according to Heidegger, there arises the possibility not to be led astray.

Errancy happens in the "between" between being and beings, between the event of truth, i.e. the unconcealment and concealment of being, and our relatedness to beings. It addresses the fact that in our daily lives, we tend to things, plan, seek, enjoy them or are driven away from them and that we don't find ourselves primarily exposed to a sense of being and the finitude of being as such, even if the latter permeate and predispose the way we relate to things.

This tendency toward things, toward relating to what we can identify and reckon with can be experienced, for instance, in moments of anxiety. When anxiety befalls us from nowhere we have the tendency to look for a cause for it; we seek to localize the fear of death in some part of our body where a cancer could be growing. This back and forth between a sense of abyssal being and something that might be threatening our life, is also a form of errancy.

There is, then, nothing wrong with errancy; it is a fact of human "life" and yet, from the thirties on, Heidegger finds that the history of being in the West, that he sees originating with the Greeks, occurs as a further and further withdrawal of being such that now, at the end of the first beginning, beings remain abandoned by being and the forgottenness of being is so entrenched that there arises the danger that a more originary sense of being remains closed off. He speaks of this as the plight of the lack of plight (*die Not der Notlosigkeit*). People feel close to life in their dealings with things and don't experience the need for a more originary questioning of being. Even more dangerous than machination (the determination of being according to which things and events always already appear to us under the paradigm of "making," that is, as calculable and useable) is lived experience (*Erlebnis*). In lived experience only that which can be incorporated into subjective life is "experienced" as "being" (see section 63 of *CP*). Subjective life in how it is "lived" thus becomes the measure for being and it forecloses any need for questioning since one "feels" close to life. Lived experience is thus different from genuine experiences (*Erfahrung*). When I think of striking examples for lived experience usually Reality TV comes to mind, but one could also think of forms of political activism. Heidegger develops much of his thought of machination and lived experience in relation to Nietzsche's notion of will to power and it is tied to the predominance of biologism and life-philosophies that Heidegger always criticized and strove to differentiate himself from.

I believe that Heidegger's thought of the historical dominance of machination and lived experience leads him, in *Besinnung*[8] (*Mindfulness*, written in 1938) to differentiate errancy from *Verkehrung* (distortion) that literally means "being turned in the wrong direction." He now rethinks errancy as nothing "human" and as belonging to the essential occurrence of the clearing of truth (the "Da-" of Da-sein), indeed to the "dignity" of the clearing of truth. "The truth (clearing) of beyng is the beyng of errancy" (*GA* 66: 11). This (dignified) errancy "is the place of origin of distortion, in which [in distortion] we are easily knocked down and in falling fall prey to exclusive predominance of what are only beings; -- powerful and powerless in the change of things and circumstances, it [the distortion] computes for us causes (drives and inclinations, pleasures and delectations) for everything and it twists everything around into the merely present to hand that everybody equally easily possesses, is accustomed to, and uses" (*GA* 66: 12).

Heidegger then goes on to say that when "what is true" (*das Wahre*) occurs and we belong to its essencing, we know of the danger of distortion rooted in the occurrence of truth and thus are able to ward off what is distorted: we "don't let the distorted enter in its unleashed power and don't fear it, dwelling in the danger of beyng, belonging to the unique service of the announced god that has not yet appeared" (*GA* 66: 12).

The differentiation Heidegger makes between truth (with its errancy) and distortion raises for me a number of questions not only when I think of how Heidegger was involved in National Socialism but also in relation to the metaphysical tradition and to experiences many of us "intellectuals" tend to share. Heidegger suggests that if we are aware of distortion, we can (out of a sense of truth) ward it off. He speaks of distortion in terms of a computing (*vorrechnen*) of causes he names "drives and inclinations, pleasures and delectations." (In "On the Essence of Truth" he wrote how in errancy we are prone to needs and goals; and needs, in German *Bedürfnisse*, have the sense of material needs.) We can safely assume that this is what he addresses as well in the notion of "lived experience." Distortions thus lead us to be entrenched in physical, bodily drives and desires relating to things. Truth, on the other hand, discloses in attunements that dislodge us from this entrenchment and open us to the mystery of being.

It is hard not to be reminded, here, of the metaphysical differentiation between physical and spiritual emotions, physical and spiritual love, for instance. Especially Heidegger's invocation of the announced god in the quote above (who is not the Abrahamic or Christian god but he calls "him" nevertheless a god) makes the reader suspicious that Heidegger is quite in line with a tradition that differentiates body and spirit and that finds in spirit a higher dignity. Many of us "intellectuals" (especially if we are sympathetic to Nietzsche and deconstruction) have to find this differentiation quite problematic and betraying a denigration of the body. But I suspect that most of us "intellectuals" would at the same time want to differentiate between people who both blindly and in a calculating way follow their "appetites" and others who are mindful of the power of emotions and attempt not to be overrun by them and we would clearly favor the latter. Furthermore, we all operate in our lives with distinctions we draw between "genuine" and "false" people, between "genuine moments" that reveal for instance "true friendship" from "fake sympathy." We base these differentiations less on reasoning than on our "gut feeling" or, I might also say, on an attunement. Somehow "we know" (or we think we know). It is in a similar sense that Heidegger repeatedly speaks of *Wissen* (knowing) also in his non-public writings. Thinking that is steadfast (*inständig*) in the truth of beyng "knows" truth (see, for instance *GA* 65: 287). Knowing thus means more a disposition than a cognitive act. However, Heidegger uses this notion of knowing not only in his non-public writings in reference to the truth of beyng but also in an address given at Freiburg University to 600 beneficiaries of the National Socialist 'labor service' program: "Knowing means: in our decisions and actions *to be up to* the task that is assigned to us, whether this task be to till the soil or to fell a tree or to dig a ditch or to inquire into the laws of nature or to illumine the fate-like force of history. Knowing means: to be *master* of the situation into which we are placed" (Wolin 1993, 58).

How do we find the measure between truth and distortion? How can we know, that our "knowing" is not entrenched in a distortion? What differentiates steadfastness in the truth of beyng from blind fundamentalism?—These are difficult questions to ask ourselves since they shake us at the very foundations of our lives. They address a fundamental trust that gives a necessary hold to our fragile existences.

Let me take a step back into questioning again the differentiation Heidegger makes between attunements on the one hand and drives, pleasures and delectations, and so on, on the other hand. When in *CP* and the volumes following it Heidegger speaks of ways of being in which we are turned away from truth and toward beings, he refrains from speaking of attunements and uses words evoking physical needs and pleasures that we relate to specific things and activities, i.e. to beings. In the earlier writings, as in *BT* or the lecture course from WS 1929/1930, however, Heidegger uses the notion of *Stimmung* as well in relation to non-fundamental attunements that relate to things: something appears as frightening or boring. We could add to these an attunement of pleasure or delight in which something appears as pleasurable or delightful. I thus would be tempted to rethink the drives, pleasures, and delectations with which our distorted being reckons as non-fundamental attunements or bodily dispositions.

Especially when it comes to non-fundamental attunements that determine how we find ourselves (*befinden*) in relation to concrete situations and things, we get the sense that this involves in a pronounced way our lived bodies. Not by chance Descartes finds the causes of passions that we feel in our minds in agitations of the body. However, causal thinking introduces a subject-object distinction that misses the whole experience and notion of Dasein and the revelatory power of attunements that concern not first a subject or object but a relationality or a dense pluriform connective tissue (as I would say) in which we always already find ourselves and out of which we come to determinations regarding ourselves and things. Let me question, then, the role of the body in Heidegger's thinking of attunements, truth, and errancy.

## 2    Attunement and the Body

There are very few places where Heidegger makes explicit the relation between the lived body (*Leib* in distinction to *Körper*, the objective body) and attunements and one cannot but wonder why.[9] Even when finally in the *Zollikon Seminars* he tackles the issue of the body, his approach to the body does not go through the question of attunement but through spatiality. Furthermore, in the places where Heidegger speaks of attunement (in the *Zollikon Seminars*), he does not mention the body but rather mostly rehashes the existentials of Dasein that are equiprimordial with *Befindlichkeit*, namely understanding (*Verstehen*) and discourse (*Rede*) and emphasizes how human beings can be addressed by beings. Since in his treatment of the body Heidegger does emphasize the existentials of understanding and discourse and how humans find themselves addressed by beings, I will first refer to passages where Heidegger speaks of attunement or disposition (*Befindlichkeit*) and how we find ourselves to be addressed by beings.

*Befindlichkeit* "is the attunedness [*Gestimmtheit*] that attunes and determines [*be-stimmende*] Dasein, its particular relation to world, to the Dasein of fellow humans and to itself" (Heidegger 1987, 182).[10] It is founded in the thrownness of Dasein into beings as a whole and thus to it belongs as well understanding (*Verstehen*). In *BT* Heidegger relates understanding to Dasein's projection, i.e. to the opening up of possibilities of being into which Dasein is always already thrown. Understanding thus is not an explicit cognitive act but a pre-theoretical disclosure of possibilities of being. In understanding is opened up a horizon of possibilities of relating to beings.[11] The unity of thrownness and projection, writes Heidegger in the *Zollikon Seminars*, is determined by language understood as a saying (*ein Sagen*) in which beings show themselves *as* being. With the notion of saying he rethinks what he calls in *BT Rede* (discourse) that precedes the spoken or written word and first makes them possible. Only in so far as something shows itself as being such and such can we find words to name it. On the basis of the unity of thrownness, projection, and language (saying) human beings can be addressed by beings (Heidegger 1987, 182f).

Heidegger highlights how humans find themselves addressed (*Angesprochensein*) also in other occasions, in which he speaks of attunement, conversing with Medard Boss. For instance, he says (July 1965): "Being attuned is not something standing for itself but belongs to being-in-the-world as a being addressed by things. Being attuned and being related are one" (Heidegger 1987, 251). (Heidegger does not refer to understanding and discourse explicitly in this passage but relates attunement directly to being addressed by things.) In a later conversation (March 1966) he highlights again being attuned as relating to the way in which one can be addressed but this time by "the claim [*Zuspruch*] of being" (Heidegger 1987, 263).

It is in the notion of being addressed (language) that I find a link between attunement and bodying (although, as I said, Heidegger does not discuss them together). But first let me indicate how Heidegger thinks the body in the *Zollikon Seminars*.

When thinking of our body out of Da-sein, i.e. out of our being, we find body to occur as what Heidegger addresses with the word *Leiben*, literally "bodying," which mostly is translated as "bodying forth." "The bodying forth of the body is a mode of being; it is a mode of Da-sein" (Heidegger 1987, 113). Da-sein cannot be reduced to bodying but on the other hand, it would not occur without the body. Using traditional language Heidegger says at some point: "The body is the necessary but not sufficient condition for the relation (to things, others, etc.)" (Heidegger 1987, 232). Bodying-forth extends much farther than our corporeal limit (our skin). Indeed "the limit of bodying forth is the horizon of being in which I dwell, a horizon that constantly changes" (Heidegger 1987, 113). Even when I make present (in distinction to imagining or remembering) the train station on the other side of town, the body participates in this making present; not in terms of brain activity, but because in this making present we are spatially oriented and such spatial orientation always involves our body. Heidegger suggests that we could not go pick up a friend at the train station if we were not there with the train station in our bodily being when making it present (Heidegger 1987, 110). Were the train station only a representation in our head, we could never get there.[12]

Although the limit of the bodying forth is the horizon of being, in which I dwell (a horizon of being that discloses in thrown projection involving a "saying"), the understanding of being, according to Heidegger, goes beyond the bodying forth: "To being-in-the-world belongs understanding of being, understanding that I stand in the clearing of being and in each case understanding of being, of how being is determined in the understanding. This limitation is the horizon of the understanding of being. Thereby no bodying forth occurs [*Hierbei geschieht kein Leiben.*]" (Heidegger 1987, 244). According to Heidegger, then, the clearing of being, that is truth reaches beyond bodying forth. One could say that truth is more originary because Heidegger would say that the way our bodying forth occurs is determined out of the clearing of being, indeed our bodying forth is determined by language in so far as our bodying forth is directed by what addresses us. He writes:

> We could not be bodily the way we are if our being-in-the-world did not fundamentally consist in always already being related in apprehension to that which speaks to us out of the openness of our world, an openness as which we exist. Thereby we are always already directed in being addressed [*Zuspruch*] by what is given to us in unconcealing. Only because of this directedness can we distinguish in front, behind, above and below, right and left. Only because of this directedness can we have a body or rather be bodily. It is not the case that we are first bodily and then have above below, right and left. (Heidegger 1987, 293f)

Our bodily orientation and the very movements of our body when we speak, look, hear, are directed out of being addressed by being and the being of other beings (including other human beings). Our bodily being is responsive to how we are addressed. Yet how we are addressed, as Heidegger said in the other passages quoted above, is determined not only by the understanding of being but also by attunement that, in fact, he relates to language (saying) even without interpellation of the understanding of being.

Especially if we consider attunement in terms of disposition (*Befindlichkeit*), this evokes human facticity, i.e. how we find ourselves to be, to dwell. This dwelling is, however, a bodily dwelling such that in bodily being-in-the-world we take place relationally in being and in being with whatever addresses us knowingly and mostly unknowingly. I would extend and "complete" Heidegger's preliminary analysis of bodying forth by saying that if our body articulates the temporal spacing of our being in relation to what addresses us (even if objectively speaking, it is far away or even if "what" addresses us cannot be geometrically located anywhere), attunements name the temporal texture of this bodily spacing (connections with Merleau-Ponty's notion of flesh could be made here), the tissue in and through which we are bodily connected with beings and overlap and variously coalesce with other modes of being in always modifying ways including modes of finding ourselves drawn out by, withdrawing from, or being like suspended in relation to what appears as fearful, desirable, indifferent, etc. Our attuned bodying forth thus precedes perception in the sense of a conscious apprehension of something. (Which does not foreclose that a conscious apprehension would alter attunements.)

If body (bodying forth) and attunement are as closely interwoven as I suggest and indeed name different aspects of the same, if furthermore attunements are revelatory, i.e. constitutive of truth, then the question of the relation between bodying and truth arises.

## 3   Bodying Forth and Truth

A discussion of the relation between the body and truth needs to draw resources from other texts and concepts we find in Heidegger and needs to address as well the "thing"—character of the body in the

Heideggerian sense of being a being (*ein Seiendes*) since there occurs a (constantly changing) delimitation with what we come to conceive as different bodies. I can only briefly sketch what I have elaborated more at length elsewhere (Vallega-Neu 2005) namely the relation between the body and what Heidegger calls the sheltering of the truth of being in beings and the (implied) relation between body and earth.

According to how Heidegger articulates it in the context of *CP*, although beyng and beings differ, there occurs no disclosure of being without beings and vice versa. "The Origin of the Work of Art" can be seen as an essay in which Heidegger thinks ahead into the possibility of how a work of art could shelter truth and thus configure a concrete site that holds open, so to speak, an event of truth in which resounds not only the coming to presence but also the concealment belonging to truth. Heidegger writes how the work of art sets up a world and brings forth the earth by setting itself back into the earth (*GA* 5: 27–36; *BW* 167–174). The work of art holds open the strife of the opening up of a world and the self-secluding of earth through which truth happens as unconcealing-concealing. Thus we can be struck by the "that-it-is" of a work of art and what is revealed through it. This account needs to be supplemented by thinking how our lived bodies are also beings that in their earthly, that is, self-secluding quality delimit, hold open and configure concrete sites of being and the way truth and errancy happens in them. Our bodies configure (in being with other beings) concrete sites of the "there-being" of truth, i.e. Da-sein. I will now add to this that our bodies happen in and through attunements such that the configuration of sites of disclosure occur through attunements in which things appear as such in differently attuned ways at the same time that the body in its earthly quality recedes, secludes itself.

"Our" attuned, ecstatically spatializing and temporalizing bodies are constitutive of truth, of the appearing and non-appearing of sites of being and the appearing and concealing of things and events. They are at the same time responsive to what addresses us from out of the opening of a world and to concealment as such. Adding Heidegger's analysis of the double concealment of truth we should also note how in our bodies are "sheltered" the double concealment of truth by virtue of our relation to death (that mirrors the finitude of being as such, the "mystery") and to errancy in which we are turned toward beings and away from death and the finitude of being as such.

The role the body plays in the happening of truth warrants that we rethink the relation between truth and errancy in light of "our" attuned and truth (and errancy) sheltering bodies. According to what Heidegger writes in the *Zollikon Seminars*, although bodying forth is a mode of Da-sein and necessary for the discovery of beings, it is different from the understanding of being through which something is disclosed as such and it is by virtue of the understanding of being but not the bodying that I can then name it, for instance, as being a window. This would mean that a disclosive aspect of truth in which something appears *as* such and such, cannot be attributed to our bodying. And yet we find ourselves addressed by virtue of *attunements*, which, according to the discussion above, means as well by virtue of our bodying forth, which I am rethinking as a dynamic connective tissue that binds us to what comes to appear, for example, as a tall window. I am thus attributing a certain primacy to attunement, which follows Heidegger's own turn in the thirties in which he no longer sees a certain primacy in the projection of Dasein over thrownness (as in *BT*), but rather attributes a certain primacy to thrownness, in so far as any projection of thought is already responsive to the throw of being (see section 122 in *GA 65* and *CP*). The throw of being he sometimes names the call of being. The following section 108 of *Über den Anfang* (*GA 70*) ("On Inception," this is a collection of non-public writings dating 1941) is the only passage (or outline) I found that indicates how the later Heidegger would think of the relation between the event (the truth of being) and human being in its bodiliness:

> *108. Da-sein and Humans*
> Provenance of the essence of humans insofar as they are experienced out of their relation to being, which relation only essentially occurs as character of the inclusion of humans into beyng "through" beyng.
> Being
> Appropriation (of Da-sein)

> Voice [*Stimme*] (word of beyng – concealment – keeping silent)
> Attunement [*Stimmung*]
> Demand of courage [or sending of mood, *Zu-mutung* means both]
> Gathered mood [*Gemüt*]
> Indwelling [*Inständigkeit* – previously translated as „steadfastness"]
> *Disposition* [*Befindlichkeit*] (bodily being)
>         (understood differently as in 'Being and Time,' where it was
> equated with attunement.)
>     Da-sein is the gathered mood of being attuned by the voice of beyng—.
> (*GA* 70: 131. My translation)

This passage indicates how Heidegger thinks attunement as rooted in the silent voice (the "word of," in the sense of "belonging to") beyng that is "sent" into being gathered by human being that is steadfast or dwells in the attuned gathered clearing of being (Da-sein). It is thus that humans are disposed in their bodiliness. Interestingly, Heidegger found it necessary to differentiate *Befindlichkeit* (bodily disposition) from *Stimmung* that arises beyond the (not yet) human being as that through which human being is appropriated (given to *be*). Thus *Stimmung* that arises as the attuning voice of being determines a provenance for further determination of bodily being as *Befindlichkeit*. What Heidegger addresses here as the attuning voice of being, in the *Zollikon Seminars* is rethought as a "being addressed" by being.

It is Heidegger's distinction between attuning being and bodily being, i.e. between attunement and bodily disposition, that I have begun calling into question by rethinking attunement as the texture of "human" bodying itself that both discloses and recedes with respect to what appears and we relate to as such. I am putting "human" in quotation marks just as I put "our" in quotation marks when writing of "our bodies" since I believe that insofar as I interpret our bodying as a dynamic connective tissue, the boundaries of the body in relation to "what" attunes us and addresses us cannot be clearly marked. There is a strange indifference of what we come to call "our bodies," an anonymous quality that Merleau-Ponty[13] was well aware of and that, in a more Heideggerian framework, I would attribute to the self-secluding earthly character of bodies. I believe that Nietzsche addressed this as unconscious drives and affects that are constitutive of what we come to identify as an "I".

The blurring of the boundaries between what addresses us and our bodying has consequences with respect to the notions of errancy and distortion we find in Heidegger, since the distinction between truth revealing attunements in which errancy or distortions are "held at bay" and attunements relating us to other beings cannot be upheld. I believe that the attunements determining our relational being are always multiple and highly complex. What weaves into attunements (into bodily being or bodily forth) are the spatio-temporal attuned-attuning occurrences of other humans, animals, configured spaces (buildings and cities), the air, the weather, the light, machines and other non-living things. I am brought to reflect as well how there are numerous conversations and messages sent on cell phones and other wireless devices that constantly invisibly permeate spaces traversing bodies. Furthermore, we need to take into account histories and expectations that are sheltered in our bodies and that are co-constitutive of relational attunements involving "our" bodies.

Heidegger's thinking always worked at gathering towards what he called fundamental attunements that in his view determined historical being. The ability to concentrate or meditate and thus somehow create a spacing with respect to various attunements is something that I cannot develop here. Let me only note that this spacing relates to what Heidegger calls "clearing." No doubt that Heidegger had great concentric power. But who meditates knows that we cannot control attunements but at best can let them be. We cannot choose which attunements become revelatory for us and much remains hidden in our dispositions. Even if there are moments of clearing, of spacing that are constitutive of an alertness with respect to various attunements, even in those very moments we inevitably remain blind with respect to many if not most of the attunements disposing our actions and thoughts. It is here, then, that I would situate what one may call Heidegger's errancies together with everybody else's.

# Notes

1. Heidegger's non-public writings on the event comprise *Contributions to Philosophy (Of the Event)* (*GA* 65) and the volumes following it. They were written between 1936 and 1944.
2. *Befindlichkeit*, literally translated means "how we find ourselves to be" either understood as a state of being in itself or as a state of being in relation to a situation.
3. Martin Heidegger, "Vom Wesen der Wahrheit," in *Wegmarken*, 3rd ed., ed. Friedrich-Wilhelm von Herrmann (Frankfurt am Main: Klostermann, 1996), *Gesamtausgabe*, vol. 9. Henceforth cited as *GA 9*. Translated as *Pathmarks*, ed. William McNeill (Ambridge: Cambridge University Press, 1998). Henceforth cited as *PM*.
4. See section two of "On the Essence of Truth."
5. The middle voice as we find it, for instance in Ancient Greek, but not in modern European languages, is a verb form that is neither active nor passive such that one cannot say that a subject acts or is acted upon. An example would be "It rains" or "A plot unfolds itself."
6. In a marginal note from 1943 Heidegger writes how between sections 5 and 6 there occurs a leap into the turning of the event. In "Deformatives: Essentially Other Than Truth" John Sallis reads this leap in terms of "a monstruous decentering of the essence of truth" (in *Reading Heidegger: Commemorations*, ed. John Sallis [Bloomington and Indianapolis: Indiana University Press, 1993], 39). It is monstruous in so far as to the essence of truth belongs the non-essence of truth, i.e. to truth belongs its "other," "non-truth" in in terms of both an originary concealment and errancy that tends to conceal the originary concealment.
7. See Daniela Vallega-Neu, *Heidegger's Poetic Writings: From* Contributions to Philosophy *to* The Event (Bloomington and Indianapolis: Indiana University Press, 2018). I would like to draw attention as well to a relation between the attuning occurring (according to the truth essay) out of the concealment of beings as a whole and what Heidegger developed in *BT* as the call of conscience, and what he addresses in *CP* as the call of beyng. Furthermore, the attuning, the call of conscience and the call of beyng all imply language understood as the very wide sense of an originary (silent) coming to be articulated even before a spoken word. Thus,

for Heidegger the disclosure of being (of the being of beings) that occurs through attunements implies language. Note that I am not suggesting that Heidegger is thinking the same phenomenon differently but rather that in *BT* and in *CP* he is rethinking similar phenomena.

8. Martin Heidegger, *Besinnung*, ed. Friedrich-Wilhelm von Herrmann (Frankfurt am Main:Vittorio Klostermann, 1997) (*GA* 66). Translated by Parvis Emad and Thomas Kalary as *Mindfulness* (New York: Continuum, 2006). All translations are mine.

9. Among the few places where Heidegger makes explicit the relation between attunements and the body is a passage in Heidegger's Nietzsche lecture from the winter semester 1936/1937: "Every feeling [*Gefühl*] is a bodying forth attuned in this or that way, an attunement bodying forth in this or that way" (*GA* 43: 118; *N1*: 100). In *Basic Questions of Philosophy* Heidegger writes that humans are determined in their bodiliness because they are taken over by attunements (*GA* 45: 154; *BQ* 133f). For a discussion of the primacy of attunements over the body in Heidegger see Michel Haar, "Le primat de la *Stimmung* sur la corporéité du *Dasein*," in *Heidegger Studies*, vol. 2, 67–80, 1986.

10. Martin Heidegger, *Zollikoner Seminare*, ed. Medard Boss (Frankfurt am Main: Klostermann, 1987). I will be citing the German pagination that can be found at the margins of the English translation.

11. In a conversation with Medard Boss, Heidegger rephrases what in *BT* he calls the understanding of being with concepts he uses in his non-public writings: "Understanding of being is the ecstatic-projecting standing in (steadfastness) in the clearing of the there" (Heidegger 1987, 236). Note how the German word for understanding (*Verstehen*) has the root "standing" (*Stehen*) in it.

12. Although the *Zollikon Seminars* don't provide us with a systematic account of different modes of being with…, that is, making present, imagining, etc., they give pointers for phenomenological differentiations. I would like to point out here, that Heidegger differentiates, for instance, the bodily being at and mere imagining, in which the bodying occurs differently (Heidegger 1987, 244f).

13. See Maurice Merleau-Ponty, *The Phenomenology of Perception* (Merleau-Ponty 223f). See as well Daniela Vallega-Neu, "Bodily Being and Indifference," *Epoché* 17, no. 1 (2012): 111–122.

# References

Heidegger, Martin. 1987. *Zollikoner Seminare: Protokolle, Gespräche, Briefe.* Edited by Boss Medard. Frankfurt am Main: Vittorio Klostermann.

Merleau-Ponty, Maurice. 2012. *The Phenomenology of Perception.* Translated by D. A. Landes. New York: Routledge.

Stolorow, Robert D. 2014. "Heidegger, Mood and the Lived Body: The Ontical and the Ontological." *Janus Head: Journal of Interdisciplinary Studies in Literature, Continental Philosophy, Phenomenological Psychology, and the Arts* 13 (2): 5–11.

Vallega-Neu, Daniela. 2005. *The Bodily Dimension in Thinking.* New York: SUNY.

Vallega-Neu, Daniela. 2012. "Bodily Being and Indifference." *Epoché* 17 (1): 111–122.

Vallega-Neu, Daniela. 2018. *Heidegger's Poietic Writings: From* Contributions to Philosophy *to* The Event. Bloomington and Indianapolis: Indiana University Press.

Wolin, Richard. 1993. *The Heidegger Controversy: A Critical Reader.* Cambridge and London: MIT Press.

# 10

## Love as Passion: Epistemic and Existential Aspects of Heidegger's Unknown Concept

Tatjana Noemi Tömmel

After the edition of Heidegger's "Black Notebooks" in 2014 and 2015, it seems necessary to justify one's research on Heidegger, especially if one writes on a topic so unpolitical as love. The revelation of Heidegger's anti-semitism, made even more appalling by its "philosophical" embedding, came as a shock even to already disillusioned Heidegger scholars. His idea of a Jewish world conspiracy shows him not only as morally condemnable, but as incapable of proper judgement, as a person eager to integrate a conspiracy theory so crude as *The Protocols of the Elders of Zion* into his "Seinsgeschichte". It is hard to believe that the same person counts as one of the greatest thinkers of the twentieth century (Trawny 2015).

There are, however, at least two reasons why it is still justifiable, maybe even necessary, to study Heidegger: First, he is one of the most influential philosophers in the past hundred years. Through his

T. N. Tömmel (✉)
Department of Philosophy, Berlin Technical University,
Berlin, Germany
e-mail: t.toemmel@tu-berlin.de

© The Author(s) 2019
C. Hadjioannou (ed.), *Heidegger on Affect*, Philosophers in Depth,
https://doi.org/10.1007/978-3-030-24639-6_10

wide and politically diverse range of students, friends and followers, he has left an indelible mark on the following generations. Without understanding Heidegger, one cannot fully understand the philosophy of the twentieth and twenty first century. Second, it is possible that Heidegger's early thought is not yet tainted by his later curious inability to think. In this case, one could gain insight from his earlier works. Given Heidegger's lasting influence, it seems in any case important to analyze the formation of his philosophy, which puzzlingly combines genuinely deep reflection with pseudo-deep babble and political views of the most primitive kind. Hence, the aim of this paper is to shed some light on an almost unknown concept of Heidegger: love.

# 1    Heidegger on Love

It seems to be a universally accepted truth that Heidegger never wrote a single word on love. The topic has been said to be "systematically excluded" (Pattison 2006, 171) from his fundamental ontology. Very few authors, among them Jacques Derrida and Giorgio Agamben (Derrida 1989; Agamben 2008), have challenged this widespread belief. However, Heidegger's philosophy is not without love: a careful reading of his writings, including lecture courses, notes and correspondence, reveals that love is not only featured as a notion among others in his works, but in fact plays a major role in the development of his thoughts. In contrast to his published work, there are parts of his personal correspondence where love becomes not just the dominant theme, but blossoms into the leitmotiv of his *philosophical* thinking, too. In scattered passages of his published work, as well, Heidegger sketches, en passant, as it were, a complex concept of love, which is cross-linked to key concepts of his thought, and whose significance goes well beyond its immediate context. Consequently, it is necessary to base the interpretation on a variety of texts. My analysis draws in equal measure on sources from published works, lectures, drafts and notes, but also draws on works that are not part of the actual oeuvre, such as letters, poems and diaries.

This chapter will focus on two aspects, namely the epistemic and the existential function Heidegger ascribes to love. The first part will analyze the relation between love and cognition. Influenced by Plato, Augustine, medieval mystics and Max Scheler, Heidegger discusses the epistemic function of love in his earliest writings and later conceives a concept of philosophy, in which love actualizes Dasein's primordial transcendence and is therefore the "foundation of phenomenological understanding" (*GA* 16: 185). The second part will focus on Heidegger's early Freiburg and Marburg years and will show how love becomes the key to leading an authentic life, usually associated with anxiety and death. Decades before 'event' or 'enowning' (*Ereignis*) becomes the focal point of his thinking, Heidegger describes the beginning of love as a true break-out, which transforms existence for good.

By discussing love's role for phenomenological understanding and *Eigentlichkeit*, the chapter aims at giving an introduction into Heidegger's little known concept of love, thus trying to gain a more differentiated image of the "socio-ontological deficits" (Schmidt 2005) of his analysis of Dasein. It will, however, have to leave out a third and equally important aspect. Time and again, Heidegger defines love as the will to the other's true self: love, he writes to Hannah Arendt in 1925, meant "volo ut sis"—"I want you to be what you are" (Arendt and Heidegger 2004, 21). Even thirty years later, Heidegger still holds on to the same definition: "Love is the letting-be [*das Sein-lassen*] in a deeper sense, according to which it calls forth the essence" (Heidegger 1960, 19; my translation). Like the kind of solicitude that 'leaps ahead' (*SZ* 122) love is focused on the *other*'s authentic existence. Given that the topic of this volume is "Heidegger on affects" and not "Heidegger on *Mitsein*", the paper will not discuss this interpersonal and social dimension of Heidegger's concept of love (Tömmel 2013, 118–144).[1]

## 2    From Logic to the *Logic of the Heart*: Heidegger's Early Works

Both historically and systematically, the concept of interpersonal love in Heidegger is preceded by a notion of love which has an epistemic function. Heidegger's earliest writings between 1912 and 1921 show that his notion of "love" played a role in his formation as a phenomenologist. Given his quest for the unity of being and thinking, I argue that Heidegger is chiefly interested in love as a philosophical 'method', a unifying force that explains the relation between subject and object. Put simply, love and cognition belong together for Heidegger, because love—understood as "devotion" or "self-abandonment"—opens up to truth or meaning.

Initially interested in epistemological questions and a fervent defender of pure logic, the young Heidegger soon harbors doubts whether logic alone can grasp truth in a full sense. During the time of his habilitation, he becomes interested in phenomenology, hermeneutics, axiology, and medieval mysticism, and soon tries to approach metaphysical problems from the point of view of "personal experience" (*GA* 1: 191). In order to create a "philosophy as living truth", Heidegger wants to "declare war" on "rationalism" (Heidegger 2005, 36; my translation). The last chapter of his habilitation (1916), marks this transition from logic to a Pascalian logic of the heart (*GA* 5: 311).[2] Heidegger describes the form of thinking of medieval men as "absolute devotion" (*Hingabe*) and "immersion" (*GA* 1: 198) into the subject matter, and points out that the medieval world view can only be grasped by a "conforming open-mindedness of empathic understanding" (*GA* 1: 408). There are many indications that in the years to follow, Heidegger modelled his idea of phenomenology after the "self-abandonment" he discovered in medieval philosophy (*GA* 26: 215). The more Heidegger becomes interested in the pre-theoretical dimension of life, the more he mistrusts theoretical, conceptual or scientific approaches. In the text "In the thou to God", written for his wife in 1918, he contrasts the alienating forces of the theoretical attitude with the foundational experience of the thou in love, which he believes to be able to heal the lost wholeness, and which he describes to have enabled him to set out from the "origin" (*Ursprung*) (*GA* 81: 15; cf. Heidegger 2005, 45).

However, Heidegger's claim that love opens up to truth, is by no means confined to personal letters. There are, in fact, many examples from his early Freiburg period, where Heidegger states that philosophy was neither science nor theoretical insight lead by principles, but "eros" or "passion" [*Leidenschaft*] (*GA* 61: 24). In this, Heidegger is influenced by Plato's *Symposion*, mystics in general and Eckhart in particular, but also by his contemporary Max Scheler whose works he seems to have read right after their publication. Giorgio Agamben was the first to point out that Heidegger's attention to the fundamental role of love for cognition was initially inspired by Max Scheler's essay *Liebe und Erkenntnis* (1916) (Agamben 2008; Scheler 1963, 77–98). Scheler assumed that love was the "uniting source of consciousness" (Scheler 1963, 94) underlying all acts of cognition, perception and willing. In his lecture on Augustine (1921), Heidegger, too, describes love as the higher form of cognition in contrast to the dissociating sciences (*GA* 60: 71, 179; Scheler 1963, 97). For his lecture course in winter 1919/1920, he noted under the heading "phenomenological intution" (*Phänomenologische Anschauung*): "Love as *motivational* foundation [*Motiv*grund] of phenomenological understanding – in its enactmental sense [*Vollzugssinn*] necessarily given" (*GA* 58: 185). Love seems to be a—or the?—basis of the phenomenological-hermeneutical process. For the same lecture course Heidegger noted: "In love there is *understanding;* in devotion – not to facts, but to meaning, as living relations of life, *winning* [...]" (*GA* 58: 168). However, Heidegger does not content himself with seeing love only as foundation of philosophy. Like Scheler, he criticizes Plato for understanding ἔρως only as motivator, being in fact the very essence of philosophy: he writes that the true philosophical attitude was never the attitude of a logical tyrant who frightens life by his stare. The true attitude of the philosopher was Plato's eros, asking for a final self-release into the last tendencies of life and its last motives. The opposite of the phenomenological attitude, he writes, was a self-harnessing into something. In contrast, philosophy demands a self-releasement into life, not into its surface, but into its originality (*Ursprünglichkeit*) (*GA* 58: 263).

This passage makes clear how far Heidegger has come from his starting point, claiming now that logic was a "tyrannic stare", not compatible with the fulness of life. But Platonic eros, too, does not exactly characterize what Heidegger wants to express, being rather the desire to catch than to release or "let-go". The true erotic attitude of the philosopher is understood as the precondition for understanding, because in contrast to the logic or scientific "stare", it is a form of openness and self-release. With Eckhart, Heidegger will later call the condition of thinking "Gelassenheit" or "letting-be" (*Seinlassen*). In substance, he did not discover it after the so-called turn, but already in 1916.

The thought that not only moods and emotions in general, but love in particular, enables cognition can be followed throughout Heidegger's work like a red thread. "The things themselves" are discovered only by someone who is passionately devoted to them. As such, Heidegger's earliest thoughts about love can be interpreted as the prologue to the disclosing role moods later play in *BT* and other texts from the 1920s and 30s. In these writings, Heidegger claims that Dasein discloses its world primarily through moods. "Dasein's openness to the world is constituted existentially by the attunement of a state-of-mind [*Befindlichkeit*]" (*SZ* 137). Hence, there is no such thing as "pure beholding" (*SZ* 138). In *Befindlichkeit*, Dasein "surrenders itself to the 'world' and lets the 'world' 'matter'" (*SZ* 139).

Heidegger criticizes psychology, physiology and biology for classifying emotions as irrational accompanying symptoms of the rationally conceived human being (*GA* 6.1: 41). In phenomenology, too, affects and feelings were still perceived as psychic phenomena, ranging in hierarchy after perception and willing. Only Scheler, "accepting the challenges of Augustine and Pascal", had pointed to the problem of the interconnection between "acts which 'represent' and acts which 'take an interest'" (*SZ* 139). In later writings, too, Heidegger praises Scheler for having been on the right track towards a primordial transcendence, which he himself did not think radically enough in *BT* (*GA* 26: 215). In his Nietzsche lectures, Heidegger does not only claim that *Befindlichkeit* or feeling precedes understanding, but that it unifies all cognitive faculties to an original unity (*GA* 6.1: 48).

It is this relation between *Befindlichkeit* and understanding, and not *Mitsein*, which makes Heidegger mention "love" in a footnote in *BT*. In this footnote, he quotes Pascal and Augustine, having been the sources for Scheler's insights, and thereby confirms the relation between love and truth. Pascal writes:

And thence it comes about that in the case where we are speaking of human things, it is said to be necessary to know them before we love them, and this has become a proverb; but the saints, on the contrary, when they speak of divine things, say that we must love them before we know them, and that we enter into truth only by charity; they have made of this one of their most useful maxims. (*SZ* 139n1)

The quote by Augustine simply states that "one does not enter into truth except through charity" (ibid.).

Heidegger will never give up the conviction that "love" is essential for philosophy discovered in his earliest years. In his later writings, he emphasizes the importance of love for thinking. Playing with the words "Vermögen" (ability, potential) and "mögen" (to like) in "What is called thinking?", he claims that man could only think if he liked his object of love, Being (*GA* 8: 5).[3] On some occasions, Heidegger even identifies thinking and loving (*GA* 75: 363), and describes the relation between man and Being as a relationship of mutual love (*GA* 6.1: 197f; *GA* 8: 5; *GA* 9: 316). In the "Letter on 'Humanism'", he states that it is by virtue of love that something is truly able to be (*GA* 9: 316).[4] The idea that love brings forth Dasein's authentic existence, can be traced back to his writings of the 1920s.

# 3    Love as an Alternative Path to *Eigentlichkeit*

The concept of *Eigentlichkeit*, or being oneself, is certainly Heidegger's best-known and most influential achievement in the Marburg period (Figal 1992, 60). The linking of *Eigentlichkeit* and existential isolation, however, provokes a conflict with another notion that blossomed in the

Marburg years: being with others. In *BT* it is clearly not the encounter with the other, but the withdrawal from them that leads to authenticity. Not surprisingly, it has been doubted if the methodological solipsism of Heidegger's approach allows for an authentic form of sociality at all (Großmann 1998, 97). This doubt, however, is not justified, as can easily be illustrated by a speech Heidegger gave on occasion of his brother Fritz's wedding day in October 1925: "The foundation of marriage is love. But what is love? Not that, what people commonly understand by it and wish of it. [...] True love does not ground in external properties, relations and circumstances. It is nothing that can mutually be given by agreement. It grows only and primarily out of an inner truthfulness towards oneself. Only where this is awake, the truthfulness towards the other becomes possible" (*GA* 16: 52; my translation).

This speech is entirely consistent with the *magnum opus* Heidegger was preparing at the time. For once Dasein has found itself in "being-towards-death", it will also be with others in an entirely new way. Heidegger tells us that being oneself is the *conditio sine qua non* for any true attachment to the beloved.

Hence, the problem every study of Heidegger's concept of being-with faces is not whether his thought leaves room for sociality at all. Rather, it is the question whether and under which conditions a *relation* with the other can be the origin of authenticity. I suggest that this is precisely the question Heidegger tries to answer in his private correspondence. An analysis of his letters, in which they are set in relation to lecture courses and other public texts, reveals that Heidegger knew an alternative path to being authentic, in addition to the self-centered way described in *BT*. In the following, I will show that, and in what way, the encounter with the beloved can be the source of true selfhood. Subsequently, I will explain why love is bestowed with this function. While at first glance it might seem as if Heidegger was merely designing a more indulgent path to authenticity in his personal correspondence, which remains philosophically irrelevant, a thorough analysis will reveal that being-in-love and being-towards-death share the same kairologic structure. I claim that Heidegger developed this kairologic concept of love (and death) through his intensive engagement with the messianism of St. Paul in 1919, and subsequently transferred it to his own philosophy. In the following, I will point out some of the structural parallels between Heidegger's lecture course on early Christianity, *BT*, and his notion of love in order to make the relation between love, time and authenticity clear.

Let's imagine for a moment that Heidegger wrote a text on love. According to his habit to introduce new concepts by contrasting them to their common, "vulgar" meaning, it could begin in the following way: "It is a complete misconception of love to believe it grown and fostered through common interests and objects – the way the bourgeois loves – one has a household together – travels together [...] one loves and is eminently happy in doing so – in which the whole life may never experience a true break-out of love" (Heidegger 2005, 99).

In this letter to his wife from 1919, Heidegger is convinced that it is not "common interests", but "a true break-out" that characterizes real love. Decades before "event" or "enowning" (*Ereignis*) becomes the focal point of his thinking, Heidegger, in his early letters, describes the beginning of love as an exceptional state, which transforms existence for good: "The other's presence suddenly breaks into our life – no soul can come to terms with that. A human fate gives itself over to another human fate, and the duty [*Dienst*] of pure love is to keep this giving as alive as it was on the first day." (Arendt and Heidegger 2004, 5) Heidegger describes the encounter between lovers as an overwhelming moment; the breaking-in of love into one's life is not merely a particular and meaningful experience, but a radical break with the continuity of existence as it was before. At the same time, a new form of life is founded, in which the other has become "a force that will influence [this] life forever" (Arendt and Heidegger 2004, 16f). The "moment of vision" (*Augenblick*) designated by this "break-in" is a new beginning that breaks with the linearity and homogeneity of time, like wonder. Such a moment or *kairos* is a crisis, in which existence can be seized or missed. Paul Tillich, who wrote about the concept of *kairos* during the same period, described it as the "irruption of eternity into time" (Tillich 1926, 35; my translation) and explained that it was characterized by fate and decision.

In Heidegger's understanding, these shocks of everyday life are precisely what offer one the prospect of living more profoundly. The "true break-out" is the onset of an exceptional state, in which the self-evidence of everyday life, its norms, values and customs, in short: the knowledge of what "one" has to do and to omit, does not count any more. As "love as such does not exist" (Arendt and Heidegger 2004, 27), the moment of the encounter is a radical appeal to be oneself: "Do you know that this [i.e. love] is the most difficult thing a human is given to endure? For anything else there are methods, aids, limits, and understanding – here alone everything means: to be in one's love = to be forced into one's innermost existence" (Arendt and Heidegger 2004, 21).

Here, Heidegger twice affirms the sole claim of love to a privilege, which, in *BT*, is granted primarily to anxiety and death: to serve as *principium individuationis* and to lead to authenticity. Love is not only the most difficult or heaviest of burdens, and therefore alone predestined to force Dasein into selfhood. What is more, Heidegger writes that "for everything else" there are conventions, "help", and "limitations" to make the path passable, i.e. to take choice and decision from the individuals' shoulders. Only in love, man has to slash his way through the thicket alone. Love is a mode of Being in which Dasein cannot be represented by someone else—and that, apparently, to at least the same measure as in its "being-towards-death". While in *BT* Dasein becomes itself by withdrawing from the diversion of interacting with others, Heidegger, in the letters, seems to sketch a form of selfhood on the basis of reciprocal transcendence toward other Dasein: "oneself becomes strong in love – a giving that is not a giving away, in whose enactment one comes to oneself for the first time" (Heidegger 2005, 112).

The fundamental role Heidegger ascribes to moods or emotions in general, and to love in particular, is based on the importance of passivity or receptivity for true understanding. When Heidegger describes love as a "passion", he wants to underline its origin from "pathos" and "paschein", meaning to suffer, endure, bear, carry or to being carried and being determined (*bestimmt*) by something (Heidegger 1963, 39f). Enduring a passion does not rule out *Eigentlichkeit*, quite the opposite: Receptivity is necessary for self-realization. In his book on Nietzsche,

Heidegger compares "passions" (*Leidenschaften*) and "affects" (*Affekte*). While affects like joy, wrath or infatuation, "affect" us in a way that we lose ourselves and are no longer master of ourselves, the "attack" of a genuine passion like love or hate was the break-out of something we had already nurtured within ourselves (*GA* 6.1: 42-44). The break-in of the presence of the other is at the same time the break-out of *Eigentlichkeit*. Therefore, the self-transcendence in passion is not a self-alienation but the manifestation of one's own will, in which Dasein becomes who it truly is (*GA* 6.1: 49).

But does this not contradict everything Heidegger has to say about "being-with-others" in *BT*? Was it not only possible for anxiety to shake the torpid existence because it illuminated the futility of *all* attachments? How then shall love—the attachment to another human being, the stability of a relationship, the confirmation of one's own existence—lead to self-realization?

In *BT* the function of death is to offer a relational structure in which the absolute, pure *possibility* is experienced. If Heidegger's concept of love should be compatible with the statements in his main work, love, too, must not tend toward making something real available, but has to make the "possibility of the possible just [...] 'greater'" (*SZ* 262). The following investigation of the temporal structure of transcendence, which Heidegger describes will show that the authenticity of love, which at first seems to contradict *BT* is, in fact, a *confirmation* of the principle of individuation outlined therein.

One of the early letters to Arendt reveals that Heidegger does not understand love as union and shared life, but as a mysterious transformation of one's own being:

> Why is love rich beyond all other possible human experiences and a sweet burden to those seized in its grasp? Because we become what we love and yet remain ourselves. Then we want to thank the beloved, but find nothing that suffices. We can only thank with our selves. Love transforms gratitude into loyalty to our selves and unconditional faith in the other. That is how love steadily intensifies its innermost secret. (Arendt and Heidegger 2004, 4f)

Heidegger describes how lovers change—but their changing is not an absorption by the other, but a realization of their own "proper" identity. The transformation is a twofold movement: in relating to what she is not, the lover comes to herself, for she wasn't herself until now. The "possibility" of love is particularly rich because the lover cannot thank the beloved but with his faithfulness to herself. Thus, the encounter with the other does not result in an annihilation of one's own identity but in its intensification—Dasein reaches a higher, an authentic form of existence. Because the lover does not escape or reduce her own existence, Heidegger characterizes love as a (even though sweet) "burden". In *BT* moods disclose the "burdensome character of Dasein" (*SZ* 134). Usually, Dasein evades this burden instead of taking it on as an occasion to evolve. The fact that love is associated with a burden that one cannot divest oneself of reconciles the concept of love with the analysis of Dasein in *BT*. Although love and death evoke rather different connotations, they structurally seem to be akin in Heidegger: for love is as strong as death – when it comes to being authentic. Love only leads to authentic selfhood because it is intrinsically linked to a kairologic understanding of time. Authenticity is not a quality that can be acquired once and for all, but rather demands a constant struggle, a constant renewal: the "duty of pure love" has to keep the event awake "like on the very first day". The dynamic of self-realization can only be maintained on the condition that the exceptional state does not get lost in shared everydayness: "Having-found-each-other [*Sichgefundenhaben*] is in itself of absolute value – the duration is immaterial. In contrast, time and duration have their truly valuable function in the stage of awaiting and hoping – the trustful preparation for the returning unification – or in the stage of thankfully thinking-back, joyfully holding-on and holding-*out* [*Durchhalten*] of the offered gift –" (Heidegger 2005, 99).

The essence of love unfolds in a specific interplay of unique encounter and retrospective conservation of this moment: outbreak and keeping awake of the state of exception. The *kairos* of the encounter is not simply a sudden turning point (von Falkenhayn 2003, 34). Although it is impossible to predict or to provoke it, it demands preparation (Arendt and Heidegger 2004, 59). Because love is always a *coup de foudre*, it will only last on condition that the "act of grace" (Heidegger and Blochmann 1990, 31) is conserved. In May 1919, Heidegger used the following words to tell Elisabeth Blochmann how one has to deal with "the secret and grace-character of life":

> We have to be able to wait for extreme intensities of meaningful life – and we have to remain in continuity with these moments of vision – not so much savour them – as rather integrate them into life – to take them into the succession of life and include into the rhythm of all coming life. [...] By that, I don't mean the triviality that one has to abide by the understood – but in a vehement life, becoming aware of the own (not theoretic) but totally experiential directedness, is at the same time the sudden stepping into it – the *expansion of a new agitatedness* over and in all stirrings of life. (Heidegger and Blochmann 1990, 14)

Hence, the transient "moment of vision" must not remain alien to daily life. From this standpoint, a repetition of the unique moment, the *kairos* becomes possible (Arendt and Heidegger 2004, 37). Heidegger takes up Kierkegaard's concept of "repetition", which he defines in *BT* as "authentic having-*been*", i.e. an authentic form of relating to the past. In contrast to a museum-like understanding of the past, the repetition rejoins that which has been by responding to the possibility of existence that has-been-there (*SZ* 385). But this repetition is not the shared renewal of love's "moment of vision". It takes place in the immanence of Dasein. The specific temporality of love does not lie in a time lived *together*, but in the fact that the lover awaits the "returning unification" (Heidegger 2005, 99; my translation) with the beloved. In love, the authentic mode of being with others turns out to be the repetitious making-present of "being-able-to-await" (*Wartenkönnen*).

What seems at first (and especially on the level of personal statements) like a way to cope with the real absence of the beloved, reveals itself as a messianic structure whose principle condition is the absence of the messiah (Tömmel 2013, 91ff): the repetition of the first *parousia* of the messiah is the awaiting of his return. The absence is not experienced as a deficit, as it makes it possible for the lover to believe in the other: "Would love still be the great faith that rises in the soul if waiting and guarding were not part of the experience of love? Being allowed to await the beloved – that is what is most wonderful – for it is in that waiting that the beloved is 'present'" (Arendt and Heidegger 2004, 18). In these lines, we do not hear the woe of a lover, mourning that his beloved is absent or unattainable, quite on the contrary: Heidegger's concept of love knows nothing about missing and longing, nor about boredom and aversion. Being ephemeral and being routine are the classical enemies of love—Heidegger suspends them both in deferring love as shared life for all eternity. The "returning unification" Heidegger speaks of, is misleading—for it does not lie ahead in the future, indeed it does not lie in time as *chronos* at all, but beyond time, in eternity: "And can you think of anything greater than this: being allowed to wait for such a being for all eternity?" (Arendt and Heidegger 2004, 19).

The other remains unattainable in love—being close to him means to preserve distance. Heidegger repeatedly calls the attitude towards the beloved "shyness" (*Scheu*), which is "that reserved, patient, astonished remembrance of that which remains near in a nearness which consists solely in keeping something distant in its fullness" (*EHP* 153). True unification is achieved when this "shyness before the other's soul does not vanish – but is heightened" (Arendt and Heidegger 2004, 23).

We would be at a loss to understand his concept of love without knowing Heidegger's lecture courses on early Christianity.[5] He uses the exact same terms in his private love letters as in his lecture courses on St. Paul: "Awaiting" and "holding-out" are the forms of enactment that preserve, 'sublate' the state of exception. Just like the believer does not wait for Christ in history, but lets him return in his own soul, love does take place in the inwardness of Dasein. Given this messianic framework, it is not necessary to bear the "burden" of factical life together—the beloved is rather the ray of the absolute that hits the lover for a moment of vision before he is alone again. Thereby, the invasion of love *isolates* the lover, who is wrested from his everyday relations without gaining the other as firm anchor in exchange. "Being close", Heidegger claims, means "being at the greatest distance from the other – distance that lets nothing blur – but instead puts the 'thou' into the mere presence – transparent but incomprehensible – of a revelation" (Arendt and Heidegger 2004, 5). Hence, it is not the other person as such who could only be experienced through her presence, but the *relation* to her that is pivotal.

Heidegger's concept of love thus clearly mirrors his concept of death: as death is not a fact at the end of life, but the relation to what is not, to what is pure possibility, love, too, is the relation to an absent presence or a present absence. The absence of the other prevents that the "true break-out" gets lost in the everydayness of "bourgeois love". As such an exception it enables the dynamic of becoming, which lets the individual ascend to less mundane regions of existence. The other who, after all, must be conceived as representative of the messiah (or, respectively, death), is unattainable—being close to him means to preserve the distance. Heidegger repeatedly describes the attitude towards the beloved as *awe,* which remained close at a distance (cf. *GA* 4: 131). With good reason, Hannah Arendt notes many years later that Heidegger, in his thinking, has made desertedness productive (Arendt 2002, 279).

It has been claimed that although all moods have a disclosing function in Heidegger, "positive" moods like joy or love could not show the limits and, thereby, the finite structure of existence so well as the "negative" ones (Rentsch 2013, 73). The analysis of his concept of love shows that this claim is based on false assumptions in so far as Heidegger's understanding of love is not linked to anything 'positive' in the usual sense: love is not a form of togetherness which eases the burden of existence, but rather a radical loneliness: The lover is close to what remains forever distant. Therefore, love brings forth the same effect as the *principle of individuation* of anxiety in *BT.*

# 4    Conclusion

In the first part, I tried to describe how love according to Heidegger is an attitude that opens up a person, makes her ready to receive a deeper understanding of life than science or logic ever could. The second part reconstructed how interpersonal love, too, transcends the everyday form of life and thereby reveals a person's own existential truth, her *Eigentlichkeit.* What links these two aspects of love, which were called the "epistemic" and the "existential"? Are they really two aspects of the same concept of love or are they rather two different concepts?

Although Heidegger's notion of love in his early years is in flux, and keeps evolving in later periods, there seems to be a basic idea, which does not change. It consists of the claim that love is essentially linked to truth: love is linked to understanding and cognition in the earliest texts, to *Eigentlichkeit* in the 1920s, and to the relation to Being in the later period.

Karl Jaspers, once a close friend to Heidegger, wrote that his philosophy was "without love" (Jaspers 1978, 34; my translation). On a philological level, he is wrong. The sources prove that Heidegger had a highly sophisticated concept of love. In fact, there are many texts indicating that Heidegger even identified philosophy with love (cf. Piazza 2003, 103; Tömmel 2013, 183–187) and conceived the true thinker as someone in love with Being. Does this rather unknown aspect of Heidegger's philosophy change his image, his persona? Does it make his thinking more "amiable"?

I fear it does not. First, his concept of interpersonal love seems to be rather counterproductive when it comes to defending Heidegger against his critics. To model intimate relationships after Pauline messianism is a strange choice, both sacralizing and marginalizing the other, who seems to be only an occasion to return to oneself. Once again, Heidegger's thinking seems to lack a sense for the need of interaction, communication and community. Second, his repeated statements that philosophy or thinking are essentially love are almost uncanny if one remembers the content of the "Black Notebooks" and other antisemitic or pro-national socialist passages. Heidegger's thinking in these writings was certainly not driven by love, but by another genuine passion, by hate.

## Notes

1. For a detailed discussion of this concept, see Tömmel 2013, 118–144.
2. Heidegger explicitly uses the term later to contrast Descartes' and Pascal's approach.
3. "Nur wenn wir das mögen, was in sich das zu-Bedenkende ist, vermögen wir das Denken."

4. "Das Vermögen des Mögens ist es, ›kraft‹ dessen etwas eigentlich zu sein vermag."
5. For a detailed comparison between the lecture courses and Heidegger's messianic concept of love, see Tömmel 2013, 83–117.

# References

Agamben, Giorgio. 2008. "The Passion of Facticity." In *Rethinking Facticity*, edited by F. Raffoul and E. S. Nelson, 89–112. Albany: State University of New York Press.

Arendt, Hannah. 2002. *Denktagebuch 1950–1973*. Munich: Pieper.

Arendt, Hannah, and Martin Heidegger. 2004. *Letters 1925–1975*. Translated by Andrew Shields. Orlando, Austin, and New York: Harcourt.

Derrida, Jacques. 1989. *Of Spirit: Heidegger and the Question*. Translated by G. Bennington and R. Bowlby. Chicago and London: The University of Chicago Press.

Figal, Günter. 1992. *Martin Heidegger zur Einführung*. Hamburg: Junius.

Großmann, Andreas. 1998. „Das (sich) verdunkelnde Licht der Öffentlichkeit. Von Heidegger zu Hannah Arendt." In *Siebzig Jahre „Sein und Zeit"*, edited by Helmut Vetter, 85–107. Frankfurt am Main: Peter Lang.

Heidegger, Martin. 1960. *Ludwig von Ficker zum Gedächtnis seines achtzigsten Geburtstages*. Nürnberg: Private Print.

Heidegger, Martin. 1963. *Was ist das – die Philosophie?* Pfullingen: Verlag Günter Neske.

Heidegger, Martin. 2000. *Elucidations of Hölderlin's Poetry [1936–1968]*. Translated by K. Hoeller. Amherst: Humanity Books.

Heidegger, Martin. 2005. '*Mein liebes Seelchen!*' *Briefe Martin Heideggers an seine Frau Elfride 1915–1970*. Edited by Gertrud Heidegger. Munich: Deutsche Verlags-Anstalt.

Heidegger, Martin, and Elisabeth Blochmann. 1990. *Briefwechsel 1918–1969*. Edited by J. W. Storck. Marbach: Deutsche Schillergesellschaft.

Jaspers, Karl. 1978. *Notizen zu Heidegger*. Munich and Zurich: Pieper.

Pattison, George. 2006. "Heidegger, Augustine and Kierkegaard: Care, Time and Love." In *The Influence of Augustine on Heidegger: The Emergence of an Augustinian Phenomenology*, edited by C. J. N. de Paulo, 153–186. Lewiston: Edwin Mellen Press.

Piazza, Valeria. 2003. "L'amour en retrait." In *L'ombre de l'amour. Le concept d'amour chez Heidegger*, edited by Giorgio Agamben and Valeria Piazza, 61–107, Paris: Rivages.

Rentsch, Thomas. 2013. "*Sein und Zeit.* Fundamentalontologie als Hermeneutik der Endlichkeit." In *Heidegger-Handbuch. Leben - Werk - Wirkung*, edited by Dieter Thomä, 48–74. Stuttgart and Weimar: Metzler.

Scheler, Max. 1963. „Liebe und Erkenntnis." In *Schriften zur Soziologie und Weltanschauungslehre*, edited by Max Scheler, 77–98. Bern: Francke Verlag.

Schmidt, Michael. 2005. *Ekstatische Transzendenz. Ludwig Binswangers Phänomenologie der Liebe und die Aufdeckung der sozialontologischen Defizite in Heideggers Sein und Zeit.* Würzburg: Königshausen & Neumann.

Tillich, Paul. 1926. *Kairos. Zur Geisteslage und Geisteswendung.* Darmstadt: Otto Reichl.

Tömmel, Tatjana Noemi. 2013. *Wille und Passion. Der Liebesbegriff bei Heidegger und Arendt.* Berlin: Suhrkamp.

Trawny, Peter. 2015. *Heidegger and the Myth of a Jewish World Conspiracy.* Translated by Andrew J. Mitchell. Chicago: The University of Chicago Press.

von Falkenhayn, Katharina. 2003. *Augenblick und Kairos. Zeitlichkeit im Frühwerk Martin Heideggers.* Berlin: Duncker und Humblot.

# 11

# The Ethics of Moods

François Raffoul

## 1 Introduction

We know the ontological import of moods (*Stimmungen*) for Heidegger: moods or affective dispositions are not superficial additions to existence, not restricted to our "emotional" lives, not inner subjective feelings, but manifest an *ontological* truth of Dasein. Moods represent a fundamental feature of existence, which is never without a mood, always situated and disposed by a mood. Existence is never neutral, but always already "moved" by a mood. "Dasein is always already in a mood," says Heidegger (*SZ* 134).[1] Heidegger talks of *Grundstimmungen*, fundamental moods, because they are fundamental to existence and pertain to our very being. Moods are the fundamental manner, "the *fundamental way in which Dasein is as Dasein*" (*GA* 29/30: 101; *FCM* 67). To that extent, Heidegger seeks to remove the investigation of moods from psychology, which has traditionally enframed their study. "Prior to all psychology of moods, a field which, moreover, still lies fallow, we must see this phenomenon as a fundamental existential and outline its structure"

F. Raffoul (✉)
Louisiana State University, Baton Rouge, LA, USA

© The Author(s) 2019
C. Hadjioannou (ed.), *Heidegger on Affect*, Philosophers in Depth,
https://doi.org/10.1007/978-3-030-24639-6_11

(*SZ* 134). Heidegger pursued in the *Beiträge zur Philosophie (Vom Ereignis)* this critique of psychology as a mode of access to moods, explaining how moods, affective dispositions, "attunement," must be removed from the horizon of psychology so as to be grasped as modes of our being itself. "Yet now and then we must speak 'about' disposition in order to point the way, but only because psychology has for a long time restricted the scope of the word 'disposition' (*Stimmung*), i.e., only because the craving for 'lived experiences' today, without a meditation on disposition, would all the more drag astray everything said of it" (*GA* 65: 21; *CP* 19). Every external or psychological representation of moods "is to be avoided here." Moods are never merely the modality that accompany, illuminate, and shade "all-supposedly already fixed-human behavior" (*GA* 65: 35; *CP* 28). Far from being but a superficial accompaniment of our existence, and of our thinking, moods represent the way our Dasein is "attuned," disposed, and ultimately disclosed along with the whole of beings. "The mood has already disclosed, in every case, Being-in-the-world as a whole" (*SZ* 137).

Further, moods are also said to determine thinking itself, which is not an abstract reflection on objectivity, but is disposed out of a mood to think being. "All essential thinking demands that its thoughts and utterances be newly extracted each time, like an ore, out of the basic disposition [*Grundstimmung*]. If the basic disposition is lacking, then everything is a forced clatter of concepts and of the mere shells of words…" (*GA* 65: 21; *CP* 19). Far from the notion, as found in Descartes for instance, of thought as pure intellection, as "pure inspection of the mind alone," under the authority of "clear and distinct ideas," Heidegger stresses the determinative role of moods for thinking: "Since indeed a misconception about 'thinking' has long since dominated the common opinion regarding 'philosophy,' the way disposition is represented and judged can therefore be absolutely nothing other than a scion of this misinterpretation of thinking (disposition is weak, erratic, unclear, and dull, versus the acuity, certainty, clarity, and nimbleness of 'thought'). In the best case, disposition might be tolerated as an embellishment of thinking." Far from being external to thinking, "the basic disposition *disposes* Da-sein [stimmt *das Da-sein*] and thereby disposes *thinking* as a projection of the truth of beyng in word and concept" (ibid.).

As early as the 1929/1930 course, Heidegger had stressed the disposing nature of moods for thinking, even naming "homesickness" (*Das Heimweh*) as the fundamental mood of philosophy. Thinking must be "gripped" by a mood to think. "Above all, however, we shall never have comprehended these concepts [*Begriffe*] and their conceptual rigor unless we have first been gripped [*ergriffen*] by whatever they are supposed to comprehend. The fundamental concern of philosophizing pertains to such being gripped, to awakening and planting it. All such being gripped, however, comes from and remains in an attunement [*Stimmung*]" (*GA* 29/30: 9; *FCM* 7). Further in that course, Heidegger presents his understanding of philosophizing as grounded in moods in this way: "We determined philosophizing as comprehensive questioning arising out of Dasein's being gripped in its essence. Such being gripped however is possible only from out of and within a fundamental attunement of Dasein" (*GA* 29/30: 199; *FCM* 132). In other words, conceptual philosophical thinking "is grounded in our being gripped, and this is grounded in a fundamental attunement." For Heidegger, conceptual work or philosophizing cannot be some "arbitrary" enterprise among others, but "happens in the *ground* [*Grunde*] of human Dasein" (*GA* 29/30: 9–10; *FCM* 7). Such a ground is to be found in moods, which are what "constantly, essentially, and thoroughly attune human beings, without human beings necessarily always recognizing them as such. *Philosophy in each case happens in a fundamental attunement*" (*GA* 29/30: 10; *FCM* 7).

Apart from this stress on the ontological dimension of affective dispositions and their constitutive role for thinking and for philosophy, I would like in the following essay to reveal the *ethical* scope of moods. Indeed, I will argue that to be in a mood, to be thrown in a mood, engages a certain response, already a responsibility, an ethical relation. In the Zollikon seminars, Heidegger thus explains that "Attunement is not only related to mood, to being able to be attuned in this or that way. Rather, this attunement, in the sense of moods, at the same time contains the relationship toward the way and the manner of being able to be addressed and of the claim of being" (*GA* 89: 263; *Zo* 211). Being in a mood is at once being called to a response, to an original responsibility. Now it may be objected from the outset that moods seem to foreclose any possibility of ethical responsiveness, because as we will see they display a kind of radical obscurity, opacity or withdrawal, and even unintelligibility (one does not know or understand why one is in such or such a mood) that seem to prevent any possible appropriation in an ethical response. Whenever Heidegger describes moods (*Stimmungen*) or affective disposition (*Befindlichkeit*) in *Being and Time* (*BT*), it is in order to emphasize the element of opacity that seems to foreclose any possibility of appropriation, whether theoretical or practical. Heidegger explains that moods are beyond the reach of both will and cognition, leading Dasein before the pure "that" of its There, that is, before the pure facticity of its existence, which as such, Heidegger writes in a striking formulation, "stares at it [Dasein] with the inexorability of an enigma" (*SZ* 136). In the phenomenon of moods, there is an expropriation of our being that is irreducible. I will nonetheless argue that this expropriation precisely calls us to an *ethical* response, an original responsibility that allows us to speak of an "ethics of moods." Ultimately, I will argue, this ethics of moods engages the task of becoming responsible for the facticity and finitude of existence.

## 2    Part I

Heidegger explores the phenomenon of affective disposition (*Befindlichkeit*),[2] and of "moods" (*Stimmungen*) in paragraph 29 of *BT*. To be precise, Heidegger explains at the beginning of the paragraph that disposition is the *ontological* characterization of the *ontical* phenomenon of mood. "What we indicate *ontologically* with the term disposition is *ontically* what is most familiar and an everyday kind of thing: mood, being in a mood" (*SZ* 134). The ontical phenomenon of moods manifest an "ontological disposition." Disposition is a mode of disclosure. It is, in fact, the more originary kind of disclosure for Dasein's being, Heidegger stating in the 1929/1930 course that moods "are the 'presupposition' for, and 'medium' of thinking and acting. That means as much as to say that they reach more primordially back into our essence, that in them we first meet ourselves-as being-there, as a Da-sein" (*GA* 29/30: 102; *FCM* 68). Moods are a mode of disclosure though which the self is revealed to itself, as one always *finds oneself* in a mood. As a mode of self-disclosure, disposition is more primordial than the traditional immanent reflectivity of consciousness: "ontologically mood is a primordial kind of Being for Dasein, in which Dasein is disclosed to itself *prior* to all cognition and volition, and *beyond* their range of disclosure" (*SZ* 136). Dasein can become aware of itself only on the basis of a self-disclosure in moods. "From what has been said we can see already that a disposition is very remote from anything like coming across a psychical condition by the kind of apprehending which first turns round and then back [*sich um- und rückwenenden Erfassens*]. Indeed it is so far from this, that only because the 'there' has already been disclosed in a disposition can immanent reflection come across 'Experiences' [*Erlebnisse*] at all" (*SZ* 136). This passage clearly shows Heidegger's critique of intellectualism or theoreticism. Yet it does not amount to positing some privilege of affectivity over intellectuality: what is at stake is to seize moods in their *ontological* scope (the disclosure of a There, the weight of an existence thrown into itself) and *not* merely in their classical opposition to the so-called "rational" faculties. The issue is to show that any reflection takes place on the basis of Dasein's self-disclosure in moods: "Disposition is so far from being reflected upon [*reflektiert*], that precisely what it does is assail [*überfällt*] Dasein in its unreflecting devotion to the 'world' with which it is concerned..." (*SZ* 136). In the 1924 lecture *The Concept of Time* (*CT*), Heidegger explained that in Dasein's everydayness "there lies no reflection upon the ego or the self," but that instead Dasein "*finds* itself *disposed* alongside itself [*Es befindet sich bei sich selbst*]" (*CT* 9E). Moods disclose Dasein's being, prior to any reflection.

In fact, moods pervade any comportment: in the Zollikon seminars, Heidegger states that "ontological disposition (*Befindlichkeit*) or attunement (*Gestimmtheit*) is a basic character of Da-sein and belongs to every comportment. *Every comportment is always already in a certain attunement beforehand*" (*GA* 89: 210; *Zo* 165, my emphasis). One could go even further and say that disposition or attunement is relationality itself, as Heidegger suggests: "Attunement [*Gestimmtheit*] is not something standing for itself but belongs to being-in- the-world as being addressed by things. Attunement and being related [*Bezogensein*] are one and the same. Each new attunement is always only a reattunement

[*Umstimmung*] of the attunement always already unfolding in each comportment" (*GA* 89: 251; *Zo* 203).

Attunements and feelings are traditionally placed alongside thinking and willing, and they are considered to be the third class of experience, under the authority and preeminence of reason and will.[3] This classification of experiences is itself based upon on the traditional representation of the human being as a rational animal. For Heidegger, however, moods are not to be classified as psychological feelings and do not designate some sentimentality. As he states in *Hölderlin's Hymns. "Germania" and "The Rhine"*, "With regard to this and every fundamental attunement, however, it must be said from the outset that what is at issue here is not some weak resignation that submerges itself in so-called feelings, a kind of sentimentality that merely 'broods over' the state of one's own soul" (*GA* 39: 81–82; *HGR* 75). Heidegger takes issue with the subjectivizing of moods, as well as with the dualism between body and soul. "Because we have long been misled and regard the human being from the outset as a corporeal thing fitted out with a soul and its processes, and because in addition we take the soul to be an 'I' in the first instance, we locate 'moods' within this 'I-subject'" (*GA* 39: 89; *HGR* 81). Moods are relegated to the subjective, leaving the objective to be the concern for cognition and knowledge: "Since cognition and willing as subjective processes at least always relate to and have to do with objects, yet moods, for the most part, also lack this relation to objects—they are naturally something purely 'subjective.'" Hence the notion that moods are the mere coloring of objective processes: "'Moods' come to be located in the subject, and this subject in turn transfers them into the objects with the aid of so-called empathy. Attunements are then something like gloves: sometimes worn, sometimes set aside somewhere" (*GA* 39: 89; *HGR* 81).

Not only are moods not merely subjective, they deconstruct as well the subject-object opposition, an opposition that is at the basis of the notion of moods as 'coloring' an objective state of affair: "the attunement and its arising or receding is what is originary, first drawing the object into the attunement in its own particular way in each instance, and making the subject that which is attuned. Considered more profoundly, however, the subject–object relationship that is commonly represented is here altogether inadequate for comprehending the essence of attunement. That relationship was conceived with respect to the representational relation between subject and object, so that the attunement, conceived as a feeling, is then merely something added on — a coloring" (*GA* 39: 83; *HGR* 76). It is artificial to think of a subject split from an object. "Yet far more fantastical—that is, far more remote from all true reality—is that representation of the human being as a corporeal thing endowed with a soul, a representation that is so commonplace and that leaves us so completely at a loss if our task is indeed to intimate the essence of attunement in the right way, that is, as it concerns the Dasein of the human being" (*GA* 39: 89; *HGR* 81). It would also be artificial to "place attunements in the subject as only 'subjective appearances'—as appearances arising in the interiority of the subject, like air bubbles in a glass of water—or to seek to explain them in terms of the effects of things acting upon our nerves" (*GA* 39: 89–90; *HGR* 81). This is why Heidegger rejects the term "affect," insofar as it implies an impression made on the subject from the outside. In the Zollikon seminars, he thus explains: "Even the term 'affect' is already disastrous. *Af-ficere* means 'to do something to someone.' Joy is not brought upon me from the outside, but this attunement belongs to my ecstatic relationship, to my being-in-the- world" (*GA* 89: 211; *Zo* 166). Therefore, having a mood is not primarily related to the psychical, is not "an inner condition" that would, then enigmatically color an objective state if affair. In the course on Hölderlin, Heidegger stresses that moods are neither inside nor outside: attunement "is not at all 'inside' in some interiority, only to appear in the flash of an eye; but for this reason it is not at all outside either" (*GA* 29/30: 100; *FCM* 66). Moods are neither inside nor outside: they disclose being-in-the-world *as a whole*. In *BT*, Heidegger already stated: "A mood assails us. It comes neither from 'outside' nor from 'inside', but arises out of Being-in-the-world, as a way of such Being" (*SZ* 136).

Let us clarify this claim. Moods are neither on the side of the subject nor on the side of the object, because they are originary to both. Far from being a superficial accompaniment of existence, they constitute the ground of the being of Dasein: "We now also have the counterthesis to our second negative thesis that attunement is not something inconstant, fleeting, merely subjective. Rather because attunement is the originary way in which every Dasein is as it is, it is not what is most inconstant, but that which gives Dasein *subsistence and possibility* in its very foundations" (*GA* 29/30: 101; *FCM* 67). Moods pervade the world, which is neither subjective nor objective. They originally dispose us as being in the world. "Attunements are not placed into the subject or into objects; rather we, together with beings, are *trans-posed* into attunements. Attunements are powerful forces that permeate and envelop us; they come over us and things together with one fell swoop" (*GA* 39: 89; *HGR* 81). Attunement, as Heidegger puts it, "imposes itself on everything," and discloses both the human being and things in an originary dis-position: "the Dasein of the human being is transposed into attunements equiprimordially together with beings as such" (*GA* 29/30: 100; *FCM* 66). This is why Heidegger, returning in the Zollikon seminars to the meaning of *Befindlichkeit*, explains that with "ontological disposition [*Befindlichkeit*] in *BT*, it is a matter of being in the world as a whole, and thereby of beings as a whole": what matters "is the attunement determining Da-sein in its particular relationship to the world, to the Da-sein-with [*Mitdasein*] other humans, and to itself. Ontological disposition founds the particular feelings of well-being and discontent yet is itself founded again in the human being's being exposed [*Ausgesetzheit*] (thrownness) toward beings as a whole [*das Seiende im Ganzen*]" (*GA* 89: 182; *Zo* 139, translation modified). Moods reveal Dasein's being and beings as a whole.

## 3 Part II

After this brief characterization of the ontological scope of moods, I would like to explore what I have called the "ethics of moods," an ethics that may already be included within the ontology of moods, if it is the case that ontology for Heidegger harbors an original ethics, as he famously claimed in the "Letter on Humanism." What I hope to demonstrate is that the ethical, in the sense of an original responsibility, pervades through and through our factical experience of moods. Nonetheless, as we alluded to above, a paradox immediately appears: do moods, with their senses of opacity, finitude, and expropriation, not challenge the very *possibility* of a response or responsibility, since they represent precisely not only what I am not responsible for, but also what I cannot in principle appropriate? How can I be responsible for a phenomenon of which I am not the author, and which presents itself as an irreducible enigma? The project of laying out an ethics of moods may seem aporetic if not impossible, as the very facticity of moods could indeed be seen as an expropriation, a challenge to the very possibility of responsible appropriation.

As we mentioned, the first extensive engagement with moods, with "disposition," *Befindlichkeit*, takes place in paragraph 29 of *BT*. What is most striking in those descriptions is how Heidegger precisely describes moods by emphasizing the element of opacity and withdrawal in them that seems to interrupt and foreclose any possibility of cognitive or practical appropriation. As he puts it, moods are "beyond the reach of both will and cognition." Although moods are said to be an originary mode of disclosure, they nonetheless display a radical opacity. Moods are the disclosure of a concealment: they disclose Dasein's being in its pure "that," which itself is a fact without a reason upon which the will is powerless. Moods disclose the being of the there in its "that it is." Heidegger writes: "A mood makes manifest 'how one is, and how one is faring.' In this 'how one is,' having a mood brings Dasein to its 'there'" (*SZ* 134). Moods lead Dasein before the pure "that" of its There, which as such, Heidegger writes in a striking formulation, "stares at it [Dasein] with the inexorability of an enigma" (*SZ* 136).

With respect to this facticity of moods, to the fact of finding oneself in a mood, "one does not *know why*" (*SZ* 134). In fact, Dasein "*cannot know why*" (*SZ* 134; my emphasis). Cognition falls "far short," not because of some weakness of our cognitive powers which somehow could be improved, but because of the peculiar phenomenon of moods as they exhibit the facticity of Dasein. And what is peculiar with this phenomenon is that the "that" of our being is given in such a way that "the whence and whither *remain obscure*" (*SZ* 134; my emphasis). This is why cognition falls short: in the phenomenon of moods, there is a remaining withdrawn or obscure that is irreducible. It is, Heidegger writes, a characteristic of Dasein's being (*SZ* 135). Against this darkness, or opacity, any enlightenment, whether theoretical or practical, is powerless. Moods are "beyond the range of disclosure" of both cognition and volition, beyond their possibilities of mastery. This explains why only a "counter-mood" can master a mood, as Spinoza had already shown. Heidegger explains: "Factically, Dasein can, should, and must, through knowledge and will, become master of its moods; in certain possible ways of existing, this may signify a priority of volition and cognition. Only we must not be misled by this into denying that ontologically mood is a primordial kind of Being for Dasein, in which Dasein is disclosed to itself *prior* to all cognition and volition, and *beyond* their range of disclosure. And furthermore, when we master a mood, we do so by way of a counter-mood; we are never free of moods" (*SZ* 136). This indicates that "against the phenomenal facts of the case," all the ideals of rational enlightenment "count for nothing." Moods reveal the opacity and inappropriability of our origins. In a 1928 course entitled "Introduction to Philosophy" (*Einleitung in die Philosophie*), Heidegger states that the fact "that by its own decision Dasein has nothing to search for in the direction of its origin, gives an essential prod to Dasein from the darkness of its origin into the relative brightness of its potentiality-for-Being. *Dasein exists always in an essential exposure to the darkness and impotence of its origin, even if only in the prevailing form of a habitual deep forgetting in the face of this essential determination of its facticity*" (*GA* 27: 340).

Moods reveal the thrownness and facticity of Dasein, which manifest a radical expropriation for the human being. The "enigma" of moods—of thrownness—weighs upon Dasein like a burden, Heidegger explaining that in being-in-a-mood, "Being has become manifest as a burden [*Last*]" (*SZ* 134). Let us dwell on the motif of weight, as it seems to harbor the expropriation of moods (but also, paradoxically, as we will see, the possibility of ethical responsibility: ordinary language does speak of the connection between responsibility and weight, as one speaks of responsibility in the sense of carrying a weight, of "shouldering" a burden). In his early lecture courses, Heidegger stated that factical life (later renamed Dasein) is marked by the difficult weightiness of a task, affected by an irreducible problematicity or questionableness. That weight, Heidegger explained in a 1921–1922 Winter semester course, "does not accrue to life from the outside, from something that lacks the character of life, but is instead present in and with life itself" (*GA* 61: 100; *PIA* 75). Due to this burdensome character of factical life, Heidegger explains that, "Factical life is always seeking the easy way" (*GA* 61: 108; *PIA* 81). One sees this phenomenon in the so-called "difficulty of life." With respect to such difficulty, Heidegger stresses the following in the 1922's "Phenomenological Interpretations in Connection with Aristotle. An Indication of the Hermeneutical Situation": "A characteristic of the being of factical life is that it finds itself hard to bear. The most unmistakable manifestation of this is the fact that factical life has the tendency to make itself easy for itself. In finding itself hard to bear, life *is* difficult in accord with the basic sense of its being, not in the sense of a contingent feature. If it is the case that factical life authentically is what it is in this being-hard and being-difficult, then the genuinely fitting way of gaining access to it and truly safekeeping it can only consist in making itself hard for itself" (*Supp* 113). The weight is here the weight of existence itself, an existence which is, as Heidegger puts it, "worrying about itself" (*Supp* 118).

Heidegger describes the human being as a being who is burdened or heavy with a weight, in a situation of care and concern, in contrast to the lightness or care-lessness of inauthentic being (in *BT* he describes inauthenticity as a "disburdening of one's being" [*Seinsentlastung*], *SZ* 128). Heidegger thus evokes the fundamental "burdensome character of Dasein, even while it alleviates the burden" (*SZ* 134). So-called "moods of elation," which do lighten the burden, are said to be possible only on the basis of this burdensome character of Dasein's being. "Furthermore, an elevated mood can alleviate the manifest burden of being. But the possibility of this mood, too, discloses the burdensome character of Dasein even when it alleviates that burden" (*SZ* 134). Further in *BT*, analyzing the mood of "hope," Heidegger insists: "The fact that hope *brings relief* from depressing apprehensiveness only means that even this attunement remains related to a burden in the mode of having-been. Elevated or elevating moods are ontologically possible only in an ecstatic-temporal relation of Dasein to the thrown ground of itself" (*SZ* 345). Moods manifest the burden of existence, a weight that indicates the expropriation to which existence is exposed.

The weight designates the facticity of our experience, a facticity that carries a radical expropriation for the human being. In "The Passion of

Facticity," Giorgio Agamben underlines the expropriation of such facticity, which always entails an element of non-originarity, and therefore of non-propriety. "What is important here," Agamben writes, "is that for Heidegger, this experience of facticity, of a constitutive non-originarity, is precisely the original experience of philosophy, the only legitimate point of departure for thinking" (Agamben 2002, 93). Drawing from an etymological analysis of the term, Agamben shows that "originally," facticity, or *facticius*, is opposed to *nativus*, and signifies: "what is not natural, what did not come into Being by itself" (ibid.), but rather was produced or made. The factical means what is made (Descartes, in the third meditation, speaks of those ideas which are "*factae*," or "produced" by me), and therefore what is non-originary, if not non-true of false (as in the English "factitious": one speaks of a "factitious illness or disorder"). Agamben traces Heidegger's account of facticity to Augustine, who contrasted *facticius*—that which is made by humans and is unnatural and artificial—with *nativus* as that which is natural and created by God. This indicates that the term factical can be situated in "the semantic sphere of non-originarity and making" (ibid.). For Agamben, the "originary facticity" of Dasein signifies that Dasein's opening is marked by an original *impropriety*. Such is the passion of facticity, a passion "in which the human being bears this nonbelonging and darkness" (Agamben 2002, 107; modified). This allows Agamben to claim that on the account of facticity, "Dasein cannot ever appropriate the being it is, the being to which it is irreparably consigned" (Agamben 2002, 100). Moods reveal the inappropriability of Dasein's being. I am thrown into existence from a completely opaque basis that resists all attempts of appropriation, as manifested in moods.

Moods reveal the dimension in our being that resist appropriation, i.e., our very coming into being, our "birth." It is often said that Heidegger neglected the phenomenon of birth, that he privileged being-towards-death. In fact, the central notion of throwness is the name for Heidegger's ontological understanding of birth. Any discussion of moods and throwness already includes a reflection on birth. The question of birth is addressed explicitly in paragraph 72 of *BT*, where Dasein is said to exist *between* birth and death. Being that between, Dasein exists towards each of them: it exists towards death, and it exists towards birth, Heidegger speaking of a "Being-towards-the-beginning" (*Sein zum Anfang*) (*SZ* 373). There is thus a *relation* to our thrownness, our inappropriable birth. Heidegger explains that very clearly: "Understood existentially, birth is not and never is something past in the sense of something no longer present-at-hand" (*SZ* 374). As relating to my birth, "Factical Dasein exists as born" (*SZ* 374). I thus exist in a "natal" way, and relate to my own birth. But is it my "own"? In fact, it remains for Heidegger inappropriable: I cannot go back behind my coming into being in order to appropriate it. Dasein is thrown. Dasein is a not a self-posited ego, but a thrown existence. This means that it "has been brought into its 'there,' but *not* of its own accord" (*SZ* 284). Dasein can never go back "behind its thrownness in such a way that it might first release this 'that-it-is-and-has-to-be' from *its Being*-its-self and lead it into its 'there'" (*SZ* 284). There lies the fundamental and irreducible impotence or powerlessness of Dasein. Dasein can never overcome the finitude of thrownness. Moods, understood in terms of thrownness, reveals that Dasein can never go back beyond this "throw" to recapture its being from the ground up. Dasein can never become master of and appropriate its own ground and origins. It would then seem that in being in a mood I am expropriated from my own being, thereby rendering any meaningful sense of responsible appropriation impossible.

# 4   Part III

Yet, the possibility of an ethical relation to moods is paradoxically opened by this expropriation. For it is at this juncture, at this very *aporetic* moment, that Heidegger paradoxically situates the arch-ethical responsibility of Dasein, a responsibility as it were arising from its own impossibility. Derrida stressed that, in principle, ethical responsibility arises out of aporia and paradox (Derrida 2008, 68).[4] How does such a paradox appear in Heidegger's text? In "Introduction to Philosophy," Heidegger explains that precisely that over which Dasein is not master must be "worked through" and "survived." He writes: "Also that which does not arise of one's own express decision, as most things for Dasein, must be in such or such a way retrievingly appropriated, even if only in the modes of putting up with or shirking something; that which for us is entirely not under the control of freedom in the narrow sense… is something that is in such or such a manner taken up or rejected in the How of Dasein" (*GA* 27: 337). The inappropriable is thus carried by Dasein. The inappropriable in existence (facticity), as seen in the phenomena of moods, is primarily felt as a weight or a burden. It is no accident that when Heidegger analyzes the disclosedness of existence into a There, that is, into an affective disposition, he speaks of a "burden" (*Last*). The being of the there, we are told, "become[s] manifest as a burden" (*SZ* 134). But, interestingly, the very concept of weight reintroduces, as it were, the problematic of responsibility (as we alluded to above, responsibility is often characterized as the carrying of a weight, of "shouldering" a burden). In a marginal note added to this passage, Heidegger later clarified: "Burden: what weighs; the human being is charged with the responsibility of Dasein, appropriated by it. To carry: to take over one's belonging to being itself [*'Last': das Zu-tragende; der Mensch ist dem Da-sein überantwortet, übereignet. Tragen: übernehmen aus der Zugehörigkeit zum Sein selbst*]" (*SZ* 134). The burden of moods is described as "what weighs," as what has to be carried (*das Zu-tragende*), Heidegger indicating the taking on of facticity as the carrying of the weight. The weight is facticity; the carrying is the taking on of facticity: such is the "facticity of responsibility." The weight of moods weighs, and is carried by an original responsibility, an original "ethics of moods."

When it comes to the motif of an ethics of moods, everything hinges on the meaning to be given to thrownness. As we know, affective dispositions or moods are translated by Heidegger into the existential vocabulary of *BT* as *Geworfenheit*, thrownness. As Thomas Sheehan rightly notes, "Thrownness bespeaks *Befindlichkeit*, the a priori fact that we are affectively attuned to the world-of-meaning and whatever we encounter within it" (Sheehan 2018, 45). What is felt in a mood is thrownness. Moods, Heidegger states, are the "disclosing of thrownness" (*SZ* 137). The withdrawal we saw occur in moods is understood by Heidegger in terms of "thrownness": "We shall call this character of being of Dasein which is veiled in its whence and whither, but in itself all the more openly disclosed, this 'that it is,' the thrownness [*Geworfenheit*] of this being into its there" (*SZ* 135). Such thrownness of moods is made apparent when

Heidegger writes: "whenever we awaken an attunement, this entails that it was already there" (*GA* 29/30: 93, *FCM* 62). Moods are the "already" where we find ourselves, already disposed. Heidegger insists on this thrownness of being in a mood: "It seems as though an attunement is in each case already there, so to speak, like an atmosphere in which we first immerse ourselves in each case and which then attunes us through and through" (*GA* 29/30: 100, *FCM* 67).

How are we to describe such thrownness? And how does it display an original ethicality? If thrownness does not designate some fall from a higher realm, but the very facticity from which Dasein becomes a care and a responsibility for itself, then the weight of existence is from the outset an original responsibility. Heidegger states that in moods, Dasein is said to be able to "burst forth as a naked 'that it is and has to be' ['*Daß es ist und zu sein hat*']" (*SZ* 134). I am thrown into a fact *that I have to be*. In a mood, one is thrown into a fact, a facticity, a "that." However, Dasein is not thrown like a brute fact and is not thrown only once and for all. Rather, it is thrown in such a way that *it has to be* this being-thrown (not being itself the basis for its self) each time in the sense of carrying it or of assuming it as its own. This gives from the outset a motion or e-motion to the "that" of moods: "Far from signifying the immobility of a factual situation (as in Sartre or Husserl), facticity designates the 'character of Being' [*Seinscharakter*] and 'e-motion' [*Bewegtheit*] proper to life" (Agamben 2002, 94). It is in this sense that thrownness "does not lie behind it as some event which has happened to Dasein, which has factually befallen and fallen loose from Dasein again" (*SZ* 284). Rather, "as long as Dasein is, Dasein, as care, *is* constantly its 'that-it-is'" (*SZ* 284). I am thrown into existing, that is, into a possibility to be, a "having-to-be." I am delivered over to an existence that, because it has no ground, puts me in the situation of having to appropriate this absence of ground. It appears—and this is why facticity is not the same as factuality—that Dasein is not thrown like a brute fact and is not thrown only once and for all. Rather, it is thrown in such a way that it has to be this being-thrown each time, in the sense of carrying it or of assuming it as its own. Heidegger is very clear on this point. "The 'that it is and has to be' disclosed in the attunement of Dasein is not the 'that' which expresses ontologically and categorially the factuality belonging to objective presence; the latter is accessible only when we ascertain it by looking at it. Rather, the that disclosed in attunement must be understood as an existential attribute of *that* being which is in the mode of being-in-the-world. *Facticity is not the factuality of the* factum brutum *of something objectively present, but is a character-istic of the being of Dasein taken on in existence, although initially thrust aside. The that of facticity is never to be found by looking*" (*SZ* 135). Agamben rightly stresses that Heidegger's understanding of thrownness and facticity is radically different from that of Husserl or Sartre:

> The references to Husserl and Sartre that one finds in philosophical dic-tionaries under the heading 'Facticity' are misleading here, for Heidegger's use of the term is fundamentally different from theirs. Heidegger dis-tinguishes Dasein's *Faktizität* from *Tatsächlichkeit*, the simple factual-ity of intraworldly beings. At the start of his *Ideas*, Husserl defines the *Tatsächlichkeit* of the objects of experience. These objects, Husserl writes, appear as things found at determinate points in space and time that pos-sess a certain content of reality but that, considered in their essence, could also be elsewhere and otherwise. Husserl thus insists on contingency [*Zufälligkeit*] as an essential characteristic of factuality. For Heidegger, by contrast, the proper trait of facticity is not *Zufälligkeit* but *Verfallenheit*. Everything is complicated, in Heidegger, by the fact that Dasein is not simply, as in Sartre, thrown into the 'there' of a given contingency; instead, Dasein must rather itself be its 'there,' be the 'there' (*Da*) of Being. Once again, the difference in modes of Being is decisive here (Agamben 2002, 92).

Dasein has to be its thrownness in moods, in a relation that is at once a response and a responsibility.

This is why the inappropriability of moods does not indicate the fail-ure and impossibility of responsibility. On the contrary: what one has to be, and be responsible for, is precisely the withdrawal—the secret—in moods, since as we know it is the withdrawal that calls one to responsi-bility. As Heidegger put it in *What Is Called Thinking?*, "Whatever with-draws, refuses arrival. But withdrawing is not nothing. Withdrawal is an event. In fact, what withdraws may even concern and claim man more essentially than anything present that strikes and touches him" (*GA* 8: 10; *WCT* 9). Heidegger speaks of the event of withdrawal (*Das Ereignis des Entzugs*) as that which is closest to us: "The event of withdrawal could be what is most present in all our present, and so infinitely exceed the actuality of everything actual" (*GA* 8: 11; *WCT* 9). It is the event of withdrawal that calls us: "What withdraws from us, draws us along by its very withdrawal, whether or not we become aware of it immediately, or at all" (*GA* 8: 11; *WCT* 9). Being happens by and in withdrawing. Being is the withdrawal, being withdraws (*Entzieht sich*) (*GA* 8: 10; *WCT* 8), and from such a withdrawal it calls us to be responsible for thrownness. What Dasein has to be, and what it has to be responsible for, is then precisely its very facticity, its being-thrown as such. What I have to appropriate, ultimately, is facticity, that is, the inappropriable itself.

There lies the "being-guilty" of which Heidegger speaks in *BT*, i.e., the taking over of one's thrownness. Dasein "has been brought into its 'there,' but *not* of its own accord" (*SZ* 284). Dasein can never go back "behind its thrownness in such a way that it might first release this 'that-it-is-and-has-to-be' from its Being-its-self and lead it into its 'there'" (*SZ* 284). This represents the fundamental and irreducible impotence or powerlessness of Dasein, who can never overcome the finitude of thrownness, the withdrawal of moods. Nonetheless, Dasein also exists in such a way that it projects itself towards possibilities in which it is thrown. What it has to be, then, what it has to assume and be responsible for, is precisely its being-thrown as such. Dasein is thrown in such a way that, each time, it *has to be* this being-thrown, that is, *it has to be not being itself the basis for its being*. "Although it has *not* laid that basis *itself*, it reposes in the weight of it, which is made manifest to it as a burden by Dasein's mood" (*SZ* 284). At this point, we need to stress the paradox of being-guilty, the paradox of being a "thrown basis." It is this very thrownness that I will have to appropriate, the very lack of authorship that I will have to make myself the author of. This is the very weight of moods as given to a responsibility: it registers this incommensurability of being a thrown origin, of having to make myself the basis of that of which I am not—and cannot be—the basis: being-a-basis means "*never* to have power over one's ownmost Being from the ground up" (*SZ* 284) and making of that "never" the task of an each time in existing. "The Self, which as such has to lay the basis for itself, can *never* get that basis into its power; and yet, as existing, it must take over Being-a-basis" (*SZ* 284). Ultimately for Heidegger, being-a-basis, that is, "never existing before its basis, but only from it and as this basis" (*SZ* 284), or existing (projecting) as thrown (projected), presents the paradox or aporia of a responsibility of having to appropriate the inappropriable, in an experience of the impossible which Derrida thematized as the very experience of responsibility.

## 5     Conclusion

We saw how moods are characterized by a withdrawal and an irreducible opacity, an opacity that ultimately one has to be responsible for. The opacity of moods reveals Dasein's finitude, a finitude which Heidegger described in the 1929/1930 course as groundlessness (*Grund-losigkeit*) and as the concealment of the ground (*Grund-verborgenheit*) (*GA* 29/30: 306; *FCM* 209; modified). This withdrawal of grounds in the phenomena of moods *obligates* me. For I am not responsible, as Kant claimed, because I am a subject who is the absolute origin of a series of causes and therefore a subject to whom actions can be ascribed, but because I am thrown in an existence that I do not originate yet for which I have to answer. Ultimately, the ethics of moods is a responsibility for finitude itself, for the *secret* of moods, a being-responsible in which it is a matter, not of overcoming moods, but of assuming their mystery, of respecting their secret, and as it were being their enigma.

## Notes

1. I draw from both extant English translations: *Being and Time*, trans. John Macquarrie and Edward Robinson (New York: Harper, 1962), *Being and Time*, trans. Joan Stambaugh. Revised and with a Foreword by Dennis J. Schmidt (Albany: SUNY Press, 2010). Hereafter cited as *SZ*, followed by the German pagination.
2. I render *Befindlichkeit* by "disposition," following an indication of Heidegger himself, who, in *What Is Philosophy?* (a lecture given at Cerisy-la-Salle, in Normandy, in August 1955), proposed the word

*disposition*, and *être-disposé* (in the French original), to designate being-in-a-mood or *Befindlichkeit* (*GA* 11: 21, *WIP* 77).

3. This is how Heidegger describes this prejudice in the 1929/1930 course: "Yet people will reply: Who will deny us that? Attunements—joy, contentment, bliss, sadness, melancholy, anger—are, after all, something psychological, or better, psychic; they are emotional states. We can ascertain such states in ourselves and in others. We can even record how long they last, how they rise and fall, the causes which evoke and impede them. Attunements or, as one also says, 'feelings', are events occurring in a subject. Psychology, after all, has always distinguished between thinking, willing, and feeling. It is not by chance that it will always name feeling in the third, subordinate position. Feelings are the third class of lived experience. For naturally man is in the first place the rational living being. Initially, and in the first instance, this rational living being thinks and wills. Feelings are certainly also at hand. Yet are they not merely, as it were, the adornment of our thinking and willing, or something that obfuscates and inhibits these? After all, feelings and attunements constantly change. They have no fixed subsistence, they are that which is most inconstant. They are merely a radiance and shimmer, or else something gloomy, something hovering over emotional events. Attunements-are they not like the utterly fleeting and ungraspable shadows of clouds flitting across the landscape?" (*GA* 29/30: 96–97, *FCM* 64).

4. "The concepts of responsibility, of decision, or of duty, are condemned a priori to paradox, scandal, and aporia" (Derrida 2008, 68).

# References

Agamben, Giorgio. 2002. "The Passion of Facticity." In *Rethinking Facticity*, edited by François Raffoul and E. S. Nelson. Albany, NY: SUNY Press.

Derrida, Jacques. 2008. *The Gift of Death*. Translated by David Wills. Chicago, IL: The University of Chicago Press.

Sheehan, Thomas. 2018. "But What Comes *Before* the 'After'?" In *After Heidegger?* edited by Gregory Fried and Richard Polt. London and New York: Rowman & Littlefield.

# 12

# Heidegger and the Affective (Un)Grounding of Politics

## Jan Slaby and Gerhard Thonhauser

# 1    Introduction

Heidegger's ontological account of affectivity provides a valuable angle for considering questions of politics.[1] On the one hand, one might take some of what Heidegger wrote on affectivity in the late 1920s and early 1930s—usually couched in the idiom of *Stimmungen* (moods) and *Befindlichkeit* (findingness)—as a foreshadowing of his involvement with Nazi politics, culminating in his time as *Führer-Rektor* of Freiburg University (1933/1934). For instance, Heidegger's interpretation of boredom in the lecture course *Basic Concepts of Metaphysics* (1929/1930) relates notably to his philosophical and public writings during that phase of his career.

J. Slaby (✉)
Free University Berlin, Berlin, Germany
e-mail: slaby@zedat.fu-berlin.de

G. Thonhauser
TU Darmstadt, Darmstadt, Germany
e-mail: thonhauser@phil.tu-darmstadt.de

© The Author(s) 2019
C. Hadjioannou (ed.), *Heidegger on Affect*, Philosophers in Depth,
https://doi.org/10.1007/978-3-030-24639-6_12

On the other hand, Heidegger's views on affectivity can figure as a starting point for an ontological perspective on the political as such. In particular, his account of *Grundstimmungen* (basic attunements) leads into what arguably is the founding dimension of the political. These encompassing affective conditions reveal the ungroundedness and thus radical contingency of human existence and thereby open an affective path towards the political as the sphere of the ungrounding grounds of politics. The political as such does not refer to politics as a sub-system of society, but to the questioning of the foundations of politics, which turn out to be necessarily "contingent foundations" (Butler 1992). Although Heidegger's own politics—at least in the early 1930s—did not explicitly relate to the affectively disclosed ungroundedness of existence, but rather curtailed this openness and indeterminacy in an individualistic and decisionistic closure, we argue that Heidegger's view yields to a radically political reading. Not least, this is testified by a significant current of French political thought since the 1960s which heavily draws on Heidegger's *ontological difference* (see Marchart 2007).

Obviously, then, it all depends on how the insight into this ungroundedness is concretely 'processed' and dealt with. In this regard, Heidegger himself can only figure as a bad example and a warning as to how the lack of secure foundations can underwrite a craving for determinacy and authority. Our aim in what follows is to trace the so-called 'post-foundationalist' line of political thought back to its origins in Heidegger's works, especially to Heidegger's approach to affectivity, in order to assess the potentials and pitfalls of 'Heidegger on politics'. Along the way, our exploration will yield an outlook on an understanding of what might be called 'political affect'.

The chapter is structured as follows. We begin by outlining the focal role that affectivity—*Befindlichkeit*—plays within the existential analytic. The following in-depth discussions of the *Grundstimmungen* of angst and boredom allow us to elaborate what we take to be key in this account: the affective insight into the radical ungroundedness of existence. We argue that this is, in fact, a paradigmatically political insight. In the throes of these *Grundstimmungen*, no direction, tendency or orientation appears in any way more relevant or meaningful than any other. After a brief interlude on Heidegger's own politics during the

*Rektoratszeit*, we will end the chapter with an outlook into a postfoundational account of the political. An encounter with ungroundedness throws us into a radically democratic situation (cf. Lefort 1988) in which all references to fixed foundations are necessarily suspended, and freedom—as the task of plural self-determination under conditions of indeterminacy—comes to the fore as the "*raison d'etre* of politics" (Arendt 1961, 146). It is at this very point, or rather: out of this predicament, that Heidegger takes his own fatal turn toward Nazism. We take this point of juncture in Heidegger's life as a call to reflect on the dangerous ambivalence of the ontological understanding of affectivity.

## 2   The Gist of Befindlichkeit

In his lecture course *The Fundamental Concepts of Metaphysics* (*FCM*), Heidegger introduces what he calls moods or attunements by way of a rigorous distancing from the psychology of individual 'inner' feelings, and by stressing the ubiquity and pervasiveness of moods as that which sets the stage and prepares the ground for our being and being-with (cf. *FCM* §17):

> Attunements are *not side-effects,* but are something which in advance determine our being with one another. It seems as though an attunement is in each case already there, so to speak, like an atmosphere in which we first immerse ourselves in each case and which then attunes us through and through. It does not merely seem so, it is so; and, faced with this fact, we must dismiss the psychology of feelings, experiences and consciousness. It is a matter of *seeing* and *saying* what is happening here. (*FCM* 67; *GA* 29/30: 100)

A few years earlier, and in a more systematic fashion, Heidegger had introduced *Befindlichkeit* (findingness)—his term of art for the dimension of affectivity among the constituents of dasein—in division one of *Being and Time* (*BT* §29&30) as part of an analysis of the three equiprimordial modes of being-in (*In-sein als solches*). In light of this positioning in the existential analytic, one might gloss findingness initially as something like a 'ground floor' dimension of intentionality: *Befindlichkeit* is the pas-sive-receptive dimension of Dasein's "openness to the world" (*SZ* 137).[2] As such, it prepares and structures the concrete modes of *directedness towards...* characteristic of intentional comportment: "*The mood has already disclosed, in every case, being-in-the-world as a whole, and makes it possible first of all to direct oneself toward something*" (*SZ* 137; italics in original). Few have said it nicer than Katherine Withy, who describes the world-disclosing role of Heideggerian moods as follows: "'Mood' is to be understood in a broad and deep sense, as the affective atmosphere that pervades the mise-en-scène of human life, through which we are attuned to ourselves and our world in a particular way" (Withy 2012, 201).[3]

As a constitutive dimension of being-in, findingness is entangled with its other constitutive modes, namely *understanding* and *discourse*. Accordingly, there is no such thing as a 'pure' mood; instead, dasein is always in a particular existential orientation that combines passive-receptive, active and discursive comportment: "Every understanding has its mood. Every attunement is one in which one understands. [...] The understanding which has its mood [...] articulates itself with relation to its intelligibility in discourse" (*SZ* 335).

Yet, when it comes to the role of findingness within the existential analytic, this de facto entanglement of attunements with other modali-ties of being-in is of lesser importance. What matters at this level is the ontological character of findingness, namely, that it discloses *facticity*—the brute '*that it is*' of dasein. In moods "dasein is brought before its being as 'there'" (*SZ* 134). For the most part manifest in the form of a burden (*Last*), the brute facticity of existence is disclosed—made manifest—by the moods and attunements that make up findingness. "In having a mood, dasein is always disclosed moodwise as that entity to which it has been delivered over in its being; and in this way it has been delivered over to the being which, in existing, it has to be" (*SZ* 134). Famously, this 'being delivered over' is what Heidegger then goes on to call the "throwness" (*Geworfenheit*) of dasein:

> This characteristic of dasein's being – this 'that it is' – is veiled in its "whence" and "wither", yet disclosed in itself all the more unveiledly; we call it the "throwness" of this entity into its "there"; indeed, it is thrown

in such a way that, as being-in-the-world, it is the "there". The expression "thrownness" is meant to suggest the facticity of its being delivered over. (*SZ* 135)

Most conspicuously in 'negative' moods, findingness is the unshakable manifestation of the *burdensome* facticity of one's own being, i.e. that one has no choice but to *be* here and now as *this* particular entity in this particular (i.e. specifically constrained and limited) worldly setting.

Another important characteristic of dasein is that the modes of being-in are constitutively prone to *Verfallen* (falling). What is important to note about falling is that Heidegger takes it to be a pervasive mode of being of dasein—it effectively describes the default way in which dasein comports itself towards entities in general, how each and everyone 'is' for the most part and usually. If this is the case, then a methodological problem arises for the existential analytic: How to get at an allegedly more original structure of dasein, how to even assume that there is such a structure, when it is true that the tendency to succumb to blind routine and averageness is so pervasive, even constitutive for everyday dasein? Heidegger assumes that certain affective conditions are capable of *counteracting* falling and thereby set dasein on the path to potentially deeper existential insights.

Findingness, however, is likewise prone to falling, so that its ontic concretions—particular instances of moods or emotions—will for the most part unfold in characteristically inauthentic forms. When it comes to the modes of *disclosure* transpiring in findingness, these will by and large be forms of an "evasive turning away" (*SZ* 136). In this way, then, everyday affectivity discloses exactly not by revealing our predicament lucidly; instead, affective disclosure unfolds (at best) indirectly, through thickets of distractions, by inclining to shallow diversions, thereby for the most part occluding or withholding what we are factually up to. Most conspicuous is this tendency with regard to the basic moods angst and boredom—so much so that we seldom even notice these moods at all for all the distractions and evasions that keep them for the most part in states of latency.

This uncommonness confirms that findingness is an exquisitely *ontological* condition: making manifest dasein's facticity, it enables the rare instances in which we encounter ourselves in an original way. Accordingly, it is not surprising that Heidegger grants to certain moods a methodological role within his endeavor of a fundamental analytic of dasein. Both angst and boredom—as *Grundstimmungen*—are capable of providing ontological insights.

## 3     Angst—Breakdown of Significance

In §40 of *BT*, Heidegger provides an encompassing phenomenological exposition of 'angst'—a word we leave untranslated because it is doubtful whether what Heidegger drives at with it comes close enough to what is meant by 'anxiety' in colloquial English (cf. Withy 2012). The analysis of angst occupies a central position in division one of *BT*: Despite the rarity of pure angst in everyday life, angst has the potential to disclose the being of dasein in particular clarity. Heidegger is not very explicit about why certain moods—and not others—possess this exquisite *ontological* potential. No doubt he assumes—in line with the hermeneutical circle—that this will become clear only during the phenomenological analysis of the mood in question.

In the case of angst, the 'depth' of this predicament is obvious from the get-go, namely from the contrast with fear. Whereas fear is directed at some particular approaching entity that is characterized by its being *detrimental* ('abträglich') to dasein, anxiety is not directed at any particular entity. Heidegger here builds on the intuition that angst—as opposed to fear—is *objectless*, which means that it is potentially limitless in its scope as it is anchored nowhere in particular and thus, potentially, everywhere at once. That 'in the face of which' one has angst (*das Wovor der Angst*) is totally indeterminate—angst-ridden dasein does not know what it is that it is anxious of. This indeterminacy encroaches upon everything there is—all innerworldly entities cease to be relevant, everyday significance "collapses into itself" (*SZ* 186). This leads to the impression that what one is anxious of is 'nothing and nowhere': "it is already 'there', and yet nowhere; it is so close that it is oppressive and stifles one's breath, and yet it is nowhere" (*SZ* 186). Here we glimpse for the first time the central insight that will become important in what follows: the "nothing and nowhere", stemming from the utter insignificance of all innerworldly entities, signals a baseline ungroundedness of all and everything. This is what angst, in its characteristically evasive mode of disclosure, reveals: nothing *must* be the way it is—ultimately, nothing even 'matters' at all.

Trying to counteract this horrible directedness at 'nothing', dasein succumbs to diversions and distractions, craving to remain within a comfort zone beyond the reach of angst's paralyzing premonitions. Heidegger glosses this tendency as one of 'fleeing', as "a fleeing *in the face of itself*" (*SZ* 184). While turning away into diversions, what it is that dasein flees—namely, itself—is not grasped, not consciously processed, yet, "in turning away from it is disclosed 'there'" (*SZ* 185). So the first focal insight of the angst analysis is that dasein is, as it were, stalked by itself. It is not something dangerous in the world that is fled (like in fear), but exactly the opposite: "what this turning-away does is precisely to *turn thither* towards entities within-the-world by absorbing itself in them" (*SZ* 186).

It helps to abstract the general structure of this existential condition, as this provides a preview into the everyday mode of the political. One might say that dasein is presented in the angst analysis as existing on two different planes, which are entwined in an unstable and shifting way: One existential plane pertains to the ungroundedness and insecurity of being-in-the-world; it is a mode of existing *in face of* the utter lack of foundations, in the instability of all things, oneself (and all that is familiar and dear to one) certainly included. Yet, this plane of insecure situatedness—this 'hovering over the abyss'—is overlaid with a veneer of surface activity, social practices, discourse and general 'clamor' or chattiness: routine comportment, commonplace ways of addressing and understanding others, oneself and one's surroundings. Taken together, these thickets of the commonplace institute a 'world' of everyday familiarity—an existential comfort zone, the "warp and weft of all our days" (Haugeland 2013, 54). Yet, while pervasive and all-enveloping, this paramount surface plane of existence is itself essentially unstable. It is fragile, prone to disruption, it is haunted by what is excluded and blocked out during its institution. At any time, for no particular reason, angst can break through and shake us out of our absorption in the familiar.

It is our conviction that this unstable duality of existential planes—a tectonic intertwining of ungroundedness at base and a tentative surface stability—resembles the way that politics and the political intertwine within everyday human life. For the most part, politics is a tedious matter of social organization, of regulations, rules and restrictions characteristic of governing institutions; yet, against the grain of these normalizing routines of day-to-day governance, a characteristic ontological fragility flashes up in rare moments. Suddenly, there are cracks in the edifice of social organization, an uncanny sense of contingency besets the public routines. This may then give rise to an awareness of political possibility: if things do not rest on secure foundations, they might as well be organized differently.

This resembles the consequences Heidegger ascribes to an encounter with angst. Angst is a genuinely ontological condition, as an insight dawns in this conditions that does not pertain to entities but to being as such: "What oppresses us is not this or that, nor is it the summation of everything present-at-hand; it is rather the *possibility* of the ready-to-hand in general; that is to say, it is the world itself" (*SZ* 187). Angst has taken us from the realm of entities (*Seiendes*), which is a realm of putative stability and order, to the conditions of possibility of entities (*Sein*). What is more, it reveals our uncanny involvement in the entities' constitution. The insight of angst is that it is *us* who, as being-in-the-world, enact a meaningful world *into being*, by 'finding' entities significant in the course of our activities. Our *involvement in world-constitution* is what angst is all about: "That which anxiety is anxious about is being-in-the-world itself" (*SZ* 187).

To be sure, Heidegger is not himself concerned with giving the lessons of angst a political spin. On the face of it, Heidegger's angst analysis drives us away from all things considered political, if by 'political' we mean the domain of public affairs and interpersonal relations. Heidegger channels the insight of angst into the direction of dasein's authentic existence, the possibility of freedom and of 'choosing oneself', in the sense of transitioning from unowned to owned, i.e. resolute dasein. Angst is said to *individualize*—that means angst pulls dasein out of all entanglements with public life: "This individualization brings dasein back from its falling, and makes manifest to it that authenticity and inauthenticity are possibilities of its being" (*SZ* 191).

Yet the flip side of owned existence is the active constitution of entities as meaningful, in other words, the disclosure of a world. What angst reveals is the ontological 'role' of dasein: constituting a world by way of existing authentically. Dasein's *being-free* "for the freedom of choosing itself and taking hold of itself" is both the "authenticity of its own being, and for this authenticity as a possibility which it always already is" and the being that it is required to take over, as it is "delivered over" to it (*SZ* 188). Angst discloses the ungroundedness of both dasein and world by making manifest the burden upon dasein to take over (its) being as being-in-the-world. Thus, angst lets dasein simultaneously face itself *and* confront the world *as* world. The uncanniness of angst signals with merciless inevitability that *it is upon* dasein to freely enact a world—or else have everything meaningful drain away into utter insignificance.

Thus, despite the seemingly unpolitical character of Heidegger's analysis, we can see that, on a deeper level, angst leads us into a dimension that is discernible as political *in potentia*: Angst discloses freedom, in the sense of ungroundedness and indeterminacy of being. Thereby, it discloses both the *possibility* and *necessity* to give shape to what is not otherwise determined, to create and maintain a meaningful world above the abyss of meaninglessness. This is, in effect, the essence of the political; in the words of Hannah Arendt: "The *raison d'etre* of politics is freedom" (Arendt 1961, 146). What Arendt hints at is not just the ontic requirement that political activity depends on the prior fulfillment of certain vital functions (i.e. is 'free' in the sense of not being bound entirely by the reproduction of life, or being free from manifest force and oppression), but the more fundamental ontological state of existential indeterminacy: The possibility and necessity of collective self-determination under conditions of contingency. Arendt's dictum is an echo of Heidegger's Kierkegaard-inspired insight into the ungroundedness of existence as revealed by angst.

In view of this baseline condition of the political, we can re-phrase the overall structure of the angst analysis in explicitly political terms. While the 'world' of everyday dasein is superficially sealed up against any genuine political impulse by assuming the guise of encompassing routine and regularity, at any time a premonition of contingency *might* arise, so that those immersed in regular commerce suddenly realize that public matters might as well be otherwise. A sense of groundlessness, pointlessness, maybe even annoyance with the way things are arises unexpectedly. It is not yet a premonition of revolution, but it is a 'coming to oneself' as potentially able to effect change, either directly or indirectly, and it is a sense that it is *upon oneself* to do so: a foreshadowing of one's potential agency. To be sure, this sense of potential agency does not in itself provide us with a direction as to how to intervene in the established constitution of the world. And just because things could be otherwise it is not certain that one's intervention—if one decided to move to action—would be of any effect. Nevertheless, the ontological realization that the current shape of the world is not grounded in any socio-transcendent foundation, that worldly (read: human) affairs do not need to be the way they are, might serve as the first step towards engaging actively with the messy field of politics. Thus, it is not surprising that Arendt's line on politics continues thus: "The *raison d'etre* of politics is freedom, and its field of experience is action" (Arendt 1961, 146).

Of course, as Heidegger's endeavor is that of fundamental ontology, he does not devote much space to pondering different surface manifestations of its ontological structure. And surely, his expressed purpose is not that of awakening dasein to *political* consciousness. Yet, what he strives for is to awaken dasein 'to itself', as actively in charge of its fate within worldly constellations that need not be the way they currently are. It is this sense of contingency and openness that provides an outlook into the political. We can interrogate this dimension further by discussing the related considerations pertaining to boredom.

# 4     Profound Boredom

Boredom marks another affective route into the depth of dasein that Heidegger is at pains to sketch out. It is in many respects parallel to the route charted by angst and both conditions arise out of the same existential abyss: from the utter ungroundedness of existence. Heidegger's remarks on boredom form an integral part of his lecture course *The Basic Concepts of Metaphysics. World, Finitude, Solitude* presented in

Freiburg in 1929/1930. In Heidegger's oeuvre, this lecture occupies an intermediate position between *BT* and his fatal stint as NSDAP-approved *Führer-Rektor* of Freiburg University in 1933/1934. We will soon see that, towards the end of his reflections on boredom, a fore-shadowing of this ruinous phase is clearly in evidence.

The 180 pages of the lecture script devoted to boredom do not merely offer a description of boredom. It is crucial to the functioning of the lecture course that it works as a performative evocation or enac-tive instalment of boredom. An important part of Heidegger's narrative concerns the fact that profound boredom is so catastrophically obtru-sive, so shockingly unbearable that we—everyday dasein—will throw everything we have in its way in order to prevent it from even arising. Or, in case boredom *has* managed to arise, we will try everything to pre-vent it from becoming any deeper: all sorts of routine distractions and diversions—modes of *Zeitvertreib*—are mobilized so as to ensure bore-dom won't get a good hold of us. That is why we for the most part will not 'find' boredom simply occurring in our lives, as some mental state or mood among others—because all manner of routine activities and engagements always already occupy the space on which it could mani-fest itself. Boredom is 'there' as an absence, by having distractions stand in for it. Thus, the main task of the lecture course becomes to awaken this concealed but basic attunement (cf. *FCM* §16).

We cannot retell Heidegger's full account of boredom. Instead we zoom in on a few decisive points, mostly concerning the third and deepest form of boredom. In the rare case of profound boredom—epitomized by the phrase '*it is boring for one*'—existence is modified to the point of an extreme. In the second of the three forms of boredom—'*being bored with something*'—the bored person's exist-ence is *temporarily* transformed into a circumscribed period of dead time. The *first* variety—'*becoming bored by something*'—is the mun-dane case where a thing, item, or situation holds us up and thus bores us (Heidegger's example is a shabby train station in the middle of nowhere where one is forced to wait).

Before turning to the third and deepest form, we dwell a little on the second form of boredom, because it can help give us a relatively lucid grasp of what Heidegger is driving at. Heidegger's example of the second variety of boredom is a dinner party in which we outwardly participate in a lively and engaged way, but where we afterwards admit that we were horribly bored throughout. Heidegger explicates that the bored person's 'self' is abandoned, left dangling, as it were, in an odd suspension: by superficially engaging in the dinner party activities, a portion of existence, a manifest span of lived time gets cut off from a temporal context essential for lending it meaning—from a *past* providing a reservoir of significance, and from a *future* providing direction for one's current pursuits. This is what engenders the obtrusive sense of 'losing oneself' to the situation, it is simply a lost portion of lifetime (cf. *FCM* 119; *GA* 29/30: 180). Boredom is literally the affliction of *time's becoming long*, explicit in the German term *Langeweile*. Lived time becomes oppressive as it is emptied of meaningful activity, and boredom is this gradual transformation of lived time—what Bergson described as *durée*—from the unremarkable, taken-for-granted background of our moment-to-moment existence into a conspicuous foreground matter. The less there is to do or worth our doing, the more a dense, obtrusive, all-consuming temporal 'emptiness' takes hold of us—unbearable in its suffocating presence. Consequently, in this state of being, existence is put on hold and turned into a 'standing now' (*stehendes Jetzt*), i.e. a state of existential futility (cf. *FCM* 125; *GA* 29/30: 189). Nothing happens that is *of relevance*, so nothing *matters*, nothing *fulfills* one. As profoundly unfulfilled, yet ours—after all, it is time we freely allocated in order to go to the dinner party—this span of time becomes obtrusive, arresting, suffocating. Like sand on the beach, a span of life-time runs idly through our fingers; seeing it slip away instills a cold horror in us. It seems as though time itself dimly resonates in the marrow of our bones.

Turning from the second to the third and most profound form of boredom ('*it is boring for one*'), we see that not just a limited period of life invested in one specific activity, but rather the entirety of existential temporality is modified. In this third variety of boredom, the *entire* temporal horizon of existence now stretches out indefinitely, takes on a suffocating vastness, besetting us with stasis and rendering everything there is utterly indifferent. "Entities have – as we say – become indifferent *as a whole*, and we ourselves as these people are not excepted. We no longer stand as subjects and suchlike opposite these entities and excluded from them, but find ourselves in the midst of entities as a whole, i.e., in the whole of this indifference" (*FCM* 138; *GA* 29/30: 208—translation modified). The breakdown of meaning in profound boredom is not limited to a specific situation or domain, it is related to the meaninglessness of entities as a whole. Moreover, in profound boredom not only all entities—everything there is—at once cease to matter, but also *we ourselves* are now literally transformed into a 'no one': "It is boring for one. It – for one – not me as me, not for you as you, not for us as us, but *for one*" (*FCM* 134f; *GA* 29/30: 203).

Exactly at this deepest point of an all-consuming lack of sense, however, a specific possibility emerges. Boredom issues a message to dasein: "All telling *refusal* [*Versagen*] is in itself a *telling* [*Sagen*], i.e., a making manifest. What do beings in this telling refusal of themselves as a whole tell us in such refusal? [...] The very *possibilities* of its [dasein's] doing and acting. [...] [It] makes them known in refusing them" (*FCM* 140; *GA* 29/30: 211f). Boredom's extreme transformation of existence creates a situation of heightened responsiveness in which the very features of existence that have been so radically modified are suddenly rendered salient: "[T]his peculiar impoverishment which sets in with respect to ourselves in this 'it is boring for one' first *brings* the *self* in all its nakedness *to itself* as the self that *is there* and has taken over the being-there of its Da-sein" (*FCM* 143; *GA* 29/30: 214). In this way, Heidegger suggests that profound boredom might facilitate dasein's *waking up* again.

What is it that profound boredom reveals and that has the potential of awakening dasein again? In short, profound boredom makes the very existential structure of Dasein salient: "what it *gives to be free* in its telling announcement – is nothing less than the *freedom of* Dasein as such" (*FCM* 148f; *GA* 29/30: 223). The overbearing experience of an utter lack of meaningful activities confronts dasein with the task of giving meaning to its life by projecting itself towards possibilities without ever being able to ground their meaning in any other source than its own projecting. Profound boredom has thus the potential to stir awake nothing less than our freedom by forcing us back into the very task of our existence. In colloquial terms, one might gloss the message of profound boredom as the task of 'getting one's act together', pulling oneself out of the slumber of futility into the resolute act: rising to the occasion, *no matter* how idle and futile everything might have seemed just a moment ago.

In terms of temporality, this means that we are tasked to transform the 'standing now' back into the *lived presence* of the *Augenblick*. In deep boredom, lived time flattens into vast expanse of all-consuming insignificance—while by contrast, in the *Augenblick*,[4] dasein is concentrated again into a single focal point, into an *extreme* of a self-enabling act, here and now; an act that requires our active engagement. It is that format of temporality that equals resolute and responsible agency, the very temporality of the *act* itself—its moment of truth (cf. *FCM* 149; *GA* 29/30: 223).

Again, this appears to carry us quite far away from anything concerning the political. However, in the case of boredom—in contrast to angst—a specific link to 'the political' is a constitutive feature of Heidegger's own project. Heidegger underscores that we will miss profound boredom if we search for it as if it were an individual's psychological state: "it is not necessarily an objection to our claim of a basic attunement being there in our Dasein if one of you, or even many, or all of you assure us that you are unable to ascertain such an attunement in yourselves when you observe yourselves. For in the end there is nothing at all to be found by observation" (*FCM* 60; *GA* 29/30 90f). Whereas the discussion of angst in *BT* points the reader towards an individualistic interpretation of angst as a *Grundstimmung* that pulls dasein out of the routines of everyday life and into the authentic possibilities of its existence, boredom is introduced from the start as a form of communal attunement. In contrast to *BT*, Heidegger suggests here that *Grundstimmungen* do not primarily attune an individual dasein. The 'subject' of basic attunements is rather a *Volk*, i.e. a particular community that separates itself from other communities. Moreover, whereas the possibility of angst appears to be introduced as an invariant structure of dasein—always looming in the depth of dasein's existence—, Heidegger now claims that *Grundstimmungen* are historically and culturally variable—they are always the basic attunement of a particular community in a particular age (cf. Ringmar 2017). Against the background of this modified account of basic attunements, Heidegger explains that the task of his lecture course is to awaken "one" (not "the") attunement, namely "our" attunement (*FCM* 59; *GA* 29/30: 89)—the *Grundstimmung* of the German *Volk*.

Thus, Heidegger's analysis of profound boredom is inextricably entangled with the question of *Volk* or political community. As he writes at the onset of his analysis: "We must awaken a fundamental attunement, then! The question immediately arises as to *which* attunement we are to awaken or let become wakeful in us. An attunement that pervades *us* fundamentally? Who, then, are *we*?" (*FCM* 69; *GA* 29/30: 103). We fail to appreciate the full depth of Heidegger's analysis if we ignore what is politically at stake here. According to Heidegger, the analysis of *Grundstimmungen* leads into the founding dimension of political communities: the dimension of the political, where the awakening of a basic attunement serves as the invocation of a particular community. As Heidegger states, *Grundstimmungen* can never be traced or tracked, but only invoked or awakened. Thus, neither basic attunements nor the political communities which they assemble are factual matters waiting to be empirically detected. Heidegger's *Volk* is not based on any positive foundation, it is not a matter of anthropology or sociology, nor one of history in a conventional sense. On the contrary, it is the awakening of a *Grundstimmung* itself which serves as the founding act of a particular *Volk*.

Thus, Heidegger's understanding of a people is far removed from any blood and soil ideology, but this does not mean that it does not have deeply troubling consequences of its own. Heidegger's entanglement of *Grundstimmung* and *Volk*, affective world-disclosure and political community, leads to an unsettling call for political activism. For Heidegger, answering the question 'who are we' is the same as understanding the demand profound boredom places on us. What is the demand of profound boredom? Heidegger's answer is alarmingly clear and determined: "It is that Dasein as such is demanded of man, that it is given to him – to be there" (*FCM* 165; *GA* 29/30: 246). Heidegger expands on the task he sees expressed in profound boredom's telling refusal in the following passage:

> We do not know it to the extent that we have forgotten that man, if he is to become what he *is*, in each case has to throw Dasein upon his

shoulders. [...] Yet because we are of the opinion that we no longer need to be strong or to expect to throw ourselves open to danger, all of us together have also already slipped out of the danger-zone of Dasein within which, in taking our Dasein upon ourselves, we may perhaps over-reach ourselves. [...] Man must first resolutely open himself again to this demand. The necessity of this disclosive resolution is what is contained in the telling refusal and simultaneously telling announcement of the moment of vision of our Dasein. (*FCM* 165; *GA* 29/30: 246f)

In a surprising turn, Heidegger transforms the fundamental insight of boredom—the utter absence of meaning, the realization that nothing *really* matters in and of itself—into a mobilizing appeal, a call to arms. Through his analysis of boredom, he issues a demand to his listeners: he urges them to constitute themselves, through the act of collective self-determination, as a political community, a *Volk*. With hindsight, we know well where this will lead him just a few years on, and the signs pointing in that direction are already very clear in this lecture from 1930. From about section 38 onward, Heidegger's lecture crashes down from the heights of existential ontology into what sounds like an odd mixture of philosophy and the convoluted eyewash of an aspiring Nazi party leader.

Heidegger's response to the experience of ungroundedness and radical alterability—an experience he carved out so masterfully in his analyses of angst and boredom—is the immediate closure of this space of open-ness and possibility in and though the demand for a resolute decision, which constitutes new meaning and leaves no room for pondering or doubt. It seems that Heidegger, when facing the political as such, does not bear the sense of freedom and openness which it implies. Thus, a pluralistic and democratic understanding of what angst and boredom might reveal to us is excluded from the outset. At this point, we need to remind ourselves of the warnings issued by Hannah Arendt and Claude Lefort: The response to the experience of the political does not need to be a democratic one; it can also lead on the path of totalitari-anism (Arendt 1973; Lefort 1986). Heidegger serves as a case in point. His incapability of bearing the experience of an utter ungroundedness of existence led him to the call for an immediate decision to lay a new foundation, to make life meaningful again—no matter what it is that will give life meaning. In that way, a collective sense of possibility—the modus operandi of democracy—is given no chance of arising.

## 5    The Collapse of Dasein and Work in the Rektoratszeit

It makes sense to follow this fatal route a step further and briefly take a look at Heidegger's stint as NSDAP-approved *Führer-Rektor* of Freiburg University (1933/1934).[5] What did resolute existence—the overcoming of boredom—concretely amount to for Heidegger at that time, when he decided to actively join the national socialist movement and its party? Literary critic Werner Hamacher (2002), who has provided a lucid deconstruction of Heidegger's *Rektorats-Philosophie*, is a competent guide for this purpose.[6]

The gist of what Heidegger proclaimed in that fatal year between the spring of 1933 and the spring of 1934—and how it connects to key strands of his pre-1933 thought—comes to the fore in his "Rede an Arbeitslose" (*Speech to the Unemployed*) on 22 October 1933 at Freiburg University[7]: In short, and befitting the National Socialist German Worker's party (NSDAP), dasein is and has to be *Arbeit* (work). Readily, Heidegger inscribes his existential analytic into the activism, dynamism and pan-workerism of the Nazi workers' state. In a 1934 Lecture on logic, Heidegger is particularly explicit about this, and we find here his characteristic move of ontologizing a mode of existence so as to expose it as unquestionably essential ('*wesentlich*'):

> Unsere Bestimmung erwirken, je nach Umkreis des Schaffens ins Werk setzen und ins Werk bringen – das heißt *arbeiten*. [...] Arbeit ist hier die zur Bestimmtheit unseres Wesens gewordene Bestimmung, die Prägung und das Gefüge des Vollzuges unserer Sendung und der Erwirkung unseres Auftrages im jeweiligen geschichtlichen Augenblick. [...] Geschichtliche Gegenwart erwächst als Arbeit aus Sendung und Auftrag, und so erwächst die Gegenwart aus Zukunft und Gewesenheit (*GA* 38: 128).

Notably, *Arbeit* is here positioned exactly at the place occupied by the *Augenblick*, the present-moment, in both *BT* and in the boredom lecture. The moment of the resolute act—from which the ownmost possibilities of dasein are said to spring—has now become the place of work in the service of the *NS-Arbeitsstaat*, mandated by *Volk* and *Führer*. It can be sobering indeed for those friendly to Heidegger's thought to see how readily and seamlessly even the deep layers of the existential analytic are recruited to serve this dire remnant of a philosophy. Heidegger with gleeful precision planted the political watchwords of his day—in this case: work—at the pinnacle of his conceptual edifice.

The point for present purposes is that work—and the activism and uncritical obedience to 'higher orders' it entailed—was also brought forth by Heidegger as the adequate answer to the predicament of boredom. In the years following the 1929/1930 lecture course, Heidegger sees in work the prime source of existential sense and meaning, and the point in responding to boredom, as we have seen, is an aggressive jump into collective meaning-yielding commitments. This jump, this resolute decision to have something matter to one, both collectively and individually—no matter what it is—is in this particular phase of Heidegger's thought equated with work.

It is important to remind ourselves of the fact that of all the things from Nazi Germany that German society and culture abandoned after WWII, work surely was not one of them. Hamacher (2002) diagnoses a worrisome continuity in the prizing and praising of work between the NS period and postwar Germany. This problematic is worthy of further consideration. Heidegger certainly saw this himself. Soon after he self-presented as the mobilizer and motivator of the German workers' state, and shortly after his stint as principal of Freiburg University, he reversed his views on the matter, now seeing in work the metaphysical epitome of modern subjectivity posited as an absolute. His notes on Ernst Jünger's *Der Arbeiter* are instructive in this regard (cf. *GA* 90), and likewise his writings on technology. One is surely right to chastise Heidegger for the horrific aberration of his philosophy during the early 1930s, and for his failure to ever address this phase later in a straightforward and accountable way. However, to what extent the rampant workerism of this phase and the krypto-authoritarian ethics it was packaged with actually resonated within main currents of twentieth century Western philosophy remains a matter for further exploration.

It is clear that we need a robust corrective to this delirious devotion to work as the paramount value in human existence, an antidote likewise to an austere work ethic and to the meagre vision of philosophy that has sprung up in its adjacency. Even more important is a clearer understanding of the paramount 'political moment' that Heidegger's early philosophy brings about, and likewise a grasp of the dangers inherent in this situation of affective ungroundedness.

# 6  The Affective (Un)Grounding of Politics

To sum up what we did so far: We have seen that certain *Grundstimmungen* serve a crucial ontological function. These basic attunements disclose the fundamental ontological make-up of dasein, the most basic conditions of its being-in-the-world. More specifically, the *Grundstimmungen* of angst and boredom disclose the radical ungroundedness of existence, the indeterminacy of one's life and the world one is embedded into. This uncanny sense of contingency and openness reveals the possibility and inevitability of freedom, and thereby provides an outlook into the domain of the political. Angst and boredom are rare moments in which the ontological fragility of familiar surface activities becomes apparent, making salient our existential condition of having to decide the undecidable, to give shape to what is not otherwise shaped—an act of freedom which, following Arendt, can be described as the essence of democracy: plural self-determination under conditions of contingency.

An affectively disclosed encounter with ungroundedness confronts us with the insight that no specific way of life can ultimately be justified once and for all; no direction, tendency or orientation appears, in the last resort, more relevant or meaningful than any other. On the other hand, our cohabitation of the world—what Arendt calls plurality—constitutes the inescapability of living together with one another.[8] The requirement of determining our ultimately undetermined lives under conditions of plurality leads to the possibility and necessity of organizing our sometimes coinciding, sometimes conflicting, but always overlapping and interfering modes of life (cf. Butler 2016). In this situation, the decisive question is: How do we respond to the affective disclosure of ungroundedness?

Following Claude Lefort, we can accentuate the socio-political significance of this issue in terms of the double body of the king (cf. Kantorowicz 1957) and its aftermath. Whereas the king's natural body is born, ages and dies like all human bodies, his spiritual body transcends mundane mortality. It represents the unity of the political body; it is the symbol of the divine right to rule; and allows for the succession of kings, as is symbolized in the expression: 'The king is dead, long live the king'. Lefort draws on this thought and suggests that after the "democratic revolution" society can no longer be defined in terms of such a unified social body:

> Power appears as an empty place and those who exercise it are mere mortals who occupy it only temporarily or who could install themselves in it only by force or cunning. There is no law that can be fixed, whose articles cannot be contested, whose foundations are not susceptible of being called into question. Lastly, there is no representation of a centre and of the contours of society: unity cannot now efface social division. Democracy inaugurates the experience of an ungraspable, uncontrollable society in which the people will be said to be sovereign, of course, but whose identity will constantly be open to question, whose identity will remain latent. (Lefort 1986, 303f)

The mainspring of this postfoundational line of thought is that neither foundationalism nor anti-foundationalism are viable options. Subscribing to anti-foundationalism by giving up transcendental discourse altogether leads to a form of naïve, unreflected, everyday empiricism, which is most powerfully enacted in the political doctrine of economic necessities ('there is no alternative'). On the other hand, going back to foundationalism comes at the cost of totalitarianism—the attempt to reestablish fixed foundations can only proceed by neglecting their contingent status in a totalitarian act of unification. This apparent dilemma led a number of postfoundational thinkers (cf. Lacoue-Labarthe and Nancy 1997) to proclaim the domain of *the political* as the sphere of the possible contestation of all foundations, a domain of quasi-transcendental discourse. Proclaiming the autonomy of the political against the dominant surface processes of politics underscores the need of theory, and indeed philosophizing, to enable us to continuously contest the available foundations within a given historical situation (cf. Marchart 2007).

Postfoundational theories of the political could build on Heidegger's insight that certain basic attunements, by pulling us out of the comfort of everyday routine, confront us with the abyss that lies at the basis of existence. By suspending all specific possibilities, the basic attunements of angst and boredom make "manifest for the first time what generally *makes* pure possibilities *possible* [*das Ermöglichende*]—or, as Heidegger says, 'the originary *possibilitization*' [*die ursprüngliche* Ermöglichung]" (Agamben 2004, 66). Arendt and Lefort transformed this postfoundational insight into a republican model of politics in terms of freedom and contingency. Others drew more agonistic conclusion, understanding politics—rather than as a search for consensus about the organization of our way of life—as a matter of conflict and struggle. Jacques Rancière, for example, identifies the political with the struggle of those who do not have a share in the current division of society; for him, the political only emerges in the fight over 'the part of those without part' (*la part des sans-part*) (cf. Ranciere 2004). In a similar vein, Chantal Mouffe suggests that for people to be able to enact their freedom, the political needs to be the arena of substantive conflict (cf. Mouffe 2013).

We cannot provide a discussion of those different ontologies of the political here. Instead, let us conclude by coming back to Lefort and his suggestion that twentieth century politics is characterized by a basic antagonism of democracy and totalitarianism. Indeed, he maintained that totalitarianism arose from the democratic situation (cf. Lefort 1986, 301). Whereas democracy requires that power is "an empty place" (Lefort 1988, 225) that can only be taken temporarily by one group—power is essentially contested and no group can claim to represent society as whole—totalitarianism claims that society can be reunified by a single source of power in the image of the "People-as-One" (Lefort 1986, 304).

We submit that this antagonism is latently present at the core of Heidegger's reflection on *Befindlichkeit*. Although his analyses of the affective disclosure of ungroundedness in angst and boredom represent the most salient expositions of postfoundational political affectivity, it seems as though Heidegger could not bear the openness and indeterminacy of a genuine political moment. His own response was a demand for activism, bound to a command from being as such, to establish meaning and determinacy—even at the costs of autocracy. Instead of following the encounter with contingency and indeterminacy into a configuration of democratic politics that is able to keep open the quest of the political, Heidegger responded with the appeal to intellectual and political authority and leadership that closes the space of political possibility. Whereas many postfoundational thinkers urged for an institutional configuration of politics that is able to keep open the political as such, Heidegger's fateful path highlights the power of an undemocratic response. Herein lies the inevitable ambivalence of the ontology of political affectivity.

## Notes

1. Jan Slaby's work on this article was part of the research activities of the subproject B05 of the Collaborative Research Center 1171 Affective Societies, funded by the German Research Foundation (DFG); Gerhard Thonhauser's work on this article was part of a project funded by the Austrian Science Fund (FWF): J-4055-G24. We thank several critical readers and discussants for helpful suggestions, notably Anna Bortolan, Andreas Elpidorou, Denis McManus, Nikola Mirkovic, Dermot Moran, Julian Reid, Michael Richardson, Erik Ringmar, Panos Theodorou, Tatjana Noemi Tömmel, Veronika Vasterling, and the editor of this volume, Christos Hadjioannou.
2. In the case of *Being and Time*, we refer to the page numbers of the German edition of *Sein und Zeit* published by Niemeyer (Heidegger 1953. The English translations are based on the edition by Macquarrie and Robinson (Heidegger 1962, but we took the liberty to modify them where we found it appropriate.

3. We can only provide a very brief discussion of the general notion of *Befindlichkeit* here; for more detailed elaborations on the preceding and the following points, see, for instance, Elpidorou and Freeman (2015), Freeman and Elpidorou (2015), Ratcliffe (2013), Slaby (2015, 2017a), and Withy (2014, 2015).
4. The originally Kierkegaardian notion *Augenblick* is usually translated into English as the 'moment of vision'.
5. The text of this section is reproduced with permission from Slaby (2017b).
6. The following all too brief thoughts are also inspired by Erich Hörl's (2013) re-working of some of Hamacher's thoughts in the context of a reflection on technology.
7. The original speech tellingly appeared in print in the NS journal *Der Alemanne. Kampfblatt der Nationalisten Oberbadens*, February 1, 1934. Of course, the seminal text in this phase of Heidegger's works is his infamous *Rektoratsrede* (*GA* 16: 107–117).
8. Whereas we—following Arendt—invoke an Aristotelian view on the political (understanding the political as the task of deciding about our way of life under conditions of plurality and indeterminacy), Heidegger appears to ultimately support a Platonic view on politics. Despite his groundbreaking insights into the fundamental ungroundedness of human existence, Heidegger appears to believe (at least for certain stretches of his life) that an ultimate salvation is possible if only we unconditionally submerge ourselves to an authentic understanding of the meaning that being gives to us in something like a stroke of fate (cf. Theodorou 2013).

# References

Agamben, Giorgio. 2004. *The Open*. Stanford: Stanford University Press.
Arendt, Hannah. 1961. *Between Past and Future: Six Exercises in Political Thought*. New York: Viking.
Arendt, Hannah. 1973. *The Origins of Totalitarianism*. San Diego, New York, and London: Harvest Book.
Butler, Judith. 1992. "Contingent Foundations: Feminism and the Question of 'Postmodernism'." In *Feminists Theorize the Political*, edited by J. Butler and J. W. Scott, 3–21. New York: Routledge.

Butler, Judith. 2016. "Precarious Life and the Ethics of Cohabitation." In *Notes Toward a Performative Theory of Assembly*. Cambridge: Harvard University Press.

Elpidorou, Andreas, and Lauren Freeman. 2015. "Affectivity in Heidegger I: Moods and Emotions in *Being and Time*." *Philosophy Compass* 10 (10): 661–671.

Freeman, Lauren, and Andreas Elpidorou. 2015. "Affectivity in Heidegger II: Temporality, Boredom and Beyond." *Philosophy Compass* 10 (10): 672–684.

Hamacher, Werner. 2002. "Arbeiten Durcharbeiten." In *Archäologie der Arbeit*, edited by Dirk Baecker, 155–200. Berlin: Kadmos Kulturverlag.

Haugeland, John. 2013. *Dasein Disclose: John Haugeland's Heidegger*. Edited by J. Rouse. Cambridge, MA: Harvard University Press.

Hörl, Erich. 2013. "Das Arbeitslose der Technik. Zur Destruktion der Ergontologie und Ausarbeitung einer neuen technologischen Sinnkultur bei Heidegger und Simondon." In *Prometheische Kultur. Wo kommen unsere Energien her?*, edited by C. Leggewie, U. Renner, and P. Risthaus, 111–136. Paderborn: Wilhelm Fink.

Kantorowicz, Ernst H. 1957. *The King's Two Bodies: A Study in Medieval Political Theology*. Princeton: Princeton University Press.

Lacoue-Labarthe, Philippe and Jean-Luc Nancy. 1997. *Retreating the Political*. London: Routledge.

Lefort, Claude. 1986. *The Political Forms of Modern Society: Bureaucracy, Democracy, Totalitarianism*. Cambridge, MA: MIT Press.

Lefort, Claude. 1988. *Democracy and Political Theory*. Translated by David Macey. Minneapolis: University of Minnesota Press.

Marchart, Oliver. 2007. *Post-foundational Political Thought: Political Difference in Nancy, Lefort, Badiou and Laclau*. Edinburgh: Edinburgh University Press.

Mouffe, Chantal. 2013. *Agonistics: Thinking the World Politically*. London: Verso.

Rancière, Jacques. 2004. *Disagreement: Politics and Philosophy*. Minneapolis: University of Minnesota Press.

Ratcliffe, Matthew. 2013. "Why Mood Matters." In *The Cambridge Companion to Heidegger's Being and Time*, edited by M. A. Wrathall, 157–176. Cambridge: Cambridge University Press.

Ringmar, Erik. 2017. "Heidegger on Willpower and the Mood of Modernity." In *Heidegger and the Global Age*, edited by Antonio Cerella and Louiza Odysseos. Lanham: Rowman & Littlefield.

Slaby, Jan. 2015. "Affectivity and Temporality in Heidegger." In *Feeling and Value, Willing and Action*, edited by M. Ubiali and M. Wehrle, 183–206. Phaenomenologica 216. Dordrecht: Springer.

Slaby, Jan. 2017a. "More Than a Feeling: Affect as Radical Situatedness." *Midwest Studies in Philosophy* 41 (1): 7–26.

Slaby, Jan. 2017b. "Living in the Moment: Boredom and the Meaning of Existence in Heidegger and Pessoa." In *Yearbook for Eastern and Western Philosophy*, edited by H. Feger, X. Dikun, and W. Ge, vol. 2. Berlin and New York: de Gruyter.

Theodorou, Panos. 2013. "Ἁμαρτία, Verfall, Pain: Plato's and Heidegger's Philosophies of Politics (and Beyond)." *The New Yearbook for Phenomenology and Phenomenological Philosophy* 13: 189–205.

Withy, Katherine. 2012. "The Methodological Role of Angst in *Being and Time*." *Journal of the British Society for Phenomenology* 43 (2): 195–211.

Withy, Katherine. 2014. "Situation and Limitation: Making Sense of Heidegger on Thrownness." *European Journal of Philosophy* 22: 61–81.

Withy, Katherine. 2015. "Owned Emotions: Affective Excellence in Heidegger and Aristotle." In *Heidegger, Authenticity and the Self: Themes from Division Two of Being and Time*, edited by D. McManus. New York: Routledge.

# Index

© The Editor(s) (if applicable) and The Author(s) 2019
C. Hadjioannou (ed.), *Heidegger on Affect*, Philosophers in Depth,
https://doi.org/10.1007/978-3-030-24639-6

Printed by Printforce, the Netherlands